D1564802

CONSTITUTIONALISM
IN THE
EMERGENT STATES

CONSTITUTIONALISM IN THE EMERGENT STATES

by

B. O. NWABUEZE

with a foreword by
S. A. DE SMITH

Rutherford · Madison · Teaneck
Fairleigh Dickinson University Press

Library of Congress Catalogue Card Number: 72-14221

Associated University Presses, Inc.
Cranbury, New Jersey 08512

© 1973 by B. O. Nwabueze

ISBN 0-8386-1365-9
Printed in Great Britain

CONTENTS

FOREWORD

By the mid-1960s Professor Nwabueze had already established a reputation as one of Africa's foremost academic lawyers. His books on *The Machinery of Justice in Nigeria* and *The Constitutional Law of the Nigerian Republic* were widely acclaimed, and he had distinguished himself as a teacher of law at Lagos and Nsukka. During the grievous civil war that racked his country, most of his books and papers were destroyed. Fortunately he has re-emerged as an author and a university teacher; and I am pleased to have been asked, as a friend and former teacher, to write a foreword to his new work.

The general theme of the book is inevitably discouraging, for of late we have seen it enacted so many times in so many countries. In a large majority of newly independent states, even the most modest expectations of liberal constitutionalists have gone unfulfilled. Perhaps such expectations ought not to have been entertained. Colonial authoritarianism, belatedly modified in its decline, had shown how a country could be governed even without popular backing. The nationalists who took over political power found too many seductive temptations to cling to office regardless of constitutional restraints or respect for minority interests. And the frustrations engendered by the prospect of indefinite exclusion from the privileges of office were usually too severe for a loyal opposition to develop. In such a political climate it was unrealistic to be astonished when political activity failed to exhibit a decorous regard for the rules of the constitutional game. Nor was a federal constitutional structure, which presupposed a willingness to accept restraints on the exercise of power at both the central and regional levels, at all likely to flourish. When, moreover, the principal divisive factors in the state are communal – religious, racial, tribal or linguistic – the prospects for constitutionalism are never bright, even in a developed country, as the recent history of Northern Ireland has underlined.

The constitutional and political history of Nigeria since 1960 has emphasised almost every problem that can beset a new state in Africa. Professor Nwabueze, both an observer of and a participant in those events, is especially well qualified to make a critical appraisal of the period. Although he does not mince his words, he writes without acrimony and he looks to the future in a mood that is by no means as pessimistic as the theme of the book may suggest. But this is not a book exclusively about Nigeria. He considers the experience of a number of other new states, particularly in Africa; and he examines not only the facts of political life but also the constitutional forms in which they have been encapsulated. Despite all the discouraging vicissitudes, and all the disappointments of a constitutionalist, he remains unconvinced of the superiority of single-party régimes and he offers suggestions for adapting constitutional ideas set in a European conceptual framework to meet the needs of developing plural societies.

Among the many interesting features of this book are studies of the legal analysis of revolutions, *coups d'état*, acts of secession and other manifestations of constitutional breakdown. In these shadowy areas, where constitutional law merges into politics and legal theory, a formidable body of case law has already emerged, from Pakistan, Cyprus, Rhodesia, Uganda, Nigeria and Ghana, and it is bound to expand. The unenviable position of a judge who is called upon to pronounce on the legality of a régime exercising effective political power unsanctioned by the letter of the law needs no emphasis, but it is important to understand the exact nature of his dilemma and the possible methods by which he may extricate himself from it.

I do not pretend to share every view that Professor Nwabueze has expressed on recent happenings. However, I hope that his book will be received as a serious attempt to relate the principles of constitutional government to the stressful experience and harsh realities of developing states.

Fitzwilliam College,
Cambridge   S. A. DE SMITH

x

PREFACE

When the civil war in Nigeria ended in January 1970 I was frequently confronted with problems concerning the legality of acts done during the secession by the secessionist régime and by individuals – contracts entered into, property seized or destroyed, appointments made or terminated, currency issued, and sentences or judgments passed by the regular courts and the special tribunals. This raises the whole question of the constitutionality of the secession and of the secessionist régime. If the régime was unconstitutional, could anything done under it have legal effect? Secession in Nigeria was of course preceded, if not caused, by the events of January 1966 when the civilian government handed over power to the military. That event was unique, for never before has a civilian government voluntarily abdicated in favour of the military. But what in fact was the true constitutional significance of that event? Was it a *coup d'état* or a normal change of government under the Constitution, and what is the nature of the military government established as a result? When I began probing these questions, I found myself confronted by other examples of constitutional breakdown in certain emergency situations.

Emergencies, *coups d'état* and secession are not confined to Nigeria; they are a general phenomenon which today holds the emergent nations in its grip. Hardly any of the new nations has escaped some form of violent emergency. Indeed, in some, emergencies have become a way of life. Perhaps the most interesting consequence from a constitutional point of view of the incidence of emergencies in the emergent states is the new meaning and vitality which it has given to the somewhat obscure and nebulous doctrine of state necessity. The use made of this doctrine in recent years demonstrates in a most striking manner the dilemma of constitutionalism in these nations. Pakistan, Cyprus and Rhodesia have all discovered in the doctrine a solution to the problems which threatened to bring the entire machinery of government to a standstill. It seems clear that the whole concept of constitutionalism is in danger in the new nations as authoritarian régimes replace the carefully balanced constitutions set up at independence. The

xi

attractions and temptations of power have led to a widespread and systematic perversion of the constitutional system.

These are some of the central issues discussed in this book. I have used Nigeria as a base for the discussion, though the focus of the book extends beyond that country. The choice of Nigeria may be justified on the ground that, until the collapse of the First Republic in January 1966, it had been held up as the bastion of democracy in Africa; it seemed to me that a discussion of the fortunes of constitutionalism there would provide a fair measure by which to judge other emergent nations. Admittedly my familiarity with the country and my own personal experience and involvement in some of the events could not have failed to influence the choice.

Now for the usual acknowledgments. My thanks go first to Stanley de Smith, Downing Professor of the Laws of England at Cambridge, who, as my teacher many years ago, first enkindled my interest in the study of Constitutional Law. In spite of the vast demands upon his time, he was kind enough to read the typescript and write a foreword to this book. Needless to say, this in no way implies any responsibility on his part for the shortcomings of the book; nor does it mean that he shares all my views. Indeed I have disagreed with him in various parts of the book. But perhaps he may feel some satisfaction in knowing that on the question of the partial fusion of the executive and legislature under the Westminster system, I have lately been converted to that aspect of the system, on the argument that effective government demands integrated leadership.

My thanks also go to my predecessor in the deanship of the School of Law, University of Zambia, Professor Robert Kent, who also read the typescript and commented upon various points touching upon the American Constitution and government. The staff of the University of Zambia Library, especially Mr. Newton Mwenifumbo, have been very obliging with my importunate demands. In Mr. Christopher Hurst of C. Hurst & Co., Publishers, London, I found a most delightful and keen collaborator.

BEN O. NWABUEZE

Lusaka
May 1972

xii

CHAPTER I

THE CONCEPT OF CONSTITUTIONALISM

Government is universally accepted to be a necessity, since man cannot fully realise himself — his creativity, his dignity and his whole personality – except within an ordered society. Yet the necessity for government creates its own problem for man, the problem of how to limit the arbitrariness inherent in government, and to ensure that its powers are to be used for the good of society. It is this limiting of the arbitrariness of political power that is expressed in the concept of constitutionalism. Constitutionalism recognises the necessity for government but insists upon a limitation being placed upon its powers. It connotes in essence therefore a 'limitation on government; it is the antithesis of arbitrary rule; its opposite is despotic government, the government of will instead of law.'[1] Arbitrary rule is government conducted not according to pre-determined rules, but according to the momentary whims and caprices of the rulers; and an arbitrary government is no less so because it happens to be benevolent, since all unfettered power is by its very nature autocratic. A dictatorship is thus clearly not a constitutional government, however benevolent it may be, and a totalitarian régime is even less so.

Two points which are apt to obscure the concept of constitutionalism require to be cleared at the outset, and these concern its relationship, first, with the constitution, and, secondly, with democracy. No word is more susceptible of a variety of tendentious interpretations than democracy, but perhaps the definition with the greatest universality of acceptance is that it is, in the words made classic by Abraham Lincoln, a government of the people by the people for the people. The underlying idea here is the popular basis of government, the idea that government rests upon the consent of the governed, given by means of elections, in which the franchise is universal for both men and women, and that it exists for their benefit. The distinction is thus with monarchical, aristocratic or oligarchical government. But free elections based upon universal franchise do not of themselves alone create con-

1

stitutional government. For, as Wheare has pointedly observed, 'universal suffrage can create and support a tyranny of the majority or of a minority or of one man . . . The absolutisms of the twentieth century have usually been based upon universal suffrage – and a compulsory universal suffrage at that. Have not modern tyrannies been returned to power by majorities of over 90 per cent?'[2] On the other hand, a monarchical government or an unelected oligarchy or a colonial administration, operated in the interest of the rulers and the class interests they represent, is not *necessarily* nonconstitutional. The crucial test is whether the government is limited by pre-determined rules.

The term 'constitutional government' is apt to give the impression of a government according to the terms of a constitution. That there is a formal written constitution according to whose provisions a government is conducted is not necessarily conclusive evidence that the government is a constitutional one. Again the determining factor is: Does the constitution impose limitations upon the powers of the government? There are indeed many countries in the world today with written constitutions but without constitutionalism. Normally, a constitution is a formal document having the force of law, by which a society organises a government for itself, defines and limits its powers, and prescribes the relations of its various organs *inter se*, and with the citizen. But a constitution may also be used for other purposes than as a restraint upon government.[3] It may consist to a large extent of nothing but lofty declarations of objectives and a description of the organs of government in terms that import no enforceable legal restraints. Far from imposing a brake upon government, such a constitution may indeed facilitate or even legitimise the assumption of dictatorial powers by the government.

The Soviet government provides perhaps the most glaring example of arbitrary power, and yet the Soviet Union has a Constitution of 146 articles which, somewhat in the fashion of the democratic constitutions of the Western countries, contains a guarantee of individual rights as well as procedures for the exercise of governmental functions, indeed a full paraphernalia of a seemingly regularised system of restraints. Yet all this seems to be nothing but a façade. To begin with, the constitution reads more like a political manifesto than a legal charter, and may indeed have been intended by its framers to have no more than a political existence. For example, individual rights are purported to be guaranteed under two different formulae: in the case of social and economic rights, by stating that 'citizens of the U.S.S.R. have a right to them,' and by describing the means by which the right is

ensured; e.g. 'the right to work is ensured by the socialist organisation of the national economy, the steady growth of the productive
forces of Soviet society, the elimination of the possibility of economic
crises, and the abolition of unemployment.'[4] It seems clear that
'right' here refers to a political, not a justiciable legal right. The
other formula declares certain rights as either 'an indefeasible law,'
e.g., equality of rights of citizens,[5] or as 'guaranteed or protected
by law', e.g. freedom of speech, press and assembly;[6] the inviolability of the homes of citizens and privacy of correspondence.[7]
What law is referred to here, the law of the constitution or some
other law? A proper interpretation would seem to suggest that the
constitution itself creates no legal guarantee of civil rights which
the individual may assert against the state. The so-called guarantee
of rights in the constitution of the U.S.S.R. means no more than
a declaration of objectives, a statement of what the state will,
hopefully, do for its citizens. In any case it provides no procedure
for the enforcement of these rights either by the ordinary courts
or otherwise. Assuming even that the constitution imposes legal
restraints upon government, there are worked into it nullifying
clauses designed to enable the rulers to escape from them. For
example, under the constitution the organs of government appear
to be subordinated to the Communist Party, which is declared
'the vanguard of the working people in their struggle to build a
communist society and . . . the leading core of all organisations of
the working people, both public and state'.[8] A remarkable example
of the dominating position of the Communist Party is the right
reserved to it to nominate candidates of the Supreme Soviet,[9] a
right which undermines, if it does not nullify, the system of
'universal, equal and direct suffrage by secret ballot' established
by an earlier article.[10] And the stipulation that the freedom of
speech, press and assembly is guaranteed 'in conformity with the
interests of the working people, and in order to strengthen the
socialist system'[11] makes the guarantee subject to what the Soviet
rulers consider is required by the interests of the working people
or by the socialist system.[12]

If, then, constitutionalism implies limited government, three
questions arise from this. How or in what form are the restraints
to be imposed? Must the rules limiting government be legal rules
embodied in a written, supreme constitution? Or is it enough that
there are in fact limitations, whether these are imposed by law or
by convention and usage? The second question concerns the nature
or content of the restraints themselves. What is the nature or extent
of the restraints necessary to make a government constitutional?
Are there any particular type or types of restraint that must exist

before a government can rightly be called constitutional? Thirdly, to what extent are the restraints observed in practice? The first two sets of questions will be considered here, and the third in the chapters following.

Must the limitations be legal?

The question arises essentially in relation to the legislative arm of government, which exercises, indeed, the greatest of all governmental discretionary powers, the power of law-making. A constitution, as a system of restraint upon government, may originate as a matter of organic growth from immemorial customs, embodying 'natural reason developed and expounded by the collective wisdom of many generations' or as an act of conscious creation in a written form by the people. With the former, the sanction for the limitation which it imposes upon government (i.e. the legislature) is not law, but the force of tradition. As a matter of law, the legislature is not bound to act conformably to such a constitution, and if it does act contrary to it, its act, though it may provoke public outcry, is not illegal. The sanction of public opinion is entirely extra-legal, and the true legal position recognises in the legislature a legal sovereignty, indeed a supremacy, that is at once absolute and unlimited, a power to alter the constitution as and how it pleases; the supremacy of law means no more than the supremacy of the legislature. No legal limitation based upon the law of nature can be implied in such an unwritten constitution. Natural law can have no more than a moral force, providing merely 'a basis of comparison . . . an intellectual standard.'[13] In a recent case the Judicial Committee of the Privy Council has emphatically rejected the argument that a legislature is limited by the law of nature.[14]

The effectiveness of extra-legal, as compared with legal, sanctions is of course another matter. Given ideal conditions, it is possible perhaps for a conventional sanction to compel as much obedience on the part of the government as a legal sanction. No matter how effective a conventional sanction may be, however, the question is whether the absolute sovereignty of the legislature under an unwritten constitution is compatible with constitutionalism. Since 'by definition, a constitutional democracy is one which does not grant all power to the majority,'[15] it has been argued that the absolute sovereignty of the legislature is 'incompatible with constitutionalism.' The example of England, with its unwritten constitution which accords to Parliament a sovereignty unlimited in law, makes it difficult to maintain this viewpoint as an invariable rule. For England undoubtedly has the most constitutional of all constitutional governments.

Happily England stands almost alone today as a country without a formal constitutional code. From the eighteenth century onwards, as a result of armed rebellion against the arbitrariness of monarchical absolutism, inspired in many cases by the revolutionary teachings of doctrinaire philosophers, proclaiming the message of liberty, equality and fraternity, unwritten constitutions, with their corollary of absolute, unlimited sovereignty of the government, have become discredited and have given place to written constitutions consciously framed by the people as a supreme law, creating, defining and limiting governments. 'The precedent for these, first developed in North America, was naturalised in France and from there transmitted to most of the continent of Europe, from which it has spread in our own day to much of the Orient.'[16] This development has been given a new boost by the emergence from colonialism of a host of new nations in Africa and Asia which needed written constitutions to launch them into their new, independent existence and to impose checks against majority power in the interests of tribal, racial or religious minorities.

Thus it is that constitutionalism has come by and large to presuppose a written constitution. Government is a creation of the constitution. It is the constitution that creates the organs of government, clothes them with their powers, and in so doing delimits the scope within which they are to operate. A government operating under a written constitution must act in accordance therewith; any exercise of power outside the constitution or which is unauthorised by it is invalid. The constitution operates therefore with a supreme authority.

The rationale for this supremacy has a rational basis: the constitution is (or is supposed to be) an *original* act of the people directly; an act of government is a derivative, and *ipso facto* a subordinate, act. 'There is no position,' writes Alexander Hamilton, 'which depends on clearer principles than that every act of a delegated authority, contrary to the tenor of the commission under which it is exercised, is void. No legislative act, therefore, contrary to the constitution can be valid. To deny this would be to affirm that the deputy is greater than his principal; that the servant is above his master, that the representatives of the people are superior to the people themselves; that men acting by virtue of powers may do not only what their powers do not authorise, but what they forbid.'[17]

No doubt the view of the constitution as law made directly by the people raises some conceptual difficulty. For it was generally thought that law-making was a function *only* of a political community, not of the people in their mass; in other words that only

B

a people organised as a political community can enact law through the machinery of the state. On this hypothesis, while the power of the people in their mass to constitute themselves into a political community is admitted, any such constituent act by which a constitution is established is purely a *political* act, giving the constitution only a political, as distinct from legal, existence. If it is intended that the constitution should also be a law, then it is for the resultant political creation, the state, to enact it as such through its regular procedure for law-making. Thus the American Constitution, as a law 'ordained and established' by the people, is said to have broken with 'the dominant tradition.'[18] Tradition is, however, sought to be reconciled by asserting that 'the agency by which constitutions are nowadays drawn up, namely constitutional conventions, had become such usual phenomena as to have been substantially assimilated to the machinery of organised government, so that one looking back to the State conventions that had in 1787 ratified the Constitution found it natural to regard them as organs of existing political societies, rather than as directly representative of the individuals back of these societies.'[19]

The argument smacks of excessive formalism. If the state is a creation of the people by means of a constitution, and derives its power of law-making from them, it may be wondered why the people who constitute and grant this power cannot act directly, in a referendum or otherwise, to give the constitution the character and force of law. After all, the constitution, being the starting-point of a country's legal order, its 'lawness' should not depend upon its enactment through the law-making mechanism of the state, but rather upon its recognition as such by the people to be governed by it. It is today generally accepted that the American constitution 'obtains its entire force and efficacy, not from the fact that it was ratified by a pre-existent political community or communities – for it was not – but from the fact that it was established by the people to be governed by it.'[20] There can be no doubt that today a referendum or plebiscite is a legally accepted way of adopting a constitution, though adherence to formalism still sometimes requires that, after adoption by the people, the constitution should be *formally* promulgated by a pre-existing state authority, invariably the head of state. It is pertinent to emphasise, however, that a referendum or plebiscite lacks a genuine constituent and legitimising effect unless it is preceded, at the drafting stage or after, by serious discussion on as popular a platform as possible, of the constitutional proposals. This is exemplified by the process followed in America, where the constitution was drafted by a convention after thorough discussion, followed by even more mature and long deliberation in the ratifying conventions in the various states. An equally genuine process is adoption by a constituent assembly and ratification in a plebiscite as in the case of the Swiss constitution of 1848.

The Supremacy of the Constitution and the Sovereignty of the Legislature

Is a legislature operating under a supreme constitution necessarily a non-sovereign one, or if not, does its sovereignty necessarily exclude the supremacy of the constitution? In other words, are the two concepts mutually exclusive? The use of the word sovereignty in relation to a legislature, like the British Parliament, operating under an unwritten constitution has obscured its meaning. Thus, it has been argued that the sovereignty of the legislature, even under a written constitution, implies that any act purporting to have been passed by it is valid and effective, irrespective of any defect in procedure; because, if a legislature is sovereign, a mere defect in procedure cannot operate to invalidate an act which is otherwise within the power of the legislature. The courts are bound to accept and act upon the official copy of the act, and cannot go outside it to ascertain whether it was passed in the manner and form prescribed by the constitution. On this view of sovereignty, a sovereign legislature operating under a written constitution is clearly above the constitution just like one operating under an unwritten constitution. However, the Judicial Committee of the Privy Council has in a recent appeal from Ceylon[21] emphatically rejected this view, holding that under a written constitution which prescribes a procedure for law-making, the courts are not only entitled to go outside the official copy of the act in order to enquire into the question of procedure, but have a duty to declare the act invalid if in fact it was passed without due form. For where a legislature is given power subject to certain manner and form, *whether it be a simple or special majority*, that power does not exist unless and until the manner and form is complied with. The supremacy of the constitution demands that the court should hold void any exercise of power which does not comply with the prescribed manner and form or which is otherwise not 'in accordance with the constitution from which the power derives.'[22] As the Board observed, the proposition is not acceptable that 'a legislature, once established, has some inherent power derived from the mere fact of its establishment to make valid law by the resolution of a bare majority which its own constituent instrument has said shall not be a valid law unless made by a different type of majority or by a different legislative process.'[23]

But does this necessarily exclude the sovereignty of the legislature?
In the view of the Board:

> 'No question of sovereignty arises. A parliament does not cease
> to be sovereign whenever its component members fail to produce
> among themselves a requisite majority, e.g. when in the case of
> ordinary legislation the *voting is evenly divided* or when in the case
> of legislation to amend the constitution there is only a bare
> majority if the constitution requires something more. The
> minority are entitled under the Constituion of Ceylon to have
> no amendment of it which is not passed by a two-thirds majority.
> The limitation thus imposed on some lesser majority of members
> does not limit the sovereign powers of parliament itself which
> can always, whenever it chooses, pass the amendment with the
> requisite majority.'[24]

The point can be put another way, by saying that the requirement
of a special majority for constitutional amendment is merely a
definition of what parliament is for that purpose, and not a
limitation upon the sovereignty of parliament.[25]

This case underlines the distinction between a sovereign
legislature operating under a written constitution and the British
Parliament. For since 'in the constitution of the United Kingdom
there is no governing instrument which prescribes the law-making
powers and the forms which are essential to those powers,'[26] the
courts are bound to take the validity of every act of parliament for
granted, and there could be no question of non-compliance with
any constitutionally prescribed procedure. 'There is no such
doctrine as the unconstitutionality of legislation by parliament.'[27]
The U.K. Parliament is therefore not only sovereign but supreme,
by which is meant that there is no law to which it is subject as
regards either the content of its power or the procedure for exercising
it, and it is this supremacy that really excludes the supremacy of the
constitution. A legislature operating under a written constitution may
be sovereign, even to the extent of having power to amend the constitution in the same way as it makes ordinary law, but it can hardly be
supreme, since it is invonceivable that the constitution should fail
at least to prescribe a quorum and the method of arriving at
decisions by a simple majority. Such a provision binds the legislature, and disregard of it will invalidate any purported exercise of
power. The supremacy of the constitution can co-exist with the
sovereignty of parliament, but it necessarily excludes the supremacy
of parliament. Comparing Britain with New Zealand, which has a
written constitution that is alterable by a simple majority, Wheare
says that there is no 'substantial difference' between them, because
'in both cases the legislature is supreme over the constitutional rules

of law. There are no legal limits on its powers of amendment.'[28] From what has been said, this position cannot be supported. By conceding that where a special majority is prescribed, 'the legislature is to that extent controlled by the constitution and the constitution is to that extent supreme over the legislature,'[29] Professor Wheare involves himself in self-contradiction, for a simple and special majorities are both a form of control, differing only in degree, not in nature.

However, the sovereignty of parliament cannot but attenuate the effectiveness of the constitution's supremacy, since every act of the legislature passed with due form, even if inconsistent with the constitution, will operate *pro tanto* as an amendment of it. It is not even necessary that the act should be expressed to be an amendment of the constitution,[30] unless the constitution requires amendments to be made expressly, as in Ghana (1960) and in West Germany (1949). Constitutionalism would be better entrenched if the constitution effectively excluded any notion of the sovereignty of parliament by requiring something more than a parliamentary majority for the amendment of the more fundamental of its provisions, e.g. the participation of some outside body or bodies, like the electorate at a referendum or other legislative assemblies in a federation. Some articles of the constitution might even be made altogether unalterable. For example, the German Basic Law, 1949, forbids any alteration of the territorial units of the federation, of the right of the *Länder* to participate in legislation, of the guarantee of human rights, and of the status of Germany as 'a democratic and social federal state';[31] in France under the Fifth Republic (1958) the republican form of government is not subject to amendment;[32] while in Ceylon the guarantee of freedom of religion is unalterable.[33] In Cyprus some forty-eight articles incorporated from the Zurich Agreement cannot be altered at all. It is questionable whether a total prohibition is really meaningful as a limitation upon the constituent power of the people. If the people do desire a change, can such a prohibition effectively prevent it?[34]

A high degree of entrenchment may be justified on the ground that a constitution is supposed to be a permanent charter, which is to endure for ages to come, and not to be lightly altered to meet the temporary expediency of party politics. If the procedure for its amendment is not sufficiently rigid, and the temptation to alter it in accordance with the fancy or interest of the party in power is succumbed to too readily, the constitution loses its sanctity and authority as the bedrock of constitutionalism, and may become instead a mockery of the very idea of a government of laws. It has been said that the strength of American constitutionalism lies in great measure in the 'divinity' with which it is clothed in the eyes of Americans, and in the feeling of devotion and worship with which they regard it. This is not to say that a constitution should be made unduly rigid, since that might invite its overthrow by revolutionary means when a genuine need for change has arisen and cannot be affected by constitutional methods. In relation to the Cyprus Constitution of 1960, Justice Vassiliades has remarked upon what he calls 'the sin of ignoring time and human nature in the making of our constitution.' 'Time moves on continuously,' he says; 'man is, by nature, a creature of evolution and change, as time moves on. The constitution was, basically, made fixed and immovable . . . As time and man moved on, while the constitution remained fixed, the inevitable crack came – perhaps a good deal sooner than some people may have thought – with grave and far-reaching consequences.'[35]

Nature and Content of the Restraints on Government

Professor de Smith has prescribed what he considers the minimum restraint necessary for constitutionalism, as follows:

'A contemporary liberal democrat, if asked to lay down a set of minimum standards, may be very willing to concede that constitutionalism is practised in a country where the government is genuinely accountable to an entity or organ distinct from itself, where elections are freely held on a wide franchise at frequent intervals, where political groups are free to organise in opposition to the government in office and where there are effective legal guarantees of fundamental civil liberties enforced by an independent judiciary; and he may not easily be persuaded to identify constitutionalism in a country where any of these conditions is lacking.'[36]

This is also the prescription of Professor McIlwain who maintains that all that is required is the ancient legal restraint of a guarantee of civil liberties enforceable by an independent court and the modern concept of the full responsibility of government to the *whole* mass of the governed.[37] There can be no doubt that the core and the substantive element of constitutionalism is the limitation of government by a constitutional guarantee of individual civil liberties enforceable by an independent tribunal. Deriving from the fundamental values of society, values which, articulated in public opinion, express a society's way of life and uphold its members' personality, individual civil liberties are indeed the very essence of constitutional government.

It must also be admitted that the democratisation of constitutionalism is today, together with civil liberties, its mainstay. The democratic control mechanisms of popular representation and the responsibility of the government to the governed unquestionably increase the efficacy of any system of restraints upon government. The necessity for elections at frequent intervals arises from the fact that the outlook and needs of the people change with the times. The issues upon which the government won an election may have ceased to have relevance after, say, five years, while, on the other hand, the people may have developed a new outlook diametrically opposed to that upon which their earlier decision had been based. If government is to be representative of the changing outlook and needs of the people, it is necessary therefore that the people should be able at reasonably frequent intervals to give practical expression to their changing wishes upon government. An irremovable legislature may thus rightly be regarded as a negation of democracy.

Political responsibility requires that public opinion should be one of the factors informing the actions of government. Indeed an extreme view of political responsibility postulates publc opinion as the determinant of policy, since, as it is said, a responsible person is one whose 'conduct responds to an outside determinant'![38] On this view, government should do nothing of which public opinion disapproves. This would be carrying the idea of responsibility too far, and it is both unrealistic and misconceived; unrealistic, because it attributes to the electorate a degree of ability, which it does not possess, to rationalise its wants in terms of detailed measures and of their conformity to technical requirements;[39] it is misconceived because it is based on too narrow a conception of governmental responsibility, which is not just to interpret and follow public opinion but to lead it along more rational and desirable lines. It is necessary to take a longer term view of responsibility as being owed not only to the individuals who constitute the electorate at a given time but also to its future members. 'Where the alternative lies between conducting the community along a popular path to disaster and trying to persuade it to adopt another and better one the statesman has to remember his responsibility to lead, as well as to interpret, opinion.'[40] The second element of political responsibility is the accountability or answerability of the rulers to the governed. This requires of the government to give an account of its actions to the people. Accountability should involve more than a periodic progress report by radio broadcast or during an election campaign. It presupposes freedom on the part of the people at all times directly or through their elected representatives, to question or criticise the action of the government, a duty on the part of the government to explain and try to justify its conduct, and lastly the availability of sanctions for unsatisfactory or unjustifiable conduct.

Eminently desirable as these democratic control mechanisms are, they cannot, however, like individual human rights, be regarded as a *sine qua non* for constitutional government. They are indeed a development of the last two centuries, but constitutionalism is much older than that, being originally monarchical or aristocratic. A colonial administration, in its early stages, was as irresponsible as any government can be, but it was perhaps more constitutional than many of the so-called representative and responsible governments in the emergent states today. A constitutional democracy is desirable, but a government need not necessarily be popularly elected to be constitutional.

The more controversial question concerning the concept of constitutionalism is whether human rights (and, subject to what has been said, the democratic control mechanisms) constitute its sole requirements. The main point at issue concerns the doctrine of separation of powers, that is, whether it is a necessary element of constitutionalism or not.

The Separation of Powers

'Among all the modern fallacies that have obscured the true teachings of constitutional history,' says Professor McIlwain, 'few are worse than the extreme doctrine of the separation of powers and the indiscriminate use of the phrase "checks and balances".'[41] It cannot, however, be much questioned that the functions of government are differentiable according to their distinctive features. Three categories are easily recognisable, viz. execution or measure-taking (which comprises 'political' direction and pure administration), law-making, and law-interpretation/adjudication. The idea of function is linked with that of *procedure*. The function of execution, for example, creates a good deal of room for and a tendency towards arbitrariness; it is the aspect of government – the maintenance of peace, order, the security of the state, the execution of social services, etc. – that brings government into the closest contact with the individual. Historically, the executive or police function (which originally included the settling of disputes) was the primary, indeed the only, function of government, for legislation is something of a later development, dating in the main from the sixteenth century. This makes it at once the aspect of government that stands in most need of restraint. By separating it from the law-making function, by insisting that every executive action must, in so far at any rate as it affects an individual, have the authority of some law, and by prescribing a different procedure for law-making, the arbitrariness of executive action can be effectively checked. The idea of procedure has an important controlling role. Where a procedure, separate from that involved in execution, is laid down for law-making, and must be complied with in order for the government to secure the necessary authority for measures it contemplates taking, then regularity in the conduct of affairs is ensured. It is usual in most countries to subject proposals for legislation to discussion and deliberation. The separation of functions, between execution and legislation, requiring separate procedures, is thus of the utmost importance, for even if government is regarded as a single, indivisible structure, the separation in procedure will necessarily operate as a limitation upon the incidence of arbitrariness. The conduct of affairs in accordance with predetermined rules is perhaps the best guarantee of regularity, and restraint has little or no value in constitutionalising government unless it is regularised. Regularity enables the individual to know in advance how he stands with the government, and how far the latter can go in interfering with the course of his life and activities.

A separation in procedure carries with it, however, the idea of a separate agency or structure. For although it may be theoretically possible to prescribe different procedures for the two functions of execution and legislation while at the same time vesting them in the same agency, this hardly accords with common sense or experience. A separation of the agencies to be entrusted with these functions would seem, in the nature of things, to be inescapable if constitutionalism is to be maintained. As Vile has put it, 'we are not prepared to accept that government can become, on the ground of "efficiency," or for any other reason, a single undifferentiated monolithic structure, nor can we assume that government can be allowed to become simply an accidental agglomeration of purely pragmatic relationships. Some broad ideas about "structure" must guide us in determining what is a "desirable" organisation for government.'[42] It may be concluded that constitutionalism requires for its efficacy a differentiation of governmental functions and a separation of the agencies which exercise them. For 'the diffusion of authority among different centres of decision-making is the antithesis of totalitarianism or absolutism.'[43] It must of course be admitted that, in the light of the practice and exigencies of modern government, governmental agencies are multifunctional; some overlapping in the functions of the various agencies is inevitable. Thus the executive agencies do make rules. Yet this fact is only a qualification upon, and not a negation of, the basic idea about a division of functions and of agencies, since in its ordinary application, rule-making by the executive is subordinate to that of the legislature. This subordination accords with the concept of government as consisting of a 'hierarchy of norms that will enable each of the decisions of an official to be tested against a higher rule.'[44] This fact, as Vile pointed out, is further reinforced by the internal rules of behaviour by which, notwithstanding the considerable over-lapping of functions, agencies recognise that particular functions are the primary responsibility of a given organ, and so refrain from unwarranted encroachment upon each others' primary function.

In orthodox theory, separation is extended beyond functions and agencies to the personnel of the agencies. It is insisted that the same person or group of persons should not be members of more than one agency. The most remarkable example of the application of this extreme separation is under the American Constitution, and the American application of the doctrine finds justification perhaps in its federal and presidential systems of government. But, whatever may be the objections to this extreme separation, it is no argument for complete fusion. Even the parliamentary executive of the West-minster system is not a complete fusion. Though members of the executive are also members of the legislature, separation is main-tained by the fact that such members form a very small proportion of the total membership of the legislature, and, more important, by the existence, in its British prototype, of an effective organised opposition whose role makes the legislature more than a mere reflection of the executive.

Separation of Powers in Relation to the Judicial Function

Not even the sternest critics of the doctrine of separation of powers deny its necessity as regards the judicial function. For the rule of law as an element of constitutionalism depends more upon how and by what procedure it is interpreted and enforced. The limita-tions which the law imposes upon executive and legislative action cannot have much meaning or efficacy unless there is a separate procedure comprising a separate agency and personnel for an *authoritative* interpretation and enforcement of them. The necessity for a procedure to interpret the law with finality is underlined by the fact that both the executive and the legislature have also to interpret the law in the course of carrying out their primary func-tions. An administrator will first have to interpret the law before applying it in his task of execution or administration, and so will the legislature have to determine the limits of its law-making powers. If, then, it is accepted that an act of the legislature contrary to the constitution is void, who is to exercise the function of declaring it so? The legislature in enacting the act may be said to have already given its interpretation of the limits of its powers under the constitution; in other words, it has by implication, declared that the act is within the constitution, for otherwise it would not have passed it, except as a deliberate attempt to violate the constitution. If, therefore, the legislature were to have the last word on the meaning of the constitution with respect to its own powers, the position will have been reached that every legislative act will have automatically to be accepted as within the constitution and valid. This would certainly make nonsense of the whole purpose of a constitutional limitation of government from the point of view at least of the relationship between the government and the individual. For the legislature's interpretation of its powers would naturally be coloured by self-interest, which would operate to make its interpretation biased in favour of itself. There is thus clearly an incontrovertible necessity for a procedure separate, in terms both of structure and personnel, from, and independent of, that for execution and legislation, which would enable the administrator's or the legislature's view of what the law means to be reviewed with finality.

This separate procedure is normally provided by the ordinary courts. The unique virtue of the separate procedure of the courts is that, being unaffected by the self-interest and consequent bias of the legislature or the executive in upholding their action, it can be expected to apply to the interpretation of the constitution or a statute an impartiality of mind which inhibits any inclination to vary the law to suit the whims or personal interests of either the judge or a party to a dispute, thus ensuring 'that stability and predictability of the rules which is the core of constitutionalism.' Whilst admittedly judges may not be entirely devoid of self-interest in the subject-matter of a legislative act – for no human procedure is ever completely neutral – yet this impartiality serves at once as a safeguard against the possible danger of arbitrariness on the part of the judges in the discharge of their interpretative function, and is reinforced for this purpose by the doctrine of precedent and the tradition of judicial self-restraint. Furthermore, the process by which the courts exercise their function, affording, as it does, ample opportunity for full argument by the parties or their lawyers on the possible interpretations of the law in the context of the facts before the court, ensures that the court's decision would reflect the reasonable or accepted view of the meaning of the law.

Properly conceived, the nature of the legislative function requires that laws should be made for the generality of the population. This at once implies that the making of laws is or should be a separate function from that of applying the law to the determination of the rights of individuals in given situations. The latter function requires a different kind of procedure from that of legislation, a procedure

which would ensure that the individual is to be condemned only
by an impartial tribunal and only after he has had adequate
opportunity to defend himself against his adversary. Legislation is
manifestly ill-suited for this function. If therefore the legislature
were to be able to make laws to pronounce a named individual
guilty of an offence and to punish him by, say, imprisonment, or to
confiscate his property or to deprive him of other rights enjoyed by
other citizens, the door is left wide open for arbitrariness and for
victimisation. The best guarantee against arbitrariness in the
exercise of the legislative function is to require legislation to be
made for the generality of the population, and not separately for
each individual and for each situation. Generality of application
ensures that individuals will be treated equally and uniformly in
accordance with the general law. Once admit *ad hominem* laws as a
general principle of legislation, and there will be an end to liberty.
Herein lies perhaps an even more compelling necessity for separating
the judicial from the legislative function. 'There is no liberty yet,'
writes Montesquieu, 'if the power to judge is not separated from the
legislative and executive power.' The U.S. Supreme Court has put
the point equally strongly in disallowing, as unconstitutional, a
Congressional Act which barred permanently from government
employment certain named American citizens believed to have
engaged in subversive activities against the United States. It
declared:

> 'Those who wrote our Constitution well knew the danger in
> special legislative acts which take away the life, liberty, or
> property of particular named persons, becuse the legislature thinks
> them guilty of conduct which deserves punishment. They intended
> to safeguard the people of this country from punishment without
> trial by duly constituted courts . . . And even the courts to which
> this important function was entrusted, were commanded to stay
> their hands until and unless certain tested safeguards were
> observed . . . When our Constitution and Bill of Rights were
> written, our ancestors had ample reason to know that legislative
> trials and punishments were too dangerous to liberty to exist in
> the nation of free men they envisioned. And so they proscribed
> bills of attainder.'[45]

The separation of the procedure or agency for the authoritative
interpretation of the law may therefore with justification be characterised as the most significant feature of modern government from
the legal point of view. It was the establishment of judicial restraint
upon the executive agencies of government that marked the beginning of the era of constitutionalism. There is yet another way in

which the evolution of the judicial powers as a restraint upon the executive power has contributed to the development of constitutional government. Judicial review of administrative activities has introduced into government standards of judicial behaviour, such as those of openness, fairness, reasonableness, and the more specific requirements of natural justice, viz. that a party affected by an administrative determination of a quasi-judicial nature should be given adequate notice and opportunity of being heard, and that the agency or tribunal giving such determination should be disinterested and unbiased. Constitutionalism, it has been truly said, 'is the application of judicial methods to basic problems of government; administrative justice, extending this application, attempts to extend the judicial methods to the wider sphere of activities which government is handling today.'[46]

The right of the courts to interpret the constitution with finality has not been accepted without question in many countries. In the United States much of the questioning is based on the argument that the right is not conferred by the constitution, except to a limited extent. Chief Justice Marshall's answer to this questioning is perhaps the best and most persuasive that can be given. It is, said the learned Chief Justice in language that has become classic:

'emphatically the province and duty of the judicial department to say what the law is. Those who apply the rule to particular cases must of necessity expand and interpret that rule. If two laws conflict with each other, the courts must decide on the operation of each. So if a law be in opposition to the constitution; if both the law and the constitution apply to a particular case, so that the court must decide that case conformably to the law, disregarding the constitution; or conformably to the constitution, disregarding the law; the court must determine which of these conflicting rules governs the case. This is of the very essence of judicial duty. If, then, the courts are to regard the constitution; and the constitution is superior to any ordinary act of the Legislature; the constitution, and not such ordinary act, must govern the case to which they both apply.'[47]

To avoid this sort of controversy, however, it would seem best to have a provision in the constitution expressly empowering the courts to pronounce upon the constitutionality of executive and legislative acts. It would also be necessary, by appropriate constitutional provisions, to insulate the courts from political influence and control. The constitutions of most of the new nations in the Commonwealth do this. Only if its independence is constitutionally guaranteed, would the judiciary be able effectively to discharge, without fear or favour, its heavy responsibility of acting as the sentinal of constitutionalism, and of holding the balance impartially between the government and the individual when their rights come into conflict.

Neither the inherent logic of the judicial function nor an express constitutional entrenchment of judicial review disposes completely of the attack upon the doctrine. The crux of the controversy is not, according to the argument, whether the courts should decide any conflict between a statute and the constitution in a case before them, for this is admitted, but whether their decision should be *final and conclusive* upon the political organs of government. Such finality, if it be admitted, would imply the superiority of the courts over the legislature. The argument is that the authority which can declare the acts of another void must necessarily be superior to the one whose acts may be so declared. It is intolerable, the argument further asserts, that the views of a handful of men should be allowed to over-ride those of the elected representatives of the people on so crucial a matter as the interpretation of the constitution; besides, judicial supremacy has implicit in it the danger that the courts might become something of a despotic oligarchy, and if a choice has to be made between the possible despotism of an oligarchy and the possible tyranny of an elected majority, the latter is the less intolerable of the two.

But once admit that the courts inexorably have to resolve any conflict between a statute and the constitution, should that become necessary in the ordinary course of applying the law in the settlement of disputes, it must equally inexorably follow that their decision should be final and conclusive upon the political organs of government. For the courts' decision establishes or rather declares the law of the land on the point covered by it, and a disregard of it by anyone, whether a private citizen or an organ of government, could only result in a new controversy, to be again finally determined by the courts; the conception upon which government proceeds does not admit that any one else's opinion of the law should have that quality of establishing or declaring it. And once authoritatively delared, constitutionalism demands that the government should be bound by the law. As regards the issue of superiority, Hamilton's answer in *The Federalist* only begs the question. He writes:

'Nor does this conclusion by any means suppose a superiority of the judicial to the legislative power. It only supposes that the power of the people is superior to both, and that if the will of the legislature, declared in its statutes, stands in opposition to that of the people declared in the constitution, the judges ought to be governed by the latter rather than the former.'[48]

The question is who should decide that the will of the legislature, declared in its statutes, is in opposition to that of the people, declared in the constitution. If the determination is to be made by the courts, then the argument is that this places them above the legislature. Judicial review does unquestionably create an impression of the courts' superiority to the political organs of government, but this superiority is more apparent than real. It must be remembered that the courts have no power generally, and at their own instance, to declare statutes void for unconstitutionality; they can do so only in concrete cases before them in which a conflict between a statute and the constitution is at issue. Judicial review is not 'the exercise of a substantive power to review or nullify acts of the legislature, for no such substantive power exists. It is simply a necessary concomitant of the power to hear and dispose of a case or controversy properly before the court, to the determination of which must be brought the test and measure of the law.'[49] In even more explicit words Judge Cooley has written:

> 'The courts have no authority to pass upon abstract questions, or questions not presented by actual litigation, and have therefore nothing to do with questions which relate exclusively to executive or legislative authority; nor is there any method in which their opinions can be constitutionally expressed, so as to have binding force upon either the executive or the legislature, when the question presents itself, not as one of existing law, but as one of what it is proper and politic or competent to make law for the future.'[50]

Moreover, the mere pendency of a case in court is not enough to enable a party to impugn a statute, for otherwise the court would indirectly be assuming a substantive power, which it does not possess, to review statutes. It would assume to do that only at the instance of a party who can show that he is in imminent danger of coming into conflict with the statute or that some existing right or business or other activities of his have been directly interfered with by or under the statute, and not merely that he suffers in some indefinite way in common with people generally, or that, although there is no immediate threat of it, he anticipates interference at some future date.[51] He must, in the language of the courts, establish a *locus standi* entitling him to impugn the statute. Underlying this rule is the recognition by the courts that the legislature represents the people, and that, accordingly, its acts, passed after due deliberation, ought not to be impugned except on the ground that it violates the interest or right of some person or group or of another government in a federation. For the same reason too the courts are willing to presume that the legislature would not *prima facie* want to violate the will of those they represent, as expressed in the constitution. In reviewing a statute, therefore, they start with a presumption in favour of its constitutionality, casting the onus on the person challenging it to show that it was in fact made without proper legal authority. The presumption is both expedient and wise provided it is not applied to cases of alleged violation of individual rights, since the primary purpose of guaranteeing them is to protect the minority against the tyranny of the majority.

Whatever the objections to judicial review, the truth, as Dicey has stressed, is that without an effective machinery for testing the constitutionality of statutes the limitations placed upon the powers of the legislature are a matter of policy rather than law; their sanction is moral or political.[52] And for this purpose, there is no satisfactory alternative to the ordinary courts, as the experience of France, Germany, Italy and Switzerland has shown. In all four countries there is a special Constitutional Court (or Council) but their essentially political membership deprives them of that impartiality which is the hallmark of judicial adjudication. Moreover, operating outside the main stream of the judicial system, they cannot perform the role of the American Supreme Court in maintaining the unity of the legal and judicial system. And, in Italy, for example, a decision by the Constitutional Court that a law is unconstitutional does not annul it, but merely refuses to apply it.

Checks and Balances

The idea of checks and balances seeks to make the separation of powers more effective by balancing the powers of one agency against those of another through a system of positive mutual checks exercised by the governmental organs upon one another. Thus the executive might be empowered to veto legislation or to dissolve the legislature, and the legislature to impeach the chief executive, to approve the appointment of certain other top state functionaries, to criticise and censor the executive or any member of it or, as a final weapon, to bring down the government. These are just a sample of the positive checks which the various organs might exercise upon one another, but the manner in which they may be combined vary from country to country according to the particular system of government instituted by its constitution. The idea of checks and balances presupposes that a specific function is assigned primarily to a given organ, subject to a power of *limited* interference by another organ to ensure that each organ keeps within the sphere delimited to it.

Finally, power may be limited by dividing it, not among different
organs of the same government, but among different territorial unit
governments.

The limitation of government by the various techniques outlined
above creates a dilemma—that of ensuring that government is not
thereby so weakened as to be incapable of governing effectively to
solve the complex problems of modern society. The limiting of
government, it has been said, is not to be the weakening of it.[53]
The problem is to maintain a proper balance between power and
law. As Professor Cowen has put it, 'although there is a deep chasm
between unfettered power and law, power must be reconciled with
law; for there can be neither government nor law without the
exercise of power. And freedom, too, must be under law; for otherwise it degenerates into licence and confusion. In short, unfettered
power is despotism or tyranny; unfettered freedom is licence or
anarchy. But between these two extremes there is a middle way,
where power tamed by law guarantees true freedom.'[54]

REFERENCES

1. C. H. McIlwain, *Constitutionalism: Ancient and Modern*, Cornell University Press, revised ed., 1947, pp. 21-2; also Wheare, *Modern
   Constitutions*, 1966, p. 137; Cowen, *The Foundations of Freedom*, 1961,
   p. 197.
2. *Modern Constitutions*, 1966, p. 139.
3. William G. Andrews, ed., *Constitutions and Constitutionalism*, 2nd ed.,
   1963, pp. 21-5.
4. Art. 118.
5. Art. 123.
6. Art. 125.
7. Art. 128.
8. Art. 126.
9. Art. 141.
10. Art. 134.
11. Art. 125.
12. See William G. Andrews, *op. cit.*, p. 152.
13. C. H. McIlwain, *op. cit.*, p. 35.
14. *Liyanage v. R.* [1967], 1.A.C. 259 (Ceylon).
15. Carl J. Friedrich, *Constitutional Government and Democracy*, revised ed.,
    1950, p. 123.
16. C. H. McIlwain, *op. cit.*, p. 14.
17. *Federalist 78.*
18. Edward S. Corwin, *The Doctrine of Judicial Review*, Gloucester, Mass.,
    Peter Smith, 1963, p. 105.
19. Corwin, *loc. cit.*
20. E. S. Corwin, *op. cit.*, p. 100.
21. *The Bribery Commissioner v. Ranasinghe* [1965] A.C. 172.

22. *Liyanage v. R.* [1967], 1.A.C. 259.
23. *The Bribery Commissioner v. Ranasinghe, ibid.* at p. 198.
24. At p. 200; my italics.
25. See the South African Supreme Court in *Harris v. Donges* (1952), 1 T.L.R. 1245; *Minister of the Interior v. Harris* (1952), S.A.L.R. 769.
26. *The Bribery Commissioner v. Ranasinghe, ibid.* at p. 198; see Dicey, *The Law of the Constitution*, 10th ed., Introduction by E. C. S. Wade, p. xl.
27. Dicey, *op. cit.*, p. lxxix.
28. *Modern Constitutions*, 1966, p. 5.
29. *Ibid.*, p. 19.
30. *McCawley v. The King* [1920], A.C. 691 (P.C.); *The Bribery Commissioners v. Ranasinghe, ibid.* at p. 198; *Kariappar v. Wijesinha* [1967], A.C. 717 (P.C.).
31. Art. 79 (3).
32. Art. 89.
33. S. 29 (2).
34. See Carl J. Friedrich, *op. cit.*, p. 145.
35. *Att.-Gen. of the Republic v. Mustafa Ibrahim and Others* (1964), Cyprus L. Rep., 195, 208; discussed below, Ch. VII, and p. 216, n. 56.
36. *The New Commonwealth and Its Constitutions*, 1964, p. 106.
37. *Constitutionalism: Ancient and Modern*, revised ed., 1947, pp. 141-6.
38. Carl J. Friedrich, *Man and His Government*, 1963, p. 310.
39. Carl J. Friedrich, *Impact of American Constitutionalism Abroad*, 1967, pp. 22-3.
40. H. R. G. Greaves, *The British Constitution*, 1958, p. 92.
41. *Op. cit.*, p. 141.
42. M. J. C. Vile, *Constitutionalism and the Separation of Powers*, 1967, p. 10.
43. *Ibid.*, p. 15.
44. Vile, *op. cit.*, p. 320.
45. *U.S. v. Lovett* (1945), 328, U.S. 303 at p. 318; 90 L ed. 1252 at p. 1260— per Justice Black, delivering the opinion of the Court. For decisions holding *ad hominem* laws void as a usurpation of the judicial function reserved to the courts under the Constitution, see *Liyanage v. R.* (1967) *ibid.*, and *Lakanmi v. Att.-Gen. (West)* Sc. 58/69 of April 24, 1970, discussed below at pp. 70 and 203, 247, 250 respectively.
46. Carl J. Friedrich, *Constitutional Government and Democracy*, revised ed., 1950, p. 117.
47. *Marbury v. Madison*, 1, Cranch, 137 (1803).
48. *Federalist*, 78.
49. *Adkins' Case*, 261, U.S. 525, 544 (1923) – per Justice Sutherland.
50. *Principles of Constitutional Law*, 3rd ed., 1898, p. 158; quoted in Corwin, *Court over Constitution*, 1957, p. 77.
51. See e.g., *Olawoyin v. Att.-Gen., Northern Region* (1961), 1, All N.L.R. 269; *Adegbenro v. Att.-Gen. of the Fedn.*, F.S.C. 170/1962; discussed in Nwabueze, *Constitutional Law of the Nigerian Republic*, 1964, pp. 309-10.
52. Dicey, *Law of the Constitution*, 10th ed., p. 157.
53. McIlwain, *op. cit.*, p. 142.
54. *The Foundations of Freedom*, 1961, p. 197.

CHAPTER II

THE CONSTITUTION
IN EMERGENT STATES

A discussion of constitutionalism in new states will inevitably begin with the constitution as the source of governmental powers and of the limitations upon them. The constitution is both the symbol and instrument of constitutionalism. The main problems in new states facing the constitution as an instrument of restraint on government relate to its legitimacy and the source of its supremacy. These problems arise because of the source from which the constitution in these nations derives its authority as a fundamental law regulating the organisation of government. Owing to their origin as colonial creations, the new states have had their constitutions adopted for them by the colonial power at the time of its withdrawal or by the local legislature set up by the colonial power or under the authority of a law enacted by it. Only in a few cases were the constitutions of these states established by the people at a referendum or by a constituent assembly elected specifically for the purpose. It is understandable and perhaps inevitable that a colonial territory should be launched into independent statehood under a constitution made for it by the colonial power. What is not easy to understand, however, is that when the country, after some years of independent existence, adopts a new constitution, the existing legislature created by the colonial power should still be the authority to enact it. In the ex-British colonies the adoption of a new constitution after independence is occasioned by the need and the desire to change from a monarchy to a republic. Thus, the Nigerian Constitution of 1963, which changed the country from a monarchy to a republic, was enacted by the parliament established by the Independence (Imperial) Constitution of 1960.[1] The method has been the same in the rest of the Commonwealth countries, with the exception of Ghana, Tanganyika and Uganda whose republican constitutions were enacted by a Constituent Assembly, but the Constituent Assembly was the imperially created National Assembly under a different name. The national assembly simply resolved itself into a constituent assembly, and by that name enacted the new republican constitution under the power conferred upon it by an Act of the national assembly itself. Even Guinea which, by voting against the establishment of the French Community under the constitution of the Fifth Republic in the referendum, became independent as it were by unilateral secession, had its Constitution adopted for it by the pre-existing national assembly.[2] In the peculiar circumstances of its origin, one would have expected Guinea to have wanted a clean break with its colonial past by having its constitution ordained directly by the people.

The Legitimacy of the Constitution

The importance of the source of a constitution's authority lies, not so much in a nationalistic longing or aspiration for autochthony as in its bearing upon its legitimacy. The constitution is no less law for being an act of the colonial power or of the local legislature but its moral authority, that is to say, its legitimacy, is another matter. The legitimacy of a constitution is concerned with how to make it command the loyalty, obedience and confidence of the people. It cannot be disputed that a major cause of the collapse of constitutional government in many of the new states was the general lack of respect for the constitution among the populace and even among the politicians themselves. The state itself is an alien, if also a beneficial creation; its existence is characterised by a certain artificiality in the eyes of the people and it is remote from their lives and thought. The constitution embodies ideas that are not part of the native cultural heritage of the people, ideas originating in Roman law and Greek philosophy, but which by a process of assimilation have become a common heritage of the whole of Europe but certainly not of Africa. It is not of course suggested as a condition for the legitimacy of a system of government that it must be the product of a traditional culture and philosophy; if that were so, no modern system of government could ever have legitimacy in most of the emergent countries whose traditional cultural systems have yielded nothing relevant to the organisation of the central government of a modern complex society. Yet the alien character of the system of government instituted by the constitutions of the new states and of the ideas underlying it made it necessary that something should have been done to legitimise them in the eyes of the people. What this means is that a constitution should be generally understood by the people and be acceptable to them. A constitution cannot hope to command the loyalty, respect and confidence of the people otherwise. And to achieve this understanding and acceptance, a constitution needs to be put through a process of popularisation, with a view to generating public interest in it and an attitude that everybody has a stake in it, that it is the common property of all. The people must be made to identify themselves with the constitution. Without this sense of identification, of attachment and involvement, a constitution would always remain a remote, artificial object, with no more real existence than the paper on which it is written.

The question of legitimacy has usually been viewed from the standpoint of the rulers, i.e., whether they have an accepted 'title to rule,' and according to Max Weber, 'title to rule' may be acquired in three ways, viz. through an authority sanctioned either by tradition, as in the case of a monarch or a chief, or by a faith in the leader arising from his personal prestige or charisma (the so-called charismatic authority); or through a popular acceptance of the appropriateness of the system of government.[3] As Lipset has shown,[4] the legitimacy of the American system of government owed much to the deep personal loyalty, confidence and veneration which Americans felt towards their first President, George Washington. To his countrymen of his day, the personality of Washington was almost divine, an object of worship. Factional antagonism which might have undermined or even destroyed the fledgling constitutional structure just brought into existence was held in check out of respect for his authority, thus giving the Constitution a chance to strike root and gain acceptance. The so-called charismatic leaders who have dominated the political scene in the new nations are men of a different type, with different aspirations and different dedication, and have generally been unable to perform the legitimising role. Lacking popular acceptance itself, the constitution could neither have bestowed legitimacy upon the government nor fulfilled its other function as a symbol of national unity.

It is, therefore, in relation to the question of legitimacy that the practical importance of a constitution's method of adoption mainly lies. In order that a constitution should have legitimacy in the public eye, the people should be involved in the process of its making. Its form and contents should be subjected to public discussion. Whatever body is charged with the role of drafting constitutional proposals, should invite views from the public both in the form of articles in newspapers, journals, etc., and of memoranda to the constitutional commission. That body should also move around the country and talk with the people individually and in groups. The proposals, when finally drafted, should be published, and submitted to the people at a plebiscite. It does not matter what body is going to enact it finally into law. The idea is that there should be a continuous public discussion of it up to the time of final enactment. Only thus can a constitution have reality for, and become the property of, the people whose affairs it is to govern; only so can it hope to win their confidence and, perhaps eventually, their respect and loyalty as well. 'The process of constitution-making,' it has been said, 'has been regarded as a major symbol of the formation of the new state.'[5]

If the final act of adoption is that of the people, that may conceivably enhance the constitution's legitimacy. The phrase, 'We the people . . . do hereby adopt, enact and give to ourselves this Constitution,'[6] which, since the adoption of the American Constitution in 1787, has become a familiar feature of most modern republican constitutions, is no mere incantation. It is meant to foster among the people a feeling that the constitution is their own, and not an imposition, and that as such they have a stake, a responsibility, in observing its rules. The device is nowadays often supplemented by an open avowal in the constitution of the principle that the people are sovereign and the ultimate source of all political power. With France particularly, it has become a matter of tradition, a tradition which she has bequeathed to her ex-colonies, to proclaim as a substantive provision of the constitution, that 'national sovereignty belongs to the people who shall exercise it through their representatives and by way of referendum.' The Constitutions of Germany, 1949, and the U.S.S.R., 1936, also proclaim that 'all state authority emanates from the people.' In the Convention that drafted the American Constitution, too, there had been proposed a motion to add to the preamble a declaration that 'governments rest on the consent of the governed,' but this was lost, on the ground that the words, 'We the people of the United States . . . do ordain and establish this constitution,' 'are as copious and expressive as possible; any addition will only drag out the sentence without illuminating it.'[7] Even the Nigerian Constitution proclaims: 'We the people of Nigeria, *by our representatives here in Parliament assembled,* do hereby declare, enact and give to ourselves the following Constitution.' It is, however, somewhat disingenuous to have made such reference to the people when they had nothing at all to do with its enactment. It was the prime minister and the regional premiers who, meeting for just one day, agreed among themselves that a republican constitution for Nigeria should reproduce the 1960 imperial constitution with such amendments as would conform it to a republican status. That their meeting attracted public notice at all was due to its controversial decision to incorporate into the new constitution provisions for the preventive detention of persons without trial. What public discussion there was was confined to just this issue. Thereafter Parliament proceeded to enact the proposals as agreed among the premiers, and, as was usual in that body, there was hardly any discussion of them. In the result, Nigeria had to continue its precarious life under what has been aptly described as 'artificial constitutional régimes which were created by the hidden impulse of a foreign (colonial) constituent power working through small groups of converts to Western constitutionalism,'[8] a group, indeed, whose understanding of constitutional democracy was at best vague. Is it then surprising that neither this group nor the general populace had any respect for the sysyem? Even among the Western democracies, the adoption of a new constitution is always the outcome of a long drawn-out debate at various levels.

We are told that, although the supremacy of the people as supreme lawgiver is recognised in most countries of the world, it would be an innovation to introduce it in the Commonwealth. For 'the people there, so far from being a supreme lawgiver, is not . . . a lawgiver at all.'[9] The reason given for thus denying the people of the Commonwealth a power which the rest of the world acknowledge to be their birthright, is that the Commonwealth was founded upon a conception of the Parliament of the United Kingdom as the supreme legislative authority for the whole of the Queen's dominions. And to recognise any other supreme lawmaking authority would run counter to this and destroy the legal unity of the association. The Commonwealth, thanks to its flexibility, has had to adjust itself to the fact that the status of a country as a dominion of the Queen cannot be insisted upon as a condition for membership. Accordingly, the legal unity of the Commonwealth does not embrace those member countries which have become republics; for them, there is nothing like the 'constitutional law of the Commonwealth,'[10] which will be violated by recognising the people as supreme lawgiver for the purpose, at any rate, of enacting a constitution.

However, a constitution need not necessarily have been enacted by the people to have legitimacy. As has been stated, what is important is that the people should be involved in the process of its making. The 1960 Constitution of Ghana was enacted by a constituent assembly, but only after it had been submitted to the people at a plebiscite. Not only that, it went further in institu-tionalising the people, by acknowledging them as the donors of all political power and by incorporating them as part of the legislative machinery of the state. Powers not delegated to the regular organs of the state remained with the people who could exercise them by means of a referendum; in particular of the fifty-five articles of the

Constitution no less than seventeen were made alterable only by the people, exclusive of the legislature.

The Supremacy of the Constitution

The link between the legitimacy of the constitution and its supremacy can at once be seen, since the rationale of this supremacy is that it is an emanation from the will of a body superior to the legislature, namely the people. A constitution is, or is supposed to be, the product of the exercise of the constituent power inherent in any people. It is an original, constituent act, from which all other legislative acts derive their authority. Since, as already noted, the constitution in nearly all the emergent states did not emanate from the people directly, what, then, is the source and rationale of its supremacy?

Before independence, a colonial constitution could claim supremacy because it emanated from the superior authority of the suzerian power. That superiority disappeared at independence. The new independent state acquires an authority equal to that of its former master, and can now alter any of the latter's acts. An independence constitution enacted by the outgoing colonial power cannot claim supremacy by virtue of the superior status or authority previously enjoyed by the colonial power *vis-à-vis* the dependency. The same is true of a constitution enacted by the local legislature. In enacting a constitution, the local legislature can act with no authority superior to that by which it makes ordinary laws. No doubt it is possible to differentiate the legislature which enacted the constitution from that which takes office under it. For although, for convenience, no new elections are held to return members to the new legislature, the old members remain in office only by virtue of a fresh oath to 'preserve, protect and defend the constitution,' and it is almost invariably stipulated that they cannot enter upon the performance of their office under the new constitution until they have taken the oath. The change may be described as involving an abdication by the old legislature, an act by which it both effaces itself and concurrently transfers its powers to a new body under the new constitution.

Granted that the legislature taking office under the new constitution is different from that which enacted it, the latter could claim no superior authority or status. The new legislature is bound by the new constitution, not because it is the act of a superior authority, but because it is the source from which it derives its existence and powers. This is an explanation of the supremacy of the constitution based upon logic; the constitution is supreme because it is logically prior to the organs of the government. If the government and its organs are created by the constitution, then logically they can have only such powers as are granted to them by the instrument from which they derive their existence.[11] Whilst admitting the validity of this logical explanation of the supremacy of the constitution, Sir Kenneth Wheare nevertheless asserts that a new constitution enacted for Britain by its parliament 'would not be binding upon parliament.'[12] This can only be if the enactment of a new constitution by parliament does not, as has been suggested, involve an act of abdication on its part. No doubt the new consitution will provide, as all constitutions do, that 'there shall be a parliament which shall consist . . .' Surely the parliament so created cannot be the same as the old parliament which enacted the constitution. An act of self-effacement or suicide will necessarily have occurred. And it is difficult to see on what ground parliament can deny the supremacy of the new constitution over it.

The question, however, is not as to the binding force of the constitution's supremacy in such circumstances, but whether a supremacy based upon the logical priority of the constitution is not too tenuous to bestow upon it maximum efficacy and respect. This accounts to some extent for the lack of respect for the constitution in the emergent states. Theory apart, a parliament which enacted a constitution is not likely to treat its own creation as being above it. There would naturally be a greater inclination on its part to disregard the constitutional limitations than would be the case if it had been a constituent act of the people. On the part of the people, too, the idea of a constitution enacted by parliament being supreme over its creator is hardly intelligible. To them, the constitution is on exactly the same level as any other law enacted by parliament, and is entitled to no greater or special respect. And because of the general ignorance about its provisions and the lack of interest in them, its role as the basis for ordered social life is insufficiently appreciated, with the result that it is not generally considered as entitled to any greater obedience than other laws. It is the recognition of the constitution as a superior law that compels the greater obedience which people are prepared to give to it.

In the view of Corwin, the worship and veneration which Americans accord to their Constitution owes not only to 'its rootage in popular will,' but also to the fact that it embodies 'an essential and unchanging justice.' Thus, he wrote:

'There are, it is predicated, certain principles of right and justice which are entitled to prevail of their own intrinsic excellence, altogether regardless of the attitude of those who wield the physical resources of the community. Such principles were made by no human hands; indeed, if they did not antedate deity itself, they still so express its nature as to bind and control it. They are external to all Will as such and interpenetrate all Reason as such. They are eternal and immutable. In relation to such principles, human laws are, when entitled to obedience save as to matters indifferent, merely a record or transcript, and their enactment an act not of will or power but one of discovery and declaration.'[13]

It is this heritage of natural law principles of right and justice which, according to him, form the background of the American Constitution and which, coupled with its origin as a superior, constituent act of the people, have earned for it the 'almost blind worship' of Americans. As previously stated, natural law thinking and Greek philosophy generally form no part of the heritage of the emergent states, and so cannot be a factor sustaining the supremacy of their constitutions.

The Length of the Constitution

If a constitution needs to be understood in order to be able to command the loyalty, confidence and obedience of the people, then it must be of such length and couched in such language as to make it readable and intelligible to the people. 'One essential characteristic of the ideally best form of constitution,' writes Wheare, 'is that it should be as short as possible.'[14]

In this repsect there is a marked difference between the constitutions of the ex-French and ex-British territories. The former are relatively short and framed in simple language, while the latter are characterised by an inordinate prolixity and by a technicality in expression that makes them difficult to read and understand. The former run from between 39 articles (Central African Republic) to 110 articles (Morocco), but the normal is between 60 and 80 articles. The latter have run all the way from 107 sections (Sierra Leone) to 247 (Kenya) to 395 (India exluding its nine long schedules). Also the short articles of the constitutions of the ex-French territories contrast strikingly with the overlong articles in the constitutions of the ex-British territories. Both Morocco and Malawi have the same number of articles (110), but whereas the 110 articles of the Morocco Constitution occupy only twelve pages of print, the Malawi Constitution covers fifty-five pages. The 300 pages of the Kenyan Independence Constitution (247 sections) are simply forbidding.

Why this disparity in length? The first explanation is of course tradition. The French notion of a code, especially a code of constitutional law, is that it should be as short as possible, marking only the main outlines of the subject and designating only its important objects, and leaving 'the minor ingredients which compose those objects to be deduced from the nature of the objects themselves.'[15] Aspects of governmental organisation which, though important, are not considered fundamental are left out of the constitution, but with the express stipulation that they should be regulated by 'organic laws.' In the Constitution of the Fifth French Republic, 1958, for example, matters so reserved to organic laws range over such fields as the life of parliament, the number of its members, and the organisation and operation of the constitutional council. Nearly all the ex-French territories have adopted this device. It has no doubt an advantage in limiting the constitution to fundamentals, but it may become objectionable as impairing the supremacy of the constitution where it is extended to what might be considered as a fundamental, or where it is used to qualify a general rule enacted in the constitution.[16] This is because an organic law does not enjoy the same status as the constitution. It is enacted and may be altered in virtually the same way as an ordinary law, except that (*a*) it cannot be debated and voted on until two weeks after its introduction; (*b*) the concurrence of the upper house can only be dispensed with if the bill received an absolute majority in the national assembly; and (*c*) it may only be promulgated after being declared by the constitutional council to be in conformity with the constitution.[17] The legislatures of the ex-French territories are of course mostly unicameral,[18] and most have no constitutional councils. In the absence of these institutions, the procedure relating to organic laws usually requires that they shall be passed or amended only by an absolute or two-thirds majority of the national assembly, and may not be promulgated unless the supreme court, at the instance of the president of the republic, has declared them conformable to the constitution.[19]

The British technique of drafting is markedly different. A statute should be as explicit as possible, leaving no loopholes and no ambiguities so far as that can be achieved by drafting ingenuity. As a result the statute becomes riddled with unnecessary verbiage, technicality and complexity, to the extent that few can read it with understanding, and none with relish. A constitution drafted in the British fashion will therefore remain unread and uncomprehended except by a few lawyers and professional politicians.

A second explanation is the form of executive government which they institute. The constitutions of the ex-French territories estab-

lish without exception a presidential system, while most Commonwealth constitutions have established a parliamentary executive
inherited from Westminster. The Westminster system rests perhaps
more upon vague, ill-defined conventions than upon explicit law.
A written constitution which adopts it is thus faced with the problem whether to incorporate only the legal rules or to attempt to
spell out the conventions in precise, written terms. There have
been three different approaches to the problem. The constitutions
of the older Commonwealth countries incorporate only the strictly
legal elements of the system; the conventions are of course taken
over also by necessary implication but they do not appear in the
constitution so as to lengthen and encumber it. In the constitutions
of some of the newer Commonwealth countries, such as those of
Ceylon, 1946, and Ghana, 1957, brevity is achieved by incorporating the conventions, not by mere implication, but by express
reference without explicit definition, e.g. by providing that the
powers of the head of state shall be exercised 'as nearly as may be
in accordance with the constitutional conventions applicable to the
exercise of similar powers in the United Kingdom by Her Majesty.'
Then there is the method of detailed specification adopted by the
constitutions of Nigeria and the countries which became independent
after it under the Westminster system.

Two distinctions are involved in these three approaches: between
law and convention on the one hand, and between two forms of
legislation on the other. Under the second and third approaches,
the conventions are clothed with the character and force of law,
becoming thereby justiciable. The merit of law in comparison with
convention as a sanction for constitutionalism is perhaps best stated
in the following words of Sir Ivor Jennings:

'The efficacy of judicial decisions in important governmental
matters lies not in enforcement, but in the precision of judgment,
the recognised sanctity of law, and the power of public opinion.
To break the law is to do something clearly and obviously unconstitutional . . . it is possible to rouse public opinion to indignation;
the breach would be proclaimed from every platform and
blazoned forth in every headline. Breaches of constitutional conventions are less obvious and can be more easily clouded by a
fog of misunderstanding. A judicial decision that a law has been
broken leaves no room for argument, save as to its politicial
justification; an accusation that a convention has been broken
may be met by an accusation of factious and deliberate mis-
representation.'[20]

Judicial enforcement, though the most important sanction of law,
is inappropriate for certain rules, such as those governing certain

aspects of the relationship between the head of state and his ministers. It is incompatible with the dignity of the office that the head of state should be amenable personally to the processes of the court during his tenure of office. For such rules, the inherent sanction of the sanctity of law is enough. Quite sensibly, therefore, these constitutions exlcude from judicial inquiry the question whether the head of state has in any case received, or acted in accordance with, advice. Granted, then, that law sanctions constitutionalism more effectively than convention,[21] brevity might be achieved at the same time by simply enacting the conventions by reference. But brevity would then have been achieved at the cost of much uncertainty, for the conventions of the British Constitution are notoriously uncertain. For example, it is still a debatable issue among the best constitutional lawyers and experienced politicians in Britian as to when, if at all, the Queen can constitutionally dismiss a prime minister or refuse his request for dissolution of parliament.[23] The process of codification provides an opportunity to try to establish these conventions, to make them up where they are uncertain on any point, and to adapt them to suit local conditions and needs. Prolixity and complexity are thus evils made inevitable by the Westminster system. The separation of the head of state from the head of government and the parliamentary character of the executive create complex relationships, which for the sake of precision, require to be explicitly defined. But for this system, there can be no doubt that much of this prolixity and complexity would have been avoided. One needs only refer to the republican, presidential constitutions of Ghana, 1960, and Tanganyika, 1962, to be convinced of this. Both ran to only fifty-five and sixty-nine articles (or sections) respectively, a striking contrast with their previous Westminster-type constitutions. They were without doubt the shortest constitutions in the Commonwealth, and Ghana's, drafted more in the French style, was the least technical and most readable and most easily understood.

The third reason is that, with the exception of Cameroon, all the ex-French territories have unitary constitutions, whereas many of the Commonwealth constitutions have been federal or at least quasi-federal, such as those of Australia, Canada, India, Pakistan, Malaya (and Malaysia), Nigeria, Kenya, Uganda, the South Arabian Federation, Rhodesia and Nyasaland and the West Indies, though the last two have since broken up, and some of the others have become unitary in form or substance. Federalism makes it necessary to incorporate additional articles defining the relationship of the various territorial units of government. However, it is interesting to note that Cameroon still managed to keep its federal constitution within only sixty articles covering just twelve pages of print.

Lastly, there is the concern of the British to ensure that on their withdrawal, the tribal or racial minorities were not left with insufficient protection against the tyranny of the majority, since in the plural societies of the emergent states the danger of tyranny of majority rule is markedly greater than in the homogeneous societies of Europe. Thus, in addition to the traditional checks and balances, institutional devices in the form of independent commissions have been established to insulate from political control such sensitive areas of public administration as the delimitation of electoral constituencies, the conduct of elections, the administration and the audit of public accounts; or there may be a special institutional mechanism designed to obstruct the enactment of legislation that discriminates against racial or tribal groups.[24] Such checks and balances have some value, but it is doubtful whether such value as they have really justifies the encumbrance they impose upon the constitution.

The Content of the Restraints Imposed by the Constitutions of Emergent States

The constitutions of all the emergent states institute in one form or another, and to a greater or lesser degree, popular representation in government, political responsibility of the rulers to the governed, separation of powers, and certain checks and balances; and they also all entrench a procedure, varying in rigidity, for constitutional amendment. The main difference between the former French and British territories in this regard relates to (*a*) the application of the rule of law to the executive; (*b*) judicial review of the constitutionality of executive and legislative acts, and (*c*) a constitutional guarantee of individual civil liberties.

The Executive and the Rule of Law

In all common law jurisdictions, it is an established principle that the executive has no inherent discretionary power to act against the citizen. As almost every executive act bears directly or indirectly upon citizens, the principle operates as a guarantee against arbitrariness in executive government. A re-affirmation of the principle in emphatic language was made by the Privy Council in a case in 1931 in which the colonial Governor of Nigeria claimed an inherent power (i.e. without the authority of a law) to appoint, depose and deport chiefs. 'As the executive,' said Lord Atkin, delivering the judgment of the Board, 'he [the Governor] can only act in pursuance of the powers given to him by law. In accordance with British jurisprudence no member of the executive can interfere with the liberty or property of a British subject except on the condition that he can support the legality of his action before a court of justice.'[25] Read in the light of this principle, the provision in many of the Commonwealth constitutions which define executive authority to extend to the execution and maintenance of the constitution and *to all matters with respect to which the legislature has power to make laws,* does not imply a power, independently of statute, to act in derogation of the rights of citizens. The provision does unquestionably imply the vital functions of thinking out policy, which might subsequently be given expression in legislation, and the co-ordination of the various processes of government. It might also authorise executive action where no private right is involved, but it clearly confers no power to interfere with such rights. The impression conveyed by the second leg of the provision that there is an independent executive power to act in all matters with respect to which the legislature has power to make laws, whether or not private rights are thereby encroached upon, is therefore incorrect. Under the British system therefore, executive power has mostly to be conferred by statute before it can be exercised.

Not only must the exercise of executive power be authorised by law, it must also keep strictly within the scope of that authority. This means that, when there is a law upon any particular matter, the executive, just like any private person, cannot defy it or refuse to be bound by it, and it does not matter that private rights are not thereby affected. *A fortiori,* a subordinate officer of the government who has committed a contravention of the law cannot plead in defence that he acted upon the orders of the government. With but few exceptions, designed largely to preserve the dignity of the office of the head of state, the government and its officers enjoy no special dispensation or immunity from the ordinary laws of the land.

Nor can the executive give itself the necessary legal authority to interfere with private rights. So far as it can make laws at all, its power in that behalf is a derivative and subordinate one, and depends upon express parliamentary authorisation, revocable at any time.

This position contrasts sharply with that in many of the ex-French territories where the executive has an independent power of legislation, a heritage from France. The Constitution of the Fifth French Republic divides legislative power between the legislature and the executive, reserving certain enumerated matters to the legislature while the residue is made the subject of rule-making by the executive.[26] Thus, not only is the rule-making power of the executive independent of the legislature, but it also covers a quite considerable range of matters. A law enacted by the legislature upon a matter which is properly the subject of the rule-making power may be modified or annulled by an executive decree. What is more, should parliament fail to pass a finance bill within seventy days, the government may put it into effect by ordinance.[27] It may also, with parliamentary authorisation, issue ordinances during a limited period of time on matters reserved to the legislature, in order to implement its programme.[28] Although such an ordinance has to be ratified by an act of parliament, yet this is more than a subordinate legislation as it is understood under the British system, since subordinate legislation presupposes that the legislature has legislated on the matter, leaving only certain points of detailed administration to be regulated by rules or regulations made by the executive. These provisions are reproduced in the constitutions of all the ex-French African territories[29] with the exception of Guinea, Tunisia and Cameroon. In Guinea the national assembly has exclusive jurisdiction over legislation, the domain of law being declared to be unlimited.[30] In Tunisia the president may legislate by decree for a limited period and for special reasons only by virtue of authority delegated to him in that behalf by the national assembly, and such decrees when made are subject to approval by the assembly.[31] During the recess of the assembly, the president may also legislate by order in council, subject to the ratification of the assembly when it reassembles.[32] The President of Cameroon has power to make regulations, but the domain of the law is not limited by his regulation-making power.[33]

Ghana, in its 1960 Republican Constitution, broke with the common law tradition, by the power given to the first president, Dr. Nkrumah, whenever he considered it to be in the national interest, to give directions by legislative instrument, which could override laws enacted by the legislature.[34] In Pakistan, too, under its 1962 Constitution, the president could legislate by temporary ordinance when the assembly was not in session.

There can be no doubt that an executive, invested with an independent law-making power, can become autocratic, as has been borne out in France under de Gaulle, in Ghana under Nkrumah and in almost all the former French African territories.

Judicial Review of Executive and Legislative Acts

The review by the ordinary courts of the constitutionality or legality of legislative and executive acts, and of the propriety of administrative acts of a quasi-judicial nature is the main bulwark of constitutionalism in the Commonwealth and the United States.

The principle is so deeply ingrained as to have become axiomatic. The courts' jurisdiction for this purpose may be invoked by an aggrieved party in proceedings before them, provided he can establish a *locus standi* entitling him to challenge the act in question. This condition means that what can be challenged is an actual legislative act in being; it is not in general permissible to impugn through the process of the court a bill before it has actually become law.[35] As questions concerning the interpretation of the constitution call for an authoritative determination, it is usual to require that such questions arising in proceedings before lower courts be referred to the highest court in the land which, after pronouncing upon them, will remit its opinion to the court below which will then apply it to decide the matter in controversy before it. The opinion of the court declaring an act unconstitutional renders the act void and inoperative. It is unusual, indeed almost unknown, for the executive or the legislature to invoke the courts' jurisdiction to impugn the constitutionality or legality of each other's acts.[36]

The necessity does not exist, since constitutionally their functions do not overlap. The executive has no independent power of legislation conferred directly by the constitution, the legislature does not exercise executive functions, and in the Commonwealth most laws passed by the legislature are initiated by the executive. It is only in a federal set-up in which power is divided among various territorial unit governments that the act of a government can be challenged by another government where there is a dispute concerning their respective areas of competence.

The division of legislative powers between the legislature and the executive in France and her former territories has compelled a different approach to judicial review. The right of recourse to the reviewing authority belongs normally to the president. He may request the authority to pronounce upon the constitutionality of laws and international undertakings as well as on conflicts of authority between the government and parliament. In most cases this recourse may be had either before or after a bill has been promulgated into law, but in the Central African Republic and Dahomey the submission must be before promulgation. Only in the Central African Republic and Madagascar may the right of recourse be exercised by someone other than the president, namely the president of the national assembly, or (in Madagascar which has a bicameral legislature) the president of the senate. A provision declared unconstitutional may neither be promulgated nor be put into force, and in Gabon it is expressly stated that such pronouncement shall be binding upon the governmental and administrative authorities.

D

Except in the Central African Republic, Madagascar, Tunisia, and Algeria, the reviewing authority is the supreme court (or the federal court in the Cameroon), which is the highest judicial authority.[37] The supreme court is also the administrative law tribunal. Its members are appointed and may be dismissed by the president either in his absolute discretion or on the recommendation of a judiciary council composed of judges and politicians and presided over by the president himself, but the independence of the judiciary from the executive and legislature is expressly proclaimed in most of the constitutions. The Central African Republic, Madagascar, Tunisia and Algeria follow the French example of vesting jurisdiction in constitutional matters in a body distinct from the ordinary courts – the constitutional council in the Central African Republic,[38] and Algeria[39] the high council of institutions in Madagascar,[40] and the council of state in Tunisia,[41] though the Tunisian council of state is merely an administrative judicial body. An organic law is to prescribe the composition, organisation and functioning of the Central African Republic constitutional council, but pending the enactment of such law, the powers of the council were exercised by a commission composed of the president of the court of appeal and two other members appointed, one by the president of the republic and the other by the president of the national assembly. The Madagascar high council of institutions has five ordinary members, two of whom are appointed by the president of the republic, two by the president of the national assembly and one by the president of the senate. Of these five, three must be persons with legal qualifications. All former presidents of the republic are automatically members of the council.[42] The president of the council is appointed by the president of the republic. The Algerian constitutional council is composed of the first president of the supreme court, the presidents of the civil and administrative chambers of the supreme court, and three deputies appointed by the national assembly and one member appointed by the president of the republic.

There is no express vesting in the supreme court or other reviewing authority of jurisdiction to pronounce on the constitutionality of executive and legislative acts at the instance of aggrieved parties in ordinary litigation before it, neither is the inherent jurisdiction of the ordinary courts in the matter expressly taken away. Judicial review has little value if it can only be exercised at the instance of the organs of government to decide conflicts of competence between them. Its main value is as a protection for individuals against arbitrary or unlawful exercise of power by the organs of government. In the absence of any express divesting of the courts' inherent jurisdiction, it must be assumed that the courts can, at the instance of an aggrieved party in ordinary litigation, pronounce a legislative act unconstitutional and refuse to apply it. Whether such a pronouncement will render the act void is a matter which, from the point of view of the citizen, is of little practical importance.

It should be noted that the Constitution of Guinea contains no provision vesting jurisdiction in constitutional matters in a supreme court or other tribunal. This is probably because legislative powers are not divided between the national assembly and the executive.

Congo (Leopoldville) – formerly a Belgian territory – has a special Constitutional Court of twelve councillors appointed, one third by the governors' conference, one third by the two secretariats of the national legislative chamber meeting together, and one third by the high court of the judiciary. All must be lawyers of at least ten years' standing who have either exercised judicial functions or taught law in a university or other institution of higher learning. The court decides the constitutionality of legislative acts, questions relating to the interpretation of the constitution and in particular conflicts of authority between the national and provincial governments; supervises the election of the president and of provincial governors as well as referenda, and decides disputes concerning their regularity and the regularity of the election of members of parliament. It has exclusive jurisdiction in the authoritative interpretation of laws. The jurisdiction of the court with respect to the constitutionality of laws or the interpretation of the constitution generally may be invoked by the president of the republic, provincial governors, members of the central and provincial governments, the presidents of the assemblies and by the supreme court of justice, and in cases of election disputes by any member of parliament or provincial assembly affected.[43]

Constitutional Guarantee of Human Rights:

(i) Need for a Constitutional Guarantee

Of Britain's legacies to the Commonwealth perhaps the most valuable is the libertarian tradition of the common law and its system of justice. Resting upon a *laissez-faire* conception of society, the common law has a zealous concern for private rights, not only civil and political liberty but individual freedom of action generally. It is the tradition of British justice, said Lord Atkin, that judges should not shrink from upholding the lawful rights of the individual in the face of the executive.[44]

The limitation of the common law guarantee of individual rights is that it avails only against the executive, but not against the legislature. Courts in the common law jurisdiction have never countenanced the view of individual liberty as embodying eternal reason, unalterable by the legislature.[45] To them, the authority of the legislature to interfere with private rights is unquestioned and unfettered by any speculative theorising, seeking to erect them into immutable binding law. However, although the authority of the statute law to interfere with private rights is thus acknowledged, the courts look upon it as something of 'an interloper upon the rounded majesty of the common law,'[46] and as such to be so interpreted as to avoid interference with private rights unless this should appear from the express words of the statute or from necessary intendment.

Under the British colonial administration, legislative encroachment upon private rights has never, however, gone beyond what the exigencies of administering a colonial territory demanded. The law of sedition, for example, has had to be made harsher and be more rigorously enforced than in Britain in order to guard against the possibility that the relatively small politically articulate section of the population might exploit the natural resentment against colonialism to incite the populace to disaffection. Apart from such cases it might be said that civil liberties were up to the time of internal self-government no less ample in many of the British dependencies than in Britain itself.

Yet, as self-government was being gradually conceded, the question had to be faced of how to preserve this libertarian heritage against not only the executive but also against a legislature controlled by tribal majorities. It would have been wishful thinking to imagine that such a legislature, in an atmosphere dominated by tribal or racial sentiment, would have been tolerant as the British had been, towards the right to criticise and oppose the government. Self-restraint and respect for the rights of minorities are ingrained in British tradition, but they are qualities which it would have been imprudent to expect the new legislatures to have acquired in anything like a sufficient measure to counteract the blinding sentiment of tribal, racial or religious politics and so make meaningful a 'presumption . . . that the constitutional guarantee of principles of civil and political liberty is unnecessary.'[47] It seems naïve in such circumstances to put too much faith in the 'sweet reasonableness of man.' Clearly therefore there was a demonstrable need to grope for some constitutional means of extending to the legislature what the common law has achieved in relation to the executive. That constitutional guarantees are notoriously ineffective is no argument for not trying. In any case one cannot conceive of a carefully-constructed justiciable bill of rights that would be completely without any effect whatever. 'No knowledgeable person has ever suggested that constitutional safeguards provide in themselves complete and indefensible security. But they do make the way of the transgressor, of the tyrant, more difficult. They are, so to speak, the outer bulwarks of defence.'[48] The Nigerian minorities commission has put it even more persuasively when it said: 'A government determined to abandon democratic courses will find ways of avoiding them, but they are of great value in preventing a steady deterioration in standards of freedom and the unobstrusive encroachment of a government on individual rights.'[49]

Disparaging constitutional guarantees of rights, Sir Ivor Jennings has said that 'in spite of the American Bill of Rights, that liberty is even better protected in Britain than in the United States.'[50] This seems to miss the point. Against whom is individual liberty better protected in Britain than in America? Surely liberty is not *legally* protected against the British parliament, and this is precisely what a bill of rights seeks to do. That is why in common law jurisdiction a constitutional guarantee achieves nothing if it merely says that no one is to be deprived of his civil liberties save in accordance with law. For then it does no more than re-state an existing principle that the executive cannot interfere with private rights without legal authority. But it does add something to the existing law if the prohibition is extended to the legislature as well.

Nearly all the new nations of the Commonwealth have bills of rights incorporated in their constitutions. The basis of these bills of rights is of course the common law, of which, it may be said, they are declaratory. The rights guaranteed are rights already possessed and enjoyed by the individual. The bills of rights created no rights *de novo* but declared and preserved already existing rights, which they extended against the legislature. This is borne out by the negative phraseology of some of the provisions. To say that 'no person shall be deprived of his personal liberty'[51] clearly presupposes an existing right, for it would be an abuse of language to talk of 'depriving' a person of a right which he does not have, unless we were to postulate the existence of the right by the so-called law of nature, a proposition whose untenability has already been demonstrated. It cannot be the fact, as Sir Ivor Jennings seems to imply, that when a common law jurisdiction adopts a formal bill of rights it thereby abolishes the common law on the matter completely. The implication of this is important, and it lies in the fact that the abolition or suspension of the constitution or of the fundamental rights chapter will not operate to abolish or suspend these rights as against the executive, so long as the common law remains part of the law of the country; its effect will be to free the legislature from the fetters on its legislative competence imposed by the constitutional entrenchment of the rights while leaving them in full force against the executive. Indeed, the bills of rights are by no means exhaustive of the private rights protected by the common law, rights which, in spite of their non-inclusion, have continued to be enjoyed by the individual. There is no question here of *expressio unius est exclusio alterius*, though to avoid the possibility of such implication the Americans have expressly had to declare that 'the enumeration in the constitution of certain rights shall not be construed to deny or disparage others retained by the people.'[52]

The ex-French territories stand in no less need of a constitutional guarantee of human rights. Indeed respect for human rights is less firmly ingrained in French tradition than it is under the English common law, though the French are more conscious of their civil liberties, and more ready to rise in revolt in order to assert them against any arbitrary encroachment. This love for liberty found its most revolutionary assertion in the Declaration of the Rights of Man in 1789.

(ii) *Form of the Guarantee of Rights*

The constitutional guarantee may take one of three forms—

(*a*) As a declaration of objectives in a preamble, or in a substantive provision, or in the oath of office to be taken by the head of state. A provision that the state 'shall ensure the equality of all citizens before the law, without distinction of race, religion and social condition'[53] is only a declaration of what the state should do; it confers no right on the citizen. In Cameroon the only constitutional recognition given to human rights is the affirmation of the Republic's 'adherence to the fundamental freedoms set out in the Universal Declaration of Human Rights and the Charter of the United Nations.'[54] The Ghana Republican Constitution of 1960 required the President, immediately after his assumption of office, solemnly to declare his adherence to the protection of certain human rights, including freedom from discrimination, freedom of speech, religion, assembly and the right of property. This has been held not to have any legal effect as a guarantee of these rights to the citizen,[55] which means that the constitution guaranteed no rights at all. Similarly all that the Tanzanian Constitution did was to recite in the preamble the state's recognition of individual rights and freedoms. In the 1962 Constitution of Pakistan, the justiciable rights guaranteed by the old constitution were replaced by nonjusticiable principles of law-making and principles of policy.

(*b*) As a guarantee of rights in the preamble. Under this form the preamble is used not merely to recite rights but to guarantee them. The French have adopted this form in the constitutions of both the Fourth and Fifth Republics, and have bequeathed it to many of its former dependencies, the Central African Republic, Chad, Madagascar and Mali. The Constitution of the Central African Republic has a three-page preamble which, after proclaiming the state's attachment to the rights of man, and its recognition of 'the existence of inviolable and inalienable rights of man as the basis of any human society, of peace and of justice in the world,' goes on to guarantee a long list of individual human rights. In the preamble to their own constitution the people of Chad solemnly proclaim its attachment to the principles of democracy as defined by the Declaration of 1948, and as guaranteed by the present constitution. Then follows in the same preamble a guarantee of a full complement of rights and freedoms. Has this form of guarantee any legal effect? It is difficult to see how it can confer any rights upon the individual. The normal conception of a preamble is that it forms no part of a statute, and as such can create no legal rights or obligations. Civil liberties guaranteed in a preamble can therefore have no more than a moral force.

(*c*) As a guarantee of rights in substantive provisions of the constitution. Where it is intended to protect human rights, the normal method is to guarantee them in substantive provisions of the constitution, but the efficacy of the guarantee depends upon how it is formulated.

(iii) *The Problem of Formulation*

The rights guaranteed in the Commonwealth constitutions are: life and personal liberty (including freedom from arrest and imprisonment); freedom from inhuman treatment, slavery and hard labour; freedom from discrimination; adequate compensation for property acquired compulsorily; judicial determination of civil rights and obligations; private and family life; freedom of conscience, of expression, assembly, association and movement. Except for the omission of the right to vote, the list is reasonably ample, covering most (though by no means all) of the civil and political rights protected by the common law. Yet the content of a bill of rights depends not only upon the range of the rights guaranteed but also upon the scope and sweep of the qualifications made to them. For it is obvious that rights cannot be guaranteed in absolute terms if for no other reason than to protect the rights of other persons. To guarantee rights without qualification is to guarantee licence and anarchy; 'the freedom of the just man is worth little to him if he can be preyed upon by the murderer or thief.'[56] It is not only in the interest of public order and the protection of the rights of other persons that qualification upon individual rights is necessary; the demands of the security of the state itself, of public morality, public health and the provision of social and economic services are no less worthy of recognition. It follows then that even if one were to guarantee rights in absolute terms, as does the American Bill of Rights, they cannot in fact be enjoyed without qualification. The agency entrusted with their enforcement will inevitably have to draw a line somewhere. But whether the line is to be drawn by the enforcement agency in accordance with the spirit of the pre-existing law or in the constitution itself, the problem is where to draw it so as to leave ample room for the enjoyment of individual rights and at the same time make it possible for the government to discharge its obligations towards the society and the political community itself. This would involve a delicate balancing of objectives.

One point of view is that the security of the individual, his right to have secured to him the *minimum* basic requirements for human existence – food and clothing, housing, education and medical and sanitary services – should be a paramount prerequisite for the meaningful enjoyment of all other rights. The provision of a basic minimum of social amenities cannot be incompatible with the enjoyment of civil and political rights; it can certainly be attained within the framework of a constitutional guarantee of rights. There is no reason why the provision of food and clothing, housing, education and medical and sanitary services can only be done at the cost of depriving individuals of their personal liberty or their freedom of speech. No doubt such collectivist measures as compulsory education will inexorably impinge upon certain areas of individual rights, but such encroachment cannot be destructive of the core of freedom which must find accommodation with it. It is necessary, however, to recognise that certain aspects of liberty are so fundamentally vital to the dignity and worth of an individual's personality as to merit being accorded premium.

This is the conception that underlies the Commonwealth bills of rights. The right to life, personal liberty, freedom from inhuman treatment, slavery and forced labour, freedom from discrimination, adequate compensation for property compulsorily acquired, judicial determination of civil rights and obligations and the requirements to fair trial are absolutely guaranteed subject only, in some cases, of specific exceptions based, by and large, on the common law. The provision that no person shall be deprived of his life or personal liberty or that in the determination of his civil rights and obligations a person shall be entitled to a fair hearing within a reasonable time by a court or other tribunal established by law and constituted in such manner as to secure its independence and impartiality will necessarily have imported into the guarantee the rules of law prescribing the conditions and procedure under which a person may be arrested, imprisoned or deprived intentionally of his life, and also the conditions of a fair trial. If, as is in fact the case, these rules permit of the enjoyment of individual rights to an extent considered ample for a democracy, it may be wondered whether any very useful purpose is served by re-stating them in a generalised form in the constitution. Explicitness ceases to be an advantage when it means merely summarising what is already explicit enough, and its effect may be to make the bill of rights rather laborious. Whilst it is true that the guarantee of the right to life, personal liberty and the judicial determination of rights in the terms used by the Commonwealth constitutions would have incorporated by implication the conditions and procedures prescribed by law for interference with them, what would have been so incorporated would have been the law as amended from time to time. By expressly formulating these conditions and procedures, the constitution provides a standard – generalised no doubt but nonetheless meaningful enough – for testing the validity not only of future enactments but of the existing law as well. Thus, the provision in the Nigerian Commissions and Tribunals of Enquiry Act, 1961, empowering a commissioner appointed thereunder to punish by imprisonment or fine anyone who failed or refused or neglected, upon summons, to attend as a witness or to produce a book, document, etc., or to answer any question put to him by or with the concurrence of the commissioner was declared to be unconstitutional and void as not coming within one of the specific exceptions to the right of personal liberty.[57] So also the provision that the fact of a commission having been appointed shall be 'sufficient proof of the proper exercise by the prime minister of his authority to do so; and neither the commission itself nor any action of the prime minister in relation thereto shall be enquired into in any court of law' was likewise declared void as being in derogation of the right to judicial determination of rights.

The other rights, viz. the right to private and family life, freedom of conscience, of expression, assembly, association and movement, are guaranteed in the Nigerian Constitution subject to certain specific exceptions, and to the proviso that the guarantee is not to invalidate any law that is reasonably justifiable in a democratic society in the interest of defence, public safety, public order, public morality or public health. As has been observed, a guarantee of rights must needs be balanced against the demands of public safety, public order, etc., but the question is whether the phraseology of the exceptions in the Nigerian bill of rights struck the right balance or whether it tilted the balance in favour of one or the other. The answer would turn upon the words 'reasonably justifiable in a democratic society.' These words are manifestly vague and flexible. First, what is to be the measure of the degree of freedom compatible with democracy? The common law qualifications upon these freedoms can provide no more than a rough guide. If there were a universally agreed lowest common denominator of democratic behaviour which could be formulated with precision,[58] then the only remaining problem would be whether 'reasonably justifiable' does not leave too much scope for derogation from those minimum standards. It has been suggested that the qualifying word 'necessary' used in the European Convention on Human Rights or 'reasonably required' used in the constitutions of some of the Commonwealth countries which adopted bills of rights after Nigeria, such as Sierra Leone, Uganda, Jamaica, Kenya, Malta and Nyasaland (as it then was), are more restrictive than the Nigerian 'reasonably justifiable.'[59] But the high court of Northern Nigeria has laid it down that 'a restriction upon a fundamental human right must before it may be considered reasonably justifiable (*a*) be necessary . . . , (*b*) not be excessive or out of proportion to the object which it is sought to achieve.'[60] A measure may be justifiable either because it is expedient or necessary, from which it follows that 'reasonably necessary' is more restrictive than 'reasonably justifiable.' Yet, in line with the view of the Northern Region high court, some of the neo-Nigerian bills of rights provide that a law which is reasonably necessary will still be invalid if it is shown not to be reasonably justifiable.[61] As Professor de Smith remarked, 'it is very hard to see how a law can itself be both reasonably required and not reasonably justifiable.'[62]

However this may be, it needs to be emphasised that the test of justifiability is made more exacting by the accompanying word 'reasonably;' to be valid, a law has to be not only justifiable but reasonably so. The Northern Region high court's definition of 'reasonable' as 'not excessive or out of proportion' must be extended to include 'not arbitrary.' This is important as it is with the arbitrariness of discretion that the concept of constitutionalism is essentially concerned. It may be said therefore that the phrase 'reasonably justifiable' imports the aspect of the American concept of due process which has enabled the U.S. Supreme Court to strike

down any law considered to have unreasonably or arbitrarily interfered with liberty. American reports abound with cases illustrating
this, and in the interpretation of the Commonwealth bills of rights
the courts will find the American precedents of immense assistance.

A further objection to the exceptions to the Nigerian and neo-
Nigerian bills of rights is that by their phraseology more emphasis
appears to be placed on the exceptions than on the substantive
rights. 'Nothing in this section shall invalidate any law . . . ' seems
to imply a presumption in favour of the validity of a derogatory
law, thereby casting the onus on the person challenging it to show
that it is not reasonably justifiable. Had it read instead, 'any law
derogating from a guaranteed right shall be invalid unless it is
reasonably justifiable,' etc., the onus of proving the reasonable
justifiability of the law would have been cast upon the authorities,
and the guaranteed right would have been enhanced in value. It is
submitted that that is the way the courts should read the exceptions.
As with the U.S. Supreme Court, their guiding principle should be
that 'liberty is the rule and restraint is the exception.'[63]

It will be noticed that the Nigerian and neo-Nigerian bills of
rights contain little to inhibit the provision by the state of the basic
requirements for human existence. A government wishing to pursue
a collectivist programme would encounter hardly any embarrassment from the bills of rights. This point deserves to be emphasised
because it has been one of the strongly urged objections to a constitutional guarantee of human rights. Thus, in rejecting the demand
for a bill of rights in the Indian Constitution, the Joint Parliamentary Committee on Indian Constitutional Reform (1934)
declared: 'either the declaration of rights is of so abstract a nature
that it has no legal effect, or its effect will be to impose an embarrass-
ing restriction on the powers of the legislature.'[64] Sir Ivor Jenning
has cited in this connection the experience of India where a law
abolishing the *zamindari* or landlord system, generally accepted to
have been undesirable, was found to be forbidden by the constitution, and 'the unusual step had to be taken of validating by constitutional amendment no less than thirteen legislative Acts.'[65] If this
objection is intended as an argument against all restrictions on
governmental powers, then it is entirely misplaced. Surely the
purpose of a bill of rights and of the whole concept of constitutionalism is to restrict or limit the powers of the government. What
must be conceded is that restriction should not be carried to a point
where it unreasonably embarrasses or frustrates legitimate and
desirable programmes for social and economic development, as will
be the case where liberty based upon a *laissez-faire* conception of
unrestrained free private enterprise is guaranteed. In the U.S.A.,

liberty under the clause of the constitution forbidding the deprivation of 'life, liberty or property, without due process of law' has
not been confined to its common law connotation of freedom of
the person but has been used by the supreme court to protect
freedom of private enterprise, of contract, and indeed of all the
ordinary rights of a citizen in a free government.[66] Thus, statutes
regulating working hours, wages, workmen's compulsory compensation, prices, and a host of other measures of a socialist or welfare
character have been declared void as an unreasonable and arbitrary
interference with liberty. The New Deal legislation, aimed at
implementing certain desirable collectivist policies of the Roosevelt
administration, initially ran foul of the constitutional guarantee of
liberty and was only saved from being completely frustrated by the
appointment to the bench of the supreme court of progressive-
minded judges.

The prohibition in the Fourteenth Amendment of any law
abridging 'the privilege or immunities of citizens' has also reinforced
the protection of freedom of private enterprise, as has the prohibition
of involuntary servitude in the Thirteenth Amendment. For
example, the former has been held to protect the right to engage in
inter-state and foreign commerce,[67] and the latter, the right of an
employee to give up one employment in order to take up another.[68]
Commenting on this aspect of the American Bill of Rights, Dicey
has written:

> 'The principle that legislation ought not to impair obligation of
> contracts has governed the whole course of American opinion.
> Of the conservative effect of such a maxim when forming an
> article of the constitution we may form some measure by the
> following reflection. If any principle of the like kind had been
> recognised in England as legally binding on the courts, the Irish
> Land Act would have been unconstitutional and void; the Irish
> Church Act, 1869, would, in great part at least, have been
> from a legal point of view so much waste paper, and there would
> have been great difficulty in legislating in the way in which the
> English parliament has legislated for the reform of the uni-
> versities. One maxim only among those embodied in the
> constitution of the United States would, that is to say, have been
> sufficient if adopted in England to have arrested the most vigorous
> efforts of recent parliamentary legislation.'[69]

In contrast to the American bill of rights, the liberty guaranteed
in the recent Commonwealth constitutions is personal liberty only
(i.e. freedom of the person), while the prohibition of forced labour
cannot possibly afford protection to freedom of contract generally.

Nor is there anything equivalent to the German guarantee of the right of the individual to the 'free development of his personality'[70] or the right of citizens 'freely to choose their trade or profession, their place of work and their place of training.'[71] The claim of the individual upon the state for social services and amenities, such as the right to be given employment, education, medical attention, etc., is not mentioned either. These bills of rights cannot therefore be said to have entrenched any particular brand of economic philosophy, whether *laissez-faire*, capitalism, socialism or communism. They leave the government free to pursue the one or the other as the changing circumstances of the society may demand, though at the moment the common law tradition of free private enterprise still prevails. Whilst admittedly it is a principle of democracy, as a philosophy of government, that the object of government should be the maintenance of the personality, dignity and creative capacity of the individual, the creation by the state of conditions enabling individuals to act freely within the law for themselves,[72] it may be doubted whether a constitution could or ought to try to transmute this philosophy in its fullest extent into living principles of political behaviour.

The formulation in all the ex-French territories which guarantee rights in substantive provisions of the constitution leaves the rights with very little content. Most of the rights are guaranteed subject to the ordinary law. As a typical example, the Morocco Constitution guarantees to all citizens freedom to circulate and settle in all parts of the kingdom, freedom of opinion, of expression in all its forms, and of assembly; freedom of association and freedom to belong to any trade union or political organisation of their choice; and then declares that 'no limitation in the exercise of these freedoms may be imposed except by law.'[73] Even less restrictive of governmental power is the provision in the Tunisian Constitution that the individual has all the rights to which the law entitles him, freedom of thought and expression, of the press, printing and meetings and freedom to found societies. 'These rights,' it declares, 'are only limited by other laws, made to safeguard the rights of others, or to promote public well-being, national defence, economic prosperity or social advancement.'[74] Article 7 of the Dahomean Constitution provides that the republic 'guarantees the fundamental liberties. It guarantees freedom of speech, press, assembly, association, procession and manifestation under conditions determined by law.' Even the right to life and physical integrity is guaranteed subject to conditions defined by law.[75] This is the pattern all through, and it would be tedious to multiply examples. Only a few rights are guaranteed without reference to the ordinary law, e.g. freedom of religious belief, the presumption of innocence, and property. The Senegalese Constitution, for example, guarantees the right of property, and prohibits any infringements of it 'except in cases of legally attested public necessity and after just and prior compensation.'[76]

(iv) *The Problem of Enforcement*

The Commonwealth constitutions guaranteeing human rights have all implemented the common law view that rights are protected, not by merely declaring them, but by providing a means for their enforcement; the rule is *ubi jus ibi remedium*. 'The Habeas Corpus Acts,' writes Dicey, 'declare no principle and define no rights, but they are for practical purposes worth a hundred constitutional articles guaranteeing individual liberty.'[77] And so we find that the procedure of the ordinary courts has in every case been entrenched for the enforcement of the guaranteed rights. Under the Nigerian bill of rights, for example, any individual whose guaranteed right had been infringed, can apply for redress to the high court, and the high court is empowered to make such orders, issue such writs and give such directions as it may consider appropriate for enforcing the right, including a declaratory judgment.[78]

The constitutions of the ex-French territories make hardly any provision for the enforcement of the guaranteed rights. The nearest they have come to doing so is the following provision in the constitutions of the Ivory Coast, Guinea and Mauritania: 'The accused shall be presumed innocent until his guilt is established . . . The judicial authority, guardian of individual liberty, shall ensure respect for this principle under conditions stipulated by law.'[79] The Guinean provision is not restricted to just one right: the 'judicial authority, guardian of individual liberty, shall ensure the respect of the rights of citizens under conditions stipulated by law.'[80]

REFERENCES

1. The constitutions of the regions were enacted by the respective regional legislatures with the concurrence of parliament signified by resolution.
2. Constitution of 1958.
3. Cited in Lipset, *The First New Nation*, p. 19. For further discussion of this, see Carl J. Friedrich, *Some Reflections on Constitutionalism for Emergent Political Orders*, pp. 11-12.
4. *Op. cit.*, Ch. 1.
5. Edward Shils, 'The Fortunes of Constitutional Government' in the Political Development of the New States, in John Hallowell, ed., *Development: for what?*, 1964, p. 104.
6. Constitution of Eire, 1937.

7. Madison, quoted in E. S. Corwin, *The Doctrine of Judicial Review*, 1963, p. 96.
8. Carl J. Friedrich, *op. cit.*, p. 29.
9. Wheare, *Modern Constitutions*, 1966, p. 60.
10. *Ibid.*, p. 54.
11. *Marbury v. Madison*, 1, Cranch 137 (1803) – per Chief Justice Marshall.
12. *Modern Constitutions*, 1966, p. 12.
13. *The 'Higher Law' Background of American Constitutional Law*, 1957, Cornell University Press, pp. 4-5.
14. *Op. cit.*, p. 34.
15. See Chief Justice Marshall in *McCulloch v. Maryland*, 4, Wheaton 316.
16. *Cf.* Jennings, *The Approach to Self-Government*, 1958, p. 22.
17. Art. 46, Constitution of the Fifth French Republic, 1958.
18. Only Madagascar has a bicameral legislature consisting of a National Assembly and a Senate.
19. See, e.g., Art. 67, Constitution of the Republic of Senegal, 1963; Art. 33, Chad, 1962; Art. 60, Dahomey, 1964; Art. 56, Togo, 1963.
20. *Cabinet Government*, 3rd ed. (1961), p. 4.
21. Contrast John Fletcher-Cooke, 'Parliament, the Executive and the Civil Service,' in Alan Burns, ed., *Parliament as an Export*, 1966, p. 150.
23. See, for example, the letters in *The Times*, London, in April 1950, by Lord Simon, former Lord Chancellor, Lord Chorley, Roy Jenkins and Sir Alan Lascelles; also Marshall and Moodie, *Some Problems of the Constitution*.
24. S. A. de Smith, *The New Commonwealth and Its Constitution*, 1964, Ch. 4.
25. *Eshugbayi Eleko v. Government of Nigeria* [1931], A.C. 662, at p. 670.
26. Arts. 34-37.
27. Art. 47.
28. Art. 38.
29. Arts. 16-18, Central African Republic; Arts. 33-4, Chad; Arts. 53-9, Congo (Brazzaville); Arts. 61-5, Dahomey; Arts. 37-42, Gabon; Arts. 41, 44-6, Ivory Coast; Arts. 32 and 33, Madagascar; Arts. 24, 27-9, Mali; Arts. 34, 35 and 36, Mauritania; Arts. 47-50, Morocco; Arts. 41, 44-6, Niger; Arts. 56, 65 and 66, Senegal; Arts. 49, 54 and 55, Togo; Arts. 41, 44-6, Upper Volta.
30. Art. 9.
31. Art. 28.
32. Art. 12.
33. Art. 55.
34. Art. 31.
35. *Hughes and Vale Pty. Ltd. v. Gair* (1954), Argus L.R. 1094; but contrast *Trethowan v. Peden* (1930), 31, S.R. (N.S.W.) 183, and *McDonald v. Cain* (1953), V. L.R. 411.
36. Cyprus is an exception, see below Ch. VII.

37. Art. 14, Cameroon; Art. 55, Chad; Arts. 30 and 72, Congo (Brazza-ville); Arts. 67 and 84, Dahomey; Art. 60, Gabon; Art. 46, Ivory Coast; Art. 44, Mali; Art. 51, Mauritania; Arts. 100 and 101, Morocco; Art. 46, Niger; Arts. 63 and 82, Senegal, Art. 59; Art. 46, Upper Volta.
38. Art. 28.
39. Arts. 63 and 64.
40. Arts. 45-7.
41. Art. 57.
42. The French Constitutional Council consists of all former Presidents of the Republic and nine members appointed in equal numbers by the President of the Republic, and the Presidents of the National Assembly and the Senate: Art. 56, Constitution of the Fifth French Republic, 1958; also Arts. 61 and 62.
43. Arts. 177-81.
44. *Eshugbayi Eleko v. Government of Nigeria, ibid.* at p. 672.
45. *Liyanage v. R.* [1967], 1.A.C. 259 (P.C.).
46. R. T. E. Latham, 'The Law and the Commonwealth' in *Survey of British Commonwealth Affairs*, Vol. 1 (1937), pp. 510-11.
47. Jennings, *Approach to Self-Government*, 1958, p. 100.
48. Cowen, *The Foundation of Freedom*, 1960, p. 119.
49. *Report Cmnd.* 505 (1958), p. 97.
50. *Op. cit.*, p. 20. See also Wheare, *Modern Constitutions*, 1966, Ch. III.
51. S. 21 (1). Nigerian Constitution, 1963.
52. IXth Amendment.
53. Art. 6, Ivory Coast; Art. 1, Mauritania; Art. 6, Niger; Art. 6, Upper Volta.
54. Art. 1.
55. *Re Akoto*, 1, Civil Appeal No. 42/61.
56. Denning, *Freedom under the Law*, 1949, p. 5.
57. *Balewa v. Doherty* (1961), 1, All N.R.R. 604 (F.S.C.); [1963], 1 W.L.R. 949 (P.C.).
58. A meeting of nearly 200 distinguished lawyers held in Delhi in 1959 was reported to have formulated such a lowest common denominator: see Cowen, *op. cit.*, p. 129.
59. S. A. de Smith, *The New Commonwealth and Its Constitutions*, 1964, pp. 189, 194.
60. *Cheranci v. Cheranci* (1960), N.R.N.L.R., 24 at p. 29 – per Bate, J.
61. See, for example, s. 18 (2), Constitution of Sierra Leone, 1961.
62. *Op. cit.*, p. 194.
63. Corwin, *The Constitution and What It Means Today*, 1958, p. 221. In point of fact the U.S. Supreme Court has alternated between this approach and the presumption of constitutionality: Corwin, *loc. cit.*
64. (1933-4), 5, H.C. 216.
65. *The Approach to Self-Government*, 1958, p. 107.
66. Corwin, *op. cit.*, p. 218 *et seq*: p. 248 *et seq*.
67. Corwin, *op. cit.*, pp. 248-9.
68. *Ibid.*, p. 246.

69. *The Law of the Constitution*, 19th ed., p. 174.
70. Art. 2 (1), German Basic Law, 1949.
71. Art. 12 (1); Cyprus is excepted.
72. Cowen, *The Foundations of Freedom*, Ch. V.
73. Art. 9.
74. Art. 3.
75. Art. 6, Senegal.
76. Art. 12; also Art. 14, Tunisia.
77. *Op. cit.*, p. 199.
78. *Olowoyin v. Att.-Gen.* (1961), 1, All N.L.R. 269.
79. Art. 62, Ivory Coast; Art. 49, Mauritania, which refers to arbitrary detention.
80. Art. 37.

CHAPTER III

THE WESTMINSTER EXPORT MODEL AND CONSTITUTIONALISM IN THE NEW COMMONWEALTH

'In developing countries,' writes Professor de Smith, 'constitutional factors will seldom play a dominant role in the shaping of political history.'[1] Could the role of the Westminster export model in the political history of the new Commonwealth nations be said not to have been dominant? It is the aim of this chapter to consider how far this has been borne out by actual experience. For convenience, the discussion will be based on the model as embodied in the Constitution of Nigeria and its operation there. The main features of the system are the diffusion of executive power, the partial fusion of the organs of government, and the responsibility of the executive to the legislature. These features and their impact upon the political history of Nigeria will now be considered in turn.

Diffusion of Executive Power

A characteristic feature of the organisation of executive power under the Westminster system is its diffusion among various persons. First there was under the Nigerian Constitution a head of state, namely, the president, but he was not the head of government. His titular position was the product of two factors. Although executive authority was formally vested in him he had virtually no personal discretion in the exercise of it. With but few exceptions, this authority was exercised largely on his behalf by others, and when he acted directly it had to be on the advice of others. Furthermore, the executive authority thus vested in him, though it implied the vital function of policy formulation and the co-ordination of the many processes of government, conferred no actual power necessary for the execution of policies. As has been explained, executive action has to be based upon power conferred by statute if interference with private rights, which such action must inevitably involve, is to be justified. The necessary powers conferred by the enabling statutes mostly devolve on persons other than the president; and, in order that there might be no suggestion of inconsistency with the vesting of executive

55

authority in the president, the Constitution provided that this was
not to preclude parliament from conferring functions on persons or
authorities other than the president. It must not be supposed that
powers were never conferred upon the president by statute. Indeed,
before the attainment of internal self-government, the bulk of
executive powers created by statute were conferred upon the
colonial governor or upon the governor in council; these were
inherited by the president upon the attainment of self-government.
However, as whatever powers he possessed, whether conferred upon
him directly or inherited from the colonial governor or governor
in council, had to be exercised on his behalf by others, it was
necessary to have them transferred formally to such others. This
was done under the Ministers' Statutory Powers and Duties (Miscellaneous Provisions) Act.[2]

The second aspect of this diffusion was that the exercise of
executive functions and powers was collective. The responsibility
for the business of government belonged to a cabinet of ministers
and to individual ministers acting under the general authority of
the cabinet, headed by a prime minister who became in effect the
head of government. It was on the cabinet's advice that the president
had to act whenever he acted directly, it was on the cabinet and
the individual ministers that powers were conferred by statute, and
it was to them that those powers conferred upon or inherited by the
president were transferred.

It might be said that diffusion of executive power is conducive
to constitutionalism inasmuch as, by preventing the concentration
of power in the hands of one man, it guards against autocracy and
dictatorship. Yet, as has been said, the limiting of government does
not require that it should thereby also be rendered weak or unstable.
The diffusion of executive power had both of these results.

*Instability Arising from the Separation of the Head of State and Head of
Government*

Conflict is necessarily to be expected in an arrangement whereby
executive authority is vested in one person and exercised by another.
It is a wholly unnatural arrangement. That this inherent conflict
has been held in check in Britain is due to certain historical factors.
The Queen's position in the British Constitution was the product of
historical evolution. The monarch once embodied in himself the
entire sovereign power of the state, which he exercised at his
discretion as a personal ruler. The government was his in every
sense of the word, and he was synonymous with the state. He
possessed and exercised over his ministers, other public servants and

subjects generally, a power that was at once absolute and complete. Allegiance was owed to him personally, and he could destroy, elevate and honour whom he pleased. His person was invested with pomp and majesty and awe. This position of sovereign power and majesty had created a definite pattern of relationship between himself and his ministers, and between himself and his subjects generally, a relationship which imposed upon the ministers conformity with certain norms of propriety in their behaviour towards him. These norms of court manners accorded him veneration, respect and courtesy. In the course of centuries of constitutional evolution, the monarch has lost his personal discretion in the exercise of sovereignty. In law, sovereign power still reposes in him, the government is still his own, but he no longer governs personally, most of his powers having devolved upon elected ministers, yet these ministers still regard themselves, as of old, as the Queen's ministers, and the government which they administer as Her Majesty's Government. This is no mere formality. The pattern of relationship has remained unchanged, and is still characterised by the same attitude of reverence, respect and personal allegiance. It would be unthinkable for a British prime minister or any other minister to conduct himself rudely or indecorously before the Queen, or to make insulting or derogatory remarks about her in public or to appear openly to defy her authority. If it happens that she should not share the Government's view upon any policy matter, her views and warning will be treated with respect and consideration, and the Government will, so far as practicable, try to accommodate them, though it is not bound to do so. These, then, are the factors upon which the separation of the head of state from the actual exercise of executive power is sanctioned in Britain; they operate to avoid or minimise conflict in the working of the system. They are, however, conditions not likely to be reproduced in a country lacking the historical background upon which the relation between the head of state and the government is patterned. Ministers in Nigeria never regarded themselves as the president's ministers or the government as his own. If anything, the prime minister regarded himself as the president's superior and often behaved as such towards him. There was hardly any attitude of personal allegiance, of reverence or of courtesy towards him; he lacked the attribute of kingly majesty in the eyes of the people, even more so in the eyes of the ministers. They had been either colleagues or opponents in partisan politics, and the differences in tribal sentiment and loyalty intruded to make still more difficult the cultivation of the attitudes that should inform the relationship. 'The main difficulty,' said Tansey and Kermode, 'was that mutual distrust between the main ethnic groupings in the country was and still is so great that few are willing to credit impartiality to a non-member of their own group.'[3] Nor, indeed, could any president be found who could maintain the same impartiality, aloofness and serenity in partisan politics as the Queen. Her upbringing within the seclusion of palaces, among a highly exclusive circle of people, and away from the humdrum of ordinary life accounts for that. It is futile to try to reproduce what clearly cannot be reproduced. It is not surprising therefore that the separation should have produced disturbing conflicts. Of these it will be sufficient to mention two instances for purposes of illustration.

(i) *Authority to Maintain and Preserve the Constitution*

The maintenance of the constitution was the first function and duty implied in the executive authority vested in the president. By his oath of office he swore 'to preserve, protect and defend the constition'. What, then, was expected of him by his duty and oath when the provisions of the constitution were being perverted by the government contrary to the duty enjoined upon them by their own oath of office? Was he to sit by and acquiesce in the acts of perversion? He could of course warn, as did President Azikiwe when in his national broadcasts he told politicians that their 'tribalism, nepotism, perfidy, bribery and corruption' were disgracing the nation. But perversion might be carried to a point where mere warning was not enough. This was the point that appeared to have been reached during the 1964 federal election crisis. The election had been marked by blatant irregularities which even the supposedly independent electoral commission admitted. There had been widespread intimidation and violence, refusal of electoral officers to accept nomination papers from the supporters of opposition parties, abduction of prospective candidates or their sponsors, denial of freedom of campaigning and even of movement, use of illegal ballot papers and other kinds of perverse practices. The final culmination was the boycott of the election by the opposition parties on the ground of these well-attested irregularities. The election was a complete travesty of democracy. What was the constitutional duty of the president in the circumstances created by these acts of perversion? As he had good ground to anticipate that the electoral system was going to be perverted, it has been suggested that the president should have acted in time to appoint a caretaker government to supervise the election.[4] That would certainly have altered nothing. For, although the president had unfettered power to dismiss the prime minister during a dissolution when no question of support in the lower house could arise, he could only appoint as successor a member of the cabinet. A caretaker government might have been useful if a neutral, non-partisan person could have been appointed. But since the choice was limited to members of the cabinet, there would have been no good ground for preferring one partisan minister to another. Moreover, 'it is hard to see how such a "caretaker" government could have enforced its will upon the regional civil servants conducting the election or upon the supposedly independent electoral commission.'[5]

The president could not therefore but allow the election to continue under the authority of the old government. Admittedly, he did suggest that it should be postponed, but the prime minister insisted that it should go on, and his was constitutionally the overriding voice. When the results were announced, indicating that the government party had 'won' – a foregone conclusion – should the president then, consistently with his oath, ignore the well-attested irregularities and re-appoint the prime minister as the leader of the winning party? That was what the letters of the law of the constitution required of him. But was that in consequence with its spirit? The position of the president in this situation was a most unenviable one. At first he refused to re-appoint the prime minister, and from that refusal there ensued a crisis full of tension. It has been contended that in these circumstances the president could have dismissed the prime minister, and, there being nobody with a legitimate claim to be called upon to form a government on the basis of the irregular election, could have assumed executive powers himself. The dismissal of the government and the absence of anyone else entitled to be called upon to form a government would have created a vacuum, leaving the president as the sole lawful functionary of the executive. With no cabinet to advise him, the president, by the imperative necessity of avoiding an abeyance of government, would have been justified in assuming the supreme function of policy formulation, and could appoint ministers to assist him. By so doing, it was argued, the president would have been doing no more than discharge his oath to 'preserve, protect and defend' the constitution. This contention might have had great plausibility and perhaps validity,[6] had it not been based upon the false premise that a vacancy in the premiership would have arisen after a general election by the president merely informing the prime minister that he was not going to re-appoint him. What the constitution actually provided was that the office of the prime minister should be vacated 'when, after any dissolution of the house of representatives, the prime minister is informed by the president that the president is about to re-appoint him as prime minister or to appoint another person as prime minister.'[7] If an election was vitiated by irregularities so that nobody could legitimately be appointed prime minister on the basis of it, the president would have no grounds for informing the prime minister that he was about to re-appoint him or to appoint someone else, from which it follows that the prime minister would have to continue in office, perhaps until fresh elections had been held. No doubt, during a dissolution the president could dismiss a prime minister, especially if he was believed to have been responsible for the irregularities in the election, by simply informing him that he was about to appoint someone else. Yet, having done that, he could not turn round and assume executive functions himself; he would have been obliged to appoint a new prime minister who, as previously stated, must be a member of the outgoing cabinet.

In a conflict between the clear letter of the constitution and its spirit, the former should prevail, and President Azikiwe was right in adopting eventually the course dictated by the law. But the crisis did shake the fabric of Nigerian government and society, and inflicted a wound from which the Republic never recovered. There was yet another aspect of it which provides a striking illustration of the conflict inherent in separating the head of state from the head of government.

(ii) *The President as Commander-in-Chief*

So serious was the crisis provoked by the president's initial refusal to re-appoint the prime minister that both had openly to solicit the loyalty and support of the armed forces. The constitution designated the president as commander-in-chief of the armed forces, and provided that his functions as such would be such as might be prescribed by parliament. In the statutes governing the armed forces, however, no reference was made to the commander-in-chief. Under them overall responsibility for the operational use of the forces was vested in the council of ministers, though at the same time the prime minister was empowered to direct the commanders of the various units of the armed forces – the army, navy and air force – with respect to the operational use of the forces for the purpose of maintaining and securing public safety and public order, notwithstanding that the directions of the council of ministers had not been obtained. Was the implication of vesting the control of the operational use of the forces in the commanders, subject to the direction of the council of ministers and the prime minister, that the commander-in-chief had no functions or powers whatever in regard thereto? Was the president commander-in-chief just in name, and not in fact? The commanders of the army and the navy (the air force was still in the process of formation) had sought and obtained advice that that was in fact the true legal position, and, on the basis of that advice, they assured the prime minister of their loyalty and support for him as the rightful authority to dispose of the armed forces. The commander of the army, Major-General Welby-Everard, instructed his officers and men accordingly in a circular letter. Convinced as the General was of the correctness of the position he had adopted, the matter was not altogether free from doubt in the minds of some of his subordinates, to whom the idea of a commander-in-chief without powers of command was hardly intelligible. Ordinarily the commander-in-chief is a well-recognised position in the hierarchy of the armed forces, implying indeed the supreme command of the forces; he can directly command any unit or member of the armed forces, even over the head of the commander. The mere designation of the president in the constitution as commander-in-chief attracted these powers; they followed inherently and necessarily from the name. The invidious question, then, was whether, if the commander-in-chief should so command any member of the armed forces, such a member, trained as he had been to obey superior military orders without question, could properly refuse to obey. To him, it was irrelevant that the Armed Forces Acts made no reference to the commander-in-chief. If there was a commander-in-chief designated by the supreme law of the land, his orders were lawful, superior orders which every member of the armed forces was duty bound to obey. It was equally irrelevant to a soldier whether, in giving such orders, the commander-in-chief had received or acted in accordance with the advice of the council of ministers or of the prime minister. Neither of these latter held command positions in the armed forces. It is true that by law they could give direction to the commander of a unit of the armed forces, but such direction could only become a military order if re-issued by recognised command officers, of whom the commander-in-chief was the most superior. In view of these considerations, many of the officers of the army considered that the course of action best calculated to uphold the integrity and impartiality of the army lay in non-commitment to either side. Happily, in the event, the armed forces were saved the unpleasantness of a division in their ranks which an unavoidable military intervention would have produced.

The Weakening of Leadership by Collective Responsibility

As has been observed, the responsibility for the business of executive government belonged collectively to the cabinet and to the individual ministers acting under its general authority. The prime minister was only one of such ministers, though the *prime* one. Any other minister to whom any business of government had been assigned had a direct constitutional responsibility for it, in the performance of which he stood in relation to the prime minister, not in the role of adviser or assistant, but as co-beneficiary of the executive power. The overall authority was that of the cabinet, and the prime minister was as much subject to its general authority as any other minister. The authority of the cabinet was of course a general one, and specific policies affecting a department were usually decided by the minister in charge of the department, who had discretion as to what to refer to the cabinet and how frequently to do so, unless the issue was a major one likely to have repercussions outside the particular department primarily concerned. It is thus with co-ordination rather than with initiation of policy that the cabinet was concerned.

Yet, although the prime minister was only a co-beneficiary with the other ministers of the executive authority, his position as the creator and chairman of the cabinet gave him pre-eminence over his colleagues, a pre-eminence which was not just a matter of dignity but of real authority, the authority of a *de facto* head of government. It was by him as chairman that meetings of the cabinet were convened and its agenda settled. His exceptional authority arose partly from his personal prerogative in the appointment and dismissal of ministers, and in the allocation of offices and functions to them; from his leadership and control of his party as the majority party in the legislature; from his power of convention, prorogation and dissolution of the legislature; and lastly through his control of the patronage of the state. A prime minister possessed of a forceful character and dominating personality could easily exploit his peculiar authority to make himself the effective wielder of the political power of the state. Nonetheless his authority was subject to certain inherent limitations. In exercising his power to appoint and dismiss ministers or to dissolve the legislature he had to consider the interest of his party whose collective effort had put him in that position, the claim of other party leaders, and the stability of his government. There is also a certain psychological element of inferiority arising from the fact that the executive power belongs not to him but to the cabinet. There is, too, a popular mass psychology which is always looking for a single national figure with whom to identify the government, a person who embodies in himself the aspiration, the unity and power of the community in a real, and not merely symbolic, sense. Besides, modern government requires a single directing authority which can oversee the entire administration and gear it to the need for progress;

nowhere is this necessity more evident and pressing than in developing countries. To combat poverty, ignorance, and disease 'demands strong government, operating in an atmosphere of urgency.'[8] It is little wonder that many of the nationalist leaders in the ex-British territories became disillusioned with the diffusion of executive power. They wanted concentrated power, not always in order to be tyrannical or autocratic, but in many cases out of a genuine desire to be able to quicken the process of development unimpaired by the dissipation of power and energy inherent in the cabinet system. As Blackstone said concerning the organisation of executive power under the British Constitution during his time:

> 'This is wisely placed in a single hand by the British Constitution, for the sake of unanimity, strength, and despatch. Were it placed in many hands, it would be subject to many wills: many wills, if disunited and drawing different ways, create weakness in a government; and to unite those several wills, and reduce them to one, is a work of more time and delay than the exigencies of state will afford.'[9]

These advantages are secured by the American presidential system. The cabinet in the American system has no constitutional existence, being merely a convenient device to assist the president in the exercise of the executive power vested exclusively in him. 'There is in American theory and practice no question of *primus inter pares*. The famous story of Lincoln consulting his cabinet and announcing, "Nos, seven; ayes, one. The ayes have it," expresses perfectly the spirit of the American Constitution.'[10] The president's government does not depend upon the support of the legislature; once elected, his tenure of office is assured for the full term of four years, and he can deal sternly with his ministers without fear that a rupture in the cabinet might lead to the collapse of the government or to his being replaced by another leader within the party.

In contrast, the weakness of the government of Nigeria's first Republic owed much to the limitations on the authority of the prime minister. Treating their ministries as though they were their personal fiefs, ministers sometimes acted and made statements in opposition not only to each other but also to the policy of the government itself, and yet they were supposed to be bound by the obligation of collective responsibility imposed upon them by the constitution. Even in the face of charges of maladministration, personal misconduct, arrogance and irresponsibility repeatedly made against ministers, Sir Abubakar Tafawa Balewa appeared incapable of enforcing discipline by dismissals. His inability to do so might have been due in part to personal weakness, but clearly there were certain ministers from his own party he dared not touch without risking his own immediate downfall. His position and authority was no doubt further undermined by the fact that he was only the deputy leader of his party, and that his party colleagues in the cabinet and in parliament owed their allegiance primarily to, and often acted on the direct instruction of, the party leader outside the federal government. The character of the government as a coalition also militated against his authority. Ministerial appointments had been apportioned upon a mutually agreed ratio between the two parties in the coalition. The NCNC ministers in the government had been nominated initially by the leader of that party, and it would have been a breach of the coalition understanding if Sir Abubakar had dismissed any of them without the consent of their party leader. When all has been said, much of the fault for the weakness must be attributed to the system. Even if the prime minister had been the leader of a single party government, he might still have found certain rivals within the party too powerful to dismiss without destroying the unity of the party upon which his own continued tenure of office depended. And so it was that for the first five years of its independent existence the country drifted without effective leadership, much to the disillusionment of the people.

The historical circumstance which justified the diffusion of executive power in Britain did not exist in Nigeria. The British monarch, once an executive ruler, had been reduced to the position of a titular head by constitutional development. Yet, while she remained the monarch of the country, it was impossible to transfer her former executive discretion to one man. The prime minister would have replaced the monarch completely both in law and in fact if executive power had been vested solely in him as under the presidential system. The cabinet system was therefore an arrangement dictated entirely by the fact of history, and it cannot but appear artificial in a context devoid of that background of history. If the qualities needed for a constitutional monarch cannot be reproduced in a country which has never been ruled by a monarch, then it might reasonably be expected that the by-product of the institution would be equally unsuitable.

These, then, are some of the explanations for the widespread disenchantment of nationalist leaders in ex-British territories with the Westminster system. Faced with this, some British writers and politicians have been at pains to stress the point that nationalist leaders had always displayed a fond enthusiasm for the Westminster type of parliamentary government, and had persistently demanded it as 'the one and only brand,' sometimes even against exhortations to consider some other alternative. The impression that they had a genuine choice in the matter is clearly not true. The assumption on the part of both the British and the nationalist leaders alike was that no real choice existed, and that the Westminster model was the one and only basis for the grant of independence.[11] Nationalist leaders were well aware that the Britishers felt profound pride in, and sentimental attachment to, their system, and had a natural desire to see it established in all their former dependencies, if for no other reason than as a common heritage binding former ward to master as equal partners in a new association, the Commonwealth of Nations. Nationalist leaders were therefore likely to regard any suggestion that they should consider some other alternative as not seriously meant, put forward perhaps as a bait, and, knowing the feeling of the British upon the matter, it might have been impolite, indeed an affront, to have opted for something else. And even assuming that there was a real choice open to them, it would be wrong to underrate the influence of past associations. One's ideas and outlook are inexorably conditioned by them. It is not easy to get away from the physical or ideological environment in which one has grown up. Having therefore been reared on the Westminster model, the nationalists might naturally be expected to have developed some vested interest in or bias for it. Such bias or interest might not have acquired very deep roots but at the time it could possibly have been an operative factor. It is hardly conceivable that, had they been reared under some other system, they would have opted to throw that over on the eve of independence in preference for the as yet untried Westminster model.

But what alternatives were there in fact to choose from? There are doubtless at least four principal methods of organising an executive government: the cabinet system, the presidential system, the Swiss council system in which the executive power is vested in a council comprising a representative from each of the cantons, with the chairmanship rotating annually; and the assembly system of the French Third Republic. The last two may be discounted at once. 'The story of modern constitutionalism,' it has been said, 'may in many ways be depicted as a great debate between American and British principles.'[12] To some people, not least the British, the American presidential system tends towards dictatorship, a tendency which might be expected to be more marked in a developing country. Could it then be supposed that the British, conscious as they were of their duty to safeguard the interest of racial or tribal minorities, would have permitted a system which they believed could conceivably lead to dictatorship? That Zambia was granted independence in 1964 on the presidential system seems perhaps to suggest that the futility of forcing every newly independent country into the straitjacket of the Westminster model has at last been realised.

The Partial Fusion of the Organs of Government
(i) *Executive Control of Law-Making*

If the cabinet system prevented the concentration of executive power in the hands of one man, it also produced the concentration of all political power, legislative and executive, in the cabinet, making the cabinet the *de facto* sovereign authority in the country. This position resulted from two factors. Under the Constitution, parliament consisted of the president (i.e. in fact the cabinet) and two legislative houses. The implication of the president being a constituent part of parliament was that his concurrence was necessary to law-making. There was in fact no way in which his concurrence could legally be dispensed with or circumvented under any situation. The constitution expressly provided that no 'bill shall become law unless it has been duly . . . assented to' by the president. Now, the prerogative of assenting to legislation imports a power, and not a duty; and a power to consent to something implies also a power to withhold consent. This result was of course expressly provided for in the constitution. The form of the president's consent was by *assent*; although this was not spelt out explicitly, it is clear that an assent had to be in writing, endorsed on the bill itself, and that an oral assent would not have sufficed.

The significance of the executive's role in legislation is underlined in the most acute form by events in Pakistan after its independence in 1947. Under its provisional constitution, a constituent assembly, created by executive order just before independence, was constituted by the Independence Act, for the time being the legislature of the country, with power to enact ordinary laws and to enact a constitution for the country. There was a governor-general representing the Queen, who, though not made a part of the legislature as so constituted, was given 'full power to assent . . . to any law of the legislature.' Proceeding from the view that the assent of the governor-general was necessary for ordinary laws but not for those of a constitutional nature, the assembly, during the seven-year period in which it was trying in vain to produce a constitution, passed forty-four constitutional laws which it put into force without submitting them for the governor-general's assent. It was decided that the governor-general's assent was requisite to all laws enacted by the assembly, and accordingly all forty-four enactments which did not receive such assent were void.[13] The result was that the constitutional and administrative machinery of the state had all but broken down, and a state of emergency had to be declared.[14]

But perhaps a more potent implication of requiring the president's concurrence to legislation was the power which it gave the executive to veto any bill passed by the legislative houses, of which it did not approve. In practice this was of little moment, since practically all bills were government bills, but it was theoretically possible for a private member's bill to find such favour with the majority of the members as to gain a passage against the wishes of the government. If that were to happen, the executive could fall back upon its reserve power of veto to prevent the bill becoming law.

The concurrence of the executive in legislation only made it in law an equal partner with the legislative houses in the law-making process, since the concurrence of the latter (or rather of the lower house) was equally indispensable. The executive's predominance in legislation arose therefore more from its control of the legislative houses, from its ability to dictate when and how the legislative houses' concurrence was to be given or withheld. The executive was able so to control the legislative houses, because its members were the leaders of the majority party in the lower house and were thus able, through the party organisation, particularly the party whip in the house, effectively to dictate how the parliamentary party members were to vote. Through his leadership of the house (i.e. the lower house) the prime minister or his deputy was able to ensure that the house moved along the lines determined by the government, giving or withholding its concurrence when the government so directed. Where, as in Britain, the conditions exist to make the system work as it is supposed to, then the role of the lower house in legislation is much less formal, much less that of a rubber stamp or a nodding automaton than is implied in this description. The ideal conditions presuppose an effective opposition party in the lower house, able to provide an alternative government, and fervently working to displace the government in the favour of the electorate by focussing public attention upon any blunders or excesses of the government. Faced with such an opposition, the government can hardly afford to take the house for granted; on the contrary, it would find itself obliged to make a genuine effort, by consultations with various interests and groups, to make its measures as widely acceptable as possible.

This is the ideal, and in Nigeria it had remained no more than an ideal. The Nigerian legislative houses had never been anything but a rubber stamp. With a feeble and frustrated opposition party consisting of a handful of members, denied any hope of ever winning an election and so forming a government; with thoroughly servile

parliamentary supporters, lacking a will of their own, whose loyalty
to the government was based more upon tribal sentiment than upon
principle; and finally with an electorate whose behaviour was
equally conditioned by tribal loyalty and prejudice, the government was inclined to ride rough-shod over the house, secure in the
belief that it would always get its way with the house and with the
electorate too. Throughout the life of the last parliament there
was not a single instance of a private member's bill passed or
indeed of any serious amendment to a government bill, and the
way in which legislative measures were always rushed through
parliament with a haste that could only be described as indecent
lends support to the view that the legislative houses' share in law-
making was entirely a formal one, and that the cabinet was the
sole *de facto* legislature. The cabinet's control of legislation was of
course rendered complete by the total subordination of the upper
house to the lower house, except in matters of constitutional amendment.

Though power was diffused among its members, the cabinet was
thus collectively more powerful than the American president. The
latter is not a constituent part of the legislature, all legislative
powers being vested in the Congress alone (i.e. the legislative
houses). The president's role in legislation is a subordinate one.
Normally a bill passed by Congress does not become law until it
has been signed by the president, but should he refuse to sign, then
the bill will become law without his signature upon its being passed
again by the votes of two-thirds majority in both houses of Congress.
So also if he should fail to return a bill within ten days of its being
presented to him, then the bill becomes law as though he had
signed it, unless its return is prevented by the fact of Congress being
in adjournment. Nor, although he is also a leader of a party which
may be in the majority in the Congress, does the president in the
U.S. exercise over Congress anything like the same degree of
control as that exercised by the cabinet over the legislature under
the Nigerian Constitution. The somewhat rigid separation of the
legislature from the executive makes it possible to have a president
whose party is in a minority in Congress. And even if his party has
a majority in Congress, Congress enjoys by virtue of this separation
almost complete independence from dictation by the president.
Not being a member of Congress he does not lead it or control its
business as does the prime minister, nor does he hold over it that
power of life and death, the power of dissolution, in which lies the
cabinet's ultimate and most effective weapon of control over the
legislature. For the American Congress cannot be dissolved before
the expiry of its normal life.

Once again it is in British history that the explanation, if not the justification, for the fusion of the executive and the legislature under the Westminster system, and the consequent control of the former over legislation, has to be looked for. It was a reflection of the days when the monarch was both the sole executive and legislature. He has, by a bitter and protracted struggle, been obliged to concede legislative authority to the people's representatives in parliament, and to hand over executive power to persons also representative of the people; it was expedient that such persons should be chosen from the houses of parliament. Yet the monarch still remains the sovereign of the country, and as the power of law-making is the main attribute of legal sovereignty, it follows by the sheer logic of his sovereignty that he has to be a constituent part of parliament. The development of the party system ensured that his ministers controlled the houses of parliament. And so the original position was virtually re-established, namely, that of an executive which also is the legislature. Now, not being a monarch, the President of Nigeria was not invested with the sovereignty of the country. What, then, was the explanation, not to say justification, for making him a constituent part of the legislature, and for making the cabinet parliamentary in character? The lack of any reason for the arrangement would probably not have mattered if it had been suitable otherwise. There can be no doubt, however, that the absolute control of the cabinet over the legislature made the latter impotent in checking the excesses on the part of the former. In a federation, the separation of the executive and the legislature is part of the system of checks and balances necessary for the satisfactory working of the system. Had the legislature been independent of the executive, had the senate not been subordinated to the House of Representatives, it might not have been possible for the party in power to pervert federal power to the extent it was able to do.

(ii) *Separation of Judicial Power*

It is remarkable that the Nigerian Constitution, unlike those of the U.S.A. or Australia, made no express vesting of judicial power in the courts. It merely created the superior courts, prescribed their constitution and the method of appointing and removing judges. This raises the question whether, under the Constitution, judicial power existed as a separate power or whether it was embraced within the ambit of the power of the legislature to make laws for peace, order and good government, which would thus enable the legislature, for example, to enact a law convicting a person of a criminal offence and imposing a sentence therefor, without trial in

F

a court of law. The latter view of the absence of an express vesting of judicial power in the courts was vigorously urged in a Ceylonese case, *Liyanage v. R.*[15] The argument in support of this view relied of course on the analogy with the British Constitution which recognises no judicial power existing independently of, and co-ordinately with, the legislative sovereignty of parliament. It was thus argued that, although the Ceylon Constitution provided for the method of appointing and removing judges, no separate judicial power was thereby created. It is certainly plausible to argue that a constitution which confers legislative power in its fullest amplitude and merely creates superior courts or prescribes the method of appointing and removing judges, without an express vesting of judicial power in them, does not intend that judicial power shall exist as a limitation upon the legislative power. All that can necessarily be predicated on the actual provisions of the constitution is that the legislature cannot abolish the courts or alter the method prescribed for the appointment and dismissal of judges except by a valid amendment of the constitution.

Alive to the danger of submerging the judicial into the legislative power, the Privy Council, happily, ruled against this argument, plausible and forceful though it is. First, it said, analogies drawn from the unwritten Constitution of England are not conclusive in interpreting a written one. Secondly, the express vesting of judicial power in the federal courts in the U.S. and Australia was made necessary by the federal character of their constitutions. No federal courts had existed before the constitution, and unless they were created and invested with power by the constitution, they could have no existence or power. Ceylon was, however, in a different position as a unitary state. The courts there had been in existence before the constitution, and had customarily exercised the judicial power before it was enacted. This hardly justifies importing into the constitution a power which it has not expressly granted, especially where the implication of such power is in derogation of a power expressly granted.

However, the decision of the Board (i.e. the Privy Council) rests mainly upon the intention and spirit of the constitution. In the board's opinion, the arrangement of the constitution into parts, among which is one headed 'the judicature,' wherein it is provided that judges are to be appointed by a judicial service commission and may be dismissed by the governor-general upon an address of both houses, imports an intention to separate the judicial power from the legislative and the executive. 'These provisions,' said the board, 'manifest an intention to secure in the judiciary a freedom from political, legislative and executive control. They are wholly appropriate in a constitution which intends that judicial power shall be vested only in the judicature. They would be inappropriate in a constitution by which it was intended that judicial power should be shared by the executive or the legislature. The constitution's silence as to the vesting of judicial power is consistent with its remaining where it had lain for more than a century, in the hands of the judicature. It is not consistent with any intention that henceforth it should be passed to or be shared by, the executive or the legislature.'[16] The legislature's power to make law for peace, order and good government does not therefore entitle it to pass legislation which usurps the judicial power of the judicature – e.g. by passing an act of attainder against some person or instructing a judge to bring in a verdict of guilty against someone who is being tried; any such legislation is *ultra vires* and void.

The facts of this case are sufficiently interesting to warrant a brief notice. Certain individuals, involved in an abortive *coup d'état* to overthrow the government of Ceylon, were indicted for this offence. After their arrest, the legislature enacted two statutes which altered the criminal law and the law of evidence, not for the generality of the citizens, but specifically for the purpose of the trial of the named individuals implicated in the coup, and their effect was to be limited solely to the particular accused persons. However, the statutes did not constitute a usurpation of the judicial power merely because they lacked generality of application, for, as the board said, such a lack of generality in criminal legislation need not usurp or infringe the judicial power.[17] In this case, however, the acts in question did not only lack generality but amounted to a special direction to the judiciary as to the trial of the particular prisoners who were identifiable. 'The pith and substance of both Acts was a legislative plan *ex post facto* to secure the conviction and enhance the punishment of those particular individuals.'[18] An act confiscating the property of a named person or attainting him of treason is rather a sentence than a law; it is a legislative judgment, and therefore an unconstitutional exercise of judicial power by the legislature.

The judgment of the Privy Council in this case constitutes a milestone of constitutionalism for countries whose constitutions are patterned upon the Westminster system. Without it and in the absence of any other express limitation in the constitution, it is difficult to see how judicial power can be excepted from the legislative power when the constitution makes no express vesting of that power in the judiciary. The decision in this case is reinforced, as regards Nigeria, by the provision of the constitution guaranteeing to every person, in the determination of his civil rights and

obligations, the right to 'a fair hearing within a reasonable time
by a court or other tribunal established by law and constituted in
such manner as to secure its independence and impartiality.'[19]

The Responsibility of the Executive to the Legislature

Political responsibility operated at two levels. As government rests
upon the consent of the governed, the constitution required that
the government should go back to the electorate for the renewal of
its mandate every five years. By this means the electorate was
enabled to exercise its supreme prerogative as the final arbiter of
who should govern. To enable it to exercise its prerogative freely
and with adequate guidance, the constitution vested responsibility
for the conduct of elections in an independent electoral commission;
it also guaranteed freedom to organise political parties, to engage
in political activities and to propagate political ideas. Furthermore,
although the constitution was itself silent upon the right to vote,
the franchise was in fact universal for both men and women (except
that women in the North did not have a vote).

At the secondary level, the executive was made accountable to
the legislature for its administration of government. The parliamentary character of the executive ensured that ministers would be
available to explain the actions and policies of the government to
parliament which could then not only criticise but also censure, if
need be, by refusing to pass a government bill laid before it or by
a formal vote of no confidence in the government. Before parliament, the executive was collectively responsible for all executive
actions, whether they emanated from the cabinet or from an
individual minister, the purpose being to maintain the unity of the
government, since only by putting forward a united front can it
maintain its control over the legislature.

(i) Problems of the Executive's Responsibility to the Legislature

Now the notion of the accountability of the government to the
legislature raises a problem as regards the sanction for it. Should
a government, faced with the loss of parliamentary support, continue in office, or resign or be dismissed or ask for dissolution? The
fate of the government in the face of an adverse vote in the legislature ought really to depend upon what purpose a parliamentary
election is intended to serve. Is it to choose a government or to
return individual members to the house? No doubt it seeks to do
both, but under modern practice the identity of individual candidates is far less important in winning an election than the standing
and programme of the party which they support. The electorate

cares less for individual candidates than for the party and its leadership. A parliamentary election is nowadays concerned more with the choice of a government than with the return of individual members to the legislature. Having been chosen upon a definite programme by the electorate, is it consistent with the maintenance of the people's choice that the government should be obliged to resign or be dismissed because the legislature has withdrawn its support from it? To subscribe to this view would seem like subordinating the will of the people to that of the legislature. Since the choice of a government is the predominant purpose of an election, the stability of the government should override whatever the legislature might think about the action of the government. The government should not therefore be obliged to resign, much less be dismissed, upon an adverse vote in the legislature, unless the party which won the election can form another government under a different leader. Should it be necessary for one to give way to the other, it is the legislature that should go. In such a situation the government should be able to ask for a dissolution, though it may mean that it too will perish along with the legislature, as a consequence of the fusion of the executive and the legislature. A dissolution is perhaps useful as a means of doing away with a government or an assembly which, in the interval before the normal expiry of its term of offices has ceased to be representative of public opinion, but it is not altogether a desirable solution. Apart from its expense, it does not make for stability in government or in the community generally. In developing countries where the political temperature is always charged, an election is an occasion for violence and destruction. The idea of an election is that it gives the government the mandate to rule (or to misrule) for a specified term, and it seems best to tolerate it for that period, however much it may be blundering. The sanction of parliamentary rejection of a government measure is enough without adding to it that of a dissolution, with its generally unsettling effects.

The Nigerian Constitution instituted the sanction of dissolution. If a government measure was rejected by the legislature, the government could ask for a dissolution, which the president might refuse if he considered that the government could be carried on without a dissolution and that a dissolution would not be in the interests of the federation.[20] Faced with such a refusal, the government might then either resign or compromise with the legislature. In the case of a vote of no confidence, the government had again a choice between resignation and dissolution. If it chose to ask for dissolution, the president must dissolve. But if it resigned instead, the president could ask someone else to form a new government, unless he considered that nobody could be found to do so within a reasonable time, in which case he must again dissolve. He must also dissolve if the premier would neither resign nor recommend a dissolution.

Those provisions represented a marked departure from those of the 1960 Independence Constitution, which empowered the governor-general or governor to dismiss a government whenever it appeared to him that the premier no longer enjoyed majority support in the elected house of the legislature. It was not stated whether the loss of support should be a permanent one. Clearly, only a permanent loss of support can destroy the popular basis of the government. This is most unequivocally expressed in a formal vote of no confidence or in some other act indicative of it, but a mere refusal to pass a particular government measure should not be conclusive unless the measure is of such importance that the fate of the government should be inseparably bound up with it or unless there have been repeated rejections occurring in such a way as to form a connected series and so lead to the inference that the legislature desires a change of government. The provision also left undefined the source from which the governor-general or governor was to form his opinion of the state of the premier's support. The dispute to which this last omission had given rise is now a familiar, if sordid, part of Nigerian constitutional history.[21] Briefly, following a squabble within the ruling party in Western Nigeria, the regional governor purported to remove the premier on the strength of a letter signed by sixty-six out of 117 members of the house of assembly to the effect that they no longer had confidence in the premier. Now, it is easy enough to imagine how the power in a non-elected head of state to dismiss an elected government on the evidence of events occurring outside the legislature can be put to mischievous and arbitrary use. It was consciousness of this not too remote possibility that led the supreme court to the conclusion that the governor's source of information as to the premier's support or lack of it among the elected MPs must emanate from the House itself. 'Law and convention,' said Chief Justice Ademola, 'cannot be replaced by party political moves outside the House.' While recognising the dangers of arbitrariness and abuse inherent in allowing the head of state so much leeway, the Judicial Committee of the Privy Council, adopting a rather literal and legalistic approach, held that the governor was free to act on other than the testimony of recorded votes.[22] A hurried constitutional amendment, nullifying with retrospective effect, the decision of the Privy Council, provided that the governor could remove the premier only in consequence of a vote of no confidence.

It is of interest to note that the Western Nigerian episode was re-enacted in Sarawak in 1966, on almost identical facts.[23] There again the governor had purported to dismiss the chief minister on the strength of a letter signed by twenty-one out of the forty-two members of the legislative council, to the effect that they no longer had confidence in the chief minister. Whereupon the governor requested him to resign, and, upon his refusing to do so, dismissed him. Under the constitution, if the chief minister ceased to command the confidence of a majority of the legislative council, then, unless at his request the governor dissolved the council, the chief minister was to tender the resignation of the members of the cabinet. It was held, distinguishing the Nigerian case, that the words 'if the chief minister ceases to command' left no discretion to the governor as to the source of his information as did the words 'if it appears' in the constitution of Western Nigeria, and that accordingly the governor was not entitled to act otherwise than on the strength of events occurring on the floor of the house; and that, in any event, a refusal by the chief minister to resign after a vote of no confidence or a defeat on a major issue, though in itself unconstitutional, gave the governor no power to dismiss him in the absence of express provision to that effect. The reinstatement of the chief minister following upon this decision triggered off a chain of events which culminated in the federal government of Malaysia, of which Sarawak is part, declaring a state of emergency in Sarawak and using its emergency power to amend the state constitution to empower the governor to dismiss the chief minister.

The question that is prompted by these unfortunate events is: is it not undesirable that such clearly avoidable sources of conflict and instability should have been built into the constitution of a young country? With all the temptations which power has for inexperienced politicians unrestrained by well-established and accepted rules and prompted by tribal or sectional impulse, should it not have been foreseen that such provisions would be inherently productive of political conflict and impasse? The Western Nigerian episode was admittedly the source of all the subsequent troubles in the country, and it was a sad reflection upon the Westminster model. Yet it is argued in favour of the system that because of the close union between the executive and the legislature, 'the dangers involved in deadlock between the law-making, tax-granting authority and the executive are absent. The right to govern flows through the legislature to the cabinet; it is not separately conferred on a popularly elected chief executive and on a popularly elected parliament; the right is not capable therefore of conflicting interpretation by two bodies having an equal moral claim to speak for the public.'[24] Is it not precisely because under the Westminster system the right to govern is capable of conflicting interpretation by two bodies having an equal moral claim to speak for the public, that dissolution has to be resorted to? It is because both the executive and the legislature claim to speak for the public that any conflict between them is sought to be resolved by an appeal to the electorate. If the right to speak for the public is vested solely in the legislature, then its views should override those of the executive and there should be no need for a dissolution. The dissolution of the legislature and with it the government in the event of conflict between them constitutes therefore another objectionable consequence of their fusion. A certain amount of conflict is of the very essence of politics,[25] and no system of government can ever hope completely to eliminate it. But the resolution of any conflict that might arise between the legislature and the executive should not involve the resignation or dismissal of the latter or the dissolution of the former. Some other solution, such as reference of the point in dispute to the electorate, is to be preferred.

It may be useful to see how other modern constitutions have dealt with the question of the relationship between the executive and the legislature.

(ii) *Mixture of the Presidential and Parliamentary Systems*

The constitution of the Fifth French Republic, 1958, is a curious mixture of features drawn from both the presidential and parliamentary systems. There is a government headed by a prime minister, with responsibility to determine and direct national policy. Its members cannot be members of parliament, but they have a right of access to, and of audience in, both houses of parliament, to which they are collectively responsible, a responsibility which is sanctioned by the provision that when the national assembly (i.e. the lower house) passes a motion of censure or rejects the programme or a general policy declaration of the government, it must forthwith resign. Except that ministers are not drawn from the national assembly, all this conforms with the parliamentary system. Yet standing above and somewhat outside the government is a president with full executive power (and a considerable measure of legislative power too), exercisable either personally or in council (i.e. the council of ministers over which he presides), and whose tenure of office, fixed at seven years by the constitution, is in no way affected by the resignation of the government or the dissolution of parliament – the president can dissolve parliament at any time provided that at least one year has elapsed since the election following the last dissolution. He is elected by universal, direct suffrage, and his responsibility is therefore to the elecotrate, not to parliament. The president is thus intended to provide the stability in executive government which is lacking in the parliamentary system. The underlying idea is that the president should stand above politics and be an impartial arbiter, ensuring 'the regular functioning of the political organs of government as well as the continuity of the state,' and protecting 'the independence of the nation, of its territorial integrity.'[26]

While the maintenance of the stability and continuity of the administration of government is commendable, the logic whereby the chief executive is to remain in office and his ministers be obliged to resign upon an adverse vote in parliament is, to say the least, difficult to follow. It looks like an irrational adherence to the parliamentary system to mulct ministers for a policy of which the president may have been the prime mover or for which he is at least jointly to blame with them. And since the president can make a direct appeal to the electorate on any issue which Parliament has refused to pass, it is also difficult to understand why he should have been given the power of dissolution. All this lends support to the assertion that the constitution was cut to de Gaulle's measure.[27] Equally characteristic of the imprint of Gaullist authoritarian personality is the provision whereby, in order to preserve the integrity of the nation in the face of grave and immediate danger, the president is given virtually unlimited power over the fundamental liberties of Frenchmen.[28]

The 1960 Ghana Republic Constitution, post-dating its French counterpart by two years, was also a curious mixture of both the presidential and parliamentary systems. It established an executive president whose right to govern derived directly from the people, though his election was combined in a single exercise with the election of members of the legislature. Excepting the first president, Dr. Nkrumah, who was elected separately by the people, the election of presidents was to be determined by the preferences for a presidential candidate given before the general election by those elected as members of parliament. The presidential candidate preferred by the majority of those so elected became president. It is of course obvious that the votes at the election would be directed more to the presidential preferences than to the parliamentary candidates. (In the event of the death or resignation of the president, his successor for the unexpired term was selected by the members of parliament.) The linkage of the executive to the legislature was reinforced by the provision requiring ministers to be drawn from the legislature. However, neither the president nor his ministers were responsible to the legislature, and so there was no question of his being forced to resign because of an adverse vote. The tying of the election of the president to that of the parliamentary members ensured that the president would have majority support in the legislature, and this, coupled with the provision requiring his ministers to be members of the legislature, assured him of control of the legislature. To complete his control over the legislature, the president was given the power of dissolution, though in that event there would also have to be a presidential election. The immunity of the American Congress from dissolution by the executive before the expiry of its normal term is a cardinal aspect of that separation of powers upon which the success of the American system to a considerable extent depends. Furthermore, the president under the Ghana Constitution was vested with an absolute veto over legislation, a veto which could not, as in America, be overriden by a special majority in the Assembly, and which, unlike the case in Pakistan under its 1962 Constitution, did not permit of the reference of the matter in dispute to the electroate at a referendum. The tendency to dictatorship of an arrangement which combines in a president full executive power and control of legislation is obvious. It is little wonder, therefore, that Dr. Nkrumah became a dictator under that constitution.

REFERENCES

1. *The New Commonwealth and its Constitutions*, 1964, p. 83.
2. Cap. 122, Laws of the Fedn., 1958, and its regional counterparts.
3. 'The Westminster Model in Nigeria' (1968), *Parliamentary Affairs*, p. 24.
4. Ohonbamu, *The Nigerian Constitution and Its Review*, 1965, pp. 20-1.
5. Tansey and Kermode, *op. cit.*, p. 24.
6. See the Common Law doctrine of civil necessity discussed below Ch. VII.
7. S. 87 (8) (a).
8. de Smith, *The New Commonwealth and Its Constitutions*, 1964, p. 237.
9. 1 Bl., Comm., p. 250.
10. Denis Brogan, 'The Possibilities of the Presidential System in Africa,' in Alan Burns, ed., *Parliament as an Export*, 1966, p. 195.
11. Is it not significant that, less than ten months after independence, the Tanganyikan national assembly passed a resolution for a presidential system?
12. Carl J. Friedrich, *Impact of American Constitutionalism Abroad*, 1966, p. 12.
13. *Federation of Pakistan v. Khan* (1955), reported in Jennings, *Constitutional Problems in Pakistan*, 1957, p. 79.
14. For further discussion, see infra, Ch. VII.
15. [1967], 1. A.C. 259.

16. *Ibid.*, at pp. 287-8.
17. For a decision directly in point, see *Kariapper v. Wijesinha* [1968], A.C. 717 (P.C.).
18. [1967], 1. A.C. at p. 290.
19. S. 22 (1). *Ex post facto* offences and punishments were also prohibited: S22 (7).
20. This represents Lord Simon's view of the relevant convention under the British Constitution. Lord Chorley and others argued that the Queen should never under any circumstances refuse a prime minister's request for dissolution. See the letters to *The Times*, London, April 24-7, 1950.
21. *Adegbenro v. Akintola*, F.S.C. 187/1962.
22. [1963], A.C. 614.
23. *Ningkan v. Openg* (1966), 2, M.L.J. 187. For a discussion of the case, see Thio, 'Dismissal of Chief Ministers,' *Malaya L.R.*, 1966, pp. 283-91.
24. H. R. G. Greaves, *The British Constitution*, 1958, p. 20.
25. See Lucy Mair, *Primitive Government*.
26. Art. 5. *Cf.* the Constitutions of Dahomey and Congo (Brazzaville).
27. William G. Andrews, ed., *Constitutions and Constitutionalism*, 1963, p. 68.
28. Art. 16. Commenting on the French Constitution, Carl J. Friedrich has said that 'the prime drafter of the constitution of the Fifth Republic, Michel Debré, preferred the British system, which de Gaulle has perverted by widening the presidential powers until they formally exceed those of the American president, being less limited by the representative assembly, and not at all by either federal or judicially enforced constitutional restraints.' *Impact of American Constitutionalism Abroad*, 1967, p. 20; also 'The New French Constitution in Political and Historical Perspective,' *Harvard Law Review*, No. 72, 1959, p. 80.

CHAPTER IV

CONSTITUTIONALISM AND NATIONAL UNITY IN NIGERIA

National Unity as a Foundation for Constitutionalism

A constitution, as has been pointed out, is not just a document in solemn form, but a living framework for the government of a people exhibiting a sufficient degree of cohesion. A constitution, however carefully constructed, cannot function among a people fundamentally at odds with one another. 'There must be some binding elements of unity in outlook which constitute the *real* constitution.'[1] National unity may thus be described as the infrastructure for constitutionalism; it is a condition precedent for viable constitutionalism. There is here again the same problem of legitimacy. The nation is vital to the state because it is only a feeling of common belonging and love for the political community which can legitimise the state. However powerful a state is in terms of its organised coercive forces, it cannot long endure unless it is accepted by the generality of the people living within its jurisdiction. Hence the need and the struggle to secure a coincidence between state and nation. 'Where,' writes Rupert Emerson, 'the state is based on any principle other than the national one, as is by definition the case in any imperial system, its foundations are immediately suspect in a nationalist age. Once the people of such a state have come to a consciousness of national identity, the presumption is that the state will shortly be swept away, to be replaced by another cleaving as closely as possible to the national foundations.'[2]

The primary problem confronting constitutionalism in emergent states is therefore one of national unity. The state, denoting a government of people inhabiting a defined territory, is of course the starting point in the making of a nation. It provides the foundation of common political, social and economic institutions and laws necessary for the organisation of communal life. The establishment of a common central government among what formerly was a collection of small, independent communities is perhaps the main beneficial legacy of the European colonisation of Asia and Africa. Yet these states are distinctly artificial by the very fact that the communities which constitute them are fundamentally different, often hostile. 'Colonialism was the glue that stuck these human units together into a shape recognisable in an atlas . . . Now the glue is dissolving and many of these units are falling apart.'³ How to transform these states into nations is one of the major problems of government in the emergent countries. It is the problem underlying the disturbing phenomena of coups and secessions which characterise government in these countries, and coups and secessions are an assault upon constitutionalism.

What is a Nation?

A nation is essentially a state of mind. It connotes, firstly, a feeling of community, a consciousness of common belonging or identity among the members of the state. This national consciousness is often the product of a common culture, language, common historical origin and tradition, a distinctive national character and a common religion.⁴ Important as are these objective factors, they are not a *sine qua non* to the development of a national consciousness.⁵ In practice they are found together only in an ideal nation. A will to live together as a corporate group has frequently to be developed as a matter of conscious effort, and it can be fostered among peoples of different cultural and national origins if there are strong enough external forces to inspire them with a sense of common destiny, such as defence against a common enemy or a commitment to a common political tradition. Switzerland (and to a lesser extent the U.S.) affords perhaps the most remarkable example of distinct linguistic and national groupings comprising Germans, French and Italians, which, under the influence of such forces, have been able to develop to a very marked degree a feeling of common belonging.

A nation requires in the second place a feeling of transcendent loyalty to the state, a love of fatherland. Conflicting loyalties to groups of various kinds, tribal, racial, religious or linguistic, are inevitable in any society, since no community is ever so homogeneous as to be completely united in the interests which its members pursue. It is, however, of paramount importance to the concept of a nation that these sectional loyalties must, for most of the population, be subordinated to a higher loyalty, the loyalty to the state. Where sectional loyalties are so strong as to override loyalty to the state, when issues affecting the state are determined by group interests rather than by those of the state, then the state is far from being a nation.

The question to be discussed in this chapter is whether there ever was a national consciousness or a desire to foster it among the peoples of the emergent states sufficient to sustain constitutional government. Nigeria again will be taken as an illustrative case.

The Social Structure of the Nigerian State

The tribe is a universal phenomenon in the social structure of African states. Whereas among the modern European states, the individual is today the unit of social relationship, in Africa, the tribe, together with its component units, the family and the clan, is the focal point of social life, with a first claim upon the loyalty of its members. Nigeria is perhaps one of the most conspicuously tribalised societies in Africa. Its tribal groups are numbered in hundreds, but the three major ones, with a population of over six million each, are the Hausa-Fulani, the Ibo and the Yoruba. From the point of view of national unity, however, the primary cleavage is between the Muslim North on the one hand and the Southern tribes on the other.

The difference between the Muslim North and the South cannot adequately be explained in terms of tribe. It lies deeper than that. Notwithstanding the absence of an agreement as to what constitutes a tribe, language seems to be universally accepted as its main constitutive element. Although difference in language is the most important disintegrative factor, yet most tribes in sub-Saharan Africa exhibit enough similarities of character and outlook to warrant referring to them, albeit loosely, as one people of a common racial stock. They belong indeed to the same Negroid race. The Hausa, Ibo, Yoruba and the smaller Nigerian tribes, fall within this category, but the Fulani, on the other hand, are in origin a Hamite race, who migrated into Hausaland and became mixed with the Hausa through a process of miscegenation. Their different cultures inevitably inter-penetrated one another. In the twelfth century Islam was introduced into Hausaland and in to many other Negroid tribes of the North, and in 1804 Hausaland was conquered by the Fulani, who then proceeded to enforce Islam as the religion of the state. All this combined to transform the character and cultural outlook of the Northern Muslim tribes to an extent that made them a people apart from the rest of the Negroid tribes in the country. The difference between the Muslim North and the South is thus not just one of language or tribe, but of *peoples*, separated by differences in racial origin, culture and religion, which are super-imposed upon that of tribe or language.

These differences are manifested, firstly, in their differing attitude to the place of the individual in society. Islam, as institutionalised in the North, has bred in the people a certain attitude of fatalism,

a belief that the life of the individual and events generally are determined by fate or Allah, and not by the individual. This fatalism
has conditioned his attitude to individual enterprise and the acquisition of individual wealth and power. His desires and aspirations
being limited and easily satisfied, he has little urge or incentive to
amass individual wealth or to acquire great political power. Islam
has inculcated in him habits and attitudes of subservience and of
political subordination to the will and authority of his master or
the chief or Emir, for whom he is content to work in return for the
latter's acceptance of responsibility for his feeding and general
welfare. The society is built upon a kind of feudalism based, not
upon land as in medieval Europe, but upon a differentiation of
society between, on the one hand, the illiterate peasants, poor,
obsequious and submissive, and, on the other, the Emirs and chiefs,
wealthy, authoritarian and aristocratic. In contrast the southerner
believes in individual self-determination, regarding the individual
as the architect of his own destiny. He places a premium, not so
much upon ascribed status, as on that acquired through his own
individual effort, whether this relates to wealth or to political power.
His individualism inclines him somewhat to self-centredness,
excessive acquisitiveness, and to a tendency to exploit others. Among
the Ibo, indeed, wealth is respected much more than traditional
authority, and so one finds that the leading figures in society are
those who have done well for themselves materially. The individualistic culture of the Ibo is probably a product of his social and
political system in which authority is diffused among family, village
and clan groups, with no large-scale states, no strong centralised
leadership or important executive chiefs. The society is an egali-
tarian one in which everyone counts equally and is entitled to a say
in public affairs. The Ibo is therefore very little inhibited by
authority or by any stratification of society based upon birth. The
political organisation of the Muslim North is, on the other hand,
characterised by the large-scale state ruled by powerful, authoritarian, hereditary Emirs, with largely hereditary subordinate chiefs
who form a council with him and administer the local units of the
emirate. The Yoruba also have a centralised political organisation
under a hereditary Oba, but it is smaller in size than the Muslim
emirate of the North. Moreover, the Oba is much less authoritarian, his power being severely limited by those of his subordinate
chiefs who form a council with him, and of the family and village
groups which, as among the Ibo, are the dominant units of social
organisation.

The difference between the Muslim North and the South is also
that between conservatives and radicals, between traditionalists

and progressives. By its out-moded customs and religious laws Islam has bred in the Muslims of the North a disinclination to change, and an apathy or even opposition to new ideas. The Islamic culture, strangling all progress, was regarded as self-sufficient, an ideal worthy of preservation in its pristine purity. The conservatism of the Muslim northerner is perhaps partly a result of the intense cultural consciousness infused into him by Islam, a consciousness born out of a belief in the inherent superiority and antiquity of the Islamic culture. The Islamic religion is intolerant of other beliefs and ideas, and its demands upon the life of its adherents are rigid and dominating. It is isolationist and segregationist in outlook, imposing among its members a sense of unity and brotherhood as against all those who are not of the faith. Between a Muslim and a non-Muslim there can, as the Sultan of Sokoto put it in his letter to the first British High Commissioner of Northern Nigeria, be 'no dealings except as between Mussulmans and Unbelievers – war, as God Almighty has enjoined on us.' All this contrasts sharply with the Southerner's progressive outlook, his radicalism, his adaptability to new ideas, and an eagerness for progress and change, a 'flexibility of response to what anthropologists euphemistically call "acculturation".'

In character, cultural outlook and emotions, therefore, the Southerners are perhaps more different from the Northern Muslims than the English are from, say, the French or the Germans. Deep as are the cultural differences, however, one would have expected that half a century of living together under a common government, with its unified administrative, economic, legal and communications system, would gradually have nurtured a consciousness of common identity among the peoples of Nigeria. It is one of the sad aspects of Nigerian history that this has not happened. Why, then, has this been the case?

Why Half a Century of British Rule Failed to Foster a Feeling of Nigerian Unity

It must be admitted that half a century is too short a period to permit of the development of a really strong and binding sense of unity, but there were, in any case, factors which militated against it.

(i) Uneven impact of modern conditions and institutions

It was to be expected from what has been said about the character and outlook of the two sets of people that contact with modern conditions and institutions would widen rather than narrow the differences between them. Because of their progressive outlook and

G

receptivity to new ideas the south became a fertile ground for heavy Christian evangelism. Millions had embraced Christianity together with its modernising culture, especially Western education which was the main instrument by which the Christian missionaries propagated their evangelising mission. The zeal for Western education was just immense. It was the hallmark of modernisation, the gateway to Western civilisation. For the Ibo in particular Western education became an obsessive concern upon which vast effort was expended by individuals and communities. A whole community would team up to build a community school and finance its courses, to institute a scholarship scheme for its sons and daughters, and even to establish a secondary school or college. A parent would slave and deny himself all comforts in life in order to send his child to school; his ambition was to make good in his child what he himself lacked. He might be a peasant farmer, a poor illiterate or semi-literate carpenter or blacksmith, but his dream was to live to see his son become a clerk or even a lawyer, doctor or an engineer. And once successfully trained, the child accepted it as a family obligation to train his brothers and sisters. This was always the driving force in the society. The standing of any community was reckoned by the number of its sons and daughters who had been to school, to college, to university, and above all to higher institutions in Britain and America. In this matter there was always something of a competitive spirit among the various communities, each struggling not to lag behind the others. The attitude of the Muslim North to both Christian missionaries and Western education was markedly different. The insularity and intolerance of Islam offered a resistance to Christian penetration, a resistance which received encouragement from official British policy. The origin of this policy was Lugard's pledge to protect the Islamic religion against Christian evangelism, but there were also reasons of expediency behind it. In the face of opposition, missionary evangelism, it was feared, might provoke social unrest.

The effect of Christianity has been to sharpen the individualism of its southern converts by emancipating them from the grip of custom and its tribal sanctions, and by infusing into them ideas about progress based upon the superior civilisation of Europe. Western education has had an even more profound impact. By his ability to read and write, the educated Southerner had a whole new vista of opportunities opened to him in commerce, in industry and in the public service of the government. Education was the stepping stone to employment, wealth and political power. It admitted its possessor to the skill and technology which have been the basis of European civilisation. Modernisation of the Southern society was also assisted by Western economic factors. The introduction and development of cash crops in the South, cocoa, coffee, rubber and palm tree, had been greatly facilitated by its favourable climate and had enabled it to achieve a *per capita* income vastly in excess of that of the North. And there was, too, the South's proximity to the sea, which greatly enhanced its superior economic position through the development of the export and import trade. 'Tribal differences,' it has been said, 'might disappear easily in the modern world if all tribes were equal economically. Where they are vastly unequal, tribal difference is called in to add protection to economic interest.'[6]

(ii) *Fear of Southern domination resulting from growing cultural differences*

As a single political entity, Nigeria originated in the amalgamation in 1914 of the two separate administrations of Northern and Southern Nigeria. This event involved not only the political association of the two countries but also the bringing together in physical contact of their peoples, separated, as they were, by basic differences in character and cultural outlook. Amalgamation meant a free mobility of people between the different parts of the country under the new peace and security afforded by the British colonial government. It was inevitable that the Eastener in particular should avail himself of the opportunity thus offered. For, while the seventeen million inhabitants of the North occupied a territory of 282,000 square miles, and the six million of the West one of 45,000 square miles, the East had to support its seven million on an area of barely 29,500 square miles.[7] The land population ratio was thus 60 persons to the square mile in the North, 130 to the square mile in the West, and 240 to the square mile in the East; indeed, in some parts of Iboland, the population density is as high as 1000 persons to the square mile. Cramped thus on insufficient, and what is more, infertile land, the Easterners saw in the North a welcome outlet for their enterprising spirit and their inherent desire for upward mobility. Over a period of time, hundreds of thousands of them had migrated to the North where they established businesses of various kinds – shops, hotels, garages, market stalls and even schools and hospitals. The advantage of the South in Western education also meant that government offices and those of the big commercial firms in the North had to be staffed mostly by educated Southerners in the capacity of clerks, technicians and artisans. Even as late as 1920 the North had not yet produced a single native sufficiently educated for appointment to the most minor clerical position in the government.

As was to be expected, this inter-mingling of peoples created a problem in human relations. It brought to the test the differences in character and culture between the peoples of the North and South. The presence of an extremely exploitative and acquisitive 'alien' minority among a simple, kindly, easily-satisfied people, the gross disparities in the level of education, and the predominance of educated Southerners at strategic points of control in the administrative, commercial and transportation sectors of the Northern society were well calculated to excite fear and resentment among the Northerners. It was fear of domination by Southerners, not only of the economy of the North, but also of its political life. Western education had produced in the Southerner a new idea about national self-determination as well as new ambitions for political power. This, coupled with ideas about acquired status and equality inherent in the traditional culture of the Easterner, was bound to pose a threat to the authority of the Northern ruling oligarchy. Nationalism was indeed becoming a potent political force among the educated elements, and its avowed aim was to capture control of the central political superstructure from the British and with it the control which it gave over the traditional authorities. The Northerners naturally saw in this Southern-dominated movement a dangerous threat to their position. They feared that in a self-governing Nigeria, administered under a unitary political framework, the educationally-backward North would be colonised by the South, and its peoples relegated permanently to a position of inferiority as second-class citizens, with no prospect of ever catching up with the South.

Fear of domination became thus the dominant factor in the relationship between North and South. The tragedy about tribal division, unlike ideological or economic divisions, is that it is not amenable to reason. Fear of domination by another tribe tends to produce resentment and misunderstanding. The Northerners had come to resent the dominating position of Southerners in the economy and public services of the region, a resentment which was accentuated by the condescending arrogance and derision with which they were regarded by the Southerners. Mallam Abubakar Imam, a leading Northerner, put it pointedly when he said in 1949: 'We despise each other; . . . we call each other ignorant; the South is proud of Western knowledge and culture; we are proud of Eastern [culture] . . . To tell you the plain truth, the common people of the North put more confidence in the white man than in . . . their Southern brothers . . .'[8] There was no love lost between North and South. Resentment of Southerners had become so strong that it erupted into violence in the Kano Riots of 1953 which claimed a casualty figure of more than fifty-two killed and about 245 wounded. An official inquiry into the disturbances observed that 'no amount of provocation, short-term or long-term, can in any sense justify the behaviour' of those engaged in them.[9] The planned campaign visit by the Action Group, the officially stated reason for the riots, only provided an opportunity for the Northerners to vent their resentment of the dominating presence in the North of Southerners, particularly Easterners who bore the main brunt of the violence.

Although this North-South cleavage was the primary factor impeding the development of a Nigerian nation, fear of domination was also an embittering factor in the relations between the other tribes, particularly between the Ibo and the Yoruba. The Yoruba were the first to come under Western modernising influence, a circumstance which secured for them a near-monopoly in educational and economic development for many decades, with the result that most of the staff of the African civil service and those of the big expatriate firms were drawn from among them. They also enjoyed a monopoly in the professions. From the early 1930s the Ibo launched a vigorous effort in education, achieving by the '40s a revolutionary break-through which enabled them, almost in one great sweep, to threaten to neutralise Yoruba dominance in the public service, commercial firms and in business. The anxiety of the Yoruba to maintain their early lead coupled with apprehensions over the growing influence and popularity of Dr. Azikiwe (an Ibo) in the nationalist movement reached fever point and nearly erupted into violence in 1948. The relations of each of the three major tribes with the minority tribes clustered around them were also embittered by a feeling of frustration which the permanent dominance of the majority tribe had created in the minorities. Under the circumstances they could not bring themselves to feel a sense of belonging with the major tribe. The estrangement in feeling was further aggravated by the disparity in the level of economic development; in each case the majority tribe was always economically more advanced, partly by reason of natural and physical advantages and partly through a discriminatory distribution of the resources of the government. We will return to this point in the next chapter.

(iii) *British Government Policy towards the development of a higher loyalty transcending tribe or region*
Colonialism is intrinsically inimical to the fostering of a sense of national identity. The framework of government which it establishes is both alien and remote from the emotions of the people,

and is intended to serve primarily the interests of the colonial power rather than those of the colonial people. A colonial constitution is essentially an instrument of subjugation with nothing of that symbolic role of unity and integrative myth associated with a constitution in an independent state. Indeed the whole notion of symbols as a psychological instrument for arousing a feeling of identity and allegiance to the state has no place under colonialism. 'Skilful handling of symbols,' writes Professor Carl Friedrich, 'is as important for constitutionalism as for other forms of government. The symbols can be of many different types . . . special celebrations greatly aid in strengthening the sense of community . . . Those patriotic occasions . . . symbolise allegiance to the community . . . The ritual of the flag, so consistently observed in the U.S., is an everyday illustration of how the symbols of communal unity are instinctively hallowed in a democracy . . . Professor Hayes' searching inquiries into the nature of nationalism have focussed attention upon the important role which flags, national anthems and the like play in rallying mass sentiment.'[10] A colonial government is of course a mere appendage of the imperial state, so that only the national symbols of the latter, its flag, anthem and ceremonial occasions, are permitted. These, like the British Empire Day celebrations, are intended to glorify the imperial state and to foster allegiance to it. Indirectly they suppress any such feeling towards the colonial political community.

Turning to actual practical administration of a people as sharply divided culturally as is Nigeria, this demands that a valiant effort should be made to try to integrate them socially. Social integration would have called for the establishment of common institutions upon which national loyalty might be focussed and a sense of unity thereby inculcated. The British colonial government in Nigeria discouraged, initially at any rate, such a policy of social integration. Southerners living in the North were segregated in separate strangers' quarters outside the walled periphery of the native towns. As a result, contact between the two peoples lacked that degree of closeness and intimacy necessary for the fostering of a consciousness of a common national identity, and the opportunity for promoting mutual understanding through a shared communal life was lost. In the schools, the same policy of tribal segregation was pursued, again to the prejudice of the promotion of mutual understanding and a national outlook among children at a formative period in their lives. Separate schools were maintained for Muslims, where instructions were orientated, not towards the emulation of the European culture as in the South, but rather to the preservation of the Islamic culture. The intention was to enable the younger generation to grow up as good, devout Muslims, unaffected by 'influences which might tend to make them careless about the observances of their religious duties, forgetful of the customs and traditions of their fellow countrymen or lacking in the respect and courtesy which they owe to their parents, to all those who occupy positions of authority, and to all old people.'[11] Religion and Arabic featured prominently in the curriculum of the Muslim schools. Thus, not only the physical separation of the children at school, but also the content of the education they were given tended increasingly to set them apart in cultural and political outlook.

The official support given to Islam at the cost of the total exclusion of Christian missionaries, was a retrograde policy. Had an early attempt been made to induce Islam to accommodate other religions and ideas, the difference between the Muslim North and the South would have been minimised. One would not of course expect a colonial government, preoccupied as it was with the maintenance of law and order, to follow the example of Kemal Ataturk of Turkey and abolish Islam altogether as the religion of the state, replacing its laws with a modern code based upon those of Western Europe, and the Arabic script with the Latin characters. The result was to revolutionise the entire Turkish society, turning it from a backward, oriental country into a modern, progressive one.

Other aspects of British policy had tended also to emphasise the separate identity of the North as against the unity of Nigeria. Such was the policy regarding land tenure, the discouragement of the nationalist movement in the North, and the undue paternalism of the British officials towards Northerners. The plain truth was that the idea of a Nigerian nation was simply inconceivable to many of the early British administrators. In official British thinking before 1945, the native authorities, rather than a Nigerian nation, were to be the focus of loyalty. The view was indeed 'urged that the native authorities be given progressively wider powers until they became self-governing, presumably with an attenuated British superstructure holding them together in a loose confederation.'[12] It is true that certain vital institutions of a national character, such as a nation-wide communication system – the railway, roads, posts and telegraphs – a common currency and an export trade in cash crops, had been established, yet, as has been noted, this was prompted primarily by a desire to further British administrative and economic interest. If they contributed to national unity, that was only a side and perhaps unwelcome effect. The official British attitude was stated in trenchant language by Sir Hugh Clifford in his famous address to the Legislative Council on December 29, 1920:

'It is the consistent policy of the Government of Nigeria to maintain and to support the local tribal institutions and the indigenous
forms of Government . . . which are to be regarded as the natural
expressions of [African] political genius . . . I am entirely convinced of the right, for example, of the people of Egbaland . . . of
any of the great Emirates of the North . . . to maintain that
each one of them is, in a very real sense, a nation . . . It is the
task of the Government of Nigeria to build up and to fortify
these national institutions . . . Assuming . . . that the impossible
were feasible – that this collection of self-contained and mutually
independent native states, separated from one another, as many
of them are, by great distances, by differences of history and
traditions, and by ethnological, racial, tribal, political, social and
religious barriers, were indeed capable of being welded into a
single homogeneous nation – a deadly blow would thereby be
struck at the very root of national self-government in Nigeria,
which secures to each separate people the right to maintain its
identity, its individuality and its nationality, its own chosen form
of government; and the peculiar political and social institutions
which have been evolved for it by the wisdom and by the accumulated experience of generations of its forbears.'[13]

The system of indirect rule was intended to implement this policy.
Built upon the Emirates, it fostered their separate identity as an
embryonic unit of a nation, emphasising in the result the cultural
and ethnic diversity of the country. The policy of discouraging a
Nigerian nation had also determined the institutional forms that
were established after the amalgamation of 1914. As has been
observed, the amalgamation had in contemplation, not the fostering
of a Nigerian nation, but British economic and administrative
expediency, and so only such forms and procedures as would
facilitate that object were established on a national basis. Amalgamation necessarily meant a single governor and an executive council,
and a central administrative machinery for departments of
common interest – railway and colliery, military, audit, treasury,
posts and telegraphs, judicial and legal, and survey. Apart from
these, each of the amalgamated units was separately administered
by a Lieutenant-Govenor, with separate departments, viz. political,
medical, public works, forestry, agriculture, education, police,
prisons and mines, and, in the Southern provinces only, marine and
customs. Considering the size of the country and the diversity of its
peoples, this might have been desirable as well as expedient, but
the same cannot be said about the absence of a unified legislative
machinery. The old Lagos Legislative Council, which had legislated

for Southern Nigeria before amalgamation, was retained for Lagos only, while the governor became the sole legislative authority for the rest of the country. Some measure of legislative unity was maintained in an arrangement which enabled the legislative council of Lagos and the governor to legislate for the whole country by means of joint ordinances, provided that the power to issue joint ordinances was not to be construed as conferring upon the legislative council power to make laws affecting the protectorate only or upon the governor power to make laws affecting the colony only. Explaining the reason for this scheme, Sir Frederick Lugard, the architect of the amalgamation, said on the occasion of the declaration of the Constitution of the amalgamated country on January 1, 1914:

'I had hoped to be able to recommend to the Secretary of State some scheme for a Legislative Council of Nigeria, but at present and until communications by railway are greatly extended the proposition is physically impossible. The Legislative Council of Nigeria, if it is to represent the public opinion of Nigeria, must draw its unofficial members alike from Calabar and Lagos in the South, and from the minefields and Kano in the North. To no place, however central, could the busy merchants and others find time to come in order to attend the Council's meetings. It would be manifestly unjust to place the Mohammedan emirates of the North and the mining interests on the Bauchi plateau under a council sitting on the coast, in which they have no representation. The only alternative is that the Legislative Council of the colony shall in the future limit its sphere to the guidance and control of the Legislature of the colony.'[14]

There may have been some truth in this, but it does not offer a complete explanation. In 1922 a Legislative Council of *Nigeria* was for the first time established, but, in spite of its name, its sphere of authority was limited to Southern Nigeria, presumably for the reason given by Lord Lugard in 1914. Nor, apart from the official members from the North, were Northerners represented in the council. The governor alone continued to legislate for the North, though the arrangement about joint legislation was retained. Had the council been allowed to legislate for the whole country, with a membership drawn from all over it, there is a chance that it might have become an instrument for inculcating a sense of Nigerian unity; it would at least have given Nigeria the opportunity to feel at that crucial period in the country's development that they were members of the same political community, which had a claim upon their loyalty. As Coleman said, 'the fact that the Northern and Southern protectorates were never effectively united has tended to perpetuate the sharp cultural differences between the people of the North and of the South.'[15]

The Second World War produced a shift in British attitude. There were now people among the British officials in Nigeria, including the war-time governor, Sir Bernard Bourdillon, who seriously entertained the idea of a Nigerian nation, however remote the prospect might have seemed at the time. Yet the idea of the native authorities as the unit of national loyalty and identity still had strong advocates. Doubtless the outlook of its advocates had broadened somewhat as a result of the experiences of the war, but only to the extent of conceding a Northern Nigerian nation, in place of the separate nationalities based upon the native authorities. The constitution of 1946, while finally rejecting the extreme view of a separate nationality for each native authority, was an attempt to reconcile the demand for a separate Northern Nigeria with the concept of a Nigerian nation. It accomplished the legislative unification of the country, bringing it under a single legislative authority, the Nigerian Legislative Council, with a membership 'representative' of the whole country. At the same time, it established for the North and for each of the two groups of provinces (now called regions) into which the South had been divided in 1939, a separate administrative machinery under a Chief Commissioner with a full complement of regional administrative and technical departments. There was also established in each of the three regions a deliberative council. Thus was regionalism formally institutionalised in Nigerian government. However, by its legislative unification of the country the 1946 Constitution made a significant contribution to the cause of Nigerian unity. The new all-Nigeria legislative council provided a forum where the representatives of all its peoples could meet together and learn to cultivate a feeling of common belonging. Unfortunately, the unifying effect which this measure would have had was all but neutralised by the advent from 1951 onwards of power politics based upon the tribe and the region. The consequences of this development for Nigerian unity will be considered in the next chapter.

(iv) *Lack of Unanimity over need for association and unity*

The introduction of power politics had painfully underlined the lack of unanimity among Nigerians for the need of the continued association of the various tribal groupings in one political organisation. Northerners were inclined to regard the amalgamation of 1914 as a 'mistake', and demanded that the union be dissolved and the North reverted to its position before 1914, with a common services organisation as the only link between it and the South. This was the substance of the now famous eight-point programme submitted to the constitutional conference in 1949. Not even the struggle for emancipation from colonial rule produced a feeling of identity strong enough to bind the people together. The nationalism which it provoked was of a negative type aimed entirely at forcing British withdrawal from the country. Inevitably, therefore, it melted away when the British began to take their exit. Even while it lasted, it was undermined by a disagreement first over leadership, and secondly over timing. Disagreement over leadership is a familiar phenomenon in nationalist movements everywhere, and so it is not surprising that it should have occurred in Nigeria. What is unusual in the Nigerian situation is that there should have been a disagreement as to timing. Here again it was the fear of domination which intruded to set the nationalist movements apart. The North desired that the rate of constitutional development should be slowed down to afford it time to catch up with the South in educational and technological advancement. For this reason they opposed the demand of the South for independence in 1956. In 1956 the North would still be lagging far behind the South, and self-government then would assuredly have meant the perpetuation of Southern domination in the higher ranks of the central civil service and police. In the event, only a spirit of compromise – one of Nigeria's notable qualities, whether for good or for bad – enabled the impasse to be resolved.

(v) *Federalism or Unitarianism*

As to the North's demand for a reversion to the pre-1914 arrangement, the compromise was found in a full-blown federal system. This, as implemented under the constitution of 1954, allowed each region full autonomy in matters of internal concern. It seems clear from the deep-rooted cultural differences between North and South, and between the two main Southern tribes, and from the disturbances in Kano in 1953, that a federal system offered the best hope of ensuring the peaceful co-existence of the various tribes. In a plural society composed of fundamentally different and mutually antagonistic groups, peace and unity is hardly possible if one group is placed in a position to control the internal affairs of the others or the destiny of the whole. It is perfectly human for any community to resent domination in its affairs by outsiders, and control by a neighbouring community is apt to hurt tribal pride much more deeply and therefore to be more bitterly resented than control by complete strangers, like the British, who might possess certain characteristics, such as colour, culture, or military might, which establish them as a superior race in the eyes of the subject community. Professor Arthur Lewis has observed, after a close study, that the basic explanation of politics in the plural societies of West Africa is that 'a society which has very wide geographical differences can live together at peace only in a federal framework;'[16] such a community, he adds, 'needs to give its provinces the opportunity to look after their own affairs, if they are to feel content with the political union.'[17]

In the case of Nigeria, the natural resentment felt by the Northerners over the dominance of Southerners in the unified public services and in the economic life of the North, might have been expected to grow increasingly worse with the inevitable march towards progressive Nigerianisation of the policy-making segment of the service. The situation would have become altogether intolerable to the North if, under the upsurge of the nationalist movement, political control of the unified machinery of government were to have passed into the hands of the Southern nationalists who led the nationalist movement. Equally, control by the North, by virtue of its superior numbers, would have been no less intolerable to the South. The economic implication of a unitary system would also have excited resentment in the South. At the time of the amalgamation the South had an annual revenue from import duties of about £1·5 million as against £·03 million from the North. Amalgamation had made it possible – and this was one of the declared objects of the merger – for resources to be pooled, thus allowing some of the revenue from the South to be used in the administration of the North. Since 1914 the South has grown richer from increased production and a boom in export crops, from the enhanced earning capacity, through education, of its population, and lately from the discovery of oil. Was it to be expected that, after the grant of self-government, the South would have continued to acquiesce in an arrangement which tied its development to the North or which permitted revenue that would otherwise have been used for its development to be diverted to subsidise development in the North? This was the main reason for the collapse of the ill-assorted Caribbean Federation. The controversy in 1954 over the apportionment of revenue accumulated by the central government from the sale of export crops illustrates the type of feeling which revenue distribution can produce. The richer regions vehemently opposed any apportionment on the basis of need, insisting that derivation should be the criterion, as in fact it had to be. If it is remembered that the revenue involved represented only a proportion of the total revenue available to a regional government, it can easily be imagined what the reaction would have been if the entire revenue of the country were to have continued to be distributed according to need. The risk of collision inherent in the political control by any one group in a plural society of the internal affairs of others or in the use of revenue from one section to subsidise the other could only be minimised in a federal framework.

This is not to say that federalism eliminates conflict altogether in a plural society. There is still the question of control of matters considered to be of common interest and requiring central administration. It must be stated that the mere fact of decentralising functions makes the question of the control of the centre less embittering than it would be under a unitary system; with the diminished powers exercisable centrally, the central government cannot become an instrument of total domination. Accordingly, the control of the centre by one group, even if it cannot be checked by appropriate devices, tends to excite less odium than if all powers are concentrated at the centre. But the federal system may nevertheless fail to promote national unity unless it is so structured as to preserve a proper balance among the component units. To minimise conflict, and strengthen unity, a federal system must not place any one of its component units in a position of dominance in the central government. Two issues are involved here: first, the extent and nature of the central powers; and secondly, the relative sizes of the component units. The intensity of conflict varies according to the scope and importance of powers left at the centre, and the bearing which they have upon life and development in the regions. If the central powers are few or unimportant from the point of view of the internal affairs of the regions, conflict will be minimised. But undue regional autonomy will tend to glorify the regions at the expense of the nation. If the regions are so powerful as almost to submerge the centre, or to cause the inhabitants to think of government in terms exclusively or mainly of the regional governments, then it will be hard for them to develop any loyalty to the nation, let alone one which would transcend loyalty to the region. This might appear to be a vicious circle; yet regional autonomy and a strong central government are not really mutually exclusive objects. It is perfectly possible to strike a balance between them; the centre can be made strong enough to act as a focus of national loyalty and consciousness, and yet prevented from interfering in matters which can, without detriment to other regions, be left with the competence of a region. If the federal system can be structured to guarantee against control of the centre by any one group, then it is desirable, in the interest of national unity, that the centre should be as strong as possible in order to be able to give effective leadership and direction to the country. In the final analysis, therefore, the relative size, population-wise, of the federating units would prove of decisive importance.

The main charge against federalism is that it recognises and crystallises tribal or group differences, thereby making it impossible for people to rise above tribal loyalty to a higher order where tribe, language, religion and geographical origin have no political significance, giving place to a common nationality as the highest loyalty. This is not entirely true. All that can be said with certainty is that federalism provides a local institutional base for an appeal to tribal or group sentiment. But what really creates the necessity for such an appeal is not federalism, but the struggle for political power, and the fear of domination. The differences and mutual antagonism between the groups create divergent interests, which make it difficult for them to come together under one party. Each group naturally wants its own party to champion its interests against those of the other groups. Reconciliation within a single party might be possible if the differences and disparity in the level of economic development are not so great and fundamental, but where they are, 'a single party supported equally by all the tribes is an impossible dream.'[18] 'Any idea,' writes Arthur Lewis, 'that one can make different peoples into a nation by suppressing the religious or tribal or regional or other affiliations to which they themselves attach the highest political significance is simply a non-starter. National loyalty cannot immediately supplant tribal loyalty; it has to be built on top of tribal loyalty by creating a system in which all the tribes feel that there is room for self-expression.'[19]

Granted that federalism is the form of political association best suited to a plural society, the question may then be asked why it failed to foster a Nigerian nation. This is the question which we will be considering in the next chapter.

Loyalty to the State and Economic Welfare

Cleavage between various social groupings is by no means the only factor working against the development of national consciousness in emergent nations. There are also economic reasons why the mass of the citizens, considered as individuals, have not developed a sense of attachment to, or identification with, the state. Whether he lives in the village or in the city, the ordinary man has certain basic needs which he expects the government to help secure for him – food and clothing, housing and medical care, employment and education. His conception of government is largely in terms of its ability to provide these needs of his existence. He is not likely to think of government as his own unless he feels that it is actively trying to cater for his material well-being. So long as the government is not doing this, he will think of it as something which has no bearing upon his material well-being, and in which, therefore, he has no stake. He cannot thus feel any sense of attachment to the state. It makes little difference to him that the government is now a fully representative one, 'a government of the people by the people.' For him election is something of a ritualistic occasion. He cares less about who is governing than how to feed and clothe his family, send his children to school and give them medical attention when they are ill. He is no more inclined to accept the government as his own because it is now administered by his own countrymen rather than by the colonial authorities. For him an independent, representative government differs from a colonial one mainly to the extent that it is able to improve his lot.

The colonial state lacked legitimacy not only because it was an alien institution but also because it was administered by foreigners for their own benefit. The colonial bureaucrats and other Europeans had an almost exclusive monopoly of all the good things provided by the modern state. They had good incomes, lived in decent houses equipped with modern amenities, owned cars, and generally enjoyed a standard of living totally different from and superior to that of the indigenous population. Western education had no doubt made it possible for a growing number of the indigenes, employed in minor positions in the government or engaged in petty trading, to rise somewhat above the village peasantry, yet so low was their income that they lived at much the same standard as the latter.

For the indigenous people the government existed only as a system of restraints to enforce the observance of law and order among the population. It had no concern for their well-being. Education, as has been observed, was largely the work of missionary and private enterprise, and so were medical services too, though to a lesser extent. There were no industrial enterprises, which meant that the government was the sole employer of labour, supplemented by the few expatriate commercial firms. With the limited range of services which it provided, the government could provide jobs only for a fraction of the product of the schools. Of the others who could not be so employed, some took to petty trading and to other kinds of occupation, as carpenters, motor mechanics, and so on, but a large and growing number, as more and more youngsters passed out of school, still remained without any kind of gainful occupation, to form a permanent class of unemployed.

The transformation of the state from a colonial to an independent one was a revolution which affected both government and society.

The state, together with its various agencies, was now administered by indigenous people who succeeded to the privileged positions previously occupied by Europeans. There emerged a crop of indigenous ministers and legislators, judges, permanent secretaries, directors of departments, chairmen and general managers of public corporations, and other high-ranking state functionaries. In the Church, universities and in the private sector generally, a similar development had taken place, as indigenous bishops and other clergy, university professors and lecturers, company directors and managers gradually replaced expatriate personnel. This development was accompanied by an expansion in the services provided by government. No longer was law and order the principal pre-occupation of government. Education was greatly expanded through the establishment of numerous new schools, colleges and universities, the institution of scholarship schemes, the introduction of compulsory free primary (and sometimes secondary) education. For the first time, a policy of industrial development was initiated. Various industrial projects were set up by the nationalist governments, either alone or in partnership with foreign entrepreneurs: printing, pharmaceutical, tourist, development corporations and marketing boards; tyre, aluminium, steel, cement, textile, glass, pottery and rubber industries as well as oil refineries. Investment and finance companies were also established with a view to liberalising credit for agricultural and industrial projects. These enterprises had opened up additional employment opportunities as well as new avenues for the acquisition of wealth by indigenous businessmen in such capacities as contractors, government agents, industrialists, transporters and traders.

Compared with the colonial régime, the nationalist government has had a good record of achievement. Yet the question remains whether the lot of the ordinary man has been improved by these developments to an extent that would make him feel that the government is now an instrument for his welfare. First, the rate of economic growth is far outstripped by the growth in manpower, with the result that there is an alarming increase in the number of unemployed, who thus constitute a grave social problem. Some of these are lured into crime, some have served the political parties as party thugs, while others just drift along, deeply disillusioned with a society which appears not to care for them. The problem has of course been aggravated by the inadequate, often indifferent attention given to agriculture, still the mainstay of the economy. Agriculture, carried on by the same old subsistence methods, could hardly be expected to attract the young school leavers. The tendency therefore has been for them to move away from the village to the townships, swelling the townships beyond what they could absorb.

Leaving aside the position of the unemployed which is like a plague upon the society, there is a depressing imbalance in the distribution of the benefits of economic progress among the population. Much of this is concentrated in the hands of a few people – the ministers, other top politicians and their associates in business. To the ordinary clerk, artisan or peasant farmer, this progress is visible only in the number of his own countrymen he now sees riding in big, expensive cars, dressed in flowing, flamboyant *agbadas* and living in lavish, ostentatious splendour. His own income and consequently his standard of living has remained substantially as it was before. Wraith and Simpkins have described in rather graphic language this disparity in income and standard of living among the various classes of the population:

'A characteristic feature of developing countries, in comparison with the more developed world, is that they are having to live in several centuries simultaneously. There are admittedly great extremes of wealth in Britain, great differences in education, and, perhaps greatest of all, differences in culture and styles of living. It is doubtful, however, whether any of these differences are as fundamental as those between the huge mass of family farmers, living very like the English peasant of the middle ages, illiterate, superstitious, handling very little money, their world bounded by the family or clan; the wage-earners and urban proletariat, living like their counterparts in nineteenth century Britain, semi-literate, underpaid, badly housed, but beginning to understand their rights and to feel their power; the growing middle class of traders, teachers and officials, whose styles and standards of living approximate to those of the privileged classes of the twentieth century; and the top professional and business men, whose material and often professional standards equal or exceed those of the Western world. It is metaphorically possible in many parts of Africa to span the centuries in the course of a short walk.'[20]

Naturally the masses of the people cannot but resent this concentration of the nation's wealth in a few hands. The struggle for freedom from colonial rule has been a period of great fervour and of high expectations of all the good things that independence would bring. Now that the much-longed-for independence has come, it has proved to be largely an illusion. A feeling of disappointment at unfulfilled expectations naturally followed, so that independence, far from bringing the masses closer in feeling and sympathy to the government, tended to alienate them even more than before. The privileged position of colonial officials did not provoke so much resentment, because they were people of a different race accustomed to a reasonably high standard of living in their own countries. Moreover, since their number was relatively small and contact with the underprivileged masses minimal, the disparity in income made little impact upon the society. But such wide disparity in the standard of living among various classes of the indigenous population was bound to produce a different kind of reaction. It was viewed as an unwarranted discrimination and accordingly was deeply resented by the underprivileged masses. It is true that the ordinary man's expectations of what the government should do for him are often out of tune with reality. He is normally unable to appreciate the limitation upon the resources of a young nation. Yet he is not entirely to blame for this. How is he to reconcile explanations of inadequate resources for the government's inability to cater for his welfare with the splendour and lavish abundance which he sees surrounding the ministers and other politicians? All around him he sees money which could otherwise have been used to improve society being diverted to corrupt purposes.

The effect of political corruption

The Coker Commission of Inquiry of 1962 into the activities of the Action Group Government of Western Nigeria provides a revealing insight into the extent of waste of public resources involved in political corruption, and its effect upon economic development and upon the attitude of the people towards government. For this reason it might be useful to consider the findings of the Commission in some detail.[21] As in other regions of Nigeria, the government of Western Nigeria had created certain statutory corporations as agencies of the government for the purposes of facilitating the development of the region. Of these the most important ones, and those probed by the Commission, were the Marketing Board, the Development Corporation, and the Finance, Housing, Broadcasting and Printing Corporations. The Marketing Board was established in 1954 with a revenue of £42 million, representing the region's share from the apportionment by the central government of money which it had accumulated over the years from the sale of agricultural produce. Between 1954 and 1962 the Board earned a further sum of £26·4 million, making a total of £68·6 million. By May 1962 the whole of this money had been dissipated, with the Board having to exist on overdrafts obtained at a high interest rate from the Bank of West Africa, Ltd. A greater part of the money – about

£46·6 million – went of course by way of loan or grant to the regional government and its other agencies. But some £11·1 million (exclusive of interest) went to four privately-owned companies, namely the National Investment and Properties Co. Ltd. (NIPC), the National Bank of Nigeria Ltd., the Merchant Bank, Ltd., and the Agbonmagbe Bank Ltd. The Commission found that these companies were owned either by the Action Group or by individual members of the party. The NIPC, in particular, to which went as much as £6·7 million of the £11·1 million, was, as the Commission found, to all intents and purposes, synonymous with the AG, existing primarily as an agency through which funds were diverted to the party from the government and its agencies. The company was promoted by the party leadership, its only four shareholders, who were also its directors, were leading members of the party, and its share capital of £100,000 was also provided by the party from money obtained from the company itself. The Commission found that between 1958 and 1962, a total sum of £4 million was made available by the NIPC to the AG through the device of a code name, Property Development Agency, which concealed the fact of the AG being the true recipient of the money. Similarly, the private accounts of the AG contained no indication of any penny having been donated by the NIPC, although they scrupulously recorded special donations by its benefactors, including a sum of £3·7 million supposedly donated by its deputy treasurer, Chief S. O. Lanlehm.

An indispensable chain in the racket was the National Bank, for it was through it that much of the money from the NIPC was channelled. The bank was in all but name an Action Group bank, most of its directors, including the Chairman, being prominent members of the party. It had received £4 million of the Marketing Board's money; how much of this was made over to the AG was, however, not disclosed. To facilitate the racket and prevent the AG from being identified as the recipient of payments made by it, the bank operated a Suspense Account and a Sundry Persons Account, which were frequenty juggled to record payments-in that were never in fact received by the bank. The deputy treasurer of the party, Chief Lanlehm, even admitted keeping a secret safe at the bank, in which large sums of money were kept for which no records existed in the books of the bank. This juggling was also done in respect of the accounts of the NIPC at the bank. The Commission found, for example, that a sum of £1·1 million shown in the bank statement of the NIPC as payment made by the NIPC to Cappa & D'Alberto Ltd. for various building projects was not in fact received by Cappa, and that at least £950,000 of it went back to the NIPC from where it was diverted to the AG.

In addition to the £6·7 million from the Marketing Board, the NIPC also obtained a further sum of £3 million from the government and the Development Corporation. This consisted in part of the sum of £2·2 million diverted from a loan of £3 million made to the Development Corporation by the Marketing Board. The loan had been intended to finance two businesses, the Nigersol Construction Co. Ltd. and the Nigerian Water Resources Development Ltd., in which the Development Corporation was interested to the extent of 60 per cent, the remaining 40 per cent being owned by an Israeli company. Only £800,000 of the total amount of the loan was in fact used by the two companies; while the balance of £2·2 million was, at the instance of the chairman of the Development Corporation, Chief Rewane, who was also the chairman of the two companies and a director of the NIPC, paid over to the NIPC by way of deposit. As the Commission found, when the NIPC could not repay the deposit, a most dishonest agreement, aimed at covering up the transaction, was executed with the Anglo-Israeli Bank in London, whereby book entries were made crediting the two companies, the Nigersol and the Nigerian Water Resources Development Ltd., with an amount of £2·1 million and debiting the NIPC with a corresponding amount, but restricting withdrawals by the former to an amount actually paid in to their debit account by the NIPC. This transaction was matched in dishonesty by another deal by which the NIPC obtained over £800,000 from the government. In October 1958 two prominent members of the AG acquired a conveyance of certain land, known as the Moba land, for £11,000 from its customary owners. Six weeks later the purchasers executed a conveyance of the land for £150,000 to one Allison who, eight months later, purported to have sold it to the NIPC for £718,000. The land was then sold by the NIPC to the government for £850,000. As the commission found, the amounts appearing on the conveyances to Allison and the NIPC were never in fact paid, both conveyances having been faked to provide cover for defrauding the government of £850,000, which amount was within a few days of its receipt by the NIPC paid over to the AG.

The Moba land deal had its analogue in the purchase by the Finance Corporation of a certain business, known as the Arab Bros. (Motors) Ltd. This business had been valued at £400,000, but the Finance Corporation was made to pay £1·1 million for it, and also to take over the liabilities of the business, amounting to £356,661, although this had not been stipulated in the sale agreement. The purchase was concluded in haste under great pressure from the Minister of Trade and Industry. The Finance Corporation had obtained the money used for purchasing this business on loan from the Marketing Board on the express understanding that it was to be invested in 'a profitable investment in a big industrial company operating in Nigeria.' Directly the loan was approved by the Marketing Board, the money was paid into the account of the Finance Corporation with the National Bank. No evidence was laid before the Commission as to how much of the £1·1 million was actually paid to the owners of the Arab Bros. (Motors) Ltd., but it may reasonably be inferred that the excess over the £400,000 estimated value of the business found its way through the National Bank into the coffers of the AG.

Apart from the amounts diverted to the AG as a party, many of its leaders as individuals shared in the plunder, in the form partly of loans and partly of illicit gains. Leaving aside loans to party members by the National Bank, which ran into hundreds of thousands of pounds, the Finance Corporation lent £120,000 to the Nigerian Fishing Co., owned by two AG members, and £50,000 to the Ikorodu Ceramic Industries in which members of the party were also interested; the NIPC granted building loans of £25,000 each to two of its directors as did the Housing Corporation to its directors, though the amount here was not disclosed. Membership of the party was an important consideration for obtaining loans for industrial and agricultural projects. It is hardly possible to quantify illicit gains by party members, as these were always secret. But it should be pointed out that members were expected to contribute to the party funds in proportion to the amount of benefit received.

It must not be thought that the fraudulent practices uncovered by the Coker Commission were a peculiar propensity of the AG. It was a vice of which all the ruling parties were guilty in varying degrees. The AG might have been somewhat more reckless and buccaneering, but the difference was only a matter of degree. At the root of these practices lay an inability or unwillingness to draw a distinction between party and government. This had tended to make politicians lose sight of the fact that it is improper to use government money for party political purposes.

Now, the funds disbursed by the statutory corporations represented only a proportion of the total revenue at the disposal of the government. One has therefore to consider government expenditure in its totality to obtain anything like a complete picture of the extent of corruption in the administration of government. This is of course not possible, but the usual forms taken by corrupt practices are well-known. There is, for example, the rake-off on land or business purchased on behalf of the government, the unofficial percentage on contracts, usually ten per cent, sometimes with a little extra.

The evil of corruption should not be viewed solely in terms of the amount of money illicitly obtained by those who engaged in it, though, as the Inquiry in Western Nigeria has shown, this often represented a substantial proportion of revenue that would otherwise have been used for the benefit of the community. Its effect must be considered in the context of the totality of loss and waste which it occasions. The Inquiry in Western Nigeria again provides an excellent illustration. Corrupt motives had led to a thoroughly inefficient disbursement and mismanagement of the funds and affairs of the Marketing Board and of the other public corporations in the Region. The corruption here consisted not just in the millions of pounds diverted into private use, but in the entire investment policy of the public corporations, which was motivated by considerations other than those of the public benefit. The investment of £9 million of public money in NIPC was criminal. But for the corrupt motive behind it, no sane person, entrusted with the management of public money, could in conscience invest £9 million of it, with inadequate security and sometimes none at all, in a private business owned by four private individuals. 'We think,' observed the Coker Commission of Inquiry, 'that the investments in the NIPC were all imprudent and but for the political considerations which certainly were uppermost, constituted a most flagrant breach of trust and an infamous design by which the peoples of the Western Region have been robbed of the financial benefits to which they are entitled from the Western Region Marketing Board.'[22] As it turned out, not surprisingly, the company became insolvent, and therefore unable to repay the moneys deposited with it. Its assets were worth substantially less than the £9 million of public money invested in it, and even part of these insufficient assets was put beyond the reach of the public by a fraudulent deed of arrangement whereby rents accruing from the NIPC properties were mortgaged to Cappa. A takeover of the company's assets would not therefore have provided a full satisfaction for its debts to the public. In 1963 the government of Western Nigeria sought to minimise the public loss by means of a compulsory acquisition of certain properties, the Maryland Estate, in which the NIPC had a part interest. The estate was worth about £1 million. But the attempt failed because, as the court held, the estate was owned, not by the NIPC, but by Sonny Investment and Properties Company, and moreover the acquisition was not for public purposes nor did it envisage the payment of compensation as required by law.

The investment in the three banks of £4·3 million, consisting of £3·08 million worth of shares and £1·26 million deposit, was also extremely careless of the public interest. None of the banks was able to repay the deposits – one of them, the Merchant Bank, had indeed gone into voluntary liquidation with £200,000 of public money. And, because of their inability to pay, the Marketing Board was forced to take overdrafts at a high interest rate from the Bank of West Africa. The Board's initial capital of £68·6 million had melted away through various dubious channels. The Arab Bros. (Motors) Ltd., purchased at the cost of £1·4 million (including the liabilities of the business) proved to be anything but the profitable investment which it was represented to be, and the Finance Corporation had been unable to repay the Marketing Board the loan of £1·2 million with which the business was purchased. The other investments by the Finance Corporation as well as those made by the Development Corporation had been hardly more successful. This is not surprising, since in each case consideration of party or personal gain had made it impossible for a careful and objective assessment of the prospects for success and profit to be made before the investments were embarked upon.

It is true, as Wraith and Simpkins said, that inefficiency and corruption do not necessarily go together. Yet the evidence disclosed by the Inquiry in Western Nigeria conclusively shows that corruption of the type and extent practised by ruling political parties and their members inevitably produced inefficiency and waste. Money that would have been used in development along lines beneficial to the public was wasted in unprofitable, politically-motivated enterprises or diverted into private coffers for electioneering or propaganda purposes of the ruling party or otherwise for the enrichment of its members.

By far the most tragic consequence of political corruption was its mental effect upon the masses of the country. There had been widespread feeling of frustration, of disgust and cynicism, which had in its turn undermined enthusiasm for, and faith in, the state. To the masses, independence has simply meant the transformation of the state from an instrument of subjugation by an alien people into one of plunder by elected representatives who are supposed to administer it as a trust for the people. The ordinary man could hardly be blamed if he continues to think of government in terms of 'they,' and not of 'we.'

It is no use trying to mitigate the obnoxious character of corruption by saying that it is merely an extension or an adaptation of the custom whereby 'a person in authority is entitled to expect (and not merely demand) and to receive some form of consideration . . . for something done, in the course of exercising his authority, to the benefit of the giver.'[23] Corruption as a social phenomenon was unknown in the traditional society before the introduction of

modern government. The conditions for its existence simply did
not exist; opportunities for its indulgence were either non-existent
or far too limited. Its specific manifestation, bribery, is essentially
an incident of the cash economy, which came into existence with
the establishment of modern government. The attempt to explain
corruption in the form in which it is practised today as part of the
traditional culture is wholly untenable. The relationship between a
customary gift of, say, a fowl or a pot of palm wine, by a villager
to his traditional ruler in return for some favours bestowed, and
the giving of money, say, five pounds, by a job-seeker to a clerk
for help in securing employment is pretty remote. First, the objects
used have totally different social significance. A fowl suggests a
motivation, namely a gift, which is normally not morally reprehensible, whereas money, which has its value clearly impressed
upon its face, has the implication of a deal or bargain; it implies
a *price* without the payment of which the service will not be rendered.
Secondly, the receipt of a fowl by the chief finds approval in custom
because it expresses a courtesy and obeisance traditionally required
by the relationship of villager and chief. The clerk has no colour of
title, traditional or otherwise, to the five pounds, and the taking of it
partakes indeed of the nature of extortion; to regard it as an adaptation of custom is therefore to do violence to the custom of exchanging
gifts for chiefly favours. The difference becomes even more evident
where the money is taken to pervert the due course of the law, as
where a policeman takes money to let off someone who has broken
the law, e.g. a traffic offender, or where in return for a bribe, a tax
or sanitary inspector reduces the tax assessment of a wealthy trader
or refrains from prosecuting an offender against sanitary regulations.

Bribery and corruption is therefore a concomitant of modern
government and the harsh economic forces which it has unleashed.
The indigenous functionaries engaged to help administer the
services and amenities of the modern government found themselves
exposed to certain pressures and temptations unknown in the traditional social and political structure. Their appointment placed them
in positions of influence and comparative wealth *vis-à-vis* their
brethren in the villages who had then to look up to them for financial
and other assistance. Their contact with urban life created in them
a desire to acquire the comforts and other amenities of modern life,
such as a modern concrete house, a bicycle, etc. These, though
legitimate ambitions, with their meagre salaries could only be
accomplished by illicit means. To these were added 'the slow,
insidious pressures of a society in which material success is adulated
. . . and where moreover material failure is ruthlessly mocked; the
pressure of increasing defeatism, on realising that public opinion

stigmatises the transgressor so lightly, and that so little seems to be gained from trying to swim against the tide.'[24] On the part of the giver of a bribe, it is the fact that jobs and other amenities are far less than the number of people seeking them that impels him to corruption. His need is desperate, and any means of satisfying it is readily seized, whether it is fair or foul.

These factors pressed so heavily upon the new élite, unaccustomed as they were to the standards of the new role that has been thrust upon them, and, what is more important, unaided by any counter-acting forces, such as the force of tradition or of a developed sense of loyalty to the government. For modern government was regarded as the white man's enterprise, in which the indigenous people felt they had no stake except what they could get out of it in terms of material benefit. The attitude to the government was that anyone connected with it should try to get as much from it as possible by plunder or by fraud; to do that was considered legitimate, and not morally reprehensible; those who had the opportunity and failed to utilise it were mocked. The bearing that this absence of loyalty to the state had on the origin and practice of corruption is illus-trated by the fact that whereas the treasurer of a local council might cheerfully make away with its fund and feel no remorse about it, the treasurer of a village union dared not, since, if he did, he would incur moral condemnation and possible ostracisation by the village. This demonstrates, as Wraith and Simpkins rightly said, that developing nations have in such matters the same regard for ethical behaviour as the civilised countries, provided their deepest loyalties were engaged.

It was politics however that gave corruption a new flavour and vastly extended its incidence, by creating new incentives and avenues for it. The desire for personal enrichment, which has always been the primary incentive, was now given an added and more vigorous stimulus. It was no longer confined to the ambition to acquire the modest comforts of modern life or to meet family financial pressures. There is now the ambition to win elections, to become a minister and thereby to attain a high standard of living. Elections cost money in bribes to electors or in payment to thugs or for the purchase of ballot papers or of candidatures. This huge expenditure has to be recouped by corrupt means. The cost of an election to an individual candidate represents a negligible pro-portion of its cost to the party, and this is the main motivation for the plunder perpetuated by ruling parties. They now have the entire revenue of the state to disburse. Corruption at this level ceased, therefore, to be a matter of persons in subordinate positions abusing their small authority in a petty and rather squalid way.

Corruption has acquired in the words of Wraith and Simpkins, a 'buccaneering flavour,' involving millions of pounds, sometimes taken straight from the coffers of the state. The ordinary public servant could not but be infected by the new flavour given to corruption. He too wanted to share in the plunder. Loyalty to the state suffered a corresponding decline both for the plunderers and for the cheated masses.

REFERENCES

1. Carl J. Friedrich, *Constitutional Government and Democracy*, revised ed., p. 164; also p. 10, p. 15. W. G. Andrews, *Constitutions*, 1963, pp. 11-12.
2. *From Empire to Nation*, 1962, p. 96.
3. Elspeth Huxley, 'Africa First Loyalty,' *New York Times Magazine*, Sept. 18, 1960, p. 14; quoted in Burke, *Africa's Quest for Order*, 1964, p. 29.
4. *Nationalism*, An R.I.I.A. Report (1963), Ch. 14; Emerson, *op. cit.*, Chs. V-X.
5. Hans Kohn, *Nationalism: its Meaning and History*, revised ed., p. 9.
6. Arthur Lewis, *Politics in West Africa*, 1965, pp. 24-5.
7. Population figures based on 1952 Census.
8. Quoted in Coleman, *Nigeria: Background to Nationalism*, 1963, p. 360.
9. Report on the Kano Disturbances, Govt. Printer, Kaduna, 1953, para. 109, p. 21.
10. *Constitutional Government and Democracy*, revised ed., p. 170.
11. Sir Hugh Clifford, Address on the occasion of the formal opening of the Katsina College for Mohammedan Teachers, March 5, 1922; quoted in Bello, *My Life*.
12. Coleman, *op. cit.*, p. 273.
13. Quoted in Coleman, *op. cit.*, p. 194.
14. *Extraordinary Gazette* No. 17, January 1, 1914, p. 48; quoted in Nwabueze, *Constitutional Law of the Nigerian Republic*, 1964, p. 46.
15. *Op. cit.*, p. 47.
16. *Politics in West Africa*, 1965, p. 53.
17. *Ibid.*, p. 55.
18. Arthur Lewis, *op. cit.*, p. 50.
19. *Ibid.*, p. 68.
20. *Corruption in Developing Countries*, 1963, p. 196.
21. Report in IV Volumes, Fed. Ministry of Information, Printing Division, Lagos (1962); also Comments of the Fed. Govt. on the Report, Sessional Paper No. 4 of 1962.
22. Report, *op. cit.*, Vol. 1, p. 36.
23. Report on the Lagos Town Council, 1952, p. 49, para. 280.
24. Wraith and Simpkins, *op. cit.*, p. 11.

CHAPTER V

INEFFECTIVENESS OF FEDERALISM TO FOSTER NATIONAL UNITY, STABILITY AND CONSTITUTIONALISM IN NIGERIA

It has been shown that in a plural society marked by sharp cleavage between its various groupings, that form of political association is to be preferred which will enable each major grouping to look after its own internal affairs within the unity of the whole. Only so can the mutual antagonism or even hostility inherent in cultural, racial or linguistic differences and the disparity in the level of economic development be checked or minimised. Federalism, it has been suggested, offers a better hope of achieving this than a unitary system, however widely powers may be decentralised within the latter. If, as has been pointed out, the primary political problem in all emergent states, given their alien, artificial and feeble foundations, is the survival of the state itself, its preservation against the forces of division and disintegration, then, of the two conflicting objectives of unity and regional autonomy, the balance must lie in favour of unity. Federalism should therefore be so structured as to favour unity against diversity. How far, however, unity should be pushed at the expense of diversity is a difficult problem calling for a careful and delicate weighting of all the relevant factors in any given situation, including particularly those of stability and constitutionalism, which are the underlying objectives for unity. For unity presupposes stability. It is only in an atmosphere of political stability that a consciousness of national identity and loyalty to the state can be fostered. Subject to this caveat, unity should be the overriding consideration in the structuring of a federal system in an emergent state. Nigerian federalism proved ineffective for this purpose because, by giving primacy to diversity as against unity, it inverted what in an emergent state should be the proper scale of priority. It placed the centre of gravity in political activity in the regions, relegating the centre to a subordinate position, which then lacked sufficient inducement and attraction for the leaders of the major parties, who chose to remain in the regions, from where they tried to control the actions of their lieutenants at the centre. The

111

predominance of the regions over the centre was the result of a combination of factors which we will now examine.

A Structure of Three Large Regions

If federalism is to be meaningful at all and be effective in achieving its objectives, a certain minimum number of constituent units would seem to be necessary. It can easily be perceived that to form a federation of two units, as was the case in Pakistan after 1955, is to pitch them against each other in a continual battle for ascendancy. A federation of three regions is much the same thing. Federalism thrives upon a multiplicity of interest–groups reacting upon one another to produce an equilibrium. A multiplicity of units creates a feeling of inter-dependence, which in turn encourages co-operation and mutual tolerance. A union of fifty states, as in the United States of America, must inevitably force upon each state an awareness of its relative insignificance *vis-à-vis* the whole, and the futility of a policy of separatism, which in such circumstances would be like the act of an individual ostracising himself from his society and thereby denying himself the comradeship and co-operation of communal life. In Nigeria the three states structure had created an attitude of self-sufficiency, of separatism and of intolerance among the regions. There was not enough scope for that interplay of interests upon which a lasting equilibrium could be based. The influence of numbers in promoting a communal outlook and in preventing the victimisation of a member was lacking. Two regions agreeing could gang up against the third to make life uncomfortable for it, as was indeed the situation produced in relation to the Western Region by the North-East coalition from 1959 to 1964. Pitched thus against the combined strength of the two regions, the third (the Western Region) became an object of victimisation by the coalition.[1] Such acts of victimisation could not but alienate from the federal state the loyalty of the region and its citizens. How could they be expected in the circumstances to feel a sense of belonging? It is needless to say that such ganging up, flagrantly and unquestionably violating the spirit and purpose of federalism, would have been inconceivable in a federation composed of a multiplicity of units. The interplay of a multiplicity of interest-groups would have imposed sufficient equilibrium in the system to ensure against that.

The enormous size of the regions had also determined the powers assigned to them *vis-à-vis* the centre. Being large and representing powerful interests, the claim of the regions for greater autonomy at the expense of the centre prevailed at the conference table. In a federal system, it is futile to give to any unit of government powers which it cannot exercise either because of its small size in territory and population or because of its limited resources in terms of revenue and qualified personnel. Had the regions of Nigeria been small, they would certainly not have been given such wide powers as they had under the Constitution; the demands of unity as against diversity would then have prevailed. Of the actual content of regional powers in relation to the central powers, something will be said later.

The Majority – Minority Tribes Structure in the Regions

Federalism in Nigeria failed in its objective of building governmental units upon fairly homogeneous social groupings in order that they should manage their internal affairs within the unity of the whole. It is of course recognised that complete homogeneity in the social composition of the regions may not always be feasible. There may be social groupings which, because they are so small as to be incapable of standing on their own as separate governmental units, will have of necessity to be grouped under major tribes to which they are contiguous. Where, however, there are within one area a number of such small groups of fairly equal size numerous enough to form a viable unit of state government, it seems better that they should be so treated than that they should be submerged under a major tribe in the same governmental unit. The regions in the Nigerian Federation were structured, unhappily, upon the nucleus of a major tribe, commanding about two-thirds of the population of the region, with a number of minority tribes clustered around it. 'Not one of the existing Regions,' write Buchanan and Pugh, 'approaches the ideal of an ethnic or linguistic unity; rather does each present a dual personality, consisting in each case of a regional nucleus occupied more or less compactly by a dominant group – Yoruba in the West, Ibo in the East, Hausa-Fulani in the North – with a peripheral zone occupied by minority groups.'[2] The minority groups in each region were of such size and location as to form one or more viable units of government, with something approaching linguistic or cultural homogeneity in some cases. For example, there were in the Eastern Region the Efik-Ibibio speaking groups with a population of one and a half million, the Ijaw-speaking and the Ekoi-Yakurr groups numbering about half a million each; the West, before the creation of the mid-West Region in 1963, contained about one million Edo-speaking people, half a million Urhobo, 365,000 Ibo and about 80,000 Ijaw; whilst in the North, there were 1·2 million Kanuri, 400,000 Nupe, and about seven million others including the Tiv of the Middle Belt and the Yoruba in Illorin and Kabba provinces.[3]

Tension was inevitable in a majority-minority tribes structure because it entrenches the permanent control of the regional government by the majority tribe. The regional minorities in Nigeria naturally felt they had no place in such an arrangement. The mere fact of being a permanent minority is in itself both demoralising and frustrating. No amount of concession could ever completely remove the feeling of frustration inherent in such a situation. Only an opportunity to be in control sometimes or to share substantially in exercising such control, and not the grant of favours or concessions, could do that. When a minority is actually discriminated against on that ground, then discontent and disaffection is added to frustration to aggravate the strained relationship between the majority and minority tribes. Allegations of discrimination, oppression, neglect and general maladministration made by minority groups against the majority-tribe-dominated regional governments in Nigeria had a substantial degree of truth in them, though there had been a tendency to exaggerate them.[4] Dictatorial treatment of minorities by the regional governments could hardly be compatible with constitutionalism. Discrimination in the distribution of social and economic amenities was evidently practised in varying degree in all the regions. This was partly the result of the natural inclination to favour the members of one's group in the distribution of amenities which are so limited in proportion to the number of persons to be benefited. Barring corruption, ten loaves of bread, distributed among fifteen people, might be fairly adequate to go round and to give reasonable satisfaction to every one, but if only one loaf is available for distribution, it is perhaps to be expected that the divider might be inclined to favour his own relations to ensure they would not starve. Even were he imbued with such a degree of impartiality as to be disinclined to favour members of his own group, the fact that there is not enough bread to satisfy everybody's want might still render him open to accusations of favouritism, nepotism and discrimination. The insufficiency of resources is one of the pressing problems in developing countries, and accounts for a good deal of the misunderstanding and disaffection in the relations between governments and minority groups.

Minority grievances and the agitation for the creation of more states constituted a major feature of Nigerian politics, necessitating the appointment by the British Government in 1958 of a commission of inquiry, the Minorities Commission as it was rather fittingly called. The Commission found the allegations of discrimination, victimisation and oppression made by the minority groups to have been either unfounded or exaggerated, but nevertheless recognised the genuineness of their fear about their position in the regional set-up.[5] It recommended certain safeguards for allaying this fear, notably the centralisation of the police, a constitutional guarantee of rights, decentralisation of functions to provincial authorities, and establishment of a development board to advise on the physical development of the Niger Delta area of Eastern and Mid-Western Nigeria. These recommendations were incorporated into the Constitution, but they proved ineffective as a protection for minority interests,[6] with the result that the strained relations between the majority and minority tribes within each region continued, creating instability in government and in the community. In the Tiv area of the Northern Region, the situation actually erupted into violent disturbances in 1960 and again in 1964. So widespread and destructive were the riots on both these occasions that troops had to be called in. The first took the form mainly of burning the houses of all those considered to be agents of NPC (the ruling party in the North) oppression, and involved an estimated loss of £5 million, but with little loss of life. The second was more violent, taking a heavier toll of lives and defying even the power of the troops. Peace was not restored in the area until the army coup of January 1966.

The situation in the Mid-West, created out of the Western Region in August 1963, was more bizarre, and so perhaps deserves to be described in some detail. The Region comprises five different linguistic groups, Edo, Ibo, Itsekiri, Ijaw and Kwale, of whom the first, Edo, were in a majority of about two-thirds. (The Edo subdivide into three sub-groups, Bini, Ishan and Urhobo.) For the first six months of its existence, the region was governed under an interim administration set up by the federal government,[7] and headed by Chief Dennis Osadebey, an Ibo. The first election in the region in February 1964 produced an NCNC government, with Chief Osadebey, the leader of the party in the Mid-West, as Premier. At the time of the election the NCNC operated under a special arrangement in Benin Division with a local political organisation, the Etu-Edo. The arrangement was originally one of alliance, but the Etu-Edo was later fused into the NCNC, though still maintaining a measure of individuality under the name NCNC (Etu-Edo), to distinguish it from the NCNC (pure). The Etu-Edo had a militant wing, the Owegbe Society, which appeared to have been formed in 1954 to counter the oppression and persecution of the Action Group government of Western Nigeria and the party's agent, the Ogboni Secret Society. The Owegbe Society practised a cult, known as the Owegbe Cult, which was manifested mainly in certain illegal oaths and in acts of intimidation. By these oaths, a member, upon initiation into the Society, swore upon the Owegbe *juju* to vote at elections for a candidate sponsored by the leader of the society and for no other; to denounce parties opposed to the Etu-Edo; to obey all orders of the Society without question; and that, should he fail to observe any of the injunctions of the oath, may Owegbe kill him. In a society gripped by superstition and *juju* worship, as was Benin, the oaths had very great influence. Adherents of the cult strongly believed in the power of the Owegbe *juju* to kill defaulters, and so unwaveringly observed their oaths. The psychological sanction was reinforced, when occasion demanded, by violence organised against defaulters by the managers of the cult and executed by a certain gang, known as the 'trouble-makers.' The danger to peace, order and good government in the activities of the Society can easily be imagined. Since the oaths enjoined upon the members unquestioning obedience to their leaders, there was a distinct danger that, should the leadership think it expedient to cause civil disorder, the members would be obliged by their belief in the power of the Owegbe *juju* to kill defaulters, to carry out their leaders' behest without regard to its propreity or consequences. For this reason, the Society was banned by the government of Western Nigeria in 1959. Nonetheless its practice continued clandestinely.

After the creation of the Mid-West and the installation of the NCNC government, relations between the NCNC and the Etu-Edo became increasingly strained, due partly to the ambition for power on the part of the Etu-Edo leaders, who considered Chief Osadebey's government as in effect a minority government. The leader of the Etu-Edo, Chief Omo-Osagie, who was the supreme authority and head of the Owegbe Society as well as being the Minister of Local Government in the regional government, felt that he should have been the rightful premier of the region, and so began to work to bring about the fulfilment of his ambition. In Benin Division where the Society had its stronghold and where in fact it originated, the Etu-Edo had been able, through the use of the cult and its oaths, to capture all the thirteen seats in the division in the regional parliamentary election in 1964. Such was the influence of the cult that no opposing candidate had a chance against an Etu-Edo candidate in a constituency where the Owegbe machine functioned fully. With Benin Division under its firm control, the Owegbe Society embarked upon a massive recruitment drive in other divisions while at the same time intensifying its activities in Benin Division itself. The plan was that when the Society had recruited enough people to assure the Etu-Edo of victory to enable it to supplant the NCNC government, an election would be forced upon the regional government. Force and intimidation were therefore mounted to compel people to join the Society. Whole communities were terrorised, and everywhere people lived in fear for their lives. Allegations were also widely circulated of a plot to overthrow the government by force, using tactics similar to those employed in the Western House of Assembly in 1962. Matters were brought to a head when an anonymous letter was written to the regional premier alerting him of a plot by the Society to assassinate him. In the event a commission of inquiry, with a Lagos High Court judge, Mr. Justice Alexander, as sole commissioner, had to be appointed to investigate the Society's activities. The inquiry[8] revealed the alarming state of instability and unrest, of mutual antagonism and the struggle for power and patronage which had been seething in the region. It revealed, too, that Owegbe had permeated the executive council, the house of assembly and the house of chiefs, certain customary courts and local government bodies, and that numerous lawless and unlawful acts had been committed in the practice of the cult. It exposed the rottenness of politicians, their predilection for falsehood and perversion. As the Commissioner observed, 'the idea of using *juju* for the purpose of achieving political ascendancy is retrograde, and contrary to the tenets of true democracy and abhorrent to its ideals.'[9] It is difficult to predict how the political situation in the Mid-West would have developed under the menace of the Owegbe had the military takeover not intervened.

Eastern Nigeria had had its own share of minority trouble, but the general unrest inherent in the relations of the dominant and minority tribes had not been given expression in violence of the kind that occurred in the North and Mid-West.

Imbalance Between the North and the Other Regions

Perhaps the most astonishing peculiarity of Nigerian federalism was the imbalance in size and population between the North and the rest of the regions. As has been observed, the North was larger than the rest of the regions put together, encompassing seventy-five per cent of the land area and sixty per cent of the population of the country. Of the danger of such an imbalance, Sir Kenneth Wheare has written:

'The capacity of states to work a federal union is also greatly influenced by their size. It is undesirable that one or two units should be so powerful that they can override the others and bend

I

the will of the federal government to themselves . . . The essential
is, as John Stuart Mill says, "that there should not be any one
state so much more powerful than the rest as to be capable of
vying in strength with many of them combined. If there be such
a one, and only one, it will insist on being master of the joint
deliberations: if there be two, they will be irresistible when they
agree; and whenever they differ everything will be decided by a
struggle for ascendancy between the rivals." The size of the units
concerned – in wealth, area and population – is therefore of prime
importance. There must be some sort of reasonable balance
which will insure that all the units can maintain their independence within the sphere allotted to them and that no one
can dominate the others.'[10]

The boundaries of the North were the result partly of the accident
of its origin and partly of sheer gerrymandering by the British.
It is true that the North had been acquired and (until 1914)
administered as a separate country, yet one would have expected
that after its amalgamation with Southern Nigeria in 1914 there
should be a general redrawing of boundaries. When the Protectorate of Southern Nigeria and the Colony and Protectorate of Lagos
were merged in 1906, the old boundary between them was not
preserved. Rather the resultant entity, known as Southern Nigeria,
was simply divided into three provinces, Eastern, Central and
Western. This precedent was not followed in 1914. On the contrary, Lord Lugard in 1918 extended the boundary of Northern
Nigeria South-East-wards to include a good part of the territory
that previously lay in the Eastern Province of Southern Nigeria.
But he rejected demands for the revision of the boundary between
the North and the South-West, although the people of Illorin and
Kabba divisions of the North belonged to the same tribal stock –
Yoruba – as those of the South-West. The only concession was the
transfer of the tiny community of Otun from the North to the
South-West in 1936. The boundary between the North and the
South, as altered in 1918, 1924 and 1936, was confirmed in 1942
and again in 1950 against agitation from the Yorubas that their
fellow tribesmen in Illorin and Kabba should be joined with them.
Agitation over Illorin and Kabba continued unabated, and was
again investigated in 1958 by the Minorities Commission which,
although it found considerable support for the merger among the
people in Illorin and Kabba, nevertheless declined to recommend
the holding of a plebiscite on the matter 'unless there was a considerable measure of agreement in Nigeria that this was the right
course to follow.'[11] The Commission knew of course that no such

agreement was possible in the face of the uncompromising opposition of the NPC. The refusal of the Commission to recommend a plebiscite is all the more surprising in view of its finding that 'if no solution is found to this dispute . . . relations within the Federation may be embittered for some time to come.'[12]

There was clearly no compelling reason why the North should have been preserved intact. Its boundary with the South was not natural. If one were in fact looking for natural boundaries, the rivers Niger and Benue provided the obvious ones, yet the North extended far beyond the Benue into the South-East, and far beyond the Niger into the South-West. When in 1939 the South was divided into two, East and West, the boundary was drawn along the natural frontier of the River Niger. Nor did the boundary of the North follow upon tribal distribution. The Hausa-Fulani were the dominant tribe, but as previously pointed out, there were a host of others, the Kanuri, the Nupe, Tiv, the Yoruba of Illorin and Kabba and over 200 others. Indeed the tribal distribution in the North offended against the main feature of Nigerian federalism, in that, instead of the normal majority–miniority tribes structure, the Hausa-Fulani, though the largest single group, were actually a minority *vis-à-vis* the rest of the Northern tribes put together, the proportion being roughly eight million Hausa-Fulani to nine million others.[13] Neither were the tribes united by the fact of a common traditional religion, as was the case in the South where animism was the universal traditional religion. Religious unity based upon Islam embraced no more than seventy per cent of the population; the remaining thirty per cent were traditionally animists. There could therefore be no other explanation for the refusal of the British to alter the boundaries of the North than that it was a deliberate design to foist Northern domination upon the country. It has quite rightly been described as 'one of the greatest acts of gerrymandering in history.'[14]

When, pursuant to a recommendation of the Constitutional Conference in 1957, a Commission of Inquiry was appointed to go into the demand for the creation of more states, together with other minority grievances, the British Government settled the terms of reference of the Commission so as virtually to preclude it from recommending the creation of more states. The Commission was directed, as 'a last resort,' to recommend the creation of not more than one region out of any existing region 'if, but only if, no other solution seems to the Commission to meet the case.'[15] In view of the known opposition of the British Government to the fragmentation of the North, it is not surprising that the Commission should have come out against the creation of more states. When the Report of

the Commission came up for consideration before the resumed constitutional conference in 1958, the secretary of state for the colonies
indicated that if the demand for more states was insisted upon either
before or after the federal election due in 1959, then the British
Government would be obliged to postpone the date for independence
to enable such new regions to gain experience in government under
British guidance. Anxious that independence should not be delayed
beyond October 1, 1960, the Nigerian delegations pressing for the
creation of more regions had to drop their demand, so that the
imbalance between North and South became written into the
Constitution as a permanent feature.

Distribution of Powers

The first principle is that matters of local concern should be placed
under the control of the regional governments, since this is a
cardinal objective and justification for federalism in a plural society.
But what matters are really of local concern? Agriculture, land
tenure, local government and cultural affairs, the law relating to
persons, personal property, contracts and markets come readily to
mind. Of these, it can be said that they are of purely local concern,
and their regionalisation should not normally impede national
integration. There are other matters of local concern to which the
local groupings may lay a legitimate claim, but the problem concerning these is that they also impinge upon the national interest,
so as not to be of *purely* local concern. Are, for example, the provision of social services and the maintenance of law and order
matters of purely or mainly local concern? Social services embrace
a wide range of matters: education, public health and medical care,
water supply, roads and other public works, unemployment relief,
workmen's compensation, social security and social welfare services.
There may be, as Watts said, 'compelling arguments for placing
the social services in the hands of the regional governments: the
personal nature of these services, the need to adapt them to local
circumstances and problems, and their close relation to other
aspects of local administration.'[16] But there are also weighty arguments for their centralisation: the greater efficiency and economy
of large-scale organisation, the maintenance of uniform and common
standards of service, and the close connection between economic and
social affairs. This brings us to the next sore point. How are economic
affairs to be dealt with? And by economic affairs one has in mind
industrialisation, technology, taxation, economic development and
planning, and the regulation of the economy in all its ramifications.
These constitute, together with the social services, the focal point
of modern life.

It is important that the citizens in each region should be made to feel the existence of the federal government and be brought to an awareness that it too is an essential part of the machinery for their government and welfare. Admittedly the focal point of modern life, the impact of economic development and planning upon the life of the ordinary man is not likely to be very great in a developing country, owing to the serious limitation in the financial resources needed for it. Government in these countries will continue for some time to be thought of largely in terms of its traditional functions – law and order – and of the social services which it provides: education, water supply, public health and medical facilities, and roads. Commerce too is important. It would seem to be necessary therefore in the interest of national integration to associate the federal government in the discharge of these functions in addition to matters clearly of common concern over which its responsibility is normally exclusive – foreign affairs, customs, money and currency, posts and telegraphs, and national defence.

The device for joint federal-regional responsibility in the field of law and order and social services should be the concurrent power. In other words, such matters should be put within the concurrent competence of both the federal and regional governments. The case for concurrent power cannot be better stated than in the following words of Watts:

'It may be argued that an additional list of concurrent legislative powers is unnecessarily cumbrous, and that it may leave regional governments in doubt about the extent of their legislative authority, since in addition to being normally excluded from the central list, they may at the same time be excluded from the concurrent list as well. Nevertheless, the advantages of such a list have outweighed these considerations. First, such a list enhances flexibility. In a new federation it permits the central government to postpone exercising its authority in a field until such time as the matter has assumed national importance, while not preventing any region which is forward-looking from going ahead and legislating in the meantime on its own account. Secondly, it provides a means whereby, in certain spheres, especially the social services, the central government may legislate to secure a basic national uniformity and to guide regional legislation, while leaving with the regional legislatures the initiative for details and for adaptation to local circumstances. Thirdly, a concurrent subject allows the general government to step into what is normally a regional field of activity, in order to provide remedies for particularly backward regions or for difficulties arising from

regional legislation which affects other regions. Fourthly, concurrent lists may facilitate "comparative federalism," by encouraging co-operative rather than independent action in these
fields. Fifthly, such a list may reduce the necessity for complicated,
minute subdivisions of individual functions assigned exclusively
to one government or another.'[17]

It is important that in developing countries one should avoid a
rigid adherence to a doctrinaire formulation of the federal principle.
The overriding problem in these countries is, as has been stated,
one of national integration. On this account, one is attracted by the
provision in the 1962 Constitution of Pakistan giving the central
government power to legislate with respect to any matter 'where
the national interest of Pakistan in relation to: (*a*) the security of
Pakistan, including the economic and financial stability of Pakistan;
(*b*) planning or co-ordination; or (*c*) the achievement of uniformity
in respect of any matter in different parts of Pakistan, so requires.'[18]
A safeguard against abuse of power by the federal government would
be to write the principle of co-operation into the Constitution itself,
by requiring the federal government to consult with the regional
governments upon any proposed exercise of a concurrent power, and
by instituting machinery for such consultation.[19] The emphasis of
modern federalism is on co-operation and comity and mutual
self-restraint.[20] It may be necessary to give the centre power to
coerce a recalcitrant regional government in order to preserve the
union, but this should be circumscribed to make it clear that it is
not intended that the federal government is to have power to take
over a regional government completely. It need hardly be said that
a law validly made by the centre should prevail over a regional one
in the event of inconsistency between them.

The distribution of powers under the Nigeria Constitution leaned
somewhat more in favour of regional power and autonomy than
was perhaps consistent with national integration. There was an
exclusive legislative list of forty-five matters exclusive to the federal
legislature, and a concurrent list of twenty-nine items; apart from
the lists, there were other matters dealt with in the body of the Constitution following the principle of concurrent power.[21] Had the
Constitution been meant for a developed country, there can be no
doubt that the powers exercisable centrally were quite ample, more
ample indeed than is the case in any of the older federations, such
as the U.S.A., Canada, Australia or Switzerland. Not only did the
federal government have financial superiority over the regions, but
it also had control over the vital aspects of the economy, money and
currency, banks and banking, customs, inter-regional and international trade, foreign borrowing, exchange control, control of

capital issues and incorporation and promotion of companies and firms. Yet, in the context of Nigeria the federal power seemed insufficient to promote national integration and discourage undue regionalism. To begin with, the implication of having only two lists,[22] one of which was exclusive to the centre, was to vest residual matters exclusively in the regions. Residuary matters have of course no inherent worth in determining the balance of power in a federation. Their importance depends upon the range and importance of the enumerated matters. Nevertheless the intention of lodging them with the regions in Nigeria was to underline regional autonomy. One would have expected that in a federal system formed by the disaggregation of an existing unitary state, the logical thing would be for the centre to surrender its former sovereignty over a specified area to the regions, while retaining the residue. This was in fact the scheme of the 1951 Constitution; its reversal in 1954 was unquestionably a surrender to the pressure for regional autonomy at the expense of national integration. Residuary powers might conceivably strengthen the government which has them through the accretion to it of functions unknown and unforeseen at the time of the adoption of the Constitution.

Secondly, when one looks at the two lists, one gets the impression that, ample though they were, the residue was equally ample and perhaps more significant in terms of its relevance to the life of the ordinary man. The general criminal law, the law of property, both personal and real, and of contracts, and the whole range of social services were virtually in the exclusive control of the regional governments. Even industrial development was concurrent to both units of government. It is hardly surprising that the average man in Nigeria should have thought of government largely in terms of the government of the region in which he resided. The main exception to this picture of regional preponderance was the concurrent power over public safety and public order and the central control of the police, the primary instrument for law and order. But even the central control of the police was undermined by the fact that a regional premier could, for the purpose of maintaining law and order in the region, direct the operational use of the contingent of the Nigeria Police Force stationed in the region. It is true that the commissioner of police in charge of the regional contingent could refuse to carry out such direction until the approval of the prime minister was obtained, but this was a qualification which was not intended to be used in practice and was never in fact used, since not only was the commissioner a native of the region but also the views of the regional premier were virtually conclusive in choosing him. Then there was the further fact that the Constitution permitted the establishment of local police forces on a provincial basis. These became indeed a potent instrument of coercion in the hands of the regional governments. (There were no local police forces in the Eastern Region.) Finally, with the exception of the Federation of Rhodesia and Nyasaland, Nigeria was the only one of the new federations in which the federal power in respect of the implementation within a region of international treaties entered into by the federal government was subject to the consent of the regional government.

The Impact of Politics upon Federalism in Nigeria
(i) The tribalisation of politics

Before 1948, budding Nigerian nationalism, which was an agitation movement for colonial emancipation, was centred around a single organisation, the National Council of Nigeria and the Cameroons (NCNC),[23] under a united leadership, with a Yoruba, Herbert Macaulay, as President, and an Ibo, Nnamdi Azikiwe (Zik as he is popularly called) as General Secretary. The NCNC was a real mass movement, uniting under its fold the masses of all the tribes in a common struggle against colonial rule. In 1946 occurred the death of Herbert Macaulay in the middle of a countrywide campaign protesting against certain 'obnoxious' legislation of the colonial government. It was the first campaign of its kind, and had a tremendous effect in rousing Nigerians to a consciousness of common identity. The accession of Zik to the leadership of the party after the death of Macaulay made the NCNC suspect in the eyes of some of the Yoruba leaders. The party's connection with Ibo cultural organisations which provided the bulk of its institutional membership, the fact that Zik was both the President of the party and of the pan-Ibo cultural organisation, the Ibo State Union, and had made statements glorifying the Ibo, were interpreted as meaning that the NCNC had become an instrument of Ibo domination. Some Yoruba leaders felt deeply apprehensive over such a prospect, and, as a counter measure, organised in 1948 a pan-Yoruba organisation, the *Egbe Omo Oduduwa*, meaning the Society of the descendants of Oduduwa, the mythical founder of the Yoruba tribe.[24] The avowed object of this organisation was, *inter alia*, to foster Yoruba nationalism. Not surprisingly, its formation heralded a period of acute Yoruba-Ibo animosity.

Then came the promulgation of the Macpherson Constitution of 1951 which introduced for the first time representative government in the country. With this, political activity ceased to be concerned solely with agitation against colonial rule. Power politics had made an appearance, and the tribe proved the most convenient medium of appeal for support by those with ambition for power in the newly created regional governments. In contemplation of the elections under the new constitution, the *Egbe* quickly organised a political wing of itself in the name of the Action Group (AG). Taking over the Egbe's ideology of Yoruba nationalism, the AG made it the dominant note in its appeal to the Yoruba electorate of the Western Region. The danger of Ibo domination, which the NCNC was said to presage, was tendentiously played up. A separate Yoruba party was necessary in order to protect Yoruba interest against this threat. In the North a similar development had also taken place in response to the grant of representative political power. A cultural organisation, the *Jamiyyar Mutanen Avewa*, the 'Northern Peoples' Congress' (NPC), formed in 1949, was quickly transformed into a political party. As with the AG, the NPC also found it expedient in its campaign at the Northern regional elections in 1951 to make the tribe its main basis of appeal. And so was launched upon the Nigerian political scene the ugly phenomenon of tribal politics which, in the words of the Donoughmore Commission on the Constitution of Ceylon (1928), was like 'a canker in the body politic, eating deeper and deeper into the vital energies of the people, breeding self-interest, suspicion and animosity, poisoning the new growth of political consciousness and effectively preventing the development of a national or corporate spirit.'[25]

The appeal to tribal sentiment in the elections of 1951 had to be cruder and uninhibited, because of the existence of an already established party which had a mass countrywide following under a mixed tribal leadership. In 1951 the NCNC had already a large following among the Yoruba, and to a lesser extent among the Northern tribes, and therefore stood a better chance of winning an election there than any new party, if tribal interests or loyalty were to be left out of the contest. An all-out appeal to tribal sentiment was thought to be the most effective weapon to dislodge the NCNC in the esteem and support of the masses of the Yoruba and Northern tribes. And so indeed it proved to be, tribal sentiment being what it is.

The split in the nationalist movement was a serious blow to the fostering of a consciousness of a common identity among Nigerians. A dominant national party, cutting across tribal, cultural and linguistic divisions, and a national hero are among the most integrating agencies in an emergent state. Writing about the integrating role of a national party and a national hero in the emergent states of Africa, Immanuel Wallerstein has observed rather pointedly:

'As one surveys the African scene today, one observes that where the party and the hero are weak, so are the process of modernisation and integration of the nation. For in this transition to a social order in which the state will be able to rely on the loyalty of a citizenry born to it and trained in it, the party and the hero can be seen somewhat as a pair of surgical clamps which hold the state together while the bonds of affection and legitimation grow . . . The party incarnates the nation, not because it is in tune with historical destiny, but because of its past and present accomplishments. In the past, it fought for freedom and helped to create a national consciousness. And in the present, it is a mass, not a class, party . . . The role of the hero is first of all to be a readily available, easily understood, symbol of the new nation, someone to incarnate in his person its values and aspirations. But the hero does more than symbolise the new nation. He legitimizes the state by ordaining obedience to its norms out of loyalty to his person. This is what people usually mean when they speak of the charismatic authority of these leaders.'[26]

In his excellent survey of the six new federations in the Commonwealth, India, Pakistan, Malaya and Malaysia, Nigeria, Rhodesia and Nyasaland, and the West Indies, Professor Watts comes to the same conclusion: 'Where a single party has been able to aggregate diverse interests and to dominate both central and regional elections so that it controls most governments at both levels, national cohesion and co-operation between governments have been facilitated. This has been the situation in India, Malaya, and until 1954, Pakistan.'[27]

The grant of political power in 1951 would have produced tribal parties in any event, whether the system was unitary or federal. However, federalism provided an institutional base for the propagation of tribalism in politics. It enabled the parties in control of the regional governments to use the institutionalised power to champion, at both the regional and federal levels, the interest of the tribes which they represented. The effect of this at the federal level was particularly unfortunate. It caused the federal government to be regarded as a single huge cake, already baked, of which it was the duty of each tribal party to secure for its tribe as large a share as possible. This was the kind of perverted attitude that characterised the relations of the parties and their members at the federal level. The resulting situation was one of continual inter-tribal enmity and hostility. Every question, whether it be the award of scholarships or contracts, appointments in the federal public service, economic development or the siting of an industrial project, was viewed from the viewpoint of tribal advantage, and support or opposition to it depended upon whether or not it advanced the interest of one's tribe. In the civil service, the tribe was always the pervading influence, intruding into questions of appointments and promotions and undermining efficiency. Much the same picture of tribal rivalry and tension prevailed in the statutory corporations. In the Airways, Railway and Electricity Corporations and in the Ports Authority, there was always a continuing state of crisis involving mainly the Ibos on the one hand and the Yorubas on the other. As always the quarrels were over jobs and contracts. An Ibo chairman of one corporation would endeavour to pack the corporation full of Ibos while a Yoruba chairman or general manager of another corporation would try to outdo him.

Perhaps the most ruinous incursion of tribal politics was upon the universities. In 1965 the young University of Lagos, then barely two and a half years old, was plunged into a mighty conflagration over the appointment of a vice-chancellor. The existing holder of the office, Professor Eni Njoku, an Ibo from the East, had been appointed for an initial term of three years. It was customary in university administration to grant tenure to the holder of the office after the initial trial period, providing he had proved himself capable and had done nothing to disentitle him to tenure. But, although Professor Njoku had got the university off to a very promising start, and had in the short space of three years built up a university community recognised throughout the academic world for the high quality of its staff and its teaching, a community, moreover, among whose members harmony had reigned and in which everybody was inspired by the eminence and the high ideals of its head, a Yoruba-dominated governing council refused to reappoint him. Determined to install a Yoruba in the job at all costs, the council proceeded, against vehement protests from the senate, the academic staff and the students' body, to appoint a Dr. Biobaku, a Yoruba, who had previously accepted a job as vice-chancellor of the University of Zambia. In the ensuing crisis, the university was closed down and remained closed from March 1965 to the end of the academic session. Practically all the non-Yoruba members of the academic staff, both expatriate and indigenous, resigned and left; most of the students left too, and the university all but collapsed. The crisis had been politically inspired. It was part of the understanding of the alliance between the NPC and the NNDP[28] in 1964 that the latter should have the vice-chancellorship of one of the two federal universities. The NNDP's appeal to the Yoruba electorate of Western Nigeria and Lagos had been based upon a pledge to secure a fair share of the 'national cake' for members of the tribe, and a university vice-chancellorship was a big prize to show in part fulfilment of its promise. Here, then, was the explanation of the Prime Minister's dilemma in all the appeals made to him to intervene to end the crisis. Much as he admired and respected Dr. Njoku, he could not intervene on his side without breaking the understanding of the alliance between his party and the NNDP. Delegations sent by the staff to the other NPC federal ministers, and even to the NPC leader, Sir Ahmadu Bello, equally produced no result. And so the young, promising university, instead of blossoming into maturity as it assuredly would have done, was allowed to wither away. The other federal university, the University of Ibadan, had had hardly any respite from tribal squabbles following the Nigerianisation of its staff. They featured in all staff appointments, eventually reaching the point of an open battle between the Ibo vice-chancellor and the Yoruba registrar, which had had to be fought out in the law courts. Subsequently in 1966 the vice-chancellor, Dr. Kenneth Dike, felt obliged to relinquish the post in disgust.

The crises in the two federal universities were part of the invigorated focus given to tribalism by the emergence of Chief Akintola's NNDP into Nigerian politics. The NNDP was first installed in power in Western Nigeria by the action of the federal government, and not by the votes of the regional electorate which remained solidly pro-Action Group. The paramount concern of the party (NNDP) was therefore how to win the support of the Western electorate from the AG. The tribe was again the convenient tool. The AG had entered into an alliance with the Ibo-dominated NCNC for the purposes of the impending 1964 federal election. This alliance was proclaimed to the Yorubas to spell Ibo domination, on the ground that a coalition federal government of the NCNC and the AG would be dominated by the Ibos, with the Yorubas occupying a subordinate position. An alliance of the Yorubas with the NPC, on the other hand, would not only offer a chance of averting the ominous spectacle of Ibo domination, but would in fact enable the Yoruba to enjoy the fruits of self-government from which they had been excluded since 1959. Thus, the AG alliance with NCNC served the NNDP as a weapon to discredit the AG with the Yoruba elecotrate. In addition to the propaganda of Ibo domination, the Yorubas were told that the Ibos in Lagos had been expropriating their lands and exploiting them in other ways. Photographs of prosperous Ibo shops were widely exhibited with the highly provocative caption: 'Lagos women sell their wares in the gutters. The UPGA[29] Ibos sell in shops.'

Regionalism

By regionalism is meant the principle which seeks to attribute to a unit within a federation a distinct individuality, with a claim upon the loyalty of its inhabitants, competing with, if not overriding, loyalty to the federal state. In this sense, regionalism was practised to a greater or less degree by all the regions of Nigeria, but it was in the North that it became a thorough-going political ideology in the hands of the NPC. We have seen how the shadow of Southern domination had always hung over the North like a nightmare. Here was an evil which called for the united effort of the entire North as one monolithic bloc. The NPC, now firmly in power in the North, felt it had a mission in such an enterprise. It proclaimed its motto to be *One North, One People irrespective of religion, rank or tribe,* and launched a vigorous effort to rally the Northern population to the cause of Northern nationalism. Northerners were told that they were one and indivisible, with a common destiny, that they were different from Southerners, and that their first and paramount loyalty was to the government of Northern Nigeria. A native of the North was primarily a Northerner, and only secondarily a Nigerian.

The ideology of One North, One People, had two main objectives. First, it implied a policy of exclusiveness, of separatism. The North must be for Northerners only. The second objective was the control of the Northern electorate by an exclusively Northern party, which was of course to be the NPC itself, the aim being to enable the North to dominate the government of the centre in perpetuity. The methods adopted towards the achievement of these objectives had rather tragic consequences for the cause of a Nigerian nation.

The policy of the North for Northerners meant that measures had to be initiated to neutralise the Southerners resident in the North. The first step was the Northernisation policy, which had its early beginning in May 1952 when, very soon after taking office, the newly constituted Northern Region executive council decided that in appointments to posts in the region suitable and qualified Northerners should be given preference over all others, and that in any case no appointments of Southerners should be made without prior consultation with the council. This was at a time when the country was still served by a single, undivided public service. But in 1954 there occurred the regionalisation of the public service, by which the NPC gained full control of the public service of the North. In the event Northernisation of the region's public service was made not only a matter of the first priority but also more thoroughgoing. No longer was it just a matter of giving preference to Northerners; no appointments of Southerners were to be made at all while at the same time steps were taken to replace completely those already serving. Where no suitable and qualified Northerners were available, expatriates were preferred to Southerners. It is perhaps, as Phillipson and Adebo remarked in their celebrated Report on the civil service, a perfectly natural desire for any community to want to staff its own public services mainly with people of that community. Yet, Northernisation stands discredited by its underlying philosophy of the North for Northerners, and by its preference for expatriate over fellow compatriots from the South. The explanation given for this preference was that 'foreigners do their job and then go back home, leaving a vacancy to be filled. Southerners want to stay for ever.'[30] The main reason seems, however, to have been the desire to exclude Southerners from the North in accordance with the policy of the North for Northerners. Evidence in support of this was afforded by the demand that Northernisation should be extended to petty traders; that 'foreign firms in the region be given a time-limit to replace all Ibos in their firms;' and that Ibos should be barred from operating hotels and from doing contract works for the government, native authorities or private enterprises.[31] To these demands, the Premier of the Region, Alhaji Sir Ahmadu Bello, replied in the Northern House of Assembly that it was his 'most earnest desire that every post in the region, however small, is to be filled by a Northerner.'[32] It is fair to mention that similar tendencies were not unknown in the other regions, but in its thoroughgoing nature, Northernisation differed from other such practices, and so constituted a severe blow to the cause of Nigerian unity.

The second weapon in the neutralisation of Southerners in the North was the imposition of restrictions upon the acquisition and tenure of land by non-natives of Northern Nigeria. A long-standing policy dating back to 1910, it denied to Southerners (and other non-natives) the right to acquire title to the occupation and use of land[33] in the North except with the consent of the government. It was a criminal offence for a non-Northerner to occupy or use any land without such consent. Any right of occupancy acquired by him might be, and often was, revoked at will and without compensation by the government. During debates in the Northern house of assembly in 1964, demands were made that Ibos should not be granted occupancy rights, and that those already held by them should be revoked. The minister of lands and survey assured members that his ministry 'will do all it can to see that their demands are met. How to do this, when to do it, all this should not be disclosed. In due course, you will all see what will happen.'[34]

It is hardly surprising that Northernisation should have won for the NPC the overwhelming support of the Northern masses, especially the job-seekers and public servants who stood to gain most by it. It helped to confirm the NPC as the party for the North. Yet the objective of making it the *exclusive* party for the North was far from achieved, and to this it now addressed itself, harnessing for the purpose all the forces of persuasion and coercion available to a regional government, including victimisation, discrimination, intimidation, physical violence and electoral malpractices. Southern-based parties must be prevented from gaining a foothold in the North, and Northern-based minority parties must be incapacitated or enfeebled. The 1959 federal election was looked upon by all the parties as a test and challenge for the ambition of the NPC to become the exclusive party for the North. Since the British were still in control, there was a good chance that the contest might be fairly conducted. The Action Group took up the challenge with much earnestness and vigour, allying itself with a Northern minority party, the United Middle Belt Congress (UMBC). The NCNC chose to operate through its long-standing ally, the Northern Elements Progressive Union (NEPU). The result of the election, when the contest was at last concluded, could hardly have been encouraging for the NPC, but it must have been distinctly disappointing for the AG in view of the money and effort it put into it. It showed 134 seats for the NPC, 25 for the AG/UMBC and 8 for the NCNC/NEPU. The overall strength of the parties in the House of Representative was NPC 134, NCNC/NEPU 89, and AG/UMBC 73. In the result, although it emerged as the single largest party, the NPC fell short of the number of seats which would have given it a majority in the House in order to be able to form a government. This of course augured well for the country, since a federal government formed by one region alone is a positive evil. Such a government would have been simply the regional government projected into the centre. The idea of a federal government is that it should be an institutional device for securing the welfare of the associated units and their consequent integration into a single national entity. The aim is to provide a machinery for joint effort in dealing with matters of common interest in order to ensure an integrated social policy inspired by the common benefit of all. Federal government is not a platform for projecting and implementing purely regional as against national interests. Unhappily, subsequent events were to produce this evil phenomenon.

In the circumstances resulting from the fact that no party had an overall majority in the house of representatives, the then British governor-general, Sir James Robertson, invited Sir Abubakar Tafawa Balewa, the deputy leader of the NPC, to form a government, as the leader of the party with the largest support in the House. It is not proposed to comment upon the constitutional propriety of this action, but the effect was to place the NPC in a position of advantage *vis-à-vis* the other parties in the manoeuvres which followed upon the election. It induced the two other dominant parties to make overtures to the NPC for a coalition, although it appeared too that the possibility of an alliance between the former was discussed. The situation amply demonstrates the undesirability of a federal system composed of only three units. Any federal government formed by the NPC alone or by a coalition of the two Southern parties might conceivably have provoked a head-on collision between North and South. The coalition that did eventually result was between the NPC and the NCNC. This avoided the risk of a North-South collision, and enabled the country to enjoy some stability for the first two years after independence, even if rather uneasily.

Yet tension was clearly in-built in the system mainly by reason of the population imbalance between the North and the rest of the regions. The NPC-NCNC coalition could provide no more than a precarious expedient, operating to hold off a major clash only for a while. The risk of a clash was accentuated by the exclusion from the coalition of the majority Yoruba elements represented by the AG. Left as it were in the cold, and disconcerted by its failure to win sufficient votes in the North at the 1959 election, the AG became increasingly radical in its opposition to the preponderant size of the North, a preponderance which was facilitated by the electoral system which, based upon single member constituencies, operated to deprive the not inconsiderable Southern population resident in the North of the weight to which their numbers would have entitled them under a system of proportional representation. Frustration over Northern dominance was also heightened by the fact that its electoral advantage was not matched by a proportionate contribution to the national revenue. Indeed the North was heavily subsidised by the South when need rather than derivation alone was recognised as a relevant factor in revenue allocation.[35]

With its ally, the UMBC, the AG mounted a rather vicious campaign in Tivland (a minority area of Northern Nigeria) against the NPC and the Hausa-Fulani tribe which it represented. The Tivs, a fiercely individualistic people, were whipped up to a frenzy of indignation, and erupted in 1960, giving vent to their indignation in wholesale burning of over 30,000 houses belonging to chiefs and other agents of NPC persuasion in Tivland. The aim was to force the creation of a Middle Belt state which, taking away a sizeable portion of the population of the North, would terminate its dominance. The AG had also sponsored a similar agitation for the creation of a new state in the minority areas of the East where it had much support. It appeared too that the party had conceived violence as a possible means of overthrowing Northern hegemony. There was evidence, admitted by its leaders at their trial for treason in 1962, of the importation of large quantities of arms and of the training of persons in their use. It seemed inconceivable, however, from the inadequate preparations alleged to have been made, that there had been any real intention to overthrow the federal government by force of arms. The importation of arms and the military training of persons were explained on the ground of self-defence. They were, so the party claimed, a precaution against the eventuality that the federal government might want to take over the government of Western Nigeria by force.

These actions by the AG provoked from the coalition partners retaliatory measures of a most repressive type. An internal crisis within the AG provided the pretext for intervention by the federal government. When Chief Awolowo moved to the centre in 1959 to become leader of the opposition in parliament, the premiership of Western Nigeria devolved upon his deputy, Chief Akintola. Following charges of insubordination and refusal to carry out party policy decisions made against him at the party conference, Chief Akintola was deposed from the deputy leadership of the party. Next he was removed from the regional premiership by the regional governor following a letter signed by sixty-six AG members of the house of assembly to the effect that they no longer had confidence in him. The governor then proceeded to appoint as the new premier Chief Adegbenro, who had earlier replaced Chief Akintola as deputy leader of the party. Chief Akintola refused to accept his dismissal, and took court action to challenge it. A meeting of the house of assembly, called to approve the new government, resulted in fighting and violence among members in the chamber of the House, necessitating intervention by the police which then cleared the House and locked it up. On the strength of these facts, the federal government took the view that it had become impossible to carry on the government of Western Nigeria, and so moved parliament to declare a state of emergency, which was duly done. Armed with its virtually unlimited powers during an emergency, the federal government took over the administration of the government of Western Nigeria, and suspended the governor and all the representative political functionaries of the AG government. It is possible that the take-over might have been justified in law,[36] but it was undoubtedly ill-motivated. Its consequences were disastrous both for the Western Region and for Nigeria as a whole. It had opened the region to the floodgates of political unrest and violence, which culminated in the débâcle of 1965-6.

K

Federal intervention in Western Nigeria had also altered the balance of power in the country, first between the centre and the regions, and between the partners in the federal coalition government. It certainly could not have been contemplated by the framers of the Constitution that the federal government was to have power to take over the government of a region. The take-over destroyed two of the cardinal objectives of federalism – viz. as a means of enabling each group in a plural society to look after its own internal affairs free from outside interference, and as a device for constitutionalism in limiting the powers of the centre, so as to prevent it from becoming an instrument of total domination and tyranny. Emphasising this last role, Carl Friedrich has said: 'the hope that one can employ it merely as a gadget, a mechanism for resolving group antagonism and conflict, in Nigeria as elsewhere, is doomed at the outset.'[37] Moreover the emergency administration was both unrepresentative, autocratic and authoritarian. The take-over demonstrated the alarming potentiality of federal power *vis-à-vis* the regions. By it the authority of the federation was enormously enhanced. But much of this increased authority enured to the benefit of the North and the NPC. The federal take-over in Western Nigeria was aimed at destroying the AG as a political party. With its leader, Chief Awolowo, and many of his principal lieutenants under detention by the emergency administrator, the parliamentary membership both at the centre and in the region was thrown into disarray. At the end of the emergency administration the AG did not regain the government of Western Nigeria. Chief Akintola, leading a splinter group of the AG, was put into power with the collaboration of the NCNC. The exclusion of the AG from its power base was the most fatal blow the party received at the hands of the federal coalition government. But more was to follow. A commission of inquiry was instituted into its administration of the government of Western Nigeria; its leadership was arrested, tried and sentenced to various terms of imprisonment for treasonable felony. The AG had become a sinking ship. The prevailing philosophy among Nigerian politicians being to jump into any bandwagon that seemed to be going, its parliamentary members in the House of Representatives began to defect to the NPC and the NCNC until, of the seventy-three elected in 1959, only thirteen were left.

The defection of AG members to the NPC gave the latter an absolute majority in the House. Given the altered strength of the parties in the House, the NPC, feeling it could now do without the NCNC, became intensely arrogant towards its partner. It now thought of itself as the senior partner, and the NCNC as the junior. Among individual NCNC ministers there was a growing sense of dependence. Actuated by a selfish love for power, prestige and wealth, some indeed curried the favour of the NPC in order to insure their continuance in office. As the NPC, encouraged by its absolute majority in Parliament, began to ride roughshod over the NCNC, the partners became increasingly estranged. The precariousness of the coalition as a basis for unity and stability began to show up. The first open crack in the coalition occurred over the census in 1962, when the figures obtained from the East were summarily rejected as 'false and inflated.' The census was cancelled, but the acrimonious controversy over the new census in 1963 drew the partners further apart. The figures from the North under the new census were hardly likely to be less false and inflated; they were in fact more distinctly so, but the census was nevertheless upheld against vehement protest from the East which rejected it, and sought through a court action to have it invalidated. Because it was the basis for representation in parliament, the census, otherwise a normal exercise in economic planning, had become almost a matter of life and death. From the time of the census on, one crisis followed another; the controversy over the proposal for preventive detention, the general strike of 1964, the federal election crisis in 1964 and the Western Region election crisis in 1965.[38] The federation had managed to survive these crises, yet with each one it came nearer and nearer to disintegration, swaying precariously upon the brink.

The census controversy, the 1964 federal election and the 1965 West Region election crises may all be traced to one cause: the desire of the NPC to perpetuate its hegemony in the affairs of the federation. Having got itself re-confirmed in power on the strength of the irregularly conducted election of 1964, the NPC now feared that a Southern-dominated senate would greatly undermine its power in the federal government. This danger could only be avoided by ensuring that its ally, Chief Akintola's NNDP, was confirmed in power in Western Nigeria.[39] Yet, given the lack of support for the NNDP among the people of Western Nigeria, the necessary confirmation could be obtained only by a wholesale rigging of the election due in 1965. As expected, the election was rigged wholesale with the active encouragement of the NPC. In the widespread violent disturbances which followed the refusal of the electorate of Western Nigeria to accept this flagrant denial of their right to choose who should govern them, the NPC-controlled federal government maintained an indifference which contrasted most tellingly with its ready, unsolicited intervention in the relatively minor crisis of 1962. The prime minister rejected demands that the federal government should declare an emergency and take over the government as it did in 1962. Yet, while maintaining that the widespread killings and arson in the region were the internal concern of the regional government, the prime minister did not hesitate to send in the police and army to help bolster up the tottering Akintola government.

The attitude of the NPC in all these crises showed quite unmistakably that its overriding interest in Nigerian government and politics was the maintenance of Northern, and consequently of NPC, hegemony. Provided this object was achieved, it did not seem to matter to the party whether the chances of evolving a Nigerian nation were thereby jeopardised. It set its face against any device that might have made its domination less odious, such as equal representation of the regions in the house of representatives or in the executive council. It was prepared to consider coalition, but only with itself as the senior partner appropriating the premiership and the strategic ministries.

With NPC's absolute majority in the House of Representatives, the federal government became more and more the reflection of Northern interest. A government of reaction, its directing spirit lay outside the cabinet – with the NPC leader and the emirs in the North. Nothing of importance could be matured that was not acceptable to these groups. The federal government had become a mere appendage of the North, an instrument for the projection of Northern interests. With hardly a will of its own, it had ceased to represent the nation or to serve as an agency for an integrated administration dedicated to securing the common welfare of all its component parts. As a mere reflection of Northern interest, the federal government had no legitimacy whatever in the eyes of the citizens of the South, nor had it the capacity to give effective leadership; and, since it could not control the North, it could not provide the basis for co-operation and integrated planning in the country. The result was that the country's economic and industrial programme became confused by uncontrolled regional competition. There was no planning authority to exercise central direction over the siting of industrial projects with a view to avoiding uneconomic duplications. The delay involved in obtaining direction from the North on matters that called for prompt action increased the government's ineffectiveness. The emir's control was a kind of spanner in the wheel of progress, since their interests dictated the preservation of the *status quo*. Progress based upon socialist ideology was inimical to their interest, because it might have led to the emancipation of the Northern peasantry and to a consequent weakening of their authority over them. To strike a balance between the conflicting demands of conservatism and radicalism, the federal government settled for a policy of gradualism. But in a society where the highest premium was placed upon modernisation, a policy of gradualism was definitely out of tune, and so it was fiercely attacked not only by the radicals but by the moderate liberals as well.[40]

As disillusion over the policy of gradualism deepened, it gave rise to a mood of subversion on the part of the radicals, who appeared to have been receiving financial support from outside. The secret police were of course set upon their trail, but their inadequacy in dealing with subversion had inclined the government to contemplate preventive detention, a plan which, happily, had to be abandoned in the face of sustained public outcry.

In conclusion, it may be said that the ineffectiveness of federalism to foster national integration, stability and constitutionalism in Nigeria was the result of a combination of structural defects and an unwillingness on the part of politicans to accept its obligations. For federalism involves not only rights but also obligations of mutual tolerance and self-restraint, which alone make co-operation and co-existence possible in a plural society.[41]

REFERENCES

1. See below.
2. *Land and People in Nigeria*, 1955, p. 94.
3. 1952 Census figures.
4. For such an exaggerated account of the minorities' plight, see Arikpo, *The Development of Modern Nigeria*, 1967, pp. 87 *et seq*.
5. Report, Cmnd. 505 (1958).
6. See Nwabueze, *Constitutional Law of the Nigerian Republic*, 1964, pp. 405-6, pp. 434-40.
7. See s. 5 (5), Constitution of the Federation, 1963, empowering Parliament to make laws for the peace, order and good government of the new region for six months after its creation.
8. See Report, Owegbe Cult Commission of Inquiry, Printing Division, Ministry of Information, Benin City, 1966.
9. Report, *op. cit.*, p. 95.
10. Federal Government, 4th ed., pp. 50-1. The quotation from John Stuart Mill is from *Representative Government* (Everyman ed., pp. 367-8).
11. Minorities Commission Report, Cmnd. 505, 1958, p. 85.
12. *Ibid.*, p. 86.
13. 1952 Census.
14. Bretton, *Power and Stability in Nigeria*, 1962, p. 124. See also Tansey and Kermode, 'The Westminster Model in Nigeria,' 1968, Parliamentary Affairs, for an equally critical viewpoint.

15. Report, *op. cit.*
16. *New Federations: Experiments in the Commonwealth*, 1966, p. 183.
17. *Op. cit.*, pp. 174-5.
18. Art. 131 (2).
19. *Cf.* Art. 79, Constitution of Malaya, 1957.
20. See McWhinney, *Comparative Federalism*, 2nd ed., particularly Ch. VII.
21. Executive powers were defined to be co-extensive with the legislative. This is the usual practice in most federations, but see India and Malaysia.
22. Contrast India and Malaysia which have three lists – federal, regional and concurrent lists.
23. Later renamed the National Council of Nigerian Citizens after the excision of the Cameroons.
24. An organisation of the same name had been formed in London earlier in 1945 by Obafemi Awolowo.
25. Report, Cmnd. 3131, 1928, p. 39. This remark was made with reference to communal representation in Ceylon.
26. *Africa: the Politics of Independence*, 1961, p. 95, p. 97, and p. 99. For the use of this argument to support the one-party state, see Ch. VI below.
27. *New Federations: Experiments in the Commonwealth*, 1966, p. 337.
28. The Nigerian National Democratic Party formed by Chief Akintola in 1964.
29. UPGA, i.e. The United Progressive Grand Alliance, was the name of the alliance of the NCNC and the AG.
30. Ahmadu Bello, *My Life*, 1962.
31. Northern Nigeria Parliamentary Debates, House of Assembly Official Report, Session 1964-5 (Govt. Printer, 1965).
32. *Ibid.*
33. Acquisition of title of ownership was out of the question for both natives and non-natives alike.
34. Debates, *op. cit.*
35. For the history of revenue allocation, see Arikpo, *op. cit.*, pp. 96-103.
36. Nwabueze, *Constitutional Law of the Nigerian Republic*, p. 174.
37. *Constitutionalism for Emergent Political Order*, p. 28.
38. For details, see Mackintosh, *Nigerian Government and Politics*, 1967, perhaps the most exhaustive account; Schwarz, *Nigeria*, 1966; Nwankwo and Ifejika, *The Making of a Nation: Biafra*, 1969.
39. This was also part of the motive behind the federal ratification of the amendment to the constitution of Western Nigeria which nullified the decision of the Privy Council upholding the validity of Chief Akintola's dismissal as premier by the Governor.
40. See Bretton, *op. cit.*
41. McWhinney, *Comparative Federalism*, 2nd ed., pp. 85, 100.

CHAPTER VI

THE PRACTICE OF CONSTITUTIONALISM IN EMERGENT STATES GENERALLY

Experience has amply demonstrated that the greatest danger to constitutional government in emergent states arises from the human factor in politics, from the capacity of politicians to distort and vitiate whatever governmental forms may be devised. Institutional forms are of course important, since they can guide for better or for worse the behaviour of the individuals who operate them. Yet, however carefully the institutional forms may have been constructed, in the final analysis, much more will turn upon the actual behaviour of these individuals – upon their willingness to observe the rules, upon a statesmanlike acceptance that the integrity of the whole governmental framework and the regularity of its procedures should transcend any personal aggrandisement. The successful working of any constitution depends upon what has aptly been called the 'democratic spirit', that is, a spirit of fair play, of self-restraint and of mutual accommodation of differing interests and opinions. There can be no constitutional government unless the wielders of power are prepared to observe the limits upon governmental powers. Already in the preceding chapters we have seen how political corruption and the waste and inefficiency which it engenders have undermined the ability of the government to secure the welfare of the people, tainting the state in the public eye as an instrument of plunder and thereby alienating the people's loyalty; how tribal politics has, like a canker, eaten into the body politic, sapping its vital energies and the entire fabric of society, pitching tribe against tribe in mutual antagonism, making impossible the development of a national spirit. All these were but a manifestation of one cardinal evil, namely, the struggle for political power and the unwillingness of the rulers in emergent states to relinquish it. Once in, they keep a tight hold upon the reins of power. As a result the society tends to become stratified into a permanent class of rulers on the one hand and ruled on the other. The aim of this chapter is to discuss the methods adopted to achieve the perpetuation of their power by the rulers and the underlying reasons for it.

Perversion of the Processes and Institutions of Constitutional Government

Liberty, it has been stated, is the substantive core of constitutionalism, and liberty in political matters means freedom to propagate political ideas and to organise politically even in opposition to the government; it means freedom in an electorate to choose who should govern, a choice which can be effectively exercised only where political parties are free to organise and to compete with one another for the favour of the electorate. But political liberty and a desire and determination by the rulers to perpetuate their rule are mutually exclusive. The latter can be achieved only by stifling opposition, especially organised opposition. The methods adopted to this end vary between outright suppression or absorption of organised opposition and its toleration under conditions which make it virtually impossible for it to be effective. All emergent countries practise one or other method. The former, being openly avowed and somewhat more repressive, has caught the attention and therefore the condemnation of the Western World much more readily. The insidiousness of the latter has enabled the countries which practice it to retain the public image of a practising democracy. Thus, until the final collapse in 1966, Nigeria had been able to beguile the Western World as a bastion of democracy in Africa. Insofar as there was some scope for independent political action which permitted parties and trade unions to be organised and dissident opinions to be voiced without fear of outright suppression or of preventive detention without trial, there was perhaps some justification for treating Nigeria as a noble exception in a continent where the one-party state and preventive detention hold the stage. But it was unmerited to have regarded it as a bastion of democracy in Africa, unless one meant to be cynical in the sense that in the country of the blind the one-eyed man is king. As, however, Nigeria was held up as a model of constitutional democracy in Africa, perhaps an account of its practice there will provide a fair measure of democratic behaviour in those parts of the emergent world where constitutional democracy still maintains a precarious existence. The conditions in the one-party states will be considered later.

In perpetuating their rule and thereby incapacitating or enfeebling the opposition, the ruling parties in Nigeria had used three main instruments of perversion: political coercion, electoral malpractices and the undermining of the individual right of speech and assembly.

(i) *Political coercion*

Ruling parties came to power in the first instance by persuading the electorate to vote for them, but once elected they harnessed, in the interval before the next election, all the forces at the disposal of government, to coerce dissident groups and individuals into supporting them. Victimisation, discrimination and actual physical violence were the familiar techniques. A community which voted against the government party or was otherwise known to have opposition sympathy would be victimised: its roads would be left to deteriorate, its sons and daughters would be denied scholarships, and development projects would be sited outside its area. As for individuals, opposition meant denial of jobs, contracts, loans for industrial or agricultural enterprise or even licences for certain occupations, such as the brewing and sale of native liquor; it might also mean heavy tax assessment and the imposition of heavy fines for default.

In the field of local government, perhaps the most fertile ground for political coercion, the institution of chieftaincy, which in many parts of the country still exercises a powerful influence in local affairs, was the first to be assaulted. The chief, now subordinated to the central power of the modern state, was coerced into exerting the influence and authority of his office on behalf of the ruling party. He was required to become the partisan agent of the party in power. Should he prove defiant or even unamenable, he might be exiled from his domain, as were the Alafin of Oyo and the Emir of Kano, or he might have his salary cut off or reduced to a penny a year, as happened frequently in Western Nigeria. Even the custom prescribing succession to chieftaincies was sometimes arbitrarily altered in order to disentitle families with known opposition sympathies. Not unnaturally perhaps, most chiefs considered it expedient to support the party in power, using all their traditional authority and influence to rally their subjects to the support of the government of the day, some going so far as to identify completely their office and its authority with the ruling party. Thus was the chief perverted from being the father of all his subjects into a partisan politician, inevitably losing much of the respect and sanctity traditionally attached to the office.

It may be said that local government in Southern Nigeria was concerned more with power politics than with the improvement of the local communities. This was perhaps partly the outcome of the introduction of exotic forms of local government, based upon democratically elected councils, the so-called 'local democracy,'[1] which grew out of the nationalist antipathy and agitation against local rule by traditional authorities as institutionalised by the indirect rule system. Elected local councils had tended to be mere local extensions of the regional political parties, reproducing within themselves all the bickerings that characterised the latter. The administration of local government, and in particular staff appointments and the distribution of amenities, was viewed as a patronage to be exploited for political ends. Where a council was controlled by an opposition party, the work of the council might be paralysed by undue interference by the regional government. In the Western Region, the usual technique was to institute an inquiry into the affairs of such councils, using the findings of the inquiry, which invariably were severely adverse, as a ground for dissolving the councils and replacing them by caretaker and management committees made up entirely of members drawn from the government party.

Political coercion was carried even into the civil service,[1] universally recognised as the mainstay of constitutional government, and which for that reason should be kept free from political influence. Nigerian politicians, it has been said, 'expect the bureaucracy to be a tool in the power process, including those outside the limits of legality, propriety and legitimacy. Thus, in spite of all the formal declarations and paper pronouncements, the bureaucracy is expected to be instrumental – or, at least, not to be an obstacle – in the acquisition of individual power or of group power.'[2] To this end civil servants were subjected to various types of pressure, including the threat of removal. Many, anxious for the favour of politicians, succumbed all too readily, becoming the agents of politicians; some, thinking it impolitic to resist, complied grudgingly, but quite a few stuck to the ideals of their profession and were victimised in consequence. Although the Constitution vested the appointment, promotion and disciplinary control of the civil service in an independent public service commission, these were never in fact free from policitical influence. Promotions to top positions in the service depended upon having the right political connections. There was often a disregard of the right code of behaviour governing the relationship between ministers and their civil service advisers. Particularly was this the case where the civil service expert had been unwilling to be used as a party tool. In such cases the civil servant was side-tracked and decisions were taken directly by the minister on matters which called for expert study and advice.

The extreme form of political coercion was violence. Violence was indeed a pervasive feature of Nigerian politics. Each party kept a band of thugs or party stalwarts, whose job was to act as bodyguards to top politicians and as depredators to keep party waverers in line and to make life uncomfortable for opponents. These party 'strong-arm men' were recruited mostly from the class of the unemployed, hooligans and ne'er-do-wells, and their activities gave politics a singularly ugly flavour. Operating, not as individuals, but as an organised body – the so-called youth or militant wing of the political parties – they were particularly effective, and constituted a kind of organised striking, though undisciplined, force. For the NCNC, there were the Zikist National Vanguard, whose organisation and operations were nationwide, the Okpara Youth Brigade and the Osadennis Crusade which served the Eastern and Mid-Western branches of the party respectively. The Action Group had the Awo National Brigade. The depredations of these gangs were in evidence mostly at public meetings and at election times. They would break up meetings, beating up opponents. At elections, when they were at their worst, they would create a great deal of sound and fury, intimidating opponents and sometimes even burning down houses, cars and other properties belonging to opponents. They might even abduct or kill opposition candidates or their nominators. When two opposing gangs of thugs encountered each other, something like a running battle sometimes ensued, and it was not unknown for firearms to be used.

In this nefarious work of coercion, the thugs of the ruling parties were aided and given the shelter of the law by the police and the native or customary courts. Police raids on the homes of political opponents and prosecutions on trumped-up charges were familiar techniques of political coercion. The high-water mark of police involvement in partisan politics appeared to have been reached in the Western Region in the years following Chief Akintola's restoration to the premiership after the emergency administration by the federal government in 1962. The police provided the necessary coercive support for Chief Akintola's precarious authority, they sheltered his offending supporters, and even collaborated actively in the electoral fraud of 1965. Several bundles of ballot papers deposited with the police authorities for safe custody were later discovered to have been taken from there and dumped into the boxes of the government party candidates. Among the known supporters of the ruling parties were some top police officers; senior police appointments were politically influenced for party advantage, although a supposedly independent appointing agency, the police service commission, was established by the constitution for the purpose. Political control was all but complete in the case of the local police which, as part of the machinery for local government, came under the local authorities, the native authorities in the North and local councils in the West and Mid-West,[3] which, as previously stated, were the local arms of the parties controlling the regional governments. In the North in particular the native authority police were hardly separable from the professional party thugs, with whom they closely collaborated in the intimidation, arbitrary mass arrests and detention, lynching and other acts of persecution of party opponents.

The native or customary courts were anything but a haven of judicial impartiality. They belonged indeed to the political rather than the judicial arm of the administration. Appointments to their benches were part of the political patronage at the dispensation of the ruling politicians. Thus, although native or customary court judges were supposed to be appointed by the native authority or local government service boards, the boards exercised scarcely any discretion in the matter, being obliged to appoint only those recommended to them by the politicians. Merit or suitability was thus sacrificed to political consideration. As political appointees, the judges felt themselves in loyalty bound to the ruling party; they considered their appointments as requiring them to use the machinery of the courts to support the authority of the party. There was here a complete fusion of the judiciary with the executive. The result was that in matters in which the ruling party was interested, no pretence at judicial impartiality was made. This abuse of the judicial machinery was of course more blatant in some areas than in others. In the North particularly, native court judges often behaved just like NPC party functionaries, openly bullying and victimising party opponents and letting it be known that they were doing so because the victims belonged to the wrong political party. In the Mid-West, too, certain customary court presidents used the machinery of their court to coerce people to join the Owegbe Society, the militant wing of the NCNC (Etu-Edo).

The extent of political interference in the higher judiciary is difficult to assess. Before 1963 judges were in no way dependent upon the politicians as regards either appointment or dismissal. Their appointment was by an independent judicial service commission, composed almost entirely of judges, while their dismissal lay with the Judicial Committee of the Privy Council in London after investigation and recommendation by a local judicial tribunal. Under the constitution their salary was charged permanently on the Consolidated Revenue Fund, and was thus removed from parliamentary discussion and action. In October 1963 the republican constitution altered the position by vesting the appointment and dismissal of judges in the premier and parliament respectively in place of the judicial bodies in whom the power had earlier been lodged. It must be admitted that since the change there had been no case of dismissal, and equally no evidence of politically-motivated appointments, except for the chief justice in Western Nigeria, but then the nomination of a chief justice had always, even before 1963, been the prerogative of the premier.

That there had been no dismissals and no political appointments since the new constitution is by no means conclusive of the absence or existence of political influence in the judiciary. One has also to consider the psychological effect upon a judge of the possibility that the political power of dismissal might be used against him should he prove an obstacle to the party in power. In the political atmosphere existing in Nigeria between 1962 and 1966, the ruling politicians would have stopped at nothing to perpetuate their rule, and a judge who stood in the way of the realisation of this objective would quite readily have been axed. In these circumstances it would have required an uncommonly brave judge to pronounce against the government in a matter in which its vital political interests were involved, such as the question concerning the constitutionality of Balewa's federal government after the 1964 election or of Akintola's government in Western Nigeria after the regional election in 1965. On this ground alone, whatever might have been the reason for it, the abolition of the independent appointing and dismissal machinery was objectionable.

Of actual political interference, the evidence was rather scanty, and was confined largely to Western Nigeria. At the centre the only event that might be interpreted as political interference, though of an indirect kind, was the prime minister's expression of resentment in 1964 over the court's decision invalidating the main operative provisions of the Commission and Tribunals of Enquiry Act, 1961. This had frustrated the inquiry which the Federal Government had proposed to conduct into the affairs of the National Bank, an Action-Group-sponsored bank. The prime minister had then reproached the courts for making a mockery of themselves in allowing their process to be used for 'minor things.' It is lamentable that the prime minister on this occasion should have departed from his known quality of self-restraint, and permitted himself the indiscretion of such a statement, but it cannot have had much effect on the judiciary.

It was in Western Nigeria after 1963 that politics made a noticeable intrusion into the judiciary. The precariousness of Chief Akintola's post-emergency administration had predisposed him to exert an increasing amount of pressure on the judiciary. An astute politician, Chief Akintola knew that the support of the judiciary was necessary in dealing with the more popularly based opposition party. His continuance in office could only be secured by a wholesale rigging of the election then impending in the region, and a compliant judiciary was necessary for the success of his plan to rig the election. To this end, he appointed as chief justice of the region a judge, Mr. Justice Morgan, whose support for the government proved unflagging. So very well had the new chief justice fulfilled the expectations of his political sponsors that he had to be retired from the bench by the military rulers after the coup of January 1966. The extent of the pressure on the judges can be judged by the statement of one of them, Mr. Justice Oyemade, in the course of the trial of some opposition party supporters for the murder of a government party supporter. He said:

> 'I will not allow myself to be intimidated into sending innocent persons to jail. Even if this means losing my job, I am still sure of leading a decent life. The only thing we have now in this country is the judiciary. We have seen politicians changing from one policy to another and one party to another, but the only protection the ordinary people have against all these inconsistencies is a fearless and upright judiciary.'

It would be unfair to lay the blame for the intrusion of politics into the judiciary on the politicians alone. For some of the judges themselves were personally involved in politics. Political involvement by judges had of course to be carefully masked, but it was nonetheless noticeable. The cultural organisations provided the convenient platform. Their objective being ostensibly cultural, the judges could with a good claim to propriety belong to them, yet, as was well-known, some of the so-called cultural organisations were not only affiliated to the major political parties but also served as a kind of bureau where high political policy and strategy were decided, thus providing spiritual leadership for the parties.

It is against this background of personal involvement in politics that some of the decisions of the Nigerian courts have to be viewed. It is perhaps remarkable that, with but one exception, all the cases arising from the crises in the country went in favour of the government. There is no suggestion here that every one of these decisions was necessarily wrong in law. However, that they should all have gone in favour of the government was, as has been observed, remarkable, and naturally created the impression of political bias. People began to feel, rightly or wrongly, that the justice administered in the courts was influenced by extra-legal considerations, by political or sectional interests; that its aim was not to uphold the law but to repress interests opposed to the government. The situation was all the more lamentable because most of the decisions concerned individual civil liberties. To what purpose, people were prompted to ask, were civil liberties guaranteed in the constitution if every violation of them, however seemingly flagrant, received the sanction of the courts? It began to look as if the courts were actively aiding the politicians in the persecution of opponents and in the perversion of the constitution. Confidence in their ability to decide political issues impartially had consequently been undermined, until eventually there was a general disinclination to take political complaints to them. To go to court on such matters was felt to be a vain effort, since by past experience a decision in favour of the government was considered a foregone conclusion. Moreover, the over-confident way in which the ruling politicians sometimes challenged opponents to take their complaints to the courts, as if to say they had been assured the courts would never decide against them, helped to sap still further public confidence in the courts.

This situation represented a real tragedy in Nigeria's experiment in constitutional government. For it is not enough that the judiciary, as the guardian of the constitution and of the people's rights, should be impartial; it is equally important that it should be seen to be so. Whatever the quality of its decisions in point of law, it can command no respect or acceptability if the public has no confidence in it, because of the known political involvement of its members or because of their sympathy or subservience to ruling politicians. And when things have come to such a pass that people with genuine grievances against the government are no longer willing to have recourse to the courts for redress, then that is the end of constitutional government, and the stage is set for anarchy. The tragic experience of Western Nigeria in 1965 bears testimony to this. Convinced that they would get no justice from the courts for the rape of their right to choose who should govern them – Chief Adegbenro, leader of the Action Group and the legitimate winner of the election, had been forced by Chief Justice Morgan to re-nounce the executive council which he had formed or go to prison – the people of Western Nigeria naturally resorted to violence as the only remedy open to them in the circumstances. For the them law and its guardians had lost their title to obedience and must give way to the rule of the jungle in which right had to be vindicated by might in its crudest, most uninhibited form.

Turning to the military, they can be said to have had the rare distinction of non-partisanship. They had had of course to be used to deal with the Tiv riots in 1960 and 1964 and with the disturbances in Western Nigeria in 1965, but, except for an excess of zeal dis-played by a few officers in the discharge of the duties, which might suggest a political motivation, their conduct on all these occasions left nothing for which they could be reproached. It was the federal election crisis of 1964 that attempted to suck them into the vortex of partisan politics. Fortunately, in the event, it became unnecessary for them to take a stand one way or the other in the conflict. This is not, however, to say that the army had escaped completely from political influence. It would have been surprising if it had. This was particularly evident in matters of appointment and promotion of the officer corps, where a quota system was applied to arrest, and ultimately, it was hoped, to reverse the predominance which the South had enjoyed by virtue of its educational superiority. Political influence was also the decisive factor in the location in the North of most of the country's military installations, equipment, factories and training institutions.

(ii) *Electoral malpractices*

Absolutely free elections are a dream in the developing countries, even under colonial conditions. In an atmosphere charged with so much heat and passion, with party thugs intimidating and beating up opponents, and an electorate ready to sell their votes to the highest bidder, free elections are largely an illusion. For the opposition parties, election campaigning was difficult; they might be denied permits to hold campaign meetings at all. But it was during the federal election of 1964 and the 1965 Western Region election that electoral malpractices assumed a proportion perhaps unequalled anywhere else in the world.

The federal election of 1964 was the fiercest the country had ever had. The NPC-NCNC coalition which had ruled the country since 1959 had now fallen apart, and each party had chosen a new bed-fellow for the purpose of the election and was determined to exert itself to the utmost to win it. The new alliances were the Nigerian National Alliance (NNA) between the NPC and Chief Akintola's NNDP, and the United Progressive Grand Alliance (UPGA) between the NCNC and the AG. Each party professed its desire to make the contest free and fair. At a conference of all the parties convened by the prime minister, agreements were reached on measures to be taken to ensure that the election would be conducted in a peaceful atmosphere: bans on processions and public meetings were to be lifted; discrimination in the grant of permits for election meetings was to be removed, while each party undertook to restrain its thugs. None of these agreements was ever observed. The UPGA complained that it had been unable to campaign in the North owing to the refusal of the Native Authorities to grant permits for campaign meetings, and to the mass arrest of their campaigners and agents for allegedly holding meetings without permits and for other trumped-up charges. A new element had also been introduced into the election. The technique was to get as many government party candidates as possible returned unopposed by preventing the opposition parties from filing nomination papers within the prescribed time. This result was achieved by abducting opposition candidates and their nominators and putting them away until the nomination time expired. In this way the NPC was able to get sixty of its candidates returned unopposed. In a documented memorandum submitted to the president of the republic, supported by sworn affidavits from the victims, the UPGA listed specific cases of intimidation, lynching, arbitrary arrest and imprisonment, abduction and other acts of persecution committed against its members by the NPC and its agents, and demanded the postponement of the election. When it failed to get the elections postponed, the UPGA decided to boycott them, but in spite of the boycott the elections went on in the Northern and Western Regions where the NNA governments were in control, and also in the federal territory of Lagos. The boycott was thus effective only in the East and Mid-West, the areas controlled by the NCNC. In the West the boycott enabled the NNDP to win the election as it were by default, with votes so low in many places as to make a mockery of the whole exercise. In the North too the NPC swept through virtually all the constituencies.

The techniques used in the Western Region election of 1965 were more brazen than those of 1964. The returning officers provided the main tool. Many deserted their posts after accepting nomination papers from government party candidates, thereby making it impossible for opposition candidates to file their own. Or, if a returning officer remained at his post he might refuse to accept an opposition candidate's nomination paper on some alleged technical fault. A returning officer refusing to desert his post might be abducted after having received the government candidate's nomination. And lastly returning officers who had accepted nomination papers from opposition candidates and even issued certificates of validity had their appointments revoked, and their successors refused to recognise the validity of such certificates or to accept new nomination papers. By these means, the ruling party, the NNDP, was able at the close of the nominations to get as many as sixteen candidates declared unopposed. Then there was the illegal trafficking in ballot papers by the government party agents. Mention has already been made of large bundles of ballot papers deposited with the police for safe keeping, and which eventually found their way into the boxes of government candidates. Wads of ballot papers were also found in the possession of unauthorised persons. When all this failed and an opposition candidate was elected, the result might be reversed in favour of the defeated government candidate who would then be promptly announced on the government radio as the winner. 'The most notorious example of this travesty was the case of a man who won the election in one of the Owo constituencies. His opponent was declared the victor. He thereupon announced that he had decided to join the NNDP. A few days after this announcement, the Electoral Commission declared him the successful candidate and quietly dropped his opponent.'[4] Before the election the regional premier, Chief Akintola, had boasted that 'whether the people voted for them or not, the NNDP would be returned to power.' And so it was, though the party had thereby overreached itself. For rather than swallow such an injury to their right to choose who should govern them, the people of Western Nigeria took the law into their own hands and launched a régime of violence and arson that held the region in its bloody grip until the military take-over of Janaury 1966 intervened to flush out the politicians.

Thus, by the closing year of the Nigerian First Republic the institution of free elections, that cornerstone of democracy, had ceased to have any meaning in Nigeria, so blatantly had it been perverted. The real tragedy of the matter was not so much that the government party had won an election by rigging as that faith in free elections had been killed not just for the present but for the future as well. As long as an election posed any possibility of defeat for the government, the same perverse techniques, perfected at every turn, would again be called into use to avert the imminence of defeat.

(iii) *Undermining of freedom of the press and of assembly*

We have seen that the freedom to form political organisations guaranteed by the constitution had been rendered almost nugatory by the intolerance of the ruling parties. With regard to the two other political freedoms, freedom of the press and of assembly, the attitude of the ruling parties was hardly less intolerant. A rather stringent sedition law, defined without reference to the tendency to violence of words alleged to be seditious, was used to discourage criticism of the government. A heritage from the colonial past, the law was designed to strengthen the hands of the colonial government in dealing with the possibility that a handful of educated nationalists might incite the gullible populace to hatred, disloyalty or violence against the government. Because of the easy excitability of illiterate peasants and the bitter emotions which imperialism is apt to generate in the minds of colonial peoples, it was thought unnecessary that words alleged to be seditious should have a tendency to provoke violence, as is the case in English law. As was to be anticipated, the colonial administration found it necessary to make rather ample use of the law, particularly against the militant Zikists of the forties. On the attainment of independence by Nigeria under a constitution which guaranteed freedom of speech, it was thought that the law could no longer be applied in the same rigorous manner as under the colonial régime.

In 1961 Dr. Chike Obi, leader of the minority Dynamic Party, published a pamphlet, entitled *The People: Facts that you must know*, in which appeared the words: 'Down with the enemies of the people, the exploiters of the weak and the oppressors of the poor . . . the days of those who have enriched themselves at the expense of the poor are numbered.' Dr. Obi was charged with having published these words with intent to excite hatred, contempt and disaffection against the federal government. To this he replied that, having regard to the guarantee of freedom of speech in the constitution, it was not reasonably justifiable in a democratic society to punish a man for making a statement which merely exposed the government to discredit or ridicule or disaffection, without any repercussion on public order or security. Dr. Obi's attack on the government appeared clearly to have been intended simply to induce the people not to vote for it at the next election. Nevertheless he was convicted and his appeal to the supreme court was dismissed. In 1962 Professor Oyenuga and Drs. Aluko and Odumosu were also prosecuted and convicted for articles written by them suggesting that the findings of the Coker Inquiry into the activities of certain statutory corporations in Western Nigeria were designed to implicate only loyal members of the Action Group. These prosecutions created the feeling of an unwarranted interference with the individual's freedom of speech. The suggestion in the articles might have been indiscreet, but its tendency to violence or disorder was pretty remote, if not altogether non-existent.

In 1964 the freedom of the press was further eroded by the Newspaper Amendment Act which made it an offence for anyone to publish in any newspaper any statement, rumour or report, knowing or having reason to believe that such statement, rumour or report was false. Knowledge of the falsity of the statement was to be presumed against the publisher unless he proved that, prior to publication, he took reasonable measures to verify its accuracy. While it is no doubt desirable that newspapers should be restrained from wilfully disseminating lies, the new law imposed very serious limitations upon newspaper reportage, since no newspaper in Nigeria could afford to post field reporters in every part of the country to check upon the truth of every report. Besides, the truth of alleged political persecution or electoral malpractices might be difficult to prove. And so it was that the rigging of the 1964 federal elections failed to get adequate newspaper coverage.

The press itself had been aptly described as a 'captive'. It had never had much independence or freedom either. All but one of the so-called national newspapers were owned and financed by one or other of the governments or by the ruling parties: the *Daily Express* by the AG, *The Outlook* by the East Regional government, the *New Nigerian* by the North Regional government, the *Morning Post* and *Sunday Post* by the federal government. The *Pilot*, though privately owned, originated as and had remained an organ of the NCNC. The federal and regional broadcasting and television services were also state-owned. Ownership and financial control implied dependence in matters of policy and news coverage. Only such news as was in accordance with the wishes of the ruling parties was broadcast or published. There was no question of any newspaper or other news medium taking a line that was independent of, not to say adverse to, the government or party that owned it. The function of the press was first and foremost to advertise the owning government or party, and to boost its public image and popularity. Criticism was a secondary role, and when considered desirable or expedient by the political bosses, was confined to the activities of competing governments or parties in other regions, or at the centre, or of political opponents within the region. Even as so confined, much of the criticism was pure sensationalism, often motivated by tribal interest and lacking in objectivity and depth. The poor quality of journalism was partly a result of the fact that, until recently, most of the press staff in Nigeria had little education or experience, and were largely ignorant of what their job required of them; their main preoccupation was with political or private financial gain, which rendered them easily amenable to perversion. The most scandalous instance of perversion of the truth in news reportage was of course during the 1965 election in Western Nigeria when both the federal and regional broadcasting services daily blared out fraudulent results issued by Chief Akintola's NNDP government. They had been instructed to take their report of the election results from Chief Akintola's office, instead of from the counting stations, and some hand-picked officials of both broadcasting services were specially detailed to 'doctor' the reports so as to ensure that they adequately projected the ruling party. The Nigerian Broadcasting Corporation Staff Association was sufficiently outraged to have issued a protest which was of course ignored.

Even the one independent daily, the *Daily Times*, was much too cautious, as shown by its 'consistent avoidance of sensitive issues, a preoccupation with the requirements of balance in the coverage of news from the three regions and the major political parties, and a reluctance to advance criticisms other than those officially inspired. Waste and corruption, for example, are discussed in detail only with regard to small, politically insigificant groups or, where politically appropriate, in connection with tribunal or court proceedings.'[5]

More rigorous, perhaps, was the control upon the freedom of assembly and procession. Between January 1961 and December 1962 public meetings and processions had been banned in Lagos for some thirteen months, either absolutely or subject to the consent of the minister being obtained, and the ban had been almost continually renewed for successive periods of two months thereafter. In most parts of Western Nigeria public meetings and processions had been banned since 1962 as a sequal to the 1962 emergency. In the North, 'it is a permanent feature of public life that freedom of assembly is a privilege, and not a natural right, reserved almost exclusively to the members of the ruling party there.'[6]

It is perhaps worth mentioning in this connection that Nigeria had come very close to becoming a régime of preventive detention. On July 20, 1963, the country was startled by the proposal that the constitution was to be amended to allow the preventive detention without trial of persons suspected of subversive activities. At the instance of the federal prime minister, the proposal had been agreed to by the three regional premiers, all of whom spoke warmly in favour of it when they arrived in Lagos a few days later for the all-party conference on a republican constitution. In the face of vehement opposition by the press, the Bar Association and the opposition party, the AG, the prime minister promptly announced that the proposal had been shelved. Yet that the matter was mooted at all was a serious indictment of the ruling politicians, revealing their inclination to arbitrary measures.

(iv) *The resultant structure of party politics*

The result of the combination of the three factors discussed above was to incapacitate the opposition parties. The ordinary man in Nigeria as elsewhere in Africa admired the strong man, the man who could provide him with the good things of life, and so it was considered pointless to support an opposition party. With every year in power the government party became stronger, while the opposition grew correspondingly weaker, with its following among the electorate progressively dwindling and many of its parliamentarians crossing the carpet to the government party. By 1965 the picture in the regions looked very much like a one-party state. In the North the opposition had been reduced to a bare handful and that government refused to recognise anyone as leader of the opposition, on the ground that the basis for such recognition is that the opposition must be of such strength in the House as to be able to form a quorum. In the East, with the flight of the leader of the opposition, Mr. S. G. Ikoku, to Ghana to avoid prosecution for treason, and the imprisonment of his deputy, Mr. E. O. Eyo, for attempted murder, the opposition all but disintegrated, so much so that it could not muster as many as four candidates for the 1964 federal elections. In the Mid-West there was by the end of 1965 only one person left in opposition. The West was in rather a special position, partly because the government party, the Action Group, had had to contend with an older and more established party, the NCNC, which capitalised on the resentment of the AG and the fear of Yoruba domination among the minority tribes of the Mid-West as well as on local rivalries among the Yorubas themselves; and partly also because of a split within the governing party in 1962. But the final picture that emerged after the crisis and the fierce political manoeuvres in the region followed much the same pattern as in other regions. The opposition was greatly emasculated, and by early 1965 had been reduced to less than a third of the House of Assembly. The achievement of this position entailed a most ruthless and brazen application of the instrument of coercion, since at its inauguration the new government party, Chief Akintola's United People's Party (UPP), had little following either in the Legislature or among the people. The party had come to life with only ten members in the house of assembly, supported by thirty-five NCNC members against sixty-five AG members. When it was announced that arrears of salaries for the period when the House was suspended during the emergency would be paid but only to supporters of Chief Akintola, AG members began to cross over to Akintola's camp. The process was facilitated by an over-generous distribution of ministerial appointments, totalling forty-nine in a House of ninety-four. By the time Chief Akintola formed his new Nigerian National Democratic Party in 1964, there remained only twenty-seven die-hard Action Groupers in the House, and four NCNC members.

Even at the federal level, the existence of a multiplicity of parties did not result from deliberate preference but from the federal system which had given rise to a competition for federal power by parties based in the regions and representing predominantly tribal interests. As has been noted, two of these parties, the NPC and NCNC were in coalition in the federal government, while the opposition AG was virtually liquidated as a political force as a punishment for its vigorous opposition to the ruling parties. A systematic act of repression whose final culmination was the displacement of the AG from its power-base in Western Nigeria had been used to achieve this result. As a result, its members in the House of Representatives, finding the hazards of opposition intolerable, began to defect to the NPC and NCNC until there were only thirteen of them left out of the seventy-five elected in 1959. The prime minister in December 1962 withdrew official recognition from such a pitiably reduced party, arguing that a handful of thirteen members could not be expected to provide an alternative government.

Conditions in the One-Party States

The picture that emerges from our account of politics in Nigeria, the reputed bastion of democracy in Africa, is that, in spite of the formal institutional structure, carefully constructed to insure constitutional government, constitutionalism had but a tenuous existence. At least one of its main restraining devices, succession of power on a regularly recurrent basis, had been completely nullified, and in its place had been established the rule in perpetuity of the same persons. It does not seem to matter very much whether the same party is successively returned to power by means of a freely and regularly conducted election, but a change in the personnel of those members who wield the power of the state is necessary. It is undesirable that the same person or group of persons should control the destiny of the nation forever. In spite of all this, however, there was still in the Nigerian situation a redeeming feature in that, although organised opposition had been systematically disabled from ever succeeding to power, individual liberty in non-political matters had remained largely unimpaired, nor had it been completely destroyed even in the political field. Opposition parties were still able to organise, and there was quite ample scope for the criticism of the government. It only becomes absurd, in the words of Carl Friedrich, 'to speak of a living constitution when in fact the very basic characteristic of a constitutional order is no longer operative, that is to say, when its regularised restraint of governmental power in the interest of protecting a personal sphere of the individual citizen and his voluntary associations is destroyed.'[7] This is the position that exists in most of the other emergent states. A single party, by virtue of being the first in the field in the nationalist movement, had been able to rally the masses to its banner to become the dominant organisation in the agitation against colonial rule. From this vantage point, it had been able, by exploiting the emotional atmosphere of the anti-colonial struggle, to assume a monopoly of political power as the colonial government gradually moved out. With the attainment of independence which consummated its power, it proceeded to make it impossible for other political parties or indeed independent voluntary organisations to operate at all.

This was the normal pattern of political development. At independence the dominant party invariably had other parties to compete with. The usual technique was to appeal to all these others to join hands with it in the supreme task of nation-building in order to save the people from the grip of poverty, disease and ignorance. The understanding that was held out was that union was not to involve the submerging of the separate identity of the other parties. But once lured into the union, the weaker parties were sooner or later swallowed up. By the absorption of its supposed partners, the dominant party now emerged as the single party. This was the manner of the origin of the single party in Guinea, Mali, Senegal, the Ivory Coast and a host of other countries. While disdaining any intention of exclusiveness, steps were nevertheless taken to eliminate opposition in both the traditional and modern sectors of the community. The chiefs were stripped of their traditional authority and turned into party agents, voluntary associations – trade unions, Youth and Women's organisations, farmers' unions, cultural organisations, etc. – were brought under the control of the party as ancillary organisations. The tentacles of the party now reached out into practically all facets of society. The electoral system might be fashioned to exclude opposition parties completely from representation in the legislative assembly. In Guinea, the Ivory Coast, Gabon, Togo, Dahomey and indeed in most of the other ex-French African territories members of the National Assembly are elected on a composite national list. Any party contesting an election has to field a complete list of candidates to be voted for, not in local constituencies, but upon a single national slate. In other words, the entire country forms, as it were, a single constituency, in which the electors vote, not for individual candidates, but for a composite list of candidates. A list that wins the majority of the votes cast gets the entire representation, even if the majority be just 50·1 per cent. By this system, the exclusion of the minority parties was made complete. For since they have no chance of winning a majority of the votes, there is no point in entering the contest at all. And what is a political party for if it cannot even win seats in the legislative assembly?

Outright suppression is the other major technique. In Dahomey two of the three main parties in the country, after merging into a single party to form the government, proscribed the third, arrested many of its members, including its leader, and then proceeded to absorb the smaller opposition parties. In the Central African Republic, the election of 1960 had been fought by two parties; six months later the winner, using the power of the government, outlawed the other, and again arrested some of its leaders. The story was the same in Upper Volta, Tanzania, Morocco, Sudan, Mauritania, Niger, Cameroon and the UAR. Prospective new parties might be suppressed even before they come into life, by the government exercising its discretion to withhold recognition under a law requiring new parties to register first with the government.

Suppression might be effected by means short of outright proscription. Of these, the most drastic is preventive detention. There are preventive detention acts in Niger, Sudan, Upper Volta, Ghana, Gabon, and Tanzania, to mention but a few. All use the power, but none so extensively as Ghana. From July 1958 when the Preventive Detention Act came into force, it was estimated that over 1,000 persons had been in preventive detention in Ghana for periods ranging up to ten years, 'in conditions of severity worse than those laid down by law and accorded to convict prisoners.'[8] The International Commission of Jurists in a report in 1961 had commented adversely on certain features of the Ghana Preventive Detention Act, notably the long duration of detention, the fact that detention was not subject to regular review, the fact that detainees were neither told the reasons for their detention nor given opportunity to face their accusers, the inadequate, often flimsy, grounds for detention, and above all, the ousting of the court's jurisdiction to inquire into the propriety of detention in individual cases.[9] 'It is impossible,' the Commission remarked in 1964, 'to see respect for human rights and the rule of law when a man may be detained for ten years without ever being accused of any crime, let alone being tried and convicted.'[10] As the detainees were mostly members of the opposition party, the effect was naturally to disorganise the party. The power of preventive detention under the Tanganyika Act is nearly as wide as in Ghana. The minister for home affairs is empowered to detain anyone at any time and for any period of time, irrespective of whether a state of emergency has been proclaimed or not. Unlike the Ghana Act, however, the Tanganyika Act requires an annual review by an Advisory Committee but the minister is not bound to accept or act upon its advice, nor can an order of detention be inquired into in any court of law. However, the Act has been used only sparingly, the most conspicuous case being the detention of the leader of the opposition party after his party had been banned in 1963.

Preventive detention has been supplemented in some places by deportations, as has been the case in Mali, Upper Volta, Guinea, Niger, Chad, Ghana and the Ivory Coast. The pretext is usually that the deportees were not native-born citizens, though the real motive was to eliminate them as political rivals. Exile has sometimes been voluntary, induced of course by a desire to escape preventive detention. Another form of physical coercion is restriction of movement. Thus the Ghana Act empowered the president to make restriction orders against anyone if he was of the opinion that preventive detention would be unsuitable 'on account of age or health or for any other reason.'

We should note that only in Ghana, Tanganyika, Malawi and Algeria is the one-party system officially instituted by the constitution. In Ghana the proposal to make the country a one-party state had been adopted in the form of a motion by the national assembly in September 1962 and was subsequently approved by the people at a referendum in January 1964, though the evidence seems to indicate that the plebiscite had been rigged to produce an affirmative vote.[11] The result of the referendum was later incorporated into the constitution by an amendment of January 31, 1964. Section 1A of the amended constitution provided that 'in conformity with the interests, welfare and aspirations of the people, and in order to develop the organisational initiative and political activity of the people, there shall be one national party, which shall be the vanguard of the people in their struggle to build a socialist society and which shall be the leading core of all organisation of the people.' It then proclaimed the Convention People's Party (CPP) the national party. In Tanganyika it was the National Executive of the ruling party which, by a resolution of January 1963, originated the proposal that Tanganyika should become a one-party state. Subsequently, a new constitution, based upon the recommendations of a presidential commission set up in February 1964, was passed by the national assembly in July 1965, making Tanzania a one-party state.

Now although the single party has become an integral part of the machinery of control, perhaps the most important instrument of mass control, it is not, except in Guinea, Mali, Niger, Tanganyika and Ghana, above the government. It serves, however, as the main link between the government and people, providing a channel through which government is kept informed of the wishes and mood of the people, and its decisions and policies transmitted and explained to them. 'The mass party is looked on in Guinea, as in

Tunisia, the Ivory Coast, Senegal, and Tanganyika, as the purveyor of plans and precepts, the stimulator of new projects, the educator of the young and of the peasants, and the emancipator of women.'[12]

One-party government has tended in almost every case to produce one-man rule. Since it imposes a unity of purpose among the government, the assembly and the party, the leader becomes *the* political power in the country, presiding over the state and party as chief executive, legislator and party boss. As a leading Ivory Coast politician explained, 'this is why you find at the head of the government a chief, Houphouet-Boigny; at the head of the elected bodies a leader, Houphouet-Boigny; at the head of the party a president, Houphouet-Boigny.'[13] Even in countries like Guinea and Mali, where the emphasis is on the primacy of the party and collective leadership, in practice government tends to become personalised around the figure of the leader.[14] So also in Senegal where before the new Constitution of March 1963, the president had rather limited powers, in reality President Leopold Senghor, as leader of the Senegalese people and Secretary-General of the ruling party, was the virtual sole ruler of the country. 'Nothing can be done in Senegal against his open opposition. One can even imagine that with the support of the masses (which he has acquired completely) Senghor imposes his point of view on the other branches of the government. Endowed by the constitution with the feeble powers of a president of the French Fourth Republic, in fact he wields the authority of a de Gaulle.'[15] The personalisation of rule results from the need to legitimise the régime. Government is a mere abstraction, incomprehensible to the masses, but a national leader is visible to them. The idea then in making him an incarnation of the state is to create a visible focus of loyalty. 'The personalisation of loyalties and movements,' writes Rupert Emerson, 'must be attributed in large part to the lack of political experience and sophistication of the mass of the people who require the personal figure of a leader to bring political abstractions down to the level of comprehensible reality.'[16]

One-party government, with its corollary of one-man rule, not only negates freedom of individual action which is the cardinal element in the whole concept of limited government, but also erodes the supporting mechanisms of constitutional government. Where an electorate has no choice between competing sets of candidates, what role could an election have in sanctioning the accountability of the rulers to the governed? Furthermore, to whatever extent powers may have been separated in the constitution, could this be effective in practice, given the absolute control of the legislative and executive organs by a single party and the unity of goals which this imposes upon these organs? An election under such a system, whatever other functions it may perform,[17] cannot enable the electorate to throw out a government of whose policies it disapproves. Abstention from voting is the only avenue whereby those who disapprove of the government can register their disapproval, but even silent opposition is looked upon with disfavour. Voting is proclaimed a civic duty, and abstention is a betrayal. Great effort is thus expended to instil into the electorate a sense of their civic responsibility in this matter in order to induce them to turn out *en masse* to cast their votes. It is hardly surprising that in many of these countries, the turn-out often exceeds ninety per cent.[18] The assembly's role in legislation cannot be more than a formality. Zolberg records that in the Ivory Coast 'during the twenty months of the life of the Assembly elected in 1959 unanimity prevailed. Seldom was there any debate on the floor. At no time were more than three votes cast against a government proposal.'[19] It is in the *Bureau Politique* of the party, which includes most of the government and the officers of the assembly, that decisions are often made. 'Individual deputies have no business trying to discuss them in the assembly because rhetoric is a waste of time and could even be harmful.'[20] The deputy is perceived more in the role of a social figure, providing leadership within his local community in the drive towards modernisation. His is the job of educating the peasantry on how to improve their farming methods, and how to improve themselves and their standard of living generally.

It is conceded that these one-party governments are not dictatorial or totalitarian régimes, since, unlike one-party states in Eastern Europe, they are genuine mass parties, are responsive to the wishes of the people, and permit a certain measure of consultation and discussion preliminary to the formation of policies.[21] These consultations and discussions, providing as they do a broad base of popular participation and consent, enable differing views to be aired and the leaders to be informed of the popular sentiment. Yet the character of the régime is clearly authoritarian. For when once a decision has been taken at the highest level after such consultations and discussions, no further debates or criticisms are permitted, since that can only impede the effectiveness of the government. Deviations are severely punished by expulsion from the party, by imprisonment or by other means. There seems to be, in some of the countries, a genuine concern to maintain the rule of law. But, 'while in external appearance it is a government of law rather than of men, these laws, including the constitution itself, have been tailored to suit a specific set of governors and can easily be altered at their discretion.'[22]

Reasons for the Trend towards Authoritarianism and the Perpetual Rule of One Party

The desire of the ruling parties in emergent nations to perpetuate their rule by the elimination of every kind of opposition has naturally prompted much questioning as to possible motivation or justification for it. The explanation undoubtedly involves a complex of motives and ideologies, but perhaps the most operative factor is the primacy accorded to politics in these countries – the politics of power, sheer, naked power to rule for the benefit of one's self-aggrandisement and of one's group. Politics is the all-in-all in these countries, the supreme object of human existence. 'Seek ye first the political kingdom,' said Kwame Nkrumah, 'and all things else shall be added unto you.' Of course a personal love of power has always been the prime motive in politics everywhere, but in under-developed countries power offers the opportunity of a lifetime to rise above the general poverty and squalor that pervades the entire society. It provides a rare opportunity to acquire wealth and prestige, to be able to distribute benefits in the form of jobs, contracts, scholarships and gifts of money and so on to one's relatives and friends. These are very high stakes indeed in a country where money and jobs are scarce. What else could one expect when 'men who have been denied responsibility for too long, who have experienced humiliations because of the colour of their skins, who have been told that they are too immature to be entrusted with real authority, who have perhaps spent most of their lives in a condition of relative poverty, find themselves in power, dispensing favours, making big decisions, giving orders to European civil servants, addressing enthusiastic mass meetings, listened to with apparently respectful attention at international gatherings, received at the White House and the Kremlin as distinguished visitors, and also enjoying the seductive material perquisites of high office.'[23] Describing these material perquisites, Arthur Lewis, in his *Politics in West Africa*, writes:

'The power is incredible. Most West African ministers consider themselves to be above the law, and are treated as such by the police . . . The prestige is also incredible. Men who claim to be democrats in fact behave like emperors. Personifying the state, they dress themselves up in uniforms, build themselves palaces, bring all other traffic to a standstill when they drive, hold fancy parades and generally demand to be treated like Egyptian

Pharaohs. And the money is also incredible. Successful politicians receive, even if only elected to Parliament, salaries two to four times as high as they previously earned, plus *per diem* allowances, travelling expenses and other fringe benefits. There are also vast opportunities for pickings in bribes, state contracts, diversion of public funds to private uses, and commissions of various sorts.'[24]

It is not surprising then that, with so much hanging upon power, the politicians in the emergent countries should want to stick to power indefinitely once they have acquired it. Much as some of them admire democracy as an ideology of government, the wealth and prestige of power are far too great to be sacrificed upon its altar. It is thus impossible for them to develop any real commitment to its requirements, so long as that might entail the loss of power and its benefits. For them, democracy must remain a high-falutin ideal, to be talked about in lofty speeches, but not to be observed in practice. To acquire and retain power is the overriding motive in politics, and to that end opposition of any kind must be eliminated.

Such is the preoccupation with the material benefits of power, that political ideologies as to how society can be organised and ruled to the best advantage hardly enter into the calculations of the politicians. The parties are seldom divided by any ideological differences. Among the Nigerian political parties, for example, the democratic socialism of the Action Group was practically indistinguishable from the pragmatic socialism of the NCNC, and between these so-called socialists and the conservative NPC the difference was essentially one of image or outlook, and not of practical policy. For example, nationalisation and public ownership, the main issues with which socialism is concerned, formed no part of the programme of either one or the other. On the contrary, both were equally against nationalisation, as they had to be, owing to the insufficiency of capital and of managerial skill – Chief Awolowo's advocacy of nationalisation in his new role as leader of the opposition in the federal parliament was more of a political stunt than an expression of practical policy; both were equally convinced of the necessity for attracting foreign private capital, and both had had to initiate a limited amount of public enterprise, either alone or in partnership with foreign investors; both believed in a planned economy within the limits dictated by prevailing conditions. Finally, in foreign affairs, non-alignment was as much a policy of the one as of the other. The material difference between them consisted in the fact that, as regards traditional ways of life and values, the conservatives favoured the preservation of the *status quo*. This had meant that the authority of the traditional emirs should be preserved, revolutionary or radical change should be avoided, and that, in foreign affairs, the ties of the colonial past should be preserved in a special relationship with Britain. This had produced a foreign policy which, though ostensibly non-aligned, inclined strongly towards Britain and the West, often showing a certain amount of hostility to the East.

In the absence of differences in ideology, political affiliations and alliances or loyalties had tended to be too shifting, motivated largely by expediency, by a desire to get a fair share of an inadequate 'national cake' for one's tribe, or by personal opportunistic considerations. Principle and conviction counted for little in party loyalties; the primary consideration was how much one got out of politics, not what ideology one subscribed to. And so one finds politicians unabashedly jumping on to any bandwagon that seemed available. It was considered futile for anyone to be in opposition, with all the hazards involved – intimidation, victimisation and constant harassment by the government party. When, therefore, a party lost an election, many of its members joined the victorious party.

Party alliances were no more motivated by principle or ideology. The NCNC's coalition with the NPC in 1959, and with the UPP in Western Nigeria in 1963 was more a marriage of convenience than of principle. More brazenly opportunistic was the NNDP's alliance with the NPC in 1964; the NNDP had entered into it with the avowed object of securing a share of the national cake for the Yorubas. Perhaps the only redeeming event in political alliances in Nigeria was that between the progressives in 1964 – the United Progressive Grand Alliance (UPGA), made up of the NCNC, AG, NEPU and the UMBC. There was at least a community of outlook among its members, each of whom entered into it knowing that it offered some risk, rather than a real prospect of power.

The poor calibre of the people attracted to politics in the emergent nations has something to do with its character and the inordinate concern with wealth and prestige rather than with ideologies. They were often people with little education, with no profession and no independent source of income upon which to fall back should they happen to lose power. Until recently the intellectuals had little taste for politics; disgusted by the unscrupulous methods by which the game was played, they preferred to maintain a contemptuous aloofness. Thus it was that no ethical standards of behaviour were ever observed. Deceit is as much an accepted norm of political life as corruption. Politicians lie quite openly, taking advantage of the ignorance of the masses and of the inexperience and perversion of the press. Mr. Justice Alexander, inquiring into the Owegbe Cult in the Mid-West Region of Nigeria, had remarked on how 'persons of the status of cabinet ministers declare unabashedly that it is a common practice to tell political lies, that is, to indulge in falsehood to gain political ends.'[25] Indeed at the same Owegbe Inquiry many politicians, including ministers, openly confessed that 'all politicians are sinners,' and a minister and traditional chief, who had informed against the Society, confessed that, had the Society kept its promise to give him £10,000 and a paramount chieftaincy title, he would have collaborated in a planned overthrow of the government of the region. 'I would have been a happy man now with £10,000 and a promise to become a paramount ruler,' he declared.[26]

Since, as Arthur Lewis has observed, no politician will ever admit that he suppresses opponents primarily because he wants to stay in power, other reasons have been advanced to justify his action. Of these the most forceful is the argument based on national unity, admittedly the most imperative need of all developing countries. The argument is threefold. At the era of the nationalist struggle, unity was posited as vital in combating the common enemy effectively. The strength of the nationalist movement, it was claimed, lay in its unity. Only by the concerted effort of all the forces in the country could the sort of impact be created that could force the hands of the imperialists. Divided effort only weakened the nationalist movement, depriving it of the full force which it would otherwise have been able to exert upon the colonial administration.

With the attainment of independence the emphasis was transferred to the peculiar and intractable character of the problem facing the government of an underdeveloped country. In the advanced countries the pressure on the government is for more social services for a society already at an advanced stage of development, in which all its members possess and enjoy the basic necessities for a decent life. In the developing countries on the other hand, even those basic necessities for human existence are either non-existent or minimal for the vast majority of the population, for whom poverty, illiteracy, disease and apathy are an inescapable condition, hovering over the community like a plague. To free the people from these demoralising evils is an urgent and challenging task upon which the very survival of the state itself depends. For unless improvement can be effected as speedily as possible, the mood of impatience, already increasingly felt by the masses, might explode into violent hostility to endanger, if not destroy, the state itself. The imperativeness and urgency of the task, it is argued, admit of no diffusion of energies in an unbridled competition for power.

Thirdly, unity is necessary to fight neo-colonialist forces trying to subvert the newly won independence. Having taken a forced exit, the imperial powers are suspected of wanting to exploit the inexperience and poverty of the new nation in order to perpetuate their economic stranglehold or to discredit it as incapable of self-government. Neo-colonialism is represented as an insidious evil, working through paid agents among the disgruntled elements in the state, and as such is perhaps even more sinister than colonialism. Those prone to fall prey to its machinations must therefore be checked or neutralised in the interest of the state.

This is the argument, and it must be confessed that it is a compelling one. To be sure, however, no opposition party ever disputes the need for economic development. Modernisation is indeed a matter upon which all are agreed. The need for national integration is equally not in dispute. It is the ruling party's insistence that unity must be equated with political unity, that is, the forcible fusion of all political parties and groups into a common mould, that is challenged. The justification for this is said to be to enable the turbulance and tension following in the wake of change engendered by economic development to be contained. No doubt, as has been noted, a national party aggregating diverse elements in a plural society can perform an integrating role, but must it then for that purpose be erected into an exclusive, monolithic organisation, to which all other associations, groups and individuals must be compelled to belong or be suppressed? Is the need for unity so compelling that the individual's freedom of choice and expression should be sacrificed, his freedom to associate with others in the pursuit of common desires and aspirations be taken away?

In his well-argued book, *Africa: The Politics of Independence*, Immanuel Wallerstein appears to have shown a somewhat excessive indulgence towards African one-party governments. For him, the one-party system is indispensable to national integration. 'The party,' he argues, 'should run the government, not vice versa, because the party, not the government, is the emanation of the people, that is, holds their loyalty and ties them to the state. The party integrates the nation and allows the integration to be accomplished by a method that maximises the opportunity of every citizen to participate on a regular and meaningful basis in the decision-making process.'[27] Few would quarrel with the system if in fact it maximised the opportunity for popular participation in government in a meaningful way. Experience of the actual working of the system shows, however, that popular participation is far from being maximised. And in any case can participation be really meaningful where there is only minimal scope for dissent and where organised dissent is not permitted at all? Can debate conducted upon the basis of only one set of programmes lead to a really meaningful

M

consent? It is easy to imagine that a mass meeting which after debate approves a policy presented to it by the leaders can easily be swayed to a different viewpoint if a different group of leaders are given the chance to present their case for it. Clearly the meaningfulness of consent presupposes the possibility of a choice between alternative views or policies presented by different groups. And, as Professor Busia remarked, 'even where there is agreement on objectives, the differences on methods and priorities by which to achieve the objectives can be very important and fundamental.'[28]

Wallerstein's next point is that 'entry of the opposition into the government and the machinery of the governing party not only serves the interests of unity, but usually, though not always, helps to maintain within the dominant party openness of discussion and the necessary pressures for arriving at a consensus that takes into account all interests.'[29] But cannot this advantage be better achieved through the opposition entering into the government without also being absorbed into 'the machinery of the governing party?' There seems to be here an inability to distinguish a coalition from a one-party government. A coalition government which enables all the parties in a plural society to co-operate in the task of national integration and reconstruction while retaining their separate identities may indeed be the most desirable way for the problems confronting such societies to be solved within the framework of constitutional democracy. The case for it has been very ably presented by one of the most unsparing critics of the one-party system, Professor Arthur Lewis. Coalition, he says, accords with the primary meaning of democracy, which is that all those affected by a decision should participate in making it. In a plural society, majority rule, implying government by and for one class of persons at the expense of others, is not only antithetical to this primary meaning of democracy but is also immoral. The consolation of majority rule that the opposition may have its chance next time has no meaning in a plural society, for the minority may never have a chance of forming a government. And even if it had, this conception of democracy is inappropriate in West Africa where an elector in casting his vote is mainly interested, not in the ideology of the party to which his representative belongs, but in what the representative can achieve for his district in terms of material benefits. He expects that his representative, in order to be able to secure benefits for his district, will play a full part in decision-making. For him (the elector), 'these basic needs and expectations remain the same whether the representative is in the winning or the losing party. This is especially the case if the elector belongs to a community (e.g. religious or tribal) which has no chance of winning an election and forming the government, and to which therefore the game of ins and outs is completely irrelevant.'[30] Professor Lewis then concludes:

'The democratic problem in a plural society is to create political institutions which give all the various groups the opportunity to participate in decision-making, since only thus can they feel that they are full members of a nation, respected by their more numerous brethren, and owing equal respect to the national bond which holds them together. In such a society a slogan that the will of the minority should prevail would make better sense than the slogan that the will of the majority should prevail; but neither slogan is appropriate. It is necessary to get right away from the idea that somebody is to prevail over somebody else . . . Group hostility and political warfare are precisely what must be eradicated if the political problem is to be solved; in their place we have to create an atmosphere of mutual toleration and compromise.'[31]

But he maintains that this argument points, not to a one-party government, but to a coalition, because 'the single party imprisons those who oppose or criticise its policy, whereas a free coalition respects the rule of law and the right of free criticism, leaving individuals and parties free to oppose if they so desire.'[32]

Wallerstein finally postulates the one-party system as the only alternative to anarchy or military régimes in Africa. 'The choice,' he writes, 'has not been between one-party and multi-party states; it has been between one-party states and either anarchy or military régimes or various combinations of the two.'[33] Surely, it is the authoritarianism of the ruling oligarchs and their determination to perpetuate their rule that are the root causes of military coups in developing countries. As new generations of the élite come of age, they naturally develop their own aspirations for power and leadership. Finding their elders firmly entrenched in power and unwilling to retire in the foreseeable future, the young generation become restless and impatient, and their impatience tends to find an outlet in radicalism and subversion. Collaborating with their counterparts in the army, with whom they share this mood of radicalism born of frustration, they contrive to effect a coup, toppling the old guards.[34] Nor has the point about anarchy any greater validity. African opposition parties may be irresponsible and their tactics destructive of the security of the state, yet it must not be forgotten that it is the attempt by the ruling parties to impose political unanimity by force, to perpetuate their rule by the suppression of the opposition, that drives the opposition to extremism. An opposition denied any say in government except at the cost of self-effacement, or which cannot get redress for its grievances by constitutional means, may well be morally justified in revolt. The plain truth which deserves to be recognised is that, in a plural society, an attempt to erase tribal or racial loyalties by political fiat is futile. Unity can only be achieved through the evolutionary process of education, social intercourse through the medium of trade, intermarriage and other social and cultural relationships, professional and business association, a functional realignment of people which cuts across tribal or racial divisions, and a shared community life generally.

It has also been argued that the task of fighting poverty, disease and illiteracy creates a continuing state of emergency, justifying the authoritarian methods of the one-party government. Advocates of the one-party system point to the fact that even developed constitutional systems recognise that under the stress of crisis the regular procedures are suspended and the country lives under a system of constitutional dictatorship. The point has been argued with some force by President Nyerere in defending the case for the one-party system in his country. But the analogy is wholly untenable. An emergency in this context is a state of affairs, such as war or other kind of public disorder, which threatens the physical security of the state. Furthermore, even when such a state of affairs has arisen, it seldom leads in the developed democracies to a complete suspension of the machinery of constitutional government. Even conceding that the task of national integration and modernisation can be regarded as constituting some kind of 'emergency,' its solution certainly does not require the institution of what has been called a 'development dictatorship.'[35] And what guarantee is there that when the assumed emergency is over, the ruling oligarchs will be disposed to abandon their authoritarian posture? After having tasted the intoxication of personalised power and the flattering adulation of hero-worship, given the corrupting influence of authoritarian power, it would be too much, indeed contrary to the nature of man and to all human experience, to expect them to do so.

Tradition is the next argument that has been advanced in justification of the one-party system. It is said that the idea of an organised opposition is foreign to the African conception of government. Whatever the nature of the political organisation in any given African country, whether government is by a chief in council or by a council of elders or by the whole mass of the village peasantry, the process of decision-making is through lengthy and unhurried discussion among those present, during which all shades of opinion are given full expression until a consensus emerges. No votes are

ever taken and so there is no question of a majority or a minority
or of government and opposition organised as mutually competing
and warring groups.[36] While this is generally an accurate picture
of the African system of government, it is wrong to suppose that
factionalism is entirely absent at such meetings. The factions may
represent family or other kinship groups. If they are not effectively
organised, it is simply because the matters at issue are of relatively
minor importance. It is, in any case, misconceived to attempt to
justify the processes of a modern, complex state, embracing peoples
of different tribal or racial origins, with widely differing interests,
by reference to those of a small face-to-face community in which
kinship and various other kinds of intimate relationships operate to
limit disagreements, in which authority is diffused or is not backed
up by organised coercive forces, and in which the functions of
government and therefore the possible areas of conflict are severely
limited. The conditions and sanctions which make a 'consensus
democracy' possible in the traditional set-up are not present in the
modern state. If organised opposition is alien to African thought,
so is the modern state itself. Its functions, procedures and institutions, as well as the coercive powers at its disposal, have no parallel
in traditional African communities. The matters at stake are in-
comparably weightier, and are thus well calculated to provoke a
conflict of interest of a type that can never arise in the traditional
community. The modern state is a large-scale organisation, and
from this arises the necessity that those who compete to control its
power should similarly organise themselves on a large scale. If we
accept the modern state as a beneficial organisation for the development of the African continent, we will also be obliged to accept that
its politics cannot be confined within the frontiers of tradition. The
argument is not that tradition has no relevance to the government
of the modern state, but rather that it can provide no justification
for one-party rule. Indeed, given a government based upon a free
coalition, African consensus democracy can have great value in
promoting greater harmony. Decision-taking by means of the vote
has obvious disadvantages. As Professor Grey has observed:

'When issues between opposing parties are decided ultimately by
parliamentary vote, it leaves the outvoted minority with its will
or desire unsatisfied. A whole society must exist for indefinite
periods of time knowing that some of its members, who may
represent a substantial proportion, do not favour the political
action being pursued, but have only agreed to restrain their
active opposition for the time being . . . The usual procedure of
parliamentary voting makes it inevitable that at all times, part

of the society will remain in unsatisfied opposition to important decisions affecting the whole society.'[37]

The one-party system has been described as a kind of 'tutelary democracy,' as a transitional phase to prepare the ground by creating the conditions needed for the evolution of full democracy at a later stage. These conditions are said to be a relatively high standard of living, mass education, a substantial middle class, industrialisation and urbanisation.[38] Whilst these are undeniably predisposing factors for the stability of democratic institutions, they cannot by themselves create democracy if the democratic tradition has not been sufficiently nurtured among the people.[39] The democratic tradition requires a spirit of tolerance and of respect for differing opinions, which in turn depends upon the existence of a broad consensus on fundamentals. Democracy cannot thrive in a country where 'the contenders for power disagree so sharply on matters which they consider fundamental that they are not willing to allow their opponents to govern, whatever the ballot box may say.'[40] Although the disagreement among the politicians in emergent countries is not upon fundamentals, the democratic spirit is sadly lacking. But Arthur Lewis is not without hope for the future. He believes that, since the single party is incapable of containing the degree of tension which rapid change inevitably produces, the chances are that it will sooner or later split into separate groups, which may then come together again in a free coalition. Such a development could be the beginning of the democratic road, from whence a spirit of compromise and mutual tolerance may gradually be nurtured.[41]

REFERENCES

1. For an excellent account of local government in Nigeria, see Cowan, *Local Government in West Africa*, 1958.
2. Bretton, *Power and Stability in Nigeria*, 1962, p. 87.
3. There were no local police in the East.
4. Arikpo, *The Development of Modern Nigeria*, 1967, p. 141.
5. Bretton, *Power and Stability in Nigeria*, 1962, p. 102.
6. Awolowo in *West African Pilot*, August 29, 1963.
7. *Constitutionalism for Emergent Political Orders*, p. 21.
8. Quoted in Busia, *Africa in Search of Democracy*, 1967, p. 129, which gives a fairly detailed account of preventive detention in Ghana.
9. *Journal of the International Commission of Jurists*, Vol. 3, No. 2, 1961, pp. 65-81.

10. *Bulletin of International Commission of Jurists*, No. 18, 1964, p. 10.
11. See Busia, *op. cit.*, pp. 126-7.
12. Carter, ed., *African One-Party States*, 1962, p. 9.
13. Quoted in Zolberg, *One-Party Government in the Ivory Coast*, revised ed., 1969, p. 266.
14. Snyder, *One-Party Government in Mali*, 1965, pp. 92, 109.
15. Ernest Milcent, in Carter, ed., *African One-Party States*, p. 119.
16. *From Empire to Nation*, 1962, p. 281. On the role of a charismatic leader, see also Apter, *The Gold Coast in Transition*, 1963, pp. 304-6; Zolberg, *op. cit.*, pp. 323-4.
17. As to which, see Zolberg, *op. cit.*, pp. 271-2.
18. For the statistics of the votes in the one-party elections in the Ivory Coast, see Zolberg, *op. cit.*, p. 271.
19. *Ibid.*, p. 280.
20. *Ibid.*, p. 282.
21. *Ibid.*, p. 334; Carter, *op. cit.*, p. 2; Wallerstein, *Africa: the Politics of Independence*, 1961, p. 159.
22. Zolberg, *op. cit.*, p. 335.
23. S. A. de Smith, *The New Commonwealth and its Constitutions*, 1964, p. 235.
24. Pp. 31-2.
25. Report, Owegbe Cult Commission of Inquiry, Printing Division, Ministry of Information, Benin City, 1966, p. 7.
26. *The Onogie of Ewohimi, Enosegbe II*, Report, *op. cit.*, p. 94.
27. *Op. cit.*, pp. 97-8.
28. *Africa in Search of Democracy*, 1967, p. 140.
29. *Op. cit.*, p. 165.
30. *Politics in West Africa*, 1965, p. 75.
31. *Ibid.*, pp. 66-7.
32. *Ibid.*, p. 81.
33. *Op. cit.*, pp. 96, 163.
34. See further below, Ch. VIII.
35. See Carl Friedrich, *Constitutionalism for Emergent Political Orders*, p. 25.
36. See Cowan, *The Dilemmas of African Independence*, 1964, pp. 11-12; Emerson, *op. cit.*, p. 284; Fletcher-Cooke, in Alan Burns, ed., *Parliament as an Export*, 1966, pp. 145 *et seq.*
37. 'Political Parties in New African Nations: an Anthropological View,' *Comparative Studies in Society and History*, IV., No. 4, July 19, 1963, p. 457, quoted in Cowan, *op. cit.*, p. 12.
38. Lipset, 'Some Social Requisites of Democracy: Economic Development and Political Legitimacy,' *American Political Science Review*, 1959, Vol. LIII, pp. 69-105.
39. *Cf.* Zolberg, *One-Party Government in the Ivory Coast*, revised ed., 1969, pp. 338-9; Emerson, *From Empire to Nation*, 1962, pp. 278-80.
40. Arthur Lewis, *op. cit.*, p. 37.
41. *Ibid.*, p. 88.

CHAPTER VII

CONSTITUTIONALISM AND THE FREQUENT INCIDENCE OF EMERGENCIES IN NEW NATIONS

Emergent nations are having to live under an almost continual state of emergency. Their societies are not only plural, but are often riven by deep-seated division between the component groups. Tribal or racial division has been deepened still further by the action of unscrupulous politicians who, in order to achieve political ends, have exploited group sentiments, creating thereby an atmosphere charged with tension and unrest. The process of transforming a primitive, traditional society into a modern one has also imposed its own strain. The society is in a state of flux, and change, especially rapid change such as these countries are undergoing, creates tension. The forces of change, urbanisation, industrialisation, vast increases in literacy and education all have to be reconciled within the society, and they inevitably operate to undermine the traditional bases of authority and established values. On the other hand, the new political organisation, the modern state, is as yet not sufficiently rooted or legitimised to provide the alternative base of authority needed to contain the pressure of these forces, and the struggle between the various groups for the right to administer the state has weakened it still further. All these factors react upon one another to make the society of the new nations into a kind of cauldron, which continually gives off vapours of conflict and instability. Now and again the uneasy equilibrium breaks down, giving way to violence. This violence has generally taken one of three forms, or a combination of all three, viz. traditional tribal feuds and warfare, riots and revolts against constituted authority, and civil war.[1] Thus Nigeria, Guyana, Morocco, Iraq, Uganda, the Congo, Ruanda, Burundi, the Sudan, Cyprus, India, Pakistan, Ceylon, Burma, Laos and South Vietnam have all experienced the disruption of tribal, racial or communal violence, while revolutionary violence, insurrection, and guerrilla warfare have become almost a way of life in most parts of Latin America and in many parts of the Middle East and Asia. There has been a steady progression in the incidence of organised violence in the new states, and the statistics indicate that there had been thirty-four incidents in 1958, thirty-six in 1959, forty-two in 1960, forty-three in 1961, forty-seven in 1962, fifty-nine in 1963, fifty-six in 1964 and fifty-seven in 1965.[2]

Emergencies affect constitutionalism in two main respects; they attract the emergency powers under the constitution or the doctrine of civil necessity or both.

Emergency Powers under the Constitution

Even the most constitutional of constitutional régimes finds it necessary to arm itself, under the constitution, with special powers to deal with an emergency. In all countries, it is recognised that constitutionalism has to be limited by the exigencies of an emergency, since an emergency implies a state of danger to public order and public safety, which cannot adequately be met within the framework of governmental restraints imposed by the constitution. There is a good justification for this. The preservation of the state and society is an imperative necessity, which should override the need for limited government. Accordingly, all constitutions which impose limitations upon government authorise the limitations to be exceeded in times of emergency. Nonetheless it has to be accepted that emergencies pose a serious threat to constitutional government. 'A first force which works against constitutional government,' writes Wheare, 'is war. In time of war or rumours of war, the government claims full freedom of action; it does not want to be bound by limitations . . . Obviously government on these lines is opposed to the limited government which we call constitutional.'[3] Emergency powers can be accommodated with constitutionalism if they are conceived of as an ephemeral aberration occurring once in a long while, and provided they are not so sweeping as to destroy or suspend the restraints of constitutional government completely. And this is where the emergent states differ from the established constitutional orders in this connection. First, emergencies in the new states are much too frequent. As already stated, in many parts of the underdeveloped world, notably Latin America, Middle East and Asia, they have tended to become the normal order of things, thus replacing constitutional government with emergency administration as the normal system of rule. Secondly, there is a tendency in these countries to abuse the concession of emergency powers in the constitution not only by using them for purposes for which they are not intended but also by using them to suspend constitutional government altogether. To illustrate the point, we may recall the emergency proclaimed in Nigeria in 1962.

The Nigerian Constitution empowered parliament to legislate beyond the limits of its powers to an extent that might be necessary or expedient for the purpose of maintaining or securing peace, order and good government during any period of emergency, which was defined to mean any period during which the federation was at war or there was in force a resolution by parliament declaring that a state of public emergency exists or that democratic institutions in Nigeria were threatened by subversion.[4] What was to constitute a state of emergency was left undefined. In its ordinary meaning, emergency seems to presuppose some event, usually of a violent nature, endangering or threatening public order or public safety. This is the usual meaning assigned to it in most democratic constitutions, such as the 1960 Cyprus Constitution which authorises the proclamation of an emergency only 'in the case of war or other public danger threatening the life of the Republic.'[5] The danger or threat must be an imminent one, and the event giving rise to it must involve a considerable section of the public, since only so can public order or public safety be said to be in jeopardy. We may recapitulate briefly the events which gave rise to the declaration of a state of emergency in Nigeria in 1962. Owing to factional squabbles within the ruling party in Western Nigeria, the Action Group, the regional governor dismissed the Premier, Chief Akintola, and appointed another in his place. Chief Akintola, refusing to accept his dismissal, promptly commenced a court action to determine its validity. Subsequently the House of Assembly met to approve the new government, but the meeting was unable to transact any business, because of violent clashes within the chamber of the house between members of the two factions. From this the Federal Government concluded that it had become impossible to carry on the government of the region, and so proceeded to declare a state of emergency. It must be noted, first, that the disturbances in the chamber of the House were caused by only ten supporters of Chief Akintola out of a house of 117, and, secondly, that apart from the event in the House the entire region outside it remained peaceful and unaffected by the rather uncivilised behaviour of the parliamentarians. When the House was cleared and locked up by the police, the members returned to their respective homes, and there was no sign of any attempt or intention to carry the affray outside the chamber. The trouble-makers were apparently satisfied that they had achieved their object, which was to prevent the House from approving the new government.

All that could reasonably be inferred from the inability of the House to transact any business was that the legislative arm of the government had been temporarily incapacitated, but surely the government of the region could have been lawfully carried on by the new executive until the legality of Akintola's dismissal had been determined by the court. Even if it be assumed that the governer acted unlawfully in dismissing him, still it was the act of a competent authority, and Chief Akintola had no justification whatever in taking the law into his own hands by refusing to accept his dismissal. The contention that there were two executives is completely untenable. From the moment of his dismissal, Chief Akintola ceased to be premier and had no right to claim to be so. It was not as if the governor acted entirely without any colour of right in dismissing him. The only question was whether he had properly exercised his lawful power by acting on a declaration of lack of confidence in the premier contained in a letter signed by the majority of the members, instead of on a formal vote on the floor of the House. The irresponsibility of his taking the law into his own hands was amply demonstrated by the decision of the court which confirmed that the governor had acted rightly after all. One would have expected that what the federal government would have done, had it been disinterested, would have been to support the authority of the new premier, pending the determination by the court of Chief Akintola's action. It cannot be seriously doubted that the declaration of a state of emergency upon the strength of the situation prevailing in Western Nigeria at the time was ill-motivated, and that it was made for a purpose other than that envisaged by the Constitution.

The next question concerns the manner in which the emergency powers were used. In pursuance of the power granted to it to legislate outside its normal sphere of competence for 'the purpose of maintaining or securing peace, order and good government during any period of emergency,' Parliament enacted the Emergency Powers Act, 1961, authorising the President in Council to make 'such regulations as appear to him to be necessary or expedient for the purpose of maintaining or securing peace, order and good government in Nigeria or any part thereof.' It is almost unprecedented in the established constitutional orders, even in time of war, for the legislature to delegate the full amplitude of its power to the executive. For it was the entirety of its emergency powers that parliament passed on to the executive, in effect allowing itself to be supplanted by the executive for this purpose. A delegation of powers in these terms not only destroyed the already attenuated foundation of the separation of powers under the constitution. It also impaired that aspect of the rule of law which requires that executive acts be justified by law and that the executive should not be the body to confer the necessary legal authority upon itself. Indeed the Emergency Powers Act, 1961, went even further in relegating the legislature. It also empowered the President in Council to amend, suspend, or modify a law enacted by any legislature in the country; furthermore any regulation made by him had 'effect notwithstanding anything inconsistent therewith contained in any law; and any provision of a law which is inconsistent with any such regulation . . . shall . . . to the extent of such inconsistency have no effect so long as such regulation . . . remains in force.'[6] It is true that a regulation made under the Act became void if it was not approved by the resolution of both Houses of Parliament within four months, and that both Houses could at any time by *resolution* amend or revoke it.[7] Yet so long as a regulation remained unrevoked, Parliament could not legislate inconsistently with it, except by first repealing or amending the Emergency Powers Act itself.

Even more destructive of constitutional government was the manner in which the unlimited powers thus delegated to the executive were used in Western Nigeria (the emergency area). Altogether twelve regulations were made by the president in council under the Act. Of these the most far-reaching was the Emergency Powers (General) Regulations, 1962. Its provisions proceeded upon the view that the government of Western Nigeria could no longer be carried on by the representative political institutions established by the constitution of the region, a view which, as already submitted, is untenable, and appeared to have been motivated by a desire to oust the Action Group from its power base as part of a grand plan to liquidate it as a political force in the country. The regulation provided for the appointment in Western Nigeria of an administrator who was to administer the government of the region. As the government of the region, the administrator was given full executive and legislative powers. He was empowered to legislate by means of orders for the peace, order, and good government of Western Nigeria; and when so legislating, he could amend any law in force in the region or suspend its operation, whether it be an Act of Parliament, a law of the regional legislature or an ordinance. The regional governor, premier, ministers, president, speaker and members of the regional Houses were forbidden to exercise their functions except to such extent and during such period (if any) as the administrator might direct. The administrator was responsible only to the prime minister for the exercise of his functions.

Was the suspension of the government of Western Nigeria warranted by the constitution either in letter or in spirit? The most that could be said of the power given to parliament to 'make such laws for Nigeria or any part thereof with respect to matters not included in the Legislative Lists as may appear to parliament to be *necessary or expedient* for the purpose of *maintaining or securing* peace, order and good government during any period of emergency'[8] is that it brought within the sphere of concurrent powers matters ordinarily exclusive to the region. If that be the case, does the notion of concurrent powers in a federal set-up enable the unit of government with the overriding power to suspend the other completely? To admit that would be to turn concurrent power into exclusive power, and so abolish the distinction between them. Even the so-called doctrine of 'covering the field' according to which the federal legislature can, by dealing completely and exhaustively with a particular matter, exclude the regional legislatures therefrom is limited to the specific subject-matter of a particular legislation. It does not enable the federal legislature to make a general legislative declaration excluding the regions completely from the concurrent field of power. Such a declaration would be manifestly subversive of the constitution, and, given the extension of the concurrent power to the whole sphere of regional exclusive competence during an emergency, would convert the constitution from a federal to a unitary one, thereby destroying the restraining role of federalism. The doctrine of covering the field is of doubtful validity, anyway. Although under the Constitution of Nigeria a federal law on a concurrent matter prevailed over an inconsistent regional law, one could not invoke the doctrine of inconsistency unless there was actual legislation in being. Only then could a comparison be made to see if one conflicted with the other. It is even doubtful whether the emergency power of parliament extended to the whole sphere of regional exclusive competence. Surely, there is a difference, however difficult it may be to define, between a power to legislate to *maintain or secure* peace, order and good government, and a power to legislate generally for peace, order and good government. The former assumes the existence of peace, order and good government, which only needs to be maintained or secured. It is a supplemental power. In other words, parliament could only lawfully have assumed a supplementary power in support of the government of Western Nigeria to maintain or secure peace, order and good government during the emergency. And assuming that parliament had the power which it purported to exercise, suspension of the government of Western Nigeria could only be said to be *necessary or expedient* on the erroneous view that the government had been rendered inoperative.

An important element of the constitutional order established by the Nigerian Constitution was the guarantee of fundamental rights.[9] Most of the rights so guaranteed were subject to curtailment, even in normal times, by laws which were reasonably justifiable in a democratic society in the interests of defence, public safety, public order, etc. The power to curtail these rights was certainly greater during a period of emergency than during a normal time, since in an emergency the test of reasonable justifiability had to be applied in relation to the conditions of emergency. This is not to say that an emergency permitted an unlimited power of interference. As regards rights whose guarantee was not subject to this qualification, namely right to life, personal liberty, determination of rights by judicial process and freedom from discrimination, the constitution authorised derogation from them during a period of emergency, but only to an extent reasonably justifiable for the purpose of dealing with the situation as it actually existed, and provided that life was not to be taken unlawfully except in consequence of an act of war, and that *ex post facto* offences and punishments were not to be created.[10] There was another safeguard for the right to personal liberty. Anyone detained, or whose movement or residence was restricted, was entitled to have his detention or restriction reviewed within one month, and thereafter at intervals of not more than six months by a tribunal established by law and constituted in such manner as to ensure its independence and impartiality. The tribunal was to make recommendations concerning the necessity or expediency of continuing the detention or restriction to the appropriate authority, who was however not bound to act in accordance therewith.[11]

It would be tedious to review in detail the extent to which the various regulations made during the emergency administration in Western Nigeria derogated from the guaranteed rights.[12] Suffice it to say that the regulations drastically curtailed the freedom of speech, of assembly and procession; they authorised search without warrant, the detention of persons without trial, and the restriction of the movement and residence of persons. These powers were amply used. All the leading politicians in the region were either detained or had their movements or residence restricted, and public meetings and processions were banned.

Abuse of emergency powers under the constitution has not been confined to Nigeria. As previously noticed,[13] the federal government in Malaysia had used its emergency power to declare an emergency in Sarawak in circumstances similar to those in Western Nigeria. In the manner of the Constitution of the Fifth French Republic,[14] the constitutions of the ex-French African countries make the president the sole authority for proclaiming a state of emergency, and empower him to 'take all measures as he may deem necessary.'[15] But they all define an emergency to be 'a clear and present danger,' threatening the institutions or independence of the nation, the integrity of its territory, or the carrying out of its international undertakings or other situation 'when the regular functioning of the governmental authorities is interrupted.' The only safeguard against abuse is the varying requirement to consult certain authorities, such as the president of the National Assembly and of the Constitutional Council, and the requirement that the National Assembly shall meet automatically by right and remain in session throughout the period of the emergency. Unlike the case in Nigeria and some of the other Commonwealth countries where the declaration of an emergency is by a resolution of parliament and where the emergency powers of the executive are only delegated, and revocable by parliament at any time, the emergency powers of the president in the ex-French countries derive directly from the constitution and are independent of parliament. Moreover it would appear that the definition of an emergency to include a situation 'when the regular functioning of the governmental authorities is interrupted' might enable a president to declare an emergency in a situation similar to that which occurred in Western Nigeria, though it seems to be aimed primarily at a general strike of workers in the public service, as happened in Senegal in 1969. In Cameroon an emergency of the type described above is classified as 'special'; in addition the president is empowered 'when circumstances so require' to proclaim a state of emergency and to assume special powers, subject to the conditions prescribed by federal law.[16] The Constitution of the Congo (Leopoldville) also makes the same distinction, though in both cases the safeguards are more effective than in the ex-French territories in that the action of the president is subject to approval by parliament.[17]

Doctrine of Civil Necessity

Perhaps the most remarkable development in the practice of constitutional government in the emergent states is the use which has been made of the doctrine of civil necessity. In private law necessity is well-established as a legal defence for an action which would have been otherwise unlawful and actionable. Thus, where life is in danger, the necessity of saving it may justify action which will ordinarily be unlawful, such as throwing cargo overboard from a sinking boat in order to save the lives of the passengers and crew, or a doctor performing an abortion (where an abortion is an offence) to save the life of a pregnant woman. A situation creating a necessity to take action to save life is the clearest example of the application of the doctrine, but it does not follow that it is limited to such cases. It is also applicable where it is necessary to avert danger to property

or physical injury or to escape from unlawful imprisonment or
confinement. The doctrine is also recongised in public law as a
justification for an action otherwise unlawful but necessary to
preserve the life of the state or society.

On the face of it, the doctrine would appear to be inconsistent
with the law. Glanville Williams has put the point cogently:

> 'What it comes to is this, that the defence of necessity involves
> a choice of the lesser evil. It requires a judgment of value, an
> adjudication between competing "goods" and a sacrifice of one
> to the other. The language of necessity disguises the selection of
> values that is really involved.
>
> If this is so, is there any legal basis for the defence? The law
> itself enshrines values, and the judge is sworn to uphold the law.
> By what right can the judge declare some value, not expressed
> in the law, to be superior to the law? How, in particular, can he
> do this in the face of the words of a statute? Does not the defence
> of necessity wear the appearance of an appeal to the judge
> against the law?'[18]

The inconsistency is, however, only apparent, for the doctrine does
not operate from outside the law, but is implied in it as an integral
part thereof. ' "The Law",' said Glanville Williams in answer to
the questions he posed, ' . . . includes the doctrine of necessity;
the defence of necessity is an implied exception to particular rules
of law.' Furthermore, when applicable, it operates parallel to the
express letters of the law; it does not abrogate express law, but can
only qualify it for the purpose of averting the threatening danger.

The rationale of the doctrine is that, in an emergency imperilling
public order or public security, the safety of the people is the
supreme law – *salus populi est suprema lex.*[19] By this supreme law of
necessity, therefore, the organs of the state are entitled, in the face
of such an emergency, to take all appropriate actions, even in
deviation from the express provisions of the constitution, in order
to safeguard law and order and preserve the state and society. Its
application is, however, subject to the following conditions:

> (i) an imperative necessity arising from an imminent and extreme
> danger affecting the safety of the state or society;
>
> (ii) action taken to meet the exigency must be inevitable in the
> sense of being the only remedy;
>
> (iii) it must be proportionate to the necessity, i.e. it must be
> reasonably warranted by the danger which it was intended to
> avert;

(iv) it must be of a temporary character limited to the duration of the exceptional circumstances;

(v) the temporary incapacitation of the authority (if any) which normally has the competence to act.

So much appears to be settled, but the difficulty is to determine what type of action can justifiably be done in pursuance of the doctrine. In English law, it has been stated, the executive, acting out of 'an actual and immediate necessity arising in the face of the enemy and in circumstances where the rule *salus populi suprema lex* was clearly applicable,' may take possession of a citizen's property for the defence of the realm without payment of compensation, unless by statute compensation is to be paid.[20] The doctrine operates therefore as an implied qualification upon individual human rights. Rights cannot be enjoyed absolutely, even where they are guaranteed in the constitution in absolute terms, since it is inconceivable that any court will enforce them at the expense of public safety. In an emergency, such as war, endangering the safety of the state and society, the necessity for safeguarding the nation against destruction will justify actions which otherwise derogate from the guaranteed rights, and this must be so notwithstanding that the guarantee is not expressly made subject to such protective measures.

The US Constitution, for example, prohibits the deprivation of life, liberty or property 'without due process of law.' This leaves it to the courts to say in what circumstances a deprivation might be justified as being in due process of law. It cannot be questioned that a total war is one such justifying circumstance; such an emergency which threatens the very existence of the state and of society creates indeed a compelling necessity for drastic action, overriding the individual's civil liberties. The extent of this overriding effect of a total war was the question the U.S. Supreme Court has had to decide in the series of cases involving Japanese living on the West coast of the United States during the Second World War. The United States had gone to war with Japan on December 8, 1941, following the Japanese attack on Pearl Harbour the previous day. The existence of a state of belligerence between the two countries and the likelihood of a further Japanese attack created a necessity for safeguarding the West coast. Espionage and sabotage were particularly feared, a danger which was aggravated by the presence on the West coast of some 112,000 persons of Japanese origin of whom about 70,000 were American citizens by birth. The protective measures which the military authorities, with the sanction of the executive and the legislature, instituted to combat the danger were, first, to impose a night curfew on all Japanese on the West coast, and eventually, when a curfew was thought inadequate, to have them segregated at various centres, called assembly or relocation centres, which they were not to leave without military permission. These centres were a kind of concentration camp. Neither the curfew nor the segregation order differentiated between various classes of Japanese; both citizens and aliens, the loyal and the disloyal were alike incarcerated. Unquestionably these orders were an invasion of the constitutional rights of the Japanese Americans, and the question was whether this was legally justified by the danger against which it was meant to be a protection. The supreme court sustained the validity of the curfew order on the ground that it was necessary 'to meet the threat of sabotage and espionage which would substantially affect the war effort and might reasonably be expected to aid a threatened enemy invasion.'[21] For the same reason, too, the court upheld the validity of the segregation order.[22]

Although the decisions were based upon the war power expressly vested in the President and the Congress by the Constitution, the premise was clearly the doctrine that the 'state must have every facility and the widest latitude in defending itself against destruction.'[23] Whilst affirming the inviolability of the individual's civil liberties, the court nevertheless conceded that 'pressing public necessity may sometimes justify the existence of such restrictions' on them.[24] The decisions in these cases have provoked a lot of criticism,[25] particularly as regards the segregation order, which could hardly have been warranted by the exigency of the occasion. The curfew alone, it has been argued, would have met the danger adequately, especially in view of the fact that the danger of further attack seemed to have receded in the interval of five months between Pearl Harbour and the proclamation of the orders. And even if the segregation order was considered really necessary, an effort should have been made to separate the loyal from the disloyal Japanese, and to confine the order to the latter.[26] It seemed that the action of the military authorities was dictated more by the pressure of racial prejudice exerted by certain groups on the West coast. However that may be, the cases do give recognition to the doctrine of necessity as a legal justification for action otherwise contrary to the express provisions of the constitution, but which is necessary to save the nation from destruction.

Is the doctrine, then, confined to cases of invasion of individual rights, or does it enable the executive to exercise legislative power during an emergency when the legislative authority is temporarily put out of action or a non-sovereign legislature to exceed the limits of its powers?

With regard to the English common law, the view has been

expressed by Chitty that the King as head of state 'is the first person in the nation . . . being superior to both Houses in dignity and the only branch of the Legislature that has a separate existence, and is capable of performing any act at a time when the parliament is not in being.'[27] This view was expressed in 1820, but does it still represent the position today in English law? Glanville Williams thinks not. 'The prerogative of necessity,' he writes, 'is now in disuse, because it is covered by and therefore superseded by statutes.'[28] Elaborating on this, he says:

'The King cannot acquire new prerogatives by reference to state necessity . . . However necessary the behaviour, the Government must today invoke the aid of Parliament if the behaviour involves breaking the letter of the law. It can act under the doctrine of necessity only to the same extent as a private person. Parliament's alleged failure to give adequate powers cannot be an excuse for conduct, because the necessity of powers claimed is for Parliament to decide, not for the judges over the head of Parliament. The question is not whether it is necessary to do the act but whether it is necessary to do it without the sanction of Parliament.'[29]

On the other hand, in Greece, Italy, France and Germany it seems to be generally accepted among writers on constitutional law that the doctrine may justify the exercise of legislative power by the executive. 'Jurisprudence,' declares a French authority, 'was thus led to appreciate that there was a hierarchy in the juridical rules and that the executive authorities were behaving more in conformity with the spirit of constitutional institutions by a temporary encroachment on legislative prerogatives than by limiting themselves to a narrow conventionality or by remaining inactive when such inactivity imperils public order.'[30] In Greece the courts have in many cases since 1945 upheld the exercise by the executive of legislative power in times of emergency by reference to the doctrine.[31]

The danger is that the doctrine of civil or state necessity appears to be even more susceptible to abuse than emergency powers under the express provisions of the constitution. For it requires no formal declaration of an emergency, and, as will appear from the Pakistani and Cypriot cases discussed below, it may justify the assumption of powers going beyond those authorised by the constitution during an emergency. It has thus been described as the 'plea for every infringement of human freedom. It is the argument of tyrants.'[32]

As has been observed, the doctrine has had the most remarkable application recently in four of the emergent states, Pakistan, Cyprus,

Nigeria and Rhodesia. The cases are extremely illuminating on the point and deserve therefore a somewhat detailed consideration.

(i) *Application of doctrine in Pakistan, 1955*

Before 1947 what is now Pakistan was part of India. It was separated from the latter and erected into a separate state under an arrangement which formed the basis for the grant of independence to the two countries. Shortly before independence in 1947, the Viceroy of India, acting under directives from the British Government, issued an executive order setting up separate constituent assemblies for India and Pakistan. By the Indian Independence Act, which came into force on August 15, 1947, it was provided that the legislative powers of the two countries shall *in the first instance* be exercised by their respective constituent assemblies both generally and in particular for the purpose of enacting a constitution. Until a constitution was so enacted by the assembly the government of each country was to be conducted under the existing constitution contained in the Government of India Act, 1935, as amended by the Independence Act; and the governor-general for each country was to adapt the 1935 Act to bring it into conformity with the new independent status of the country. From the date of the Independence Act, the two constituent assemblies immediately took in hand the task of providing a constitution for their respective countries, but after seven long years the Pakistani Assembly was nowhere near accomplishing its task. Representations were made to the governor-general by the various representative bodies in the country that the assembly had turned itself into a permanent legislature and had thereby become unrepresentative of the people. What was more, conceiving itself as possessing the sovereign power of the state on behalf of the people of Pakistan, the assembly in the course of its seven years' existence passed some forty-four constitutional laws, which it put into force without submitting them for the governor-general's assent as the Indian Independence Act clearly required. (Ordinary enactments were duly submitted for the governor-general's assent.) These purported enactments were thus clearly invalid and were declared so by the Pakistani federal court.[33]

The governor-general then dissolved the assembly, basing his action on the ground that it had proved itself incapable of accomplishing the task set for it by the Independence Act; that it had become unrepresentative and had lost the confidence of the people, as the resolutions of the various representative bodies in the country made clear; and that it had become an illegal legislature by purporting to exclude the governor-general from the process of law-making. After dissolving the assembly, the governor-general issued an ordinance declaring a state of emergency and purporting, by virtue of his emergency powers under the Government of India Act, 1935, to validate with retrospective effect most of the void constitutional enactments of the dissolved assembly. The validation of these enactments so far as it purported to be based upon the governor-general's emergency powers under the 1935 Act was pronounced invalid by the court as going beyond the provisions of the Act.[34] 'Under the Constitutional Acts,' declared Chief Justice Muhammad Munir in the leading judgment, 'the governor-general is possessed of no more powers than those that are given to him by those Acts. One of these powers is to promulgate Ordinances in cases of emergency, but the limits within which and the checks subject to which he can exercise that power are clearly laid down in section 42 itself . . . Any legislative provision that relates to a *constitutional matter* is solely within the powers of the Constituent Assembly and the governor-general is under the Constitution Acts precluded from exercising those powers.'[35]

Thereafter the governor-general summoned a new Constituent Assembly for the purpose of making provision as to the constitution for Pakistan. He next proceeded by proclamation to re-validate the enactments which the court had earlier declared he had no power to validate. But whereas the earlier attempt at validation was based upon the governor-general's emergency powers under the 1935 Act, the basis of the new proclamation was the doctrine of state necessity. It was stated that the invalidation of the enactments having rendered unlawful all acts done thereunder, executive, administrative and judicial, the constitutional and administrative machinery had broken down, thereby threatening the state with imminent collapse; the validation of the enactments was therefore necessary in order to preserve the state and society and maintain the *status quo* until the new constituent assembly had met and enacted the necessary validating laws. The proclamation was made subject to the opinion of the federal court. The governor-general now asked for the court's opinion whether, there being no legislature in existence competent to validate the void constitutional enactments of the dissolved assembly, 'there is any provision in the constitution or *any rule of law* applicable to the situation by which the governor-general can by order or otherwise declare that all orders made, decisions taken, and other acts done under those laws shall be valid and enforceable, and those laws . . . shall be treated as part of the law of the land until the question of their validation is determined by the new constituent convention.'[36]

Among the questions referred for the court's opinion was whether the assembly had been validly dissolved. For if it had not, then the whole premise for the exercise of the power of validation claimed by the governor-general would not arise. It would suffice to say simply that the court unanimously accepted that under the circumstances the governor-general had power to dissolve the assembly and that the power had been validly exercised. Upon the crucial question concerning the governor-general's power to validate by proclamation the void constitutional enactments, the court was sharply divided, three for and two against. In the leading judgment delivered by Chief Justice Muhammad Munir, who went into a far-ranging examination of the doctrine of civil or state necessity, the majority affirmed the doctrine to be 'implicit in the constitution of every civilised community.'[37] On the premise stated in the Special Reference, namely that in consequence of the dissolution of the assembly and the invalidation of all the constitutional laws enacted by it during a period of seven years, the constitutional and administrative machinery of the state had broken down, so that the state itself stood in imminent danger of collapse, and since the measures proposed by the governor-general for dealing with the situation were only temporary until the new constituent assembly had met to decide the matter finally, they (the majority) held that the retrospective validation of the laws by the governor-general was legally justified as a temporary measure by the exigency of the situation. In coming to this conclusion they relied upon the statement of the law by Chitty quoted above, but were nevertheless at pains to emphasise that the application of the doctrine in this case in no way implies that during an emergency the head of state steps into the position of the legislature as the sovereign legislative authority. On the contrary, legal sovereignty remains with whatever authority the constitution has invested it, and no transfer of it is or can be effected by the principle of imminent state necessity; all it does is to enable the executive to exercise legislative power temporarily on behalf of the incapacitated legislative authority, in order to save the state or society from ruination, but subject to the ultimate authority of the legislature, when it recovers from its incapacitation, to ratify or annul what the executive had done on its behalf. As Chief Justice Muhammad Munir said, the law of civil necessity 'in no way interferes with, or affects, the sovereignty of the legislature.'[38] The principle does not justify any claim of power to legislate independently and exclusively of the sovereign authority.

The minority maintained that the common law of civil necessity is confined to cases where in times of war or other national disaster the executive might interfere with private rights, but that it has never been extended to changes in constitutional law; and that so to extend it would be wholly repugnant to the Government of India Act which prescribed the circumstances and the limits within which the governor-general might exercise legislative powers. Insofar as Chitty's statement of the law relied upon by the majority, implied that the executive could exercise the legislative powers of parliament when that body is not in existence, that relates to 'periods when, and to territories where, the power of the King was, in fact, supreme and undisputed. The records of these affairs are hardly the kind of scripture which one could reasonably expect to be quoted in a proceeding which is essentially one in the enforcement and maintenance of representative institutions.'[39] Once admit that the doctrine of necessity may justify executive encroachment upon the legislative field, and one may not quarrel with its application in the Pakistani situation, since what was done involved no separate legislative initiative on the part of the governor-general, but merely a confirmation of legislation already passed by the legislature.

Such, then, was the rather remarkable application which the doctrine has received in the extraordinary situation existing in Pakistan in 1955. With this may be compared the equally extraordinary experience of Cyprus in 1964.

(ii) *Application of doctrine in Cyprus, 1964*

The application of the doctrine in Cyprus was a case of the legislature itself exceeding the limits of its powers under the constitution, but the Cypriot precedent can only be understood against the background of the nature of the society and of the constitution. The island state of Cyprus, comprising mainly two peoples of different race, nationality, religion and language – Greeks and Turks – is perhaps the most deeply riven of plural societies. So sharply divided and hostile are the two racial groups that relations between them have been marked by a state of extreme tension interspersed with periods of bloody civil conflict. The situation in the island has been aggravated by the fact that the forces at work there are not confined within its boundaries, for the mother country of each of the two island communities, Greece and Turkey, have also been actively involved, and there has always been present a danger of war between the two countries on account of events in Cyprus. The other party in this tragic situation is Britain which had been administering the island (from 1878) until its independence in 1960. When independence began to be envisaged for the island the hostility between the two island communities and the involvement of their respective mother countries assumed more menacing proportions, with the Greek majority, supported by the Greek Government, demanding union of the island with Greece (*Enosis*) and the Turks pressing for partition. The fate of the island in the event of the impending British withdrawal became thus an international issue engaging the vital interests of Greece and Turkey, with Britain more or less in the role of arbitrator. Meeting in Zurich and later in London in February 1959, the three countries undertook to guarantee the integrity of Cyprus as a sovereign state on the basis of certain heads of agreement, which were to be incorporated into its independence constitution as basic articles thereof. A joint commission consisting of members from Greece, Turkey and the two island communities was commissioned to draft the Constitution, which was completed in April and initialled in Ankara on July 29, 1960, by the parties' representatives. On August 16, 1960, the island acceded to independence by virtue of an order-in-council (made under the Cyprus Act, 1960), which gave force of law to the draft constitution. The Constitution gave force of law to the treaty between Cyprus, Greece, Turkey and the United Kingdom whereby the independence, territorial integrity and con-stitution of the state of Cyprus were guaranteed by the parties, and its union with any other state or partition forbidden.[40] It reserved to each of the guarantor countries the right to intervene should there be an attempt to abrogate or subvert the 'state of affairs established by the Basic Articles of the Constitution.' The Constitution also gave force of law to the treaty of alliance between Cyprus, Greece and Turkey, providing for the stationing in Cyprus of Greek and Turkish military contingents for the defence of the island republic against any attack or aggression directed against its independence or territorial integrity.[41]

The conflicting interests represented in Cyprus have impressed upon the constitution a complexity and rigidity unparalleled any-where else in the world. The feature that runs through it is the balancing of almost every conceivable power in the interest of the Turkish minority. All powers, executive, legislative and judicial are shared between the two communities in a manner that seems to caricature reason. In the same way, all public offices and amenities are to be apportioned on a pre-determined ratio of 7 : 3. Commenting, in his usual telling language, upon this unique structure, Professor de Smith observed that 'constitutionalism has run riot in harness with communalism.'[42] 'Two nations,' he went on, 'dwell together under its shadow in uneasy juxtaposition, unsure whether this precariously poised structure is about to fall crashing about their ears.'[43] It did in fact crash between December 1963 and

1964, and it was the situation thus produced that gave rise to the application of the doctrine of civil necessity.

The specific issue concerned the impact of this crash upon the machinery for the administration of justice established by the constitution. The judicial system under the constitution consisted in its most important aspects of a supreme constitutional court composed of three judges, one Greek Cypriot, one Turkish Cypriot and a neutral president;[44] and a high court composed of four judges, two Greek Cypriot, one Turkish Cypriot and a neutral president armed with two votes as a counterpoise to the Greek majority.[45] Between them these two courts exercise the superior judicial authority of the country. There is also power given to establish inferior courts.[46] The high court is to determine the composition of such inferior courts in civil and criminal cases involving persons of different communities, but the court must in any case be of mixed composition with judges drawn from both the Greek and Turkish communities.[47] If only persons from the same community are involved in a case, the court must be composed solely of a judge or judges belonging to that community.[48] These provisions were incorporated into the constitution from the Zurich agreement, and became therefore in accordance with that agreement basic articles which 'cannot, in any way, be amended, whether by way of variation, addition or repeal.'[49] The constitution itself is proclaimed the supreme law of the republic, and 'no law or decision of the House of Representatives or of any of the Communal Chambers and no act or decision of any organ, authority or person in the republic exercising executive power or any administrative function shall in any way be repugnant to, or inconsistent with, any of the provisions of this constitution.'[50]

In July 1963 the neutral president of the Supreme Constitutional Court, a German, resigned; a successor, an Australian, appointed early in December was to have assumed duty in January 1964. Meanwhile on December 21 trouble flared up between the Greek and Turkish communities, thus making it impossible for the new president of the court to arrive in the country. And in May 1964 the neutral president of the high court, a Canadian, also resigned because of the political situation in the country. It should be mentioned here that the appointment of the president and other judges of the two superior courts is the joint responsibility of the president of the republic who must be a Greek and of the vice-president who must be a Turk. Neither can override the other in the appointment of the neutral presidents, but each has an over-riding voice in the appointment of the judges assigned to his own community.[51]

From December 21, 1963, when the troubles started, the Turkish minority immediately organised themselves in armed revolt against the Greek-dominated government. The Turkish military contingent stationed in Cyprus under the provisions of the treaty of alliance moved out of their camp and took up positions outside Nicosia, the capital. The Turks established military control over their own quarter of Nicosia and over certain other parts of the country, to which access was barred to Greek Cypriots. Armed clashes occurred between groups from the two communities, resulting in loss of life, damage to property, interruption of communications and a general breakdown of law and order in the areas affected by such clashes. To prevent further clashes while negotiations in international circles were going on to find a political settlement, a United Nations peace-keeping force was sent to the country with the consent of the government. Claiming that the Cyprus Government had lost its legality and had thereby forfeited any right to be recognised as the lawful government, the Turkish vice-president, ministers, members of the house of representatives and civil servants withdrew from participation in the government. Turkish judges of the district courts also refused to attend court except in one or two cases. The non-participation of the Turkish vice-president in the government made it impossible for the vacancy in the presidency of the high court to be filled or for a substitute to be found to the new Australian president of the supreme constitutional court who had not turned up to take up his appointment because of the troubles. The result was that the two courts had been unable to function for some fourteen months, which meant that appeals in both civil and criminal matters could not be heard, and, with the impossibility of forming mixed courts, the administration of justice and consequently the protection of the rule of law was all but paralysed.

The non-functioning of the supreme constitutional court affected the governmental structure in other respects, since the court is the pivot of the constitutional system in the country. For in it is vested exclusive jurisdiction to interpret the constitution, to adjudicate upon the constitutionality of laws, upon any conflict of power between the organs and institutions of government,[52] and upon any question whether a law or decision of the house of representatives, including a budget, discriminates against either of the two communities.[53] In this latter case, the function of the court is more than that of a judicial tribunal, for it may either confirm or annul the alleged discriminatory law or decision, or return it to the House for reconsideration. Questions (not involving any issue of constitutionality) relating to abuse or excess of their powers by administrative authorities are also exclusively for the court to decide,[54] and it also decides whether a vacant post is to be filled by a Greek or Turk where the public service commission is unable to reach a decision upon the matter.[55]

It was in these circumstances that the house of representatives, sitting with only its Greek Cypriot members, on July 9, 1964, passed a law, the Administration of Justice (Miscellaneous Provisions) Law, to enable justice to continue to be administered pending a political settlement of the controversy. The law established a supreme court composed of the three Greek and the two Turkish judges of the supreme constitutional court and the high court, and vested in it the jurisdiction and powers of those two courts. It also empowered the new court to determine the composition of subordinate courts without the requirement that in mixed cases such courts should contain a Greek and a Turkish judge. Its constitutionality was challenged on the ground that it contravened the basic articles of the constitution regulating the administration of justice and defining the jurisdiction and powers of the courts, which articles are made unalterable by the house of representatives or even at all.[56] A further ground of challenge was that the law had not been promulgated in accordance with the constitution, which required laws made by the house of representatives to be promulgated conjointly by the president and vice-president by publication in the official gazette in both the Greek and Turkish languages.[57] The law had been promulgated by the president alone and was published in the gazette only in Greek.

It was admitted that the law contravened the express provisions of the constitution in all the respects alleged, but it was nevertheless contended to have been validly enacted by virtue of the doctrine of civil necessity. In separate exhaustive judgments all three judges nominated by the full bench of the court to determine the case, examined the status and applicability of the doctrine in various jurisdictions, English, French, Italian and Greek, and came to the unanimous conclusion that, as in these other jurisdictions, the doctrine should be read into the written constitution of Cyprus as an inarticulate major premise thereof, and that so incorporated it operates to qualify, though not to abolish, the concept of the inviolability of the constitution's supremacy and consequently of the limitations which the constitution imposes upon governmental powers. Upon the question whether the situation existing in the country at the time the law was enacted justified the legislature in exceeding the limits of its power, the court held that the non-participation of the Turks in the government on account of the troubles which had developed between them and the Greek majority, had destroyed the premise upon which the constitutional structure was built, and had thereby created a situation which could not be met within the express provisions of the constitution, but which nevertheless called for action to ensure the continuance of a vital function of the state, namely the administration of justice, without which, law and order was bound sooner or later to break down. The maintenance of law and order at all times is an imperative necessity for the preservation of society and the state. As Justice Triantafyllides puts it:

> 'Organs of government set up under a constitution are vested expressly with the competence granted to them by such a constitution, but they have always an implied duty to govern. It would be absurd to accept that if, for one reason or other, an emergency arises, which cannot be met within the express letter of the constitution, then such organs need not take the necessary measures in the matter, and that they would be entitled to abdicate their responsibilities and watch helplessly the disintegration of the country or an essential function of the state, such as the administration of justice. Notwithstanding a constitutional deadlock, the State continues to exist and together with it continues to exist the need for proper government. The Government and the Legislature are empowered and bound to see that legislative measures are taken in ensuring proper administration where what has been provided for under the constitution, for the purpose, has ceased to function.'[58]

To hold otherwise, he maintains, would amount to saying that 'a state, and the people, should be allowed to perish for the sake of its constitution.'[59]

It was argued that the doctrine was not applicable in the circumstances, since its application presupposes the existence of an emergency, and that since no emergency had been proclaimed in accordance with the provisions of the constitution, it must be assumed that no public danger threatening the life of the state existed such as would justify the legislature exceeding its constitutional powers. The constitution empowers the council of ministers, subject to a veto by the president or vice-president, to issue a proclamation of emergency, 'in case of war or other public danger threatening the life of the republic or any part thereof.'[60] In the opinion of the court, however, the exercise of power by an organ of government in excess of its ordinary constitutional competence, upon the ground of necessity to save the constitution and the state from destruction, does not depend upon whether a state of emergency has been formally proclaimed. 'It would be an abdication of responsibility on the part of this court,' observed Justice Triantafyllides, 'to close its eyes to the realities of the situation, because, for any reason, no Proclamation of Emergency has been made under Article 183, and to hold that everything is normal in Cyprus.'[61] The court also held that, in any case, the provisions of Article 183 were altogether inadequate to meet the abnormal situation under consideration which had not been foreseen nor provided for by the framers of the constitution. The case therefore illustrates how much more sweeping are the powers that may be exercised by virtue of the doctrine of civil necessity than under the express emergency provisions of the constitution. For although the constitution empowers the council of ministers to legislate by ordinance on matters strictly connected with the state of emergency,[62] neither the proclamation of emergency nor any such ordinance can suspend any provisions of the constitution except certain of the articles relating to fundamental rights and liberties.[63]

Granted that the situation created a necessity justifying the legislature in exceeding its powers, the crucial question still remains whether the provisions of the law were reasonably warranted by the necessity. This is an important condition for the application of the doctrine. Since what prevented the supreme constitutional court and the high court from functioning was the vacancy in their presidentships and the impossibility of filling them, was the action called for not one that might enable those courts to function in some form or other, instead of their temporary replacement by a completely new court not contemplated by the constitution? The new supreme court, composed, as it was, of the three Greek and the two Turkish judges of the supreme constitutional court and the high court, gave the Greeks a majority. If this was considered a satisfactory solution – and it must be noted again that the new court combined all the powers and jurisdiction of the two courts – then it would have been equally satisfactory to have provided for the appointment to the supreme constitutional court of one additional Cypriot judge, preferably a Turk, since it is the Turks who stand in most need of the court's protection. The Law would then empower the president to make the appointment alone should the Turkish vice-president not be willing to countersign it. With regard to the high court, it would have been enough to empower it to function with its two Greek and one Turkish judges. The Greek majority in the high court and the absence of the neutral president's neutralising extra vote would make it all the more desirable to appoint as the additional judge to the supreme constitutional court a Turk. It is difficult to resist the inference that perhaps the main operative factor in merging the functions of the two courts in one supreme court was what Justice Vassiliades referred to as the 'obstruction,

delay and expense in ordinary litigation,'[64] caused by the dichotomy
in the judicial system and the procedure requiring all constitutional
questions arising in proceedings before the high court and the
inferior courts to be referred to the supreme constitutional court,
and Justice Triantafyllides as 'the need for maximum efficiency.'[65]

Furthermore, the provision of the law empowering the new
supreme court to assign a sole judge to try mixed cases was based
upon the impossibility of forming mixed courts owing to the non-
attendance of Turkish inferior judges. It was conceded, however,
that the Turkish inferior judges resumed sitting again in June, so
that on July 9 when the law was enacted this particular necessity
had been removed. The argument that 'it is likely that the same
factor or factors which prevented them from attending in the past
may at any moment prevent them again from carrying out their
judicial duties,'[66] does not seem convincing, much less conclusive.
Even if it were genuinely feared that they might absent themselves
again in the future, the power of the court to dispense with mixed
courts in mixed cases should have been made conditional upon that
fear materialising.

In view of all this, one is inclined to question the correctness
of the court's decision that the particular provisions of the law were
legally justified by necessity. It is true that the law was a temporary
measure, and in no way abolished the two superior courts established by the constitution, yet its provisions would appear somewhat
disproportionate to the immediate necessity they were intended to
meet. It may be conceded that the non-participation of the Turkish
vice-president in the government justified promulgation of the law
by the Greek president alone, but the justification for the non-
publication of the law in the Turkish language is not so easy to
accept, namely the absence from duty of Turkish officers in the
printing department, who should have done the translation. One
shares Justice Vassiliades' worry over this point. It was admitted
that thousands of Turkish Cypriots were still to be found in areas
controlled by the government, so that it would have been possible
to secure the services of one of them to do the translation. No effort
in that direction was made. There was good reason for requiring
laws to be published in both languages and stipulating that a law
only comes into force on the day it was so published. Accordingly,
even if we grant that the enactment of the law was justified by
necessity, it should be deemed not to have come into force as far
as the Turks were concerned. For (excepting for those of them who
could read Greek) how otherwise could they inform themselves of
its contents? The view of the court that, if the enactment of the law
itself was justified by necessity, its non-publication in Turkish

should not be allowed to defeat it seems to confuse validity with
the coming into force of the law.

(iii) *Application in Nigeria*

Nigeria had been in the throes of a crisis since the last federal
election of 1964. In 1966 the army finally struck. The action,
organised by a group of young army majors, took place simultaneously in the three capitals of the federation soon after midnight on
January 15. Led by a dashing and spirited officer, Major Chukwuma
Nzeogwu, the operations in the Northern capital, Kaduna, were
successful in overthrowing the regional government of Sir Ahmadu
Bello, who was killed when the soldiers stormed his official residence.
For a couple of days thereafter, Major Nzeogwu, as leader of the
revolting soldiers, held the reins of government in the region. In the
West and Lagos, the operations were only partially successful. The
head of the Western regional government, Chief Akintola, was
killed, and the federal prime minister, Sir Abubakar Tafawa
Balewa, and his minister of finance, Chief Festus Okotie-Ebo, were
kidnapped and taken to an unknown destination, where some days
later their bodies were discovered by villagers. But the coup
organisers had failed to gain control of the military power in Lagos
which is always the decisive factor in the success of a coup. To
their discomfiture, the General Officer Commanding the Nigerian
army, Major-General Aguiyi-Ironsi, who was to have been arrested,
escaped their dragnet, and quickly rallied the rest of the army
against the coup organisers, posting loyal troops to guard public
buildings and ministerial quarters in Lagos, Ibadan and Enugu.
With their plans thus aborted by the action of the major-general,
the coup organisers in the South were forced to go underground.
But the danger was not yet completely averted. Major Nzeogwu
remained in control of the seat of government of the North wherein
lay most of the country's military installations and equipment.
What was indeed more ominous, there were indications that he
was preparing to march down to the South.

Meeting in Lagos under the shadow of this threat of civil war,
the remnants of the federal council of ministers were given an
assessment of the situation by the General Officer Commanding.
The whereabouts of the prime minister were still at the time
unknown. The dire necessity created by his absence was for a
leader to hold the government together in order to be able to deal
effectively with the threatening situation. Among the available
ministers there was much jockeying for leadership. It soon became
clear from this that none of them was acceptable to all as leader.

They proved incapable of maintaining their own unity. How much less able would they then have been to mobilise the forces of the nation to fight an invasion of the dissident soldiers from the North! In the face of their own disunity, surely the path of reason and the one most calculated to preserve their own lives and that of the nation, was to withdraw, even if temporarily, from the helm of affairs, and let others handle the situation. In the event that was what they did. In a short but historic speech at 11.50 p.m. on January 16, the Acting President, Dr. Nwafor Orizu (the President, Dr. Nnamdi Azikiwe, was away on a convalescent holiday in Britain) announced to the anxious nation that he had 'tonight been advised by the council of ministers that they had come to the unanimous decision voluntarily to hand over the administration of the country to the Armed Forces of the Republic with immediate effect,' and expressed his 'fervent hope that the new administration will ensure the peace and stability of the Federal Republic of Nigeria and that all citizens will give them their full co-operation.'[67] He then called upon the General Officer Commanding to inform the nation of the policy of the new Administration. In his own speech, the G.O.C. stated, *inter alia*, that 'the government of the Federation having ceased to function, the Nigerian armed forces have been invited to form an interim military government for the purposes of maintaining law and order and of maintaining essential services.' 'This invitation,' he continued, 'has been accepted and I, General J.T.U. Aguiyi-Ironsi, the General Officer Commanding the Nigerian Army, have been formally invested with authority as Head of the Federal Military Government, and Supreme Commander of the Nigerian Armed Forces.'[68]

This event is open to at least two interpretations. It might be regarded either as a revolution or as a change of government under the constitution. Its character depends upon whether the hand-over could be justified by reference to the constitution. If it cannot, then it is unquestionably a revolution. It was indeed a unique event. For, as the supreme court of Nigeria has observed, 'it is no gainsay that what happened in Nigeria in January 1966 is unprecedented in history. Never before, as far as we are aware, has a civilian government invited an army take-over, or the armed forces to form an interim government.'[69]

On the view that it is a constitutional change, it is necessary to be quite clear what exactly was handed over. Judged by what the Acting President and G.O.C. said, clearly what was handed over (was purported to have been handed over) to the armed forces was not just the executive authority of the country, but the entire legislative sovereignty as well. By the hand-over, the armed forces became the sole government of the country, combining all the powers, legislative and executive, of both the federal and regional governments. As a government, whether for an interim period or not, they were invested with the totality of the country's sovereignty – absolute, undivided and unlimited sovereignty. Before this, no one single government in the Federation possessed the absolute sovereignty. That was the inevitable consequence of the federal character of the Constitution, which divided sovereignty between a federal and four regional governments.

The words used by the Acting President and the G.O.C. made it clear too that only sovereignty was being handed over. They manifested no intention to abrogate the Constitution. It must be assumed that the Constitution was to remain in force as the basic law of the country, and that the sovereignty ceded to the armed forces was to be exercised within its general framework. There is nothing inconsistent in this, for, as has been pointed out,[70] the sovereignty of government operating under a written constitution does not exclude the supremacy of the constitution. The Constitution is wider than and above the sovereignty of government. However, the ultimate mark of sovereignty is the ability to alter the constitution in its entirety. While, therefore, absolute sovereignty had been ceded to the armed forces to be exercised within the general framework of the Constitution, they acquired by the cession competence to deal with the Constitution in any way they might think fit – to preserve it, suspending or modifying only such of its provisions as are incompatible with the structure and purposes of a military government or to abrogate it completely.

Considered as an event which affected only sovereignty while leaving the constitution in force until abrogated or altered by the new sovereign authority, what the council of ministers did amounted clearly to abdication of sovereignty in favour of the armed forces. The first constitutional issue that arises then is whether sovereignty can be abdicated. Abdication implies an act of self-effacement, of self-destruction. It involves the surrender of the whole of the abdicating sovereign's power. As early as the seventeenth century, abdication has been recognised as legally feasible. Thus Sir Francis Bacon in his legal maxims drew a distinction between it and an attempt by the sovereign irrevocably to limit his sovereignty without a prior act of abdication. A sovereign cannot, *while remaining such under the constitution,* limit his sovereignty, as, for example, by transferring part of it irrevocably to another body or person.[71] 'It is,' declares Bacon, 'in the power of Parliament to extinguish or transfer their own authority, but not, whilst the authority remains entire, to restrain the functions and exercise of the same authority.'[72]

In the same vein, Dicey, writing on the occasion of the controversy over Gladstone's Government of Ireland Bill, 1886, said: 'No principle of jurisprudence is more certain than that sovereignty implies the power of abdication.'[73] In this view he was supported by the two other leading English constitutional lawyers of the time, Sir William Anson[74] and Lord Bryce.[75] Dicey takes up the point again in his *Law of the Constitution*, where he provides an exposition of the two ideas of abdication and the illimitability of sovereignty, which for its clarity and cogency perhaps deserves to be quoted *in extenso*:

'Let the reader, however, note that the impossibility of placing a limit on the exercise of sovereignty does not in any way prohibit either logically, or in matter of fact, the abdication of sovereignty. This is worth observation, because a strange dogma is sometimes put forward that a sovereign power, such as the Parliament of the United Kingdom, can never by its own act divest itself of sovereignty. This position is, however, clearly untenable. An autocrat, such as the Russian Czar, can undoubtedly abdicate; but sovereignty or the possession of supreme power in a state, whether it be in the hands of a Czar or of a Parliament, is always one and the same quality. If the Czar can abdicate, so can a Parliament. To argue or imply that because sovereignty is not limitable (which is true) it cannot be surrendered (which is palpably untrue) involves the confusion of two distinct ideas. It is like arguing that because no man can, while he lives, give up, do what he will, his freedom of volition, so no man can commit suicide. A sovereign power can divest itself of authority in two ways, and (it is submitted) in two ways only. It may simply put an end to its own existence. Parliament could extinguish itself by legally dissolving itself and leaving no means whereby a subsequent Parliament could be legally summoned . . . A sovereign again may transfer sovereign authority to another person or body of persons.'[76]

The Acts of Union between England and Scotland in 1707, and between Great Britain and Ireland in 1801, Dicey maintains, involved just such an abdication. Here again he is supported by Sir William Anson,[77] and more recently by Professor Smith, the renowned authority on Scottish law.[78]

Granted, then, that sovereignty can be abdicated, the next question is whether the hand-over was in accordance with the express provisions of the constitution. Or, putting it differently, was the Acting President, acting upon the advice of the council of ministers, competent to dispose of the sovereignty of the country?

It is clear that he had no such power under the express provisions of the constitution. The most he could do was to dissolve parliament. Dissolution is, however, only a temporary effacement of parliament, because, having dissolved parliament, he was bound under the Constitution to summon a new one within three months. Abdication of sovereignty to the armed forces required much more than the effacement of the federal parliament and government. It required also the effacement of the regional legislatures and governments as well, and the hand-over of all the legislative and executive powers of all the governments in the Federation. This would require an amendment of Sections 69 to 85 of the constitution under which sovereignty was distributed between the Centre and the Regions; the amendment would then provide that the legislative and executive authority of the republic was now vested absolutely in the armed forces; Section 4 of the Constitution, prescribing the procedure for constitutional amendment, would also have to be repealed completely. Not even Parliament alone could effect such amendments, for Sections 4 and 69 to 85 were among the fundamental provisions which were doubly entrenched in the constitution. Their amendment required not only the authority of parliament (and a two-thirds majority in both Houses was necessary) but also the consent of the legislative houses of at least three regions signified by resolution.

It is true that the creation of new states out of the existing states needed in addition the consent of 60 per cent of the registered voters in the area to be affected, but that limitation would be got rid of indirectly through the power of parliament to amend Section 3 of the Constitution, under which the regions were established and their territories defined. It may be observed in parenthesis that the power of parliament unilaterally to abolish the regions or any of them was a curious one. No doubt it was not contemplated that this power should be used, yet it is anomalous that one unit of government in a federation should be given power unilaterally to abolish the others or any of them.

Clearly, therefore, the president lacked power under the express provisions of the Constitution to cede sovereignty to the armed forces. It is true that where the cession of sovereignty is to a foreign power, the head of state is the appropriate authority to do this. This is because 'the head of a state, as its chief organ and representative in the totality of its international relations, acts for his state in its international intercourse, with the consequence that all his legally relevant international acts are considered to be acts of his state. His competence to perform such acts is termed *jus repraesentationis omnimodae*.'[79] Thus, Professor Smith maintains that the

Union between England and Scotland in 1707 derives essentially, not from the ratifying Acts passed by the English and Scottish Parliaments respectively, but from the Articles of Agreement concluded between the two countries. This Agreement, he asserts, constituted 'a treaty in international law between two sovereign states – the treaty being concluded not by the Parliaments, which did not exercise the prerogative treaty-making powers, but by Anne, Queen of Scotland, with Anne, Queen of England.'[80] Yet an international cession of sovereignty sounds not only in international law; it has also to conform with the domestic law, which will invariably require the authority of the legislative sovereign (i.e. parliament), unless parliament has been incapacitated by the event necessitating the cession.

The fact that the president had no power under the express provisions of the constitution to abdicate sovereignty to the armed forces does not, however, conclude the matter, since in addition to its express provisions, the constitution incorporated by implication the law of necessity. Was the hand-over, then, justified by necessity? It cannot be doubted that the action of the coup organisers, and in particular Major Nzeogwu's warlike preparations, created an emergency situation of the utmost gravity for the life of the republic. The object of the coup organisers was to terminate the rule of the discredited politicians, and it was not likely that any settlement short of this would have induced them to lay down their arms. Major Nzeogwu indeed made this a condition of his surrender to Major-General Aguiyi-Ironsi. The hand-over was therefore clearly warranted by the exigency. It was the only course of action that would have averted the threat of civil war.

But the doctrine of necessity requires, not only that the action taken must be warranted by the exigency, but also that the authority competent to take the necessary action must have been temporarily incapacitated. There was in fact such temporary incapacitation of the competent authority, in this case parliament and the regional legislatures. The premiers of both the North and West had been killed in the early hours of January 15. With their deaths all the other ministerial appointments in the two regions were in accordance with the Constitution vacated. There being thus no one to advise the governor of either region with regard to the exercise of his power, the regional legislature could not be summoned. To forestall operations planned in the East and the Mid-West by the coup-makers, the G.O.C. had had loyal troops posted to guard public buildings and ministerial quarters in their capitals. Afraid for their own lives, the ministers slipped out of their official residences and disappeared to their respective villages, so that the government and the legislature in both regions were also in no state to function. Only in Lagos therefore did the constitutional authorities retain some semblance of freedom of action, owing to the presence and prompt intervention of the G.O.C. Yet even there, the situation was steadily deteriorating. Parliament had met briefly on January 15, but thereafter its members had not been allowed to resume their business, the building having been cordoned off by loyal soldiers to prevent its being taken over by the coup organisers. In any case Lagos was so gripped by fear as to what might happen next, that most members felt it risky to stay in Lagos and so returned to the safety of their villages. This left the Acting President and his ministers as the only constitutional authorities in the country that remained in anything like a functioning state after January 15. In these circumstances, with parliament and the regional legislatures and governments incapacitated, it was permissible for the president, in accordance with the law of necessity, to exercise on behalf of those bodies the authority ordinarily belonging to them.

As a constitutional head, the president could act only upon ministerial advice, and the hand-over speech stated that he had been so advised. This presupposes that the ministers who advised him were still such at the time the advice was given. Their status depended of course upon the fate of the Prime Minister at that particular time. Was he still alive or dead? If the latter, then all the other ministerial appointments became automatically vacated. It was not known, however, precisely at what moment of time he died. All that was known was that he had been kidnapped, and it might reasonably be presumed that until his body was discovered he was alive. Even if he were presumed to have died at the time of the hand-over, it would still have been permissible for the president, as the only remaining constitutional authority, by virtue of the law of necessity, to act on behalf of the legislative bodies.

All the cases discussed earlier in which the doctrine of necessity has been applied are concerned with the exercise of power by an authority not otherwise competent to do so, and not with the abdication of sovereign power itself. Indeed, so far from abdication being contemplated in the Pakistani case, the basis of the decision presupposes, not the destruction, but the continued existence, of the legislature whose temporary incapacitation creates the necessity for the head of state to exercise its power pending such time as it is again in a position to express its will on the matter. However, where an emergency which has arisen can only be met effectively by the abdication of sovereignty to the armed forces or other person or authority, there is no reason why this cannot be done by virtue of the law of necessity. The object is to save the state and society from destruction, and if this can only be done by abdicating sovereign power to a body best able to achieve the object, then abdication of sovereignty ought to be within the permissible ambit of the doctrine.

In a recent case, *Lakanmi v. The Attorney-General (West)*,[81] the supreme court of Nigeria, sitting with a full bench of five judges, has had to consider the doctrine of necessity in relation to the hand-over of January 16, 1966, and the status of the military government. Against the argument of the learned attorney-general that the doctrine applies only with regard to colonial governments, the court unhesitantly affirmed it. 'We think it wrong,' said Chief Justice Ademola, delivering the unanimous judgment of the court, 'to expect that constitutions must make provisions for all exigencies. No constitution can anticipate all the different forms of phenomena which may beset a nation.' The application of the doctrine to the hand-over received, however, only a brief treatment. The court affirmed the view that the grant of power to the armed forces took place by virtue of the doctrine, and was therefore in accordance with the Constitution which for this purpose includes the law of necessity. It rejected the contention that the hand-over could not have been under the Constitution, and that it was a revolution which destroyed the constitution. In the view of the court, the event could not have been a revolution, because there was no question of seizure of power by the section of the armed forces which started the rebellion; the rebellion had indeed aborted, and it was not to the insurgents that power was handed over.

It was with the nature of the military government and the extent of the powers granted to it that the court was largely concerned. From the premise that the hand-over was effected under the Constitution, it follows that the military government created thereby was at its inception a government under the Constitution, which therefore continued in force after the hand-over. Yet, as has been pointed out, what was handed over was the entire sovereignty of the country. Just as parliament, with the concurrence of the regional legislatures, could have altered or abrogated the Constitution, so could the military government after it had been invested with the totality of the sovereignty which under the constitution had been divided between the federal and regional legislatures. However, instead of abrogating the Constitution, the military government chose to preserve and govern under it. Of course those of its provisions relating to the political organs (the legislature, president and ministers, both federal and regional) had of necessity to be suspended, and eventually dissolved;[82] so also all such other provisions that had those organs specifically in mind had to be suspended or modified in order to conform to the structure of the military government. These suspensions and modifications were effected by the Constitution (Suspension and Modification) Decrees. At the same time, by these same decrees, the military government declared its intention to use its sovereign power at any time to amend the Constitution either expressly or by means of enactments inconsistent with it. Thus, by Section 3 of the Constitution Decree No. 1 of 1966, the federal military government declares its power to make laws by decrees for the peace, order and good government of Nigeria or any part thereof with respect to any matter whatsoever; the Constitution, the section further provides, shall not prevail over a decree, nor shall anything therein contained render any provision of a decree void to any extent whatsoever. By Section 6, no question as to the validity of a decree shall be entertained by any court of law.

The supreme court took a different view of the nature and powers of the military government. First it held it to be a *constitutional interim government*, basing its finding on the reference to 'an interim military government' contained in the speech of the G.O.C., in which the acceptance of the hand-over of power was announced. From its character as an interim government arose an implied obligation on the part of the military government to preserve and uphold the Constitution; the military government must be deemed therefore never to have intended 'to rule but by the Constitution.' The cession of power to the military being thus for an interim period, no question of their power to abrogate the constitution completely could arise. 'We venture,' said Chief Justice Ademola, 'to put the attitude of the Acting President and the council of ministers to the head of the army thus – your men have started a rebellion, which we fear may spread; you have the means to deal with them. We leave it to you to deal with them and after this, return the administrative power of the government to us.'

The court conceded that the military government had power to amend the Constitution, but its power to do so was not an unfettered or unlimited one. Only amendments that could properly be justified by the doctrine of necessity whereby the federal military government was granted power were permitted to it. For it was not intended that the federal military government, in its power to enact decrees, should exceed the requirements or demands of the necessity of the case. 'The necessity must arise before a decree is passed ousting any portion of the Constitution. In effect, the Constitution still remains the law of the country and all laws are subject to the Constitution excepting so far as by necessity the Constitution is amended by decree. This does not mean that the Constitution of the country ceases to have effect as a superior norm. From the facts of the taking over, as we have pointed out, the federal military government is an interim government of necessity concerned in the political cauldron of its inception as a means of dealing effectively with the situation which has arisen, and its main object is to protect lives and property and to maintain law and order.' The provision in Section 3 of the Constitution Decree No. 1 of 1966 that nothing in the Constitution shall render any provision of a decree void to any extent whatsoever must therefore be read subject to this implied limitation.

The specific issue in the case before the court concerned a conflict between a decree and certain aspects of the Constitution which were not suspended by the Constitution Decrees, namely the fundamental rights chapter and the sections establishing and definining (in part at least) the jurisdiction of the superior courts. The decree alleged to be in conflict with these aspects of the Constitution was the Forfeiture of Assets, etc. (Validation) Decree No. 45 of 1968. The background to this decree was the policy of the military government to clean up the society of corruption, which was one of the principal causes of the abortive coup that brought the military government into existence. Not long after taking office, it enacted a law, the Investigation of Assets (Public Officers) Decree No. 51 of 1966, authorising the assets of public officers suspected of having corruptly enriched themselves at the expense of the public, to be investigated. A similar law, covering persons other than public officers, was also enacted by the military government of Western Nigeria in 1967. Under the later enactment, a tribunal of inquiry, with a judge of the high court as chairman, was appointed. By virtue of its powers under the law, the tribunal made an order attaching the properties, both real and personal, of certain persons who then brought an action challenging the validity of the law and of the order. It being feared that the regional enactment might be void through inconsistency with the Federal Decree No. 51 (actually the Supreme Court declared it void, on the ground that as Decree No. 51 manifested an intention to cover the field on this matter, it thereby excluded separate regional legislation),[83] the federal military government intervened in favour of the regional military government and enacted in 1968 three decrees, among them the Investigation of Assets (Public Officers *and other Persons*) Decree (which repealed Decree No. 51 of 1966) and the Forfeiture of Assets, etc. (Validation) Decree.

The validation decree validates certain orders (scheduled to the decree) made under various enactments, whereby some public officers or persons had had their assets forfeited or were adjudged liable to make reparation; it also validates the order made by the tribunal under the West regional enactment which had attached the plaintiffs' properties. Finally it precludes the courts from inquiring into the validity of anything done under any of the Investigation enactments, provides for the abatement of all pending proceedings arising from actions taken under such enactments, and excludes the application of the fundamental rights chapter in relation thereto.

It cannot be questioned that the decree was directed against the plaintiffs and their pending action. It was therefore impugned on the ground that it was a legislative judgment which imposed sentence (namely the attachment of properties) upon named individuals without prior trial by a court of law, and that as such it amounted to a usurpation of the judicial power under the Constitution. As the court held, the separation of judicial power from the legislative and executive powers remained, even after the hand-over, a fundamental provision of the Constitution, and by assuming to pass legislative judgment and to impose sentence on named persons, the military government was usurping the judicial power, contrary to the Constitution.[84] Furthermore, as an enactment confiscating or attaching the property of named individuals the decree violated the provision of the bill of rights which prohibits the compulsory acquisition of property without the payment of adequate compensation except under a *general law* which imposes penalties or forfeitures for breach of the law, whether under civil process or after conviction for an offence.[85] Such a usurpation of the judicial power or violation of the individual's guaranteed right could be justified only by a valid alteration of the Constitution. The question then was whether the decree was a valid exercise of the military government's power to legislate inconsistently with the constitution. As already stated, the court held that the power of the military government to amend the Constitution was limited to what was properly required by the necessity under which it took power; in its view the decree went 'beyond the necessity of the occasion,' and was accordingly *ultra vires* and void.

Accepting that the military government acquired its powers by virtue of the doctrine of necessity, it is difficult to see on what ground the doctrine can be used to limit the absolute powers thereby ceded. The necessity that compelled the hand-over of power to the armed forces was not a continuing one. It ended when, after the formation of the military government, Major Nzeogwu and his fellow coup-makers surrendered themselves to the head of the federal military government, and accepted the authority of his government, and were taken into protective custody. What other necessity was there, which imposed this limitation upon the powers of the federal military government? The judgment itself recognised that the only necessity was the insurgency created by the coup-makers. It cannot be said that the troubles in Western Nigeria were part of the necessity which compelled the council of ministers to abdicate power to the armed forces. And even those troubles as well as those in Tivland were soon quelled. Or was it the general necessity of maintaining law and order? If that was the sole justification for the existence and exercise of power by the military government, then it must follow that the vast majority of the laws and executive actions of the government, which had no bearing upon law and order, such as those relating to companies, limitation of actions, etc., would also be *ultra vires* and void. Indeed the continuance of the military government might be questioned. Clearly the view taken by the court is untenable.

Furthermore, too much appears to have been made of the reference to an 'interim military government' in the speech of the G.O.C. on the occasion of the hand-over. More weight should have been given to the words used by the acting president, since it was those which conveyed the actual decision of the council of ministers. Nor does it follow from the G.O.C.'s use of the word 'interim' that the military government was supposed merely to be holding the fort for the civilian rulers until the emergency was over. That is clearly not the ordinary meaning of an interim government. The use of the word in this context could not have been intended to mean more than the military government was a temporary or provisional one. But it clearly does not imply the existence in the background of an existing permanent government temporarily put out of action by an emergency and which is to resume its power upon the cessation of the emergency. So to hold would be to deny that the action of the council of ministers was an abdication; abdication, as already explained, means self-destruction or suicide.

Without question the decision of the court constituted a serious undermining of the power of the federal military government, and it is hardly surprising that it should have provoked an adverse reaction from the government. For, on May 9, 1970, two weeks after the decision was handed down, the government came out with a decree, entitled Federal Military Government (Supremacy and Enforcement of Powers) Decree 1970. This nullified the court's decision,[86] and declared that what took place on January 15 and 16 was a revolution which 'effectively abrogated the whole pre-existing legal order in Nigeria except what has been preserved under the Constitution (Suspension and Modification) Decree 1966 (1966 No. 1).'[87] Perhaps if the court had recognised the absolute power of the federal military government under the Constitution, the government might not have been driven to the view of the event of January as a revolution. But what exactly is the nature and constitutional effect of a revolution? It is to this question that we will turn in the next chapter, but before doing that let us consider the recent invocation of the doctrine of necessity in Southern Rhodesia.

(iv) *Application in Southern Rhodesia*

It is perhaps not without justification that necessity has been called the 'devil's authority.' A doctrine which can be invoked alike by the constituted authority and by those seeking to destroy it has something of the ring of a paradox. But it is claimed that a rebel against constituted authority who is in actual control may on the ground of necessity take measures to deal with a situation which threatens to destroy society itself.

Like the hand-over of power to the armed forces by the civilian government of Nigeria, the situation which arose from the unilateral declaration of independence by Ian Smith and his colleagues in Southern Rhodesia is in its own way unparalleled in legal history. Originally acquired by conquest by the British South African Company, Southern Rhodesia was annexed by the British Crown as a colony by an order-in-council of September 12, 1923. Under a Constitution of 1961, the territory had attained a large measure of autonomy, but it remained still a colony, and so subject to the authority of the British government and parliament. This authority the prime minister of the colony, Ian Smith, and his fellow-ministers, purported to throw off on November 1, 1965, by unilaterally declaring the colony an independent, sovereign state under a new constitution. This unilateral declaration of independence (U.D.I. as it has become known) was unquestionably illegal, and was declared so by the British authorities. For on the very day of its declaration, the governor of the colony, acting on instructions from Her Majesty, dismissed the prime minister and the other ministers from office, as he was entitled to do, since under the 1961 Constitution the ministers held office during Her Majesty's pleasure. Five days later, the British parliament itself intervened and declared its sovereignty in the colony unaffected by the U.D.I. By the Southern Rhodesia Act it enacted that 'Southern Rhodesia continues to be part of Her Majesty's dominions, and that the government and parliament of the United Kingdom have responsibility and jurisdiction as heretofore for and in respect of it.'[88] The Act authorised Her Majesty in Council to make all such provisions for the colony as might be called for by the illegal action of Ian Smith, including power to suspend, amend or revoke the 1961 Constitution.[89] Pursuant to this, Her Majesty in Council made the Southern

Rhodesia (Constitution) Order, 1965, which made provision for the government of the territory in the circumstances created by the U.D.I. After declaring Mr. Smith's new Constitution void and of no effect,[90] the order-in-council prohibited the Legislature of Southern Rhodesia from functioning, and transferred all its powers to Her Majesty in Council;[91] executive authority was to be exercised by a Secretary of State and, subject thereto, by the governor.[92] Finally it declared any law made, business transacted, steps taken or function exercised in contravention of its provisions to be void and of no effect.[93]

It is remarkable, however, that, having divested the local political organs of their power and assumed unto itself complete power over the territory, the British government took no steps to provide an alternative functioning government. Although some thirty-eight orders-in-council were made for Southern Rhodesia, none dealt with matters connected with the ordinary running of the government. Nor was there any attempt to provide political direction for the public services. In short the lawful legislature and executive remained almost completely dormant and inactive. The judiciary, the armed forces, the police and the public service had been enjoined by the governor on the day of U.D.I. 'to maintain law and order in the country and to carry on with their normal tasks,' but the lawful authority left them entirely to their own devices, with no effort to provide the needful political direction and no arrangement for the payment of their salaries.

Without such political direction and financial provision for the running of the administration, it was perhaps to be expected that a vacuum would, sooner or later, arise in the government, with a consequent chaos in society. The rebel government by supplying a functioning government prevented this from happening. They did so of course in disregard of their dismissal and the prohibition contained in the 1965 order-in-council, but under their own illegal Constitution which established in place of the old legislature, a rebel parliament, and in place of the colonial governor, an 'Officer Administering the Government,' while still recognising the British monarch as 'the Queen of Rhodesia,'[94] and also permitting the courts to continue to function under the 1961 Constitution.

Was this government a lawful one? If it was not a lawful government, was it entitled to recognition by the courts as a *de facto* one? If it was neither a lawful nor a *de facto* government, were its acts, legislative or executive, entitled to recognition to any, and if so, what, extent?

These were the questions posed to the courts in Rhodesia and the Judicial Committee of the Privy Council in London. The actual case that gave rise to these questions arose out of the detention of one Daniel Madzimbamuto, whose experiences under the Smith régime had been very sad. He was first detained in 1959 under emergency regulations then in force in the colony. From that detention he was released to a restriction area in 1961, and finally given his freedom in January 1963. In April 1964 a new restriction order was made against him, which was lifted in April 1965 to be followed two months later by yet a fresh restriction for five years. On November 5, 1965, a state of emergency was validly proclaimed by the governor, and Emergency Regulations were made, under which the minister of justice, Mr. Lardner-Burke, ordered Madzimbamuto to be detained in prison on the ground that he was, even while under restriction, 'likely to commit acts in Rhodesia which are likely to endanger the public safety, disturb or interfere with public order or interfere with the maintenance of any essential service.' Under the Constitution of 1961, a state of emergency could last only for three months in the first instance, but could be prolonged by a resolution of the Legislative Assembly. For the state of emergency declared on November 5, 1965, this three months' period expired on February 4, 1966, that is, at a time when, following the U.D.I., the Legislative Assembly had been proscribed, and so could not lawfully resolve to prolong the state of emergency. Nevertheless, 'the officer administering the government,' acting under the rebel constitution, prolonged the state of emergency, and made fresh emergency regulations by virtue of which the detention of Madzimbamuto was continued. His wife then instituted proceedings in the high court of Southern Rhodesia challenging the legality of her husband's continued detention after February 4, 1966.[95]

The case was fought all the way to the Privy Council, but throughout its various stages there was a general agreement among all the courts concerned in it (the general and appellate divisions of the Rhodesian high court and the Privy Council) that the new constitution and the régime under it were unlawful, on the ground that the rebellion had not been completely successful in displacing the lawful sovereign of the country.[96] The majority of the appellate division of the Rhodesian high court was, however, prepared to accord the status of a *de facto* government to the rebel régime, on grounds which will be explained later.[97] The Privy Council, on the other hand, unanimously denied it a *de facto* status.[98] But their Lordships of the Privy Council were divided on the question whether the denial of a *de facto* status to the rebel régime meant that no countenance of any sort was to be given to its acts.

The general division of the Rhodesian high court, while affirming the unlawful character of the rebel Constitution and government nevertheless upheld as valid the régime's emergency powers regulations and consequently Madzimbamuto's continued detention under them. The ground for this finding was necessity, which the court stated to be the need to avoid chaos and a vacuum in law. As elaborated upon by Justice Fieldsend in the appellate division:

'The necessity relied on in the present case is the need to avoid the vacuum which would result from a refusal to give validity to the acts and legislation of the present authorities in continuing to provide for the everyday requirements of the inhabitants of Rhodesia over a period of two years. If such acts were to be without validity there would be no effective means of providing money for the hospitals, the police, or the courts, of making essential by-laws for new townships or of safeguarding the country and its people in any emergency which might occur, to mention but a few of the numerous matters which require attention in the complex and modern state. Without constant attention to such matters the whole machinery of the administration would break down, to be replaced by chaos, and the welfare of the inhabitants of all races would be grievously affected.'[99]

But the learned justice of appeal emphasised that the application of the doctrine of necessity in the present case to bestow validity upon certain acts of the rebel government was subject to the qualification that (*a*) such acts must be directed to and be reasonably required for the ordinary running of the country; (*b*) the just rights of citizens under the 1961 Constitution were not defeated; and (*c*) there was no consideration of public policy to preclude the court from upholding such an act, for instance, if it were intended to or did in fact in its operation directly further or entrench the usurpation of power by the rebel government.[100]

Persuasive as this argument is, there are obstacles in the way of its acceptance. First, the vacuum in government which threatened chaos in the society was entirely of the making of the rebel government; it was a direct consequence of their illegal seizure of independence. It can scarcely be for them to set up their own wrongdoing as creating a necessity for their continued violation of the law and the Constitution. No doubt the failure of the British government to provide an effective alternative government after the dismissal of the Rhodesian ministers exposed society to the danger of chaos, yet such a danger ceased to be the responsibility of the Rhodesian ministers after their dismissal. They were no more entitled or obliged than any other Rhodesian citizens to protect society from the danger of chaos. To argue otherwise amounts to saying that after their dismissal without an effective replacement, the government of the country was at large, and was open to any group of citizens to grab and exercise its powers on the ground that society needed to be protected from chaos. The title of Ian Smith and his colleagues to exercise the powers of government in the country was no greater than that of any other group of citizens, merely because they had previously been ministers. While necessity is admittedly available to private persons in private law, it is difficult to see how it can enable a private individual to claim to exercise the legislative or executive powers of a state on the ground that that is necessary for the preservation of society.

Secondly, since the vacuum in government seemed likely to be an enduring and permanent one, the necessity for measures to protect society from it would equally be a permanent one. But a measure of a permanent nature goes beyond what can legitimately be predicated upon necessity. The doctrine envisages that the measure taken must be of a temporary character.

The most fatal obstacle in the way of the application of the doctrine in this case is the enactments of the British government and parliament. The premise for the application of the doctrine is that a constitution cannot provide for every kind of situation that may arise to threaten the fabric of ordered society, and that the occurrence of such a situation may create a necessity justifying departure from the express provisions of the constitution by the lawful or *de facto* organs of government in order to save the state or society from ruination. But where a particular situation is anticipated or has actually arisen, it would be utterly indefensible to invoke the doctrine to modify the provisions which the law has made for it. And where such provisions are couched in prohibitory terms, the application of the doctrine must result in the nullification or overriding of them, contrary to the conception underlying the doctrine, which is that it does not nullify express law. The majority of their Lordships of the Privy Council rightly therefore held that to accord validity to the acts of the rebel régime on the ground of necessity would be to enable the doctrine to override and nullify the legislation of the lawful sovereign, which not only transferred all political power in Rhodesia to the British government but also declared void 'any law made, business transacted, step taken or function exercised in convention' of the legislation. As Lord Reid stated, delivering the judgment of the Board, the result of transferring the law-making power to Her Majesty in Council was that 'no purported law made by any person or body in Southern Rhodeisa can have any legal effect, no matter how necessary that purported law may be for the purpose of preserving law and order or for any other purpose. It is for Her Majesty in Council to judge whether any new law is required and to enact such new laws as may be thought necessary or expedient.'[101]

From this conclusion, Lord Pearce dissented, holding, on the authority of the civil war decisions of the U.S. Supreme Court,[102] that the emergency powers regulations of the rebel régime were valid on the ground of necessity. But the American decisions relied upon were based upon a premise which his Lordship had earlier rejected, namely that the state governments of the seceding states in America constituted, in the strictest sense of the term, *de facto* governments, because they were not a usurpation of the powers either of the United States or of any other rival but lawful government. Even in Texas where the state government came into existence by summarily ejecting the lawfully elected governor, the latter acquiesced in his ejectment, and did not at any time attempt to assert his authority in competition with the unlawful government, which remained throughout in undisturbed and unquestioned possession of the seats of powers. The attribution of a *de facto* status to the state government was not based upon any notion of necessity. Having, however, arrived at the conclusion that the state governments possessed a *de facto* status, it was necessary to mark out the limit within which their acts were to be recognised as valid by the courts, for obviously a *de facto* rebel government cannot have the same plenitude of power as is possessed by the *de jure* government. It is here that the notion of necessity came in. As Chief Justice Chase put it, 'it is not necessary to attempt any exact definitions, within which the Acts of such a state government must be treated as valid or invalid. It may be said, perhaps with sufficient accuracy, that Acts necessary to peace and good order among citizens . . . must be regarded, in general, as valid when proceeding from an actual, though unlawful government.'[103] As to the usurping Confederate Government (the counterpart in the seceding states of the U.S. Government), the U.S. Supreme Court held it had no *de facto* status, and that no legislation enacted by it could have any legal validity whatever.[104] In view of his earlier emphatic finding that 'the *de facto* status of sovereignty cannot be conceded to a rebel government as against the true sovereign in the latter's courts of law,'[105] Lord Pearce's reliance upon the American decisions seems, with the greatest respect, to be misplaced.

His Lordship also rested his finding upon the ground that, in a situation, such as occurred in Southern Rhodesia, creating a necessity for action in order to fill a vacuum in government and protect society from chaos, the lawful sovereign is to be taken to have mandated by implication those in actual control without lawful authority to act on his behalf. And he found ample ground for the implication of such a mandate in the Governor's directive to the judiciary, the armed services, the police and the public service 'to maintain law and order in the country and to carry on with their normal tasks,' as well as in the failure of the lawful government to provide for the payment of the salaries of public officers, believing and expecting that the rebel government would make the necessary provision. It is difficult to see that the directive to the public officers to carry on with their normal task necessarily implied a mandate to the rebel government to continue to exercise authority in regard to law and order. It is true that the public officers could not be expected to carry on with their normal tasks and at the same time refuse to take orders from those responsible for their salaries, nevertheless no mandate to legislate can be implied from that. However that might be, the governor's directive must be read subject to the Order in Council, especially as it was given prior to the Order; it could therefore apply only in so far as the public officers could comply with it without acting or supporting action in contravention of the Order in Council.

The Rhodesian high court had refused to apply the decision of the Privy Council in this case, on the ground that to do so would be completely destructive of the functions of the court itself, and would result in a complete breakdown of law and order and the existence of a state of chaos throughout the country.[106] Subsequently too it held that the rebellion had become a successful revolution, and that by the efficacy of the change the 1961 Constitution had been annulled, and been replaced by the 1965 rebel Constitution; accordingly that Constitution and the government formed under it were now the *de jure* Constitution and government of the country, so that the Rhodesian courts no longer belonged to the same hierarchy of courts as the Privy Council as to be bound by its decisions.[107]

REFERENCES

1. Burke, *Africa's Quest for Order*, pp. 14-16.
2. U.S. Dept. of Defense, quoted in Huntington, *Political Order in Changing Societies*, p. 4.
3. *Modern Constitutions*, 1966, p. 138; Carl Friedrich, *Constitutional Government and Democracy*, revised ed., pp. 12-13.
4. S. 70.
5. Art. 183, 1.

6. S. 6.
7. S. 5.
8. S. 70. My italics.
9. See ante, Ch. II.
10. S. 29 (1).
11. S. 30.
12. On this, see Nwabueze, *Constitutional Law of the Nigerian Republic*, 1964, pp. 411-14.
13. Ante, p. 75.
14. Ante, p. 76.
15. See, e.g., Cameroon, 1961, Art. 15; Central African Republic, 1960, Art. 12; Chad, 1962, Art. 14; Congo-Brazzaville, 1963, Art. 37; Dahomey, 1964, Art. 27; Gabon, 1961, Art. 19; Ivory Coast, 1960, Art. 19; Senegal, 1960, Art. 47.
16. Art. 15.
17. Arts. 103 and 104.
18. 'The Defence of Necessity,' *Current Legal Problems*, 1953, 6, p. 216.
19. Glanville Williams in the article cited above has collected a host of such maxims by classical writers like Bracton, Bacon, Coke, Hale, and Hawkins upholding the doctrine.
20. *Att.-Gen. v. De Keyser's Royal Hotel* [1920], A.C. 508 – per Lord Moulton.
21. *Hirabayashi v. U.S.*; *Yasui v. U.S.*, 320 U.S. 81 and 115 (1943).
22. *Korematsu v. U.S.*, 323 U.S. 214.
23. Eugene Rostow, 'The Japanese American Cases – A Disaster,' *Yale Law Journal*, 54, 1945, pp. 489-505.
24. *Korematsu v. U.S.*, *ibid* at p. 216 – per Justice Black delivering the opinion of the Court.
25. Rostow, *op. cit.*; Nanette Dembitz, 'Racial Discrimination and the Military Judgment: the Supreme Court's Korematsu and Endo Decisions,' 1945, 45 Col. L.R. 175.
26. In *ex parte Endo*, 323 U.S. 283 (1944), the Supreme Court held that a loyal Japanese was entitled to be released unconditionally from a relocation centre.
27. *Prerogatives of the Crown*, 1820 ed., p. 68.
28. *Ibid.*, p. 231.
29. P. 229.
30. Conseiller R. Odient, *Contentieux Administratif*, 1961, Vol. 1, pp. 137-8; quoted in *Att.-Gen. of the Republic v. Mustafa Ibrahim and Others* (1964), Cyprus Law Reports, 195 at p. 272 – per Josephides J. (Cyprus), discussed below.
31. See *Att.-Gen. of the Republic v. Mustafa Ibrahim and Others*, *ibid.* at p. 235, p. 261.
32. Pitt, Speech in the House of Commons, November 18, 1783, quoted in Glanville Williams, *op. cit.*, p. 223.
33. *Federation of Pakistan v. Khan* (1955), reported in Jennings, *Constitutional Problems in Pakistan*, 1957, p. 77.

34. *Usif Patel and Two Others v. The Crown* (1955), reported in Jennings, *op. cit.*, p. 241.
35. *Ibid.*, pp. 249-50.
36. *The Special Reference by the Governor-General of Pakistan,* reported in Jennings, *op. cit.*, p. 259.
37. See *Federation of Pakistan v. Shah* (1955), reported in Jennings, *op. cit.*, pp. 353, 357.
38. *Federation of Pakistan v. Shah,* Jennings, *op. cit.*, p. 357.
39. *The Special Reference Case,* Jennings, *op. cit.*, p. 342 – per Cornelius J.
40. Art. 181.
41. Art. 181. Both these treaties were scheduled to the constitution.
42. *The New Commonwealth and its Constitutions,* 1964, p. 285.
43. *Ibid.*, p. 296.
44. Art. 133, 1.
45. Art. 153, 1.
46. Art. 152.
47. Art. 153, 3.
48. Art. 159, 1 and 2.
49. Art. 182, 1.
50. Art. 179, 1.
51. Arts. 133, 2 and 153, 1 (2).
52. Arts. 139-42, 144, 146, 147.
53. Arts. 137 and 138.
54. Art. 146.
55. Art. 25, 3.
56. *Att.-Gen. of the Republic v. Mustafa Ibrahim and Others* (1964), Cyprus Law Report, p. 195. The constitutionality of the Law arose as a preliminary issue in an appeal by the Attorney-General against bail granted to certain Turkish accused persons charged with undertaking warlike activities against the state with a view to overthrowing the government.
57. Arts. 3, 1 and 2; 47 (*e*), and 52.
58. *Ibid.*, p. 227.
59. At p. 237.
60. Art. 183, 1. The proclamation must be laid forthwith before the house of representatives, which may confirm or reject it: Art. 183, 4 and 5.
61. *Ibid.*, p. 226. See also Justice Josephides at p. 266 on this point.
62. Art. 183, 7 (1).
63. Art. 183, 2.
64. *Ibid.* at p. 206.
65. At p. 236; also p. 239.
66. At p. 267 – per Justice Josephides.
67. Govt. Notice No. 147 of January 26, 1966.
68. Govt. Notice No. 148 of January 26, 1966.
69. *Lakanmi v. Attorney-General (West),* Sc. 58/69 of April 24, 1970 (unreported).
70. *Supra,* Ch. I, p. 10.

71. *Re. Initiative and Referendum Act* [1919], A.C. 935 (P.C.).
72. *Bacon's Works*, ed. Spedding, Ellis and Heath, 1859, Vol. VII, pp. 371-2.
73. Dicey, *England's Case Against Home Rule*, 1886, p. 244.
74. Anson (1886), 2 L.Q.R. 440.
75. Bryce, *Studies in History and Jurisprudence*, Vol. 1, p. 207.
76. Dicey, *Law of the Constitution*, 10th ed., pp. 68-9, n. 1.
77. Anson, *Law and Custom of the Constitution*, 5th ed., p. 8.
78. Smith, 'The Union of 1707,' *Public Law*, 99, 1957; *The United Kingdom: Development of its Laws and Constitutions*, 1955, pp. 641 *et seq.*
79. Oppenheim, *International Law*, 8th ed., ed. Lauterpacht, Vol. 1, p. 757.
80. Smith, *The United Kingdom: Development of its Laws and Constitutions*, p. 55.
81. Sc. 58/69 of April 24, 1970 (unreported).
82. See Parliament (Dissolution) Decree, 1967 (No. 12), which with effect from January 16, 1966, dissolved Parliament and vacated the appointments of the president, ministers, parliamentary secretaries, and all office holders and office bearers of Parliament.
83. For this conclusion the Court relied upon the following Australian cases: *Ex parte McLean*, 43, C.L.R. 472 at p. 483; *State of Victoria v. Commonwealth of Australia*, 58, C.L.R. 618 at p. 630; and *O'Sullivan v. Noarlunga Meat Ltd.*; etc. [1956], 3, All E.R. 177; [1957], A.C. 1.
84. *Liyanage v. The Queen* [1966], 1, All E.R. 651; [1967], 1, A.C. 259 – discussed above at p. 70.
85. S. 31, Constitution 1963.
86. S. 1 (2).
87. For further details of the Decree, see below Ch. VIII.
88. S. 1.
89. S. 2.
90. S. 2.
91. S. 3.
92. S. 4.
93. S. 6.
94. They have since abolished the monarchy and turned the country into a republic.
95. *Madzimbamuto v. Lardner-Burke* (1968), (2) S.A. 284.
96. See below p. 292 for further discussion on this point.
97. Below pp. 290-2.
98. [1969], 1, A.C. 645.
99. [1968] (2), S.A. 284, p. 435.
100. *Ibid.* at p. 444.
101. [1969], 1, A.C. 645, p. 729.
102. *Texas v. White* (1868), 7, Wall 700 (74 U.S.); *Horn v. Lockhart* (1873), 17, Wall 570 (84 U.S.); *Baldy v. Hunter* (1898), 64, Davies 388 (171 U.S.). These cases are discussed below at pp. 271, 278, 280.
103. *Texas v. White, ibid.* at pp. 732-7.
104. For the relevant cases on this, see below pp. 278-80.
105. [1969], 1, A.C. 645, p. 732.

106. *R. v. Muzeza* (1968), (4) S.A. 206.
107. *R. v. Ndhlovu* (1968), (4) S.A. 207. There has been a vast amount of literature on the Rhodesian case. See, for example, Claire Palley, 'The Judicial Process: U.D.I. and the Rhodesian Judiciary', (1967) 30 M.L.R. 263; Alan Wharam, 'Treason in Rhodesia', *Cambridge Law Journal* (1967) 189; Donald Molteno, 'The Rhodesian Crisis and the Courts', (1969) 2 C.I.L.S.A. 254; J. M. Eckelaer, 'Rhodesia: The Abdication of Constitutionalism', (1969) 32 M.L.R. 69; L. C. Grea, 'Rhodesian Independence – Legal or Illegal?' (1968) 6, *Alberta Law Review*, 37; R. H. Christie, 'Practical Jurisprudence in Rhodesia', (1968) 1 C.I.L.S.A. 390; (1969) 2 *ibid*. 3, 206; H. R. Hahlo, 'The Privy Council and the Gentle Revolution', (1969) 86 S.A.L.J. 419.

CHAPTER VIII

COUPS D'ETAT IN EMERGENT STATES AND THEIR IMPLICATION FOR CONSTITUTIONALISM

Causes of Coups d'Etat

Organised violence is endemic in the society of the emergent states, but of the various types of violence mentioned in the preceding chapter the *coup d'état* is the most widely prevalent. But it is a phenomenon of the independence era. Before 1963, with the exception of Egypt (1952) and Sudan (1958), military interventions in the politics of the emergent states had been confined to the independent countries of Latin America, Asia and the Middle East. Since that date, however, from its first occurrence in Togo in January 1963, the military *coup d'état* has engulfed practically the whole of the African continent, and its endemicity shows no sign of foreseeable abatement. No less than nineteen countries have experienced it, some more than once. Dahomey with its four coups in six years tops the scale. The tally is distinctly disquieting:[1]

1. *Algeria:* June 19, 1965.
2. *Burundi:* (2) October 1965; November 29, 1966.
3. *Congo-Brazzaville:* (3) August 15, 1963; August 3, 1968; September 4, 1968.
4. *Congo-Kinshasa:* (1) November 25, 1965.
5. *Central African Republic:* (1) January 1, 1966.
6. *Dahomey:* (4) October 28, 1963; December 22, 1965; December 7, 1967; December 10, 1969.
7. *Gabon:* (1) February 18, 1964.
8. *Ghana:* (1) February 24, 1966.
9. *Lesotho:* (1) January 31, 1970.
10. *Libya:* (1) September 1, 1969.
11. *Mali:* (1) November 19, 1968.
12. *Nigeria:* (2) January 15 and July 29, 1966.
13. *Sierra Leone:* (2) March 24, 1967; April 18, 1968.
14. *Somalia:* (1) October 21, 1969.
15. *Sudan:* (1) May 25, 1969 (excluding the earlier one of 1958).

16. *Togo:* (2) January 1963; January 13, 1967.
17. *Uganda:* (2) February 22, 1966; January 25, 1971.
18. *Upper Volta:* (1) January 4, 1966.
19. *Zanzibar:* (1) January 12, 1964.

The total is twenty-nine in seven years, and this is exclusive of abortive or attempted coups, such as the ones in Ethiopa in December 1960, Senegal in 1962, Niger in December 1963, the Ivory Coast in 1963, Congo-Brazzaville in June 1966 and November 1969, Algeria in December 1967, Ghana in April 1967, Sierra Leone in March 1971, and the United Arab Republic in May 1971. Mention may also be made of the East African army mutinies of 1964 in Tanzania, Kenya and Uganda, though these were not aimed at overthrowing the government but at obtaining redress for army grievances mainly over pay and promotions.

The background to these coups has been described in the previous chapters of this book. They are an incident of the political situation in those states. Corruption, waste, concentration of wealth in a few hands, increasing unemployment, general maladministration especially of the economy, electoral malpractices and other types of political perversion of the constitutional system, tribalism – these are the main factors compounded in this situation. They breed disillusionment and discontent against the rule of the politicians. This discontent is widespread in the society, and is shared alike by the civilian population and the military.

Yet discontent with the discreditable performance of the ruling politicians provides only a superficial explanation of the recurrent phenomenon of coups in the emergent states. When the deeper motivations are probed, most of the coups would be found to be the product of the ambition for political power among the different elements in the society. Coup-makers usually come from the class of the young élite, both civilian and military. These have their own ambitions for power, independently of the failure of the ruling politicians. It is a characteristic of the élite in emergent states that they consider themselves as a privileged group, with a right to rule. There is some kind of a distinctly élitist outlook towards the right to rule. Army officers qualify by their training and standing in society as an élite, and so share in this outlook. They believe that they have as much right as the ruling politicians to determine the political destiny of the country, and that, when politicians begin to mess up matters, they owe it to themselves and to the country to intervene to put matters right again. Their élitist outlook tends to outweigh the tradition of non-interference in politics which the ethics of their profession are supposed to impose upon them. They are inclined to subordinate tradition to what they consider as their obligation as an élite to society. The clash between tradition and the promptings of their élitist outlook may sometimes create in them a genuine conflict of conscience, but the impulse to intervene and right matters usually prevails. The tradition of non-interference in politics is maintained only so long as the command of the army remains in the hands of the expatriate officers, as is the case for some years after independence. The presence in the top command positions of expatriate officers acts as a deterrent to the élitist impulses of the indigenous officers. It operates to stay their hands, but only temporarily. For with the eventual departure of expatriate commanders under the pressure of the policy of africanisation of the public services, this inhibition is removed, and the indigenous officers' élitist belief in their right to determine the political destiny of the country asserts itself.

No doubt the intervention of the military in politics has to be viewed in a wider territorial context. Precedent has a powerful influence upon human behaviour. An event in one country may provide a cue for a similar event in neighbouring countries. The army in one country may be spurred to an assertion of their élitist prerogative, which hitherto may have been dormant, by military seizure of power in the same geographical area. This has been particularly the case in Africa. The genesis of military intervention in politics in the continent may be traced more directly to the Congo crisis of 1960-2. The earlier military coups in Egypt (1952) and Sudan (1958) provide only a remote ancestry. But the part played by the Congolese army led by General Mobutu in the Congo crisis, the manner in which they arbitrated between or coerced the political leaders, had a direct impact. The visiting army contingents from other African countries participating in the United Nations operations in the Congo could not but have been impressed by this. It was an experience which was bound to affect their attitude towards their own governments. When, therefore, not long after the cessation of the Congo crisis, the first military coup occurred in Togo in January 1963, it proved to be the first stirrings of an event that was to contaminate the whole continent. The spread of the contagion was facilitated by the integrating forces which have brought the continent closer together, so that events in one country have a reaction in neighbouring countries. For one thing, the armies in the French- or English-speaking countries are closely linked to one another by connections and associations formed during common training in France or Britain or common service in the French Army or in the Royal West African Frontier Force or the King's African Rifles (East Africa). Old-boy relationships create an enduring fraternity which exercises one of the strongest influences on conduct. One is naturally inspired, for good or ill, by the actions or achievements of someone with whom one has shared life together as school or service mates.[2]

It must be recognised that the military's élitist belief in their prerogative to determine the political destiny of the country provides only a partial answer. They live, after all, as part of a large community, and unless there exists in the community a mood of agitation for change, the military are not likely to intervene. They can seldom act as an isolated group. There must be some external stimulus from the community outside the army, stirring them to action. Admittedly it is the mood of discontent among the community that provides this external stimulus, but this discontent is not so much with the ostensible factors of corruption, waste, etc., as with the propensity of the ruling politicians to perpetuate their rule. The issue again is about power. The greatest malady of the politics of emergent states is the unwillingness of the rulers to relinquish power. Political offices tend to become life appointments, resulting in a stratification of the society between the underprivileged masses on the one hand and a permanent class of rulers on the other. To perpetuate their rule, the politicians pervert the political and electoral systems, and stifle any kind of opposition. To be once a president is to undergo a complete personality transformation. An African president feels a kind of demi-god, occupying a pedestal high above and far removed from the rest of his community. He thinks of himself as indispensable, a messiah, an incarnation of the state; he feels it inconceivable that he can thereafter be anything else but a president. The power is so intoxicating, the adulation so flattering, and the prestige and grandeur of the office so incredibly dazzling as to be almost irreconcilable with a new life as an ordinary citizen. Hence the temptation to cling to the office for life.

This propensity to personalise rule and to perpetuate it indefinitely is perhaps the most outstanding contrast between the politics of the emergent states and those of the established democracies, especially Britain and America. In Britain politics has attained a happy equilibrium in which the alternation of government at not too distant intervals between two parties has become a political norm. This owes to the good sense not only of the electorate but of the politicians themselves. It is unthinkable that a party in power should want to rig an election in order to stay in power. But what is equally, if not more, remarkable is the frequent change in the personnel of the rulers within the governing party. A British politician would not normally want to remain prime minister for as long as his party continues to win elections. No law forbids him to do so, but there is a general acceptance that the talent for leadership is not the exclusive property of any one individual. Many would be satisfied with two terms, some indeed would prefer to retire before the expiration of their second term, as did Harold Macmillan; this may be due partly to health and other personal reasons, but there is no doubt also a desire to give others within the party a chance to succeed to the leadership. And from the point of view of the nation, a change in leadership may guarantee against sterility, complacency and the danger of the cult of personality. Change may enable a fresh vitality and a fresh approach to be brought to bear upon the problems of government. 'An untried president may be better than a tired one; a fresh approach better than a stale one.'[3] There is yet another striking feature of the system of rulership in Britain. It is not considered 'infra dig' for a person who has once been prime minister to serve as an ordinary minister under another leader. Each party has its own system of choosing its leader, and a previous appointment as prime minister carried with it no title to the continued leadership of the party in the future. A former prime minister who has lost in the contest for the party leadership will not necessarily feel embarrassment in serving as minister under a new party leader as prime minister, as happened in the case of Sir Alec Douglas-Home. The prime minister enjoys prestige and power no doubt, but he does not consider himself as uniquely set apart from the rest of the community.

In the United States the problem of succession to the rulership has received an equally happy solution, as a result again of the good sense of successive presidents from the first downwards. Until 1951 the American Constitution imposed no restrictions on the eligibility of a president to seek re-election indefinitely. At the time of the Constitution's adoption, most Americans wished indeed that George Washington, the first president, would retain his office indefinitely, so profound was the confidence and love they had for him. As a matter of general political principle, quite apart from the personality of Washington, the question of indefinite eligibility had provoked a disagreement of views. Washington himself and Alexander Hamilton favoured it while Jefferson opposed it. Hamilton, in *The Federalist*, argued that a limitation on the number of terms permitted to a president would stifle zeal and make the president indifferent to his duty; that a president, knowing he would be barred from the office for ever after, might be tempted to exploit for personal advantage the opportunities of the office while they lasted; that an ambitious president might be tempted to try to prolong his term by pervert means; that it would deprive the community of the advantage of the president's previous experience in the office; and that it would lead to a lack of continuity in policy, and consequently to instability in administration.

Washington did, however, retire after two terms, much against the wishes and expectations of his countrymen. His example was followed by Jefferson, also against appeals from eight State Legislatures that he should continue in office. 'If,' he argued, 'some termination to the services of the chief magistrate be not fixed by the Constitution, or supplied by practice, his office, normally four years, will in fact become for life, and history shows how easily that degenerates into an inheritance.'[4] Since then the tradition has stuck that no person should be president for more than two terms. Until 1940, this tradition has been consistently observed except when, taking advantage of the uncertainty as to whether two terms meant two consecutive terms, Theodore Roosevelt sought (but failed) to be elected in 1912 for a third term some years after his first two consecutive terms. Tradition was finally breached when Franklin D. Roosevelt was re-elected for a third consecutive term in 1940 and for a fourth in 1944. But those were periods of grave emergency, the period of the Second World War. It is such emergency situations that present the strongest argument in favour of indefinite elegibility. In such a situation the prestige and authority of the president's personality might be invaluable in saving the life of the nation. This was the consideration underlying the break with tradition of Franklin Roosevelt's third and fourth consecutive re-elections. Roosevelt himself professed a desire to adhere to the tradition, and to relinquish office in 1941 to a successor if only he could do so with an assurance that 'I am at the same time turning over to him as president a nation intact, a nation at peace, a nation prosperous, a nation clear in its knowledge of what powers it has to serve its own citizens, a nation that is in a position to use those powers to the full in order to move forward steadily to meet the modern needs of humanity – a nation which has thus proved that the democratic form and methods of national government can and will succeed.'[5]

These are words which might be used by any African president to justify his rule in perpetuity, and it might even be more cogent and compelling in his case. As Corwin points out this is just the 'indispensible man' argument. To accept it, he says, 'is next door to despairing of the country.'[6] In a temporary emergency, like a war, it might perhaps be condoned, but in the context of the sort of emergency created by the development crisis in the emergent states it is a positive evil. For since the development crisis is a continuing 'emergency,' the argument tantamounts to making the presidency a life appointment. In any case, the Americans, after the Roosevelt experience, had to amend their Constitution in 1951 to give force of law to the tradition limiting the presidential office to two full elective terms or one full elective term plus more than half of another term inherited from a previous president.[7]

Herein, then, lies the fundamental cause of coups in the emergent states. When a government has made itself irremovable, when at the same time it has also become destructive of the fundamental liberties and freedoms of the citizens and of their economic well-being, violence becomes the means of last resort in getting rid of it. As Colonel Afrifa puts it in justifying the military intervention in Ghana, 'where there was no constitutional means of offering a political opposition to the one-party government the armed forces were automatically made to become the official opposition to the government.'[8] No one will quarrel with this. All irremovable and tyrannical dictatorships ought to face this fate. Nkrumah, for all his good services to Ghana and Africa, had unquestionably become a dictator under the Constitution of 1960, and an oppressive one at that. He had become obsessed with power, and with how to consolidate it against all forces in the community. He was most concerned about the army. The constitution had invested him with the power of supreme command over the army, a power to dispose of it in any manner he liked, and this he made quite ample and arbitrary use of, thereby arousing the resentment of its members. To keep the disaffected under surveillance he resorted to the injection into the army of political agents whose duty was to spy on army officers and to report to him.[9] This aggravated matters and drove the army to revolt.

Admittedly tribal motives may be a relevant factor in the making of coups. One tribal group may have been entrenched in power by the constitution or it may have manipulated the political and electoral processes to perpetuate its rule. The military might then intervene to put an end to that. The experience of Nigeria exemplifies this sort of situation. By its predominant numerical size, the North was assured of perpetual domination of the federation, and the Northern leaders were determined not only to perpetuate this domination at all costs, but also to tighten the Northern grip on the federal power machine. 'It was,' wrote Gutteridge, 'the determination of the conservative Northern majority to retain power which brought into play the only forces which appeared to be capable of breaking that power. A situation which cannot be changed by constitutional means invites the use of violent measures in the same way as a life president can only be removed by force or assassination.'[10] Moreover Northern domination had had a particularly ruinous consequence for the country. It had been the cause of an endless cycle of crises, whose final culmination was the widespread killing, arson and other types of violence in Western Nigeria, which followed in the wake of the massive rigging of the regional election in 1965. In this débâcle, the Northern-dominated Federal Government displayed a partisan involvement, motivated by a desire to perpetuate Northern hegemony, an involvement which rendered it incapable of discharging its duty to the country for law and order. What was worse, as the Western Region bled steadily to death, the president of the ruling Northern Peoples Congress (NPC) met with his ally, Chief Akintola, Premier of Western Nigeria, and reportedly agreed with him upon a plan for a 'ruthless blitz' to silence the injured people of Western Nigeria. It was partly to forestall this pernicious plan that the army immediately intervened.

The military may intervene not only to keep out the politicians altogether and install themselves, but sometimes also in order to replace one class of politicians or other élite with another. The second coup in Sierra Leone on April 18, 1968, had this purpose. In the 1967 election the opposition party had won – the first time in independent black Africa in which an opposition party had won an election against the party in power. But, although it had lost, the government party was unwilling to permit the opposition to rule, and so induced the army to take over and keep out both parties. The opposition itself got to work on the privates in the army, eventually succeeding in stirring them up to overthrow their officers in control of the government and to hand power to the opposition party. Similarly, when the military, mainly the soldiers demobilised from the French army following the disbandment of French African regiments after the Algerian settlement, overthrew the Togolese Government of Olympio for its refusal to absorb them into the small Togolese army, the aim was not to take over the government. The government was handed over to Grunitsky as president (Olympio himself had been killed in the coup), though the real power in the country was the army, which eventually took over the government completely.

Political corruption, mass poverty, ministerial affluence and the plan of President Fulbert Youlou to introduce a one-party government were the factors which sparked off the coup in Congo (Brazzaville) in August 1963. To the country's militant trade unions the ban on political meetings pending the formation of the single party was an affront to the fundamental liberty of the citizens, and, with the support of the army, they forced Youlou to resign. The army take-over following upon this was not, however, with a view to rule but merely for the purpose of supervising a transfer of power to another civilian ruler, Massemba-Debat, who became president in place of Youlou. The country has since come under military rule following two further military coups. The Dahomean coup of October 1963 which overthrew the Government of President Maga was again the work of trade unions with the backing of the army under General Soglo who assumed power to administer the country pending the general election due in January 1964 which returned President Apithy. In November 1965 Apithy was deposed by the Vice-President, Justin Ahomadegbe, with the support of youth organisations and army officers. The following day the army intervened and appointed a new president, and a month later took over the government itself.

The coups in Uganda (1966) and Lesotho (1970) were of a different character. They were not a case of the military intervening on behalf either of themselves or of some other class of the élite. They were coups staged by the government itself. Although none of the other coups in Africa can be called a people's revolution, the nearest to this being the Congo (Brazzaville) and Dahomean coups of 1963, most of them were at least rooted in popular discontent against the government. In Uganda, after a motion of censure against him, the Prime Minister, Milton Obote, abrogated the constitution in violation of its provisions, and declared himself the executive authority.

In Lesotho it was the government acting against the people with the backing of foreign interests. Lesotho, formerly a British colony, is a tiny, rugged kingdom which is completely surrounded by the Republic of South Africa. In 1966 it acceded to independence, and on January 30, 1970, it had its first post-independence election. When it became clear that the opposition party had won overwhelmingly, the prime minister, Chief Leabua Jonathan, immediately declared a state of emergency, arrested the opposition leaders, put the King under house arrest and suspended the Constitution. He then went on the air and announced: 'I have seized power and I am not ashamed of it.'[11] It may well be, however, that, in this unconstitutional seizure of power, Jonathan acted as a tool of the British and the Republic of South Africa, both of whom had a vital interest in keeping the opposition out of power, since not only had it a radical outlook with leanings towards Nkrumah and Peking, but it was also avowedly anti-South African. There is some evidence that Jonathan was originally inclined to accept the verdict of the electorate, hand over power to the opposition, and flee the country to Malawi, but was prevailed upon to adopt a different course.

Nature and Constitutional Effect of a Coup

A *coup d'état*, if successful, is a revolution. And a revolution is an
abrupt political change not within the contemplation of the constitution. The change may be brought about by violence or by
peaceful means. The *Shorter Oxford Dictionary* definition of a revolution is that it is 'an overthrow of an established government by
those who were previously subject to it' or a 'forcible substitution
of a new ruler or form of government.'

But what is the precise effect in law of a revolution? What is
the nature of the change? Is it just a change directed against those
who administer the government, a change, that is to say, aimed
merely at replacing them with a new set of rulers while leaving the
constitution unaffected? The *Shorter Oxford Dictionary* definition
might appear to suggest this by its reference to 'government,'
though the word 'overthrow' points to a wider consequence involving the constitution itself. It suggests an unconstitutional change,
and an unconstitutional change or substitution of rulers cannot
leave the constitution unaffected. There is yet a further question.
Assuming that the change is one overthrowing the constitution
itself, does it also destroy the entire body of laws based upon the
constitution? In other words, does it destroy the entire existing
legal order, i.e. the constitution and all the laws enacted by or
under its authority? Finally, what is the effect of a revolution
upon the state? Does it also involve the destruction of the existing
state and the creation of a new one?

The German legal philosopher, Hans Kelsen, has made perhaps
the best exposition of the nature and effect of a revolution, and it
might be helpful at this point to look at what he has said. He writes:

> 'A revolution . . . occurs whenever the legal order of a com-
> munity is nullified and replaced by a new order in an illegitimate
> way, that is in a way not prescribed by the first order itself . . .
> From a juristic point of view, the decisive criterion of a revolu-
> tion is that the order in force is overthrown and replaced by a
> new order in a way which the former had not itself anticipated . . .
> No jurist would maintain that even after a successful revolution
> the old constitution and the laws based thereupon remain in
> force, on the ground that they have not been nullified in a
> manner anticipated by the old order itself. Every jurist will
> presume that the old order – to which no political reality any
> longer corresponds – has ceased to be valid.'[12]

Kelsen distinguishes between on the one hand the *intrinsic* effect
of a revolution, the consequences which *should* follow intrinsically
from the nature of the change, and on the other the effect which

the revolutionary rulers may deem fit to give to it, which invariably involves a modification of the consequences that should necessarily have followed. Our concern is first with the intrinsic effect. The revolutionary rulers' modification of the intrinsic effect will be considered later.

How far then does Kelsen's theory of the intrinsic effect of a revolution represent the law? For surely theory is one thing and reality may be quite another; both do not always correspond. Fortunately the question has not remained entirely in the realm of theory. In very recent years it has engaged the attention of the courts in at least four countries (Ghana, Pakistan, Uganda and Nigeria) and of the legislature in one (Nigeria).

The question arose before the Ghana court of appeal in 1970 in the case of *Sallah v. The Attorney-General*.[13] On February 24, 1966, it may be recalled, the armed forces of Ghana ousted Dr. Nkrumah and assumed the government of Ghana. They then issued a law on February 26 entitled a 'Proclamation for the Constitution of a National Liberation Council for the Administration of Ghana and for other matters connected therewith,' in which among other things, they established the national liberation council (NLC) as the new sovereign authority for Ghana, with power to legislate by decree; suspended the 1960 Republican Constitution of the Nkrumah régime, dismissed Dr. Nkrumah as president and commander-in-chief together with his ministers, dissolved the national assembly, and the presidential commission which was then acting for the absent Dr. Nkrumah (he was away on a state visit to Peking), and proscribed Nkrumah's ruling Convention People's Party, the only political party permitted by the law of Ghana. Then followed the following paragraph upon which the dispute in this case largely turned:

'Subject to any decree made under the immediately preceding sub-paragraph, any enactment or rule of law in force in Ghana immediately before the 24th of February 1966 shall continue in force and any such enactment or rule of law may by decree of the National Liberation Council be revoked, repealed, amended (whether by addition, omission, substitution or otherwise) or suspended.'

It was also provided that the public services were to continue in force subject to the decrees and any directions of the NLC. In 1969 the armed forces terminated their rule and returned the country to civilian rule under a new Constitution. Among the transitional provisions in the new Constitution for a civilian government was this one:

Q

'Subject to the provisions of this section, and save as otherwise provided in this Constitution, every person who immediately before the coming into force of this Constitution held or was acting in any office established

(*a*) by or in pursuance of the proclamation for the constitution of a National Liberation Council for the administration of Ghana, or

(*b*) in pursuance of a Decree of the National Liberation Council, or

(*c*) by or under the authority of that Council, shall, as far as is consistent with the provisions of this Constitution, be deemed to have been appointed as from the coming into force of this Constitution to hold or to act in the equivalent office under this Constitution for a period of six months from the date of such commencement, unless before or on the expiration of that date, any such person shall have been appointed by the appropriate appointing authority to hold or to act in that office or some other office.'

The plaintiff had in 1967 been appointed manager of the Ghana National Trading Corporation which was established in 1961 by executive instrument made under the Statutory Corporations Act, 1961. He was dismissed by the new civilian government of Ghana under the article of the Constitution recited above. He brought this action challenging the validity of his dismissal. For the government, the attorney-general rested his argument upon the view that the event of February 24, 1966, was a *coup d'état*, which abolished the old legal order of Nkrumah and established a new one in its place; that the effect of this was to destroy the basic law of that order (i.e. the Constitution); that all existing laws, including the Statutory Corporations Act and the executive instrument made under it perished with the Constitution. For these propositions of the legal effect of a revolution the learned attorney-general relied upon Kelsen. This reliance upon Kelsen's theory was spurned by the majority of the judges of the Ghana Court of Appeal. Justice Apaloo explained the reason for this rejection partly on the ground that 'experience of the world teaches one that there is often considerable divergence between theory and practice; between the process of authorship and judicial adjudication. The literature of jurisprudence is remote from the immediate practical problems that confront judges called upon to interpret legislation or indeed to administer any law.'

Much of this is a truism, but to inquire into the intrinsic legal effect of a revolution is no mere academic exercise, since it is only against the background of a proper understanding of this that the legislation of the new revolutionary rulers can be accurately interpreted. What, for example, is the necessity for a law saving existing offices after a revolution? If the event of February 24 in Ghana can be dismissed as a matter of dry philosophical theory, with no practical effect upon the laws and constitutional institutions of the country, then the armed forces which assumed the government of Ghana need not have decreed that existing laws and public offices 'shall continue in force' until revoked or suspended by them. If that event had no effect of its own upon the existing order, assuming that the existing laws, public offices and institutions remained with their legal authority in no way unimpaired, then the provision of the proclamation continuing them in force would be unnecessary, as it would do no more than state the obvious.

Nevertheless, Justice Archer was uncompromisingly emphatic in rejecting Kelsen. As he explained:

'Suppose we apply this juristic reasoning to the present case, it follows that when the proclamation suspended the Constitution of 1960, the old basic norm disappeared. What was the new basic norm? Was it the proclamation? It was not because it was not a constitution. How then do we trace the basic norm? Is the basic norm the people of Ghana who supported the armed forces and the police or is the basic norm to be detected from the armoured cars at Burma Camp?'

The learned judge's answer is that 'what happened in Ghana on February 24, 1966, was just the beginning of a revolution which culminated in the promulgation of the 1969 Constitution which annulled or revoked the 1960 Constitution.' The clear implication of this is that, apart altogether from what the proclamation said, the event of February 24 in Ghana had no effect of its own intrinsic force upon the 1960 Constitution of the Nkrumah régime, and that if the proclamation had not been enacted, that Constitution would have remained in force until revoked by the 1969 Constitution. Surely the event of February 24 destroyed the authority of the 1960 Constitution and with it all the laws and offices made or established under it, replacing it with a new one. This new state authority was the armed forces of Ghana. The proclamation recognised this fact when it recited in its preamble that 'whereas on Thursday the 24th day of February, 1966, the Armed Forces of Ghana in the interest of the People of Ghana and with the co-operation of the Police Service of Ghana and the support of the People of Ghana *assumed the Government* of the State of Ghana.' It cannot be suggested that the armed forces so assumed the government of Ghana under the 1960 Constitution. They assumed sovereign authority against and in opposition to that Constitution, and the success of their revolt against the Constitution destroyed it.

Since all members of the armed forces could not administer the government of Ghana, it was necessary to provide how and by whom the authority of the armed forces as the new sovereign authority of Ghana was to be exercised. This was the purpose of the proclamation, and for this it created the NLC. The proclamation was unquestionably the Constitution, the basic norm, of the military government. Its character as such was amply defined in that part of the preamble which recited that 'whereas it is expedient that due provision should be made by law for the proper administration of the country and for the maintenance of law and order therein.' What else is a constitution concerned with? It is interesting that, while repudiating Kelsen, some of the judges, perhaps unwittingly, still talked of 'the fall of the first republic.' Does this not import the destruction of the old legal order, or was the first republic just Dr. Nkrumah?

That a revolution is not a mere change in the personnel of the government is borne out by the fact that it can be staged from within the government, by the ruler himself, as happened in Germany in 1933 when Hitler, as chancellor, subverted the Constitution to assume absolute powers, or in Uganda in 1966 when Prime Minister Milton Obote abrogated the Constitution and declared himself executive president. A revolution may also be brought about by virtue of the people's constituent power. Changes in the conditions of society or in its fundamental conceptions may give rise to a popular demand for a change, which may be shared by the rulers and the governed alike. It is the essential purpose for inserting an amending procedure in the constitution to prevent such a demand from being canalised into revolutionary action. But the constitution may have been made unalterable or it may contain an amending procedure which cannot yield to the sort of change desired. In that event, recourse may be had to the residuary constituent power inherent in the community. A change brought about in this manner amounts to a revolution because it is not effected in accordance with the constitution but it is not a *coup d'état* since the hypothesis is that it is concurred in by both the rulers and the governed. It does not seek to subvert the established order, but rather to create a new order better suited to the present needs and circumstances of the society.

Repudiated by the Ghana Court of Appeal, Kelsen had, however, been upheld by the Pakistani supreme court twelve years earlier.[14]

The sad experience of that country since its creation in 1947 has already been recounted. In March 1956, at long last, the country got a constitution. The new constituent assembly, summoned in 1955, had accomplished what the old was unable to do in seven long years. Unfortunately the new Constitution, which was based on the Westminster system, was to be short-lived, for on October 7, 1958, barely two years after its promulgation, it was annulled by the President, Iskander Mirza, who, with the backing of the army, also declared martial law throughout the country, dissolved the cabinet and the national assembly (both federal and provincial), and appointed General Ayub Khan, the commander-in-chief of the armed forces, as the chief martial law administrator. Further, he promulgated the Laws Continuance in Force Order, which, among other things, empowered both himself and the chief martial law administrator to make laws. Subject to any laws so made, the existing laws other than the annulled Constitution, were continued in force. The reasons for Mirza's action were of course the familiar ones: the corruption and maladministration of the politicians, the unworkability of the Constitution as manifested particularly in the fighting in the East Pakistan Provincial Assembly, and the danger of possible future violence.[15]

These actions of the President's were clearly done outside the Constitution, since the Constitution gave him no power to annul it. The Pakistani supreme court accordingly held that the event, being a change of the Constitution otherwise than by the manner contemplated by it, was a revolution. Chief Justice Muhammad Munir puts it quite pointedly:

'A revolution is generally associated with public tumult, mutiny, violence and bloodshed but from a juristic point of view the method by which and the persons by whom a revolution is brought about is wholly immaterial. The change may be attended by violence or it may be perfectly peaceful. It may take the form of a *coup d'état* by a political adventurer or it may be effected by persons already in public positions. Equally irrelevant in law is the motive for a revolution, inasmuch as a destruction of the constitutional structure may be prompted by a highly patriotic impulse or by the most sordid of ends. For the purposes of the doctrine here explained a change is, in law, a revolution if it annuls the Constitution and the annulment is effective. If the attempt to break the Constitution fails, those who sponsor or organise it are judged by the existing Constitution as guilty of the crime of treason. But if the revolution is victorious in the sense that the persons assuming powers under the change can successfully require the inhabitants of the country to conform to the new régime, then the revolution itself becomes a law-creating fact because thereafter its own legality is judged not by reference to the annulled Constitution but by reference to its own success.'[16]

What is destroyed, the court emphasised, quoting extensively from Kelsen, is not just the constitution but the entire legal order as well as public offices, including indeed the courts. 'The revolution,' said Chief Justice Muhammad Munir, 'having been successful satisfies the test of efficacy and becomes a basic law-creating fact. On that assumption the Laws Continuance in Force Order, *however transitory or imperfect it may be, is a new legal order.*'[17]

Even the principle of effectiveness as the criterion for the validity of the new legal order is denied by Justice Archer of the Ghana court of appeal. 'If,' he said, 'any attempt is made to scrutinise the legal validity of the Proclamation itself, there will be unpleasant difficulties. What is the *Grundnorm* for the Proclamation?'[18] Surely the validity of a revolutionary constitution and government cannot be rested upon law, since there is no law anterior to it to serve as a criterion for its validity. Effectiveness must therefore be the criterion. And by effectiveness is meant that 'the individuals whose behaviour the new order regulates actually behave, by and large, in conformity with the new order.'[19] This effectiveness may have been achieved through the application or threat of force or through the active or passive support on the part of the people.

An apt illustration of the principle of effectiveness is provided by the case of Southern Rhodesia where on November 11, 1965, Prime Minister Ian Smith and his ministers unilaterally declared the territory independent of Britain whose colony it has been since its annexation in 1923. The British Government promptly dismissed Smith and his colleagues, suspended the legislature, and took over the entire legislative and executive government of the country. The lawfully appointed colonial governor continued in occupation of Government House and to assert the rights of the legitimate government, while also the judiciary continued to recognise the authority of the rightful Sovereign and of the pre-existing Constitution enacted in 1961. Yet, with the exception of the judiciary, the British Government, as the government of the country, was almost completely dormant and inactive, so that the legislative and executive powers of the country were, in a physical sense, being exercised by the rebel government. Did the rebel government thus become the lawful government of the country? In other words, had there been a successful revolution?

These were among the questions the courts had to decide in a case arising out of Smith's unilateral declaration of independence.[20] With but one exception all the twelve judges involved in the case from the court of first instance right up to the Privy Council concurred in the view that the rebellion had not been completely successful to have become a revolution. The Privy Council accepted the decision in the Pakistani case as correct in stating the effect of a revolution, quoting with approval the statement by Chief Justice Muhammed Munir to the effect that 'the essential condition to determine whether a constitution has been annulled is the efficacy of the change.'[21] But, as their Lordships rightly observed, 'it would be very different if there had been still two rivals contending for power. If the legitimate government had been driven out but was trying to regain control it would be impossible to hold that the usurper who is in control is the lawful ruler, because that would mean that by striving to assert its lawful right the ousted legitimate government was opposing the lawful ruler.'[22] To recognise the usurpation as lawful would also amount to saying that there are two lawful governments at the same time with each seeking to prevail over the other – a clearly untenable position. Furthermore, since the Rhodesia courts were still sitting as courts of the lawful Sovereign under the pre-existing Constitution, they were necessarily precluded from recognising any other Sovereign. To do so would be a manifest absurdity. It certainly does not fall within the purview of a domestic tribunal to question the legality of its own constitution.

The decision of the Privy Council was handed down on July 23, 1968, nearly three years after UDI. On September 13, 1968, the appellate division of the Rhodesian high court considered the authority of that decision and the position of the Rhodesian judiciary in the light of it. Their position as courts of Her Majesty in a territory controlled effectively by the rebel régime had, the court declared, become increasingly untenable, and the situation had been reached where, if they were to carry on at all, they had to do so on the basis of the new rebel Constitution, which meant that they had to recognise that the rebel government had become the *de jure* government. The appeal court extended this recognition, rationalising its decision on the ground that, in the factual situation then existing in Southern Rhodesia, the seizure of independence had become completely effective, and that its efficacy had annulled the 1961 Constitution.[23] Since the new Constitution recognised no appeals to the Privy Council, it follows that the Rhodesian courts are no longer in the same hierarchy of courts as the Privy Council, and accordingly are not bound by its decisions.

The decision of the Pakistani supreme court in the *Dosso Case* has also been received with approval by the Ugandan high court,[24] and by the Nigerian supreme court,[25] though in the latter's view the military take-over in Nigeria on January 15, 1966, was not a revolution but a constitutional change, and the military government a constitutional government whose powers were limited by the doctrine of necessity whereby it was granted power. The reaction of the federal military government to the supreme court's decision, as has been noted, was to enact a decree wherein it was declared that:

'Whereas the military revolution which took place on January 15, 1966, and which was followed by another on July 29, 1966, effectively abrogated the whole pre-existing legal order in Nigeria except what has been preserved under the Constitution (Suspension and Modification) Decree 1966 (1966 No. 1):

'AND whereas each military revolution involved an abrupt political change which was not within the contemplation of the Constitution of the Federation 1963 . . .

'AND whereas by the Constitution (Suspension and Modification) Decree (1966 No. 1) there was established a new government known as the "Federal Military Government" with absolute powers to make laws for the peace, order and good government of Nigeria or any part thereof with respect to any matter whatsoever and, in exercise of the said powers, the said Federal Military Government permitted certain provisions of the said Constitution of 1963 to remain in operation as supplementary to the said Decree.'

By Section 1 this recital is declared to be part of the decree.

A revolution creates the same situation as an international change of sovereignty by which one country, by conquest or cession, acquired the sovereignty of another. Such a change takes place almost invariably outside the constitution. Lord Dunedin, delivering the judgment of the Judicial Committee of Privy Council in an Indian Appeal in 1924, has stated the effect of such a change to be that 'any inhabitant of the territory can make good in the municipal courts established by the new soverign only such rights as that sovereign has, through his officers, recognised. Such rights as he had under the rule of predecessors avail him nothing.'[26]

The question whether a revolution also destroys the state must depend upon how one defines a state for this purpose, the state being capable of a variety of meanings. These various meanings have been described by the U.S. Supreme Court. Sometimes, the court observed, it is used to denote 'a people or community of individuals united more or less closely in political relations, inhabiting temporarily or permanently the same country; often it denotes only the country or territorial region, inhabited by such community; not infrequently it is applied to the government under which the people live; at other times it represents the combined idea of people, territory and government. It is not difficult to see that in all these senses the primary conception is that of a people or community. The people, in whatever territory dwelling, either temporarily or permanently, and whether organised under a regular government or united by looser or less definite relations, constitute the State.'[27]

The definition of a state to denote either people or territory alone hardly accords with the origin and development of the concept. The state is 'a concept . . . forged by political theorists . . . to give the king's government a corporate halo,'[28] i.e. a corporate existence, a distinct legal personality capable of rights and duties, of owning property and generally of being treated in like manner as a physical person. Just as when individuals incorporate a business into a company, the company, from the moment of its registration as such, becomes a distinct legal person as regards the assets, property, and liabilities of the business, and as regards rights and duties generally; the company exists separately from the persons who formed it and who therefore own its business; no one of them can claim any part of the company's assets as his own, nor can he be made personally liable for its debts. A state represents the idea of incorporation in the realm of government. It is a device which enables the machinery of government evolved by a political community for its own administration to be given a separate existence for the purpose of performing legal acts. For all legal and other purposes, therefore, the device enables the state to be separated from the members of the community generally, and from the persons who control the governmental machine from time to time. The death of any one such member or person, be he even the head of state, leaves the existence of the state unaffected. The members and rulers may come and go, but the state endures or is supposed to endure for ever. The state of course exists for the members of the community by whom after all it has been created; it also operates upon territory inhabited by them. In a loose sense, therefore, it may be equated to people and territory, or more appropriately to the combined idea of people, territory and government, but in a strict legal sense it is government conceived as a distinct legal, if a disembodied, entity.

The next development in the concept of a state was its linkage to the idea of sovereignty, a process of thought which was progressively developed to a point where the state itself was proclaimed sovereign. This is not unintelligible. Legal sovereignty is an attribute of government, and since the state is government transmuted into a corporation, the sovereignty associated with government must enure to the state. As applied to a monarchy, the concept of state and sovereignty takes a personalised character. In a monarchy the government belongs to the monarch. When the concept of the state was invented to give corporate existence to the government, the state logically stood in the same relation to the monarch as the government previously did, and so did sovereignty. So, the monarch personifies and embodies the state. He is the state and the sovereign. As such, allegiance is owed to him as a matter of personal relationship. Herein lies the fundamental difference in the position of a monarch and a president as head of state in a republic. The latter is not invested with the sovereignty of the state, the government does not belong to him, he is not the state, allegiance is not owed to him personally, and indeed he owes allegiance to the state just like any other citizen.

Since a revolution destroys the constitution and the government which it establishes, it must follow logically that it will also destroy the state, creating a new state in the place of the old. This is what is implied, when, after a revolution, people talk of the fall of the First Republic. However, the transition from the new to the old state is automatic and the break in the continuity of the state is not observable. While it must be accepted that a revolution destroys the state in domestic law, the position in international law is not so certain. Chief Justice Muhammad Munir has expressed the view in the Pakistani case referred to earlier that 'no new state is brought into existence though Aristotle thought otherwise. If the territory and the people remain substantially the same, there is, under the modern juristic doctrine, no change in the corpus or international entity of the state and the revolutionary government and the new constitution are according to international law, the legitimate government and the valid Constitution of the state.'[29] To the extent that the state will not have to seek fresh admission to the United Nations, this is true, but the recognition of other states which the state enjoyed before the revolution does not necessarily continue thereafter. How does one explain the practice of fresh recognition being granted or withheld if no change occurred in the existence of the state as a result of a coup, unless the explanation be that the fresh recognition or the denial of it relates, not to the state itself whose existence is perpetual, but to the new revolutionary government? It is not proposed to pursue this point further.

Modification of the Intrinsic Effect of a Revolution to Save Existing Ordinary Laws and Offices

The destruction of the existing laws (other than the constitution) and of the non-political public offices does not, as a practical matter, follow upon a revolution. Invariably one of the very first acts of the new revolutionary rulers is to save them by express re-enactment. But supposing that by some inadvertent omission no such express saving is made. Will the destruction nevertheless take place in practice? It seems that in that case the new revolutionary government will be deemed to have tacitly permitted them to continue in force. Acquiescence on their part in the laws and offices continuing in force will be implied. Necessity should dictate that the ordinary laws should continue in force until altered by the new sovereign. For, having been in existence before the state, society should not perish with the constitution and the state. No legal system could fail to take cognisance of the argument *ab inconvenienti* in order to avoid a result that might involve the total destruction of society. Happily this viewpoint can be rested not only upon the principle of necessity but upon authority too. The Judicial Committee of the Privy Council has laid it down that where, upon a change of sovereignty, 'there was an existing system of law, it has always been considered that there was an absolute power in the [new soverign] . . . to alter the existing system of law, though until such interference the laws remained as they were before.'[30] This does not of course negate the principle that a revolution destroys as a matter of intrinsic consequence the pre-existing legal order and offices, but it does mean that the destruction has more of a notional than a practical consequence.

It is worthwhile to reiterate that this tacit saving does not apply to the constitution. But the unusual situation may be supposed where the ordinary laws are enacted *directly* in the constitution. The 1960 Constitution of Ghana, for example, provided that the laws of Ghana should comprise (*a*) the Constitution, (*b*) enactments made by or under the authority of parliament established by the Constitution, (*c*) enactments other than the Constitution made by or under the authority of the constituent assembly, (*d*) enactments in force immediately before the coming into operation of the Constitution, (*e*) the common law, and (*f*) customary law.[31] Were the laws so enumerated (other than the Constitution itself) to be regarded as having been enacted directly by the Constitution or to have owed their origin to it? In the *Sallah case* before the Ghana Court of Appeal an affirmative answer was returned by Justice Anin, but this was emphatically rejected by Justice Sowah. His view, which must certainly be correct, is that all the 1960

Constitution did was to recognise the existence of these laws. 'To recognise the existence of a state of affairs,' he said, 'is a far cry from giving the state of affairs its validity.' The inclusion of *future* enactments in the enumeration of laws of Ghana lends support to this conclusion, since it cannot be said that such future statutes would also be deemed to have been enacted by the Constitution. Even if the laws so enumerated are construed as having been enacted in the Constitution, they would nevertheless have been saved by the implication of necessity. This is true also of non-political offices created directly in the Constitution. The non-political offices and institutions created directly by the Nigerian Constitution include the inspector-general and commissioners of the police, the judges of the supreme court and high court, the director of audit and the director of public prosecutions; the Nigeria police force, the police service commission, the supreme court of Nigeria and the high courts, and the public service commissions.

In view of the implied saving of existing laws and non-political public offices a revolutionary change of the constitution would not therefore have the effect of depriving a man of rights acquired before the change, whether such rights arose from the law of contract, property, succession, tort, marriage, etc. Nor would any alteration in the law which the new sovereign might make take away accrued rights, unless this should appear from an express provision in the relevant enactment or from necessary implication.

As regards the rights and obligations of the demised state, those devolve upon the new state. The new state is liable for debts owed by the old, and is equally entitled to any property owned by or debts owed to its predecessor. 'Every state,' said Malins, V. C., 'which takes possession of the territories of another . . . takes the annexed territories liable to the debts and loans which exist on its revenue.'[32] There is of course the impediment about enforcing a right against a foreign sovereign who has annexed the territory of another state either by force or by treaty. Annexation is an act of state, and no rights pre-existing against the old sovereign can be enforced against the new in his municipal courts except such as he has expressly recognised. All that can be properly meant by the proposition that a state which takes possession of the territory of another state succeeds to the latter's obligation 'is that according to the well-understood rules of international law a change of sovereignty by cession ought not to affect private property, but no municipal tribunal has authority to enforce such an obligation. If there be either an express or well-understood bargain between the ceding potentate and the government to which the cession is made that private property shall be respected, that is only a bargain which can be enforced by sovereign against sovereign in the ordinary course of diplomatic pressure.'[33] So where certain bankers had lent money to the King of Oudh, then an independent state, for the purposes of the state on the mutual understanding that the loan was to be paid out of the revenue of the territory, it was held that, although the East India Company when it annexed the kingdom of Oudh on behalf of the British Crown took it with such debts as existed against it, yet since annexation was an act of sovereign power, the claim for the recovery of the debt was not maintainable in the municipal courts of the new sovereign.[34] The premise upon which enforcement in the courts is denied in cases of annexation, namely that it is a matter of one sovereign against another in the ordinary course of diplomatic pressure, does not apply where the change of sovereignty is entirely internal. The new state as the successor to the liabilities of its predecessor is clearly amenable to the jurisdiction of the municipal courts for the enforcement of those liabilities. Equally, too, it is entitled to enforce the rights of the demised state.

International engagements entered into by the old state which impose obligations of a contractual nature fall into the same category as obligations owed to individuals. The new state is liable for them. But ordinary non-contractural treaty obligations may be repudiated.

In practice, as has been stated, there is invariably an express saving of existing laws, offices, etc. Even Kelsen recognises that 'usually, the new men whom a revolution brings to power annul only the constitution and certain laws of paramount political significance, putting other norms in their place. A great part of the old legal order "remains" valid also within the frame of the new order.'[35] In determining the practical effect of a revolution, it is the action of the revolutionary rulers that is therefore conclusive. They may even choose not to annul the constitution completely, but merely to suspend it, as in Ghana, or to suspend only parts of it leaving the rest still in force with necessary modifications, as in Nigiera.

But what is the true legal implication of such saving of existing laws and offices? Does it mean that those laws now owe their validity to the constitution of the revolutionary régime? Or, putting it more precisely, do they become re-enacted by the new régime, and do the existing offices become re-established? This was the crux of the question before the Ghana court of appeal in the case already referred to. The argument of the attorney-general on behalf of the new civilian government of Ghana was that the effect of the proclamation of February 26, 1966, of the new revolutionary government, which continued in force all existing laws and offices in the public services, was to re-enact those laws and to re-establish those offices; and that consequently, if the plaintiff's office as Manager of the Ghana National Trading Corporation, which had been destroyed by the revolution, was to be deemed to have been so re-established, he came within the category of persons whose offices were 'established by or in pursuance of the proclamation' within the meaning of the transitorial provision in the new constitution. Again it was on Kelsen that he relied for this proposition. It is here that Kelsen's conclusions may be questioned and are rightly rejected by the majority of the Ghana court of appeal. This is what he said:

> 'It is only the contents of these norms [i.e. those not annulled] that remain the same, not the reason of their validity. *They are no longer valid by virtue of having been created in the way the old constitution prescribed.* That constitution is no longer in force; it is replaced by a new constitution which is not the result of a constitutional alteration of the former. If laws which were introduced under the old constitution "continue to be valid" under the new constitution, this is possible only because validity has expressly or tacitly been vested in them by the new constitution. The phenomenon is a case of reception (similar to the reception of Roman law). The new order "receives," i.e., adopts, norms from the old order; this means that the new order gives validity to (puts into force) norms which have the same content as norms of the old order. "Reception" is an abbreviated procedure of law-creation. *The laws which, in the ordinary inaccurate parlance, continue to be valid are, from a juristic viewpoint, new laws whose import coincides with that of the old laws. They are not identical with the old laws, because the reason for their validity is different. The reason for their validity is the new, not the old, constitution.*'[36]

There are two issues which it is necessary to keep distinct, namely the *continued application* of existing laws and their *continued validity*. Since revolution abrogates them, their continued application is owed entirely to the new legal order. Yet they are so continued in force upon the implied condition that they had been validly enacted according to the old constitution. It is only if they were validly enacted that they qualify as 'law' under the expression 'existing law.' It can hardly be contended, for example, that a bill which had passed through parliament but which had not received the president's assent before the occurrence of the revolution becomes valid by virtue of the enactment continuing existing laws in force, or that a bill passed with less than the prescribed majority or otherwise than in accordance with the manner and form prescribed by the old constitution is validated under the saving clause. If a question should arise as to the constitutionality of such a law, the question will have to be determined by reference to the old constitution, and the court will have to pronounce it void for inconsistency with that constitution. Admittedly the new revolutionary constitution has also a bearing upon the continued validity of the existing laws, since their continued application is invariably made subject to laws made by the new government. Subject to this, the true legal implication of the saving of existing laws by the new revolutionary government is, as the majority of the Ghana court of appeal held, that they continued in force under the authority of the old constitution. They are saved from destruction; in other words, as far as they are concerned, it is as if the revolution and the consequent destruction of the old legal order had not occurred. The Proclamation of February 26 certainly did not re-enact or re-create the existing laws neither did it re-establish existing offices. It merely continued their application or operation under their old authority, subject of course to that of new legal order. 'To permit a thing to continue,' said Justice Apaloo, 'is to acknowledge its prior existence and it is an abuse of language to say that the person who permitted its continuance in fact created it.'

On this point, the Pakistani supreme court again followed Kelsen. The issue in the *State v. Dosso* concerned the validity of a law, the Frontier Crimes Regulation, enacted before the revolution, under which certain persons had been charged and convicted of certain offences. It was not disputed that the law in question, being a law which discriminated against persons on racial grounds, violated the fundamental rights provisions of the annulled Constitution, and was therefore void under Article 4 thereof. Had its validity been challenged before the revolution in appropriate proceedings, the court would have pronounced it unconstitutional and void. The accused persons contended that the law remained tainted with its original invalidity. The contention was accepted by the high court, which accordingly set aside the convictions and sentences. The supreme court reversed this, holding that the accused persons could not, after the revolution, challenge the validity of the law by reference to the annulled Constitution, on the ground that the criterion of validity of existing laws continued in force by the revolutionary government is the new legal order, and that the fundamental rights provisions having disappeared with the old Constitution, the law in question could not be impugned by reference to them.

The refusal to permit the accused persons to impugn the law is perhaps justified, but not for the reasons given. The challenge to the law involved an attempt to enforce a right which at the time of the action the accused persons no longer possessed as against the legislature. The result is that, having lost that right, the accused persons could not now seek to enforce it in order to impugn a law enacted before the abrogation of the Constitution but in violation of its fundamental rights provisions. The abrogation of the right deprived them of any *locus standi* upon which to challenge the constitutionality of the law on this ground. Secondly, the enforcement of the right was also precluded by the absence of a remedy, since no court could after the abrogation of the right issue a writ for its enforcement.

It is important to stress what has been said before, that in a common law jurisdiction the abolition of the constitution and of its guarantee of fundamental rights makes the rights unavailing against the legislature, while leaving them effective against the executive. The statement by Chief Justice Muhammad Munir that 'unless therefore the president expressly enacts the provision relating to fundamental rights, they are not a part of the law of the land'[37] cannot be supported. Before their entrenchment in the constitution, they were part of the common law received in the country, though enforceable only against the executive. When they were inserted in the constitution they became enforceable against the legislature as well. With the annulment of the constitution, they disappeared as rights against the legislature, but they resumed their original status as rights under the common law enforceable against the executive and individuals, and in that character they were continued in force along with other existing laws.

The Emergence from the Coups of Non-constitutional Military Governments

The destruction of the constitution, the instrument of restraint upon government, by a revolution would not undermine constitutionalism if the object was to create a new constitution better adapted to the current needs of the community. It is in this respect that the main difference lies between a coup, especially a military coup, and a revolution brought about by means of the people's constituent power. In the former the abolition of the constitution is usually not followed by the restoration of the limitations which it imposes upon government. Usually the motivation for the coup is the assumption of absolute powers by the coup-makers, and this is so whether the coup is staged from within or without the government. Hitler subverted the German Constitution in 1933 in order to escape from its fetters and assume dictatorial powers, so did Mirza in Pakistan in 1958, and, to a limited degree, Obote in Uganda in 1966. On the other hand, a revolution by means of the people's residuary constituent power is aimed at maintaining or even reinforcing constitutionalism. The people's participation in the revolution means that effort will be made to put restraints upon government.

Most of the coups in the emergent states have established military governments. In the result Africa has today thirteen military governments or governments with military heads – those of Algeria (headed by Colonel Boumedienne), Burundi (Captain Micombero), Central African Republic (Colonel Bokassa), Congo-Brazzaville (Captain Ngoubi), Congo-Kinshasa (General Mobutu), Libya (Captain Gaddafi), Mali (Lieutenant Traore), Nigeria (General Gowon), Somalia (General Barreh), Sudan (Colonel al Nimeiry), Togo (Colonel Eyadema), Uganda (General Amin), and Upper Volta (Colonel Laminaza). Sierra Leone, Ghana, Egypt and Dahomey have shed their military governments and returned to civilian rule.

Nature and Structure of the Revolutionary Military Governments[38]
What is the character of these governments? About one thing there can be no dispute, namely that these governments are not democracies. 'In Western terms,' writes Rupert Emerson, 'democracy has gone by the board when a group of officers seizes the government, pushes the constitution aside, and abolishes or suspends parties and elections. The counterclaim has, however, been made, as, for example, on behalf of the government of Pakistan, that, since the basic concept of democracy is rule by consent, where a government has popular support it is by definition a democracy regardless of its structure. This is a claim to be rejected. A government controlled by the military may be doing an admirable and necessary job, as in attacking corruption, undertaking land reform in West Pakistan, or cleaning up Rangoon, but it is debasing the currency of political terminology to call it a democracy, even though it has the honest intention of creating conditions under which democratic institutions can be restored.'[39] The notion of a 'military democracy'[40] is in some measure a contradiction in terms. It is not enough to establish a democracy that individual civil liberties are respected; it is necessary in addition that the government must have been freely chosen by the people by means of an election held at fairly frequent intervals under a universal adult franchise. However much a military government may accommodate popular

R

consultation or participation by civilians, however much its policies and actions may meet with popular acceptance or reflect 'the nation's feelings and sentiments and its love of democracy and freedom,' its unrepresentative character alone disqualifies it to be called a democracy.

At the same time they cannot all be labelled as dictatorships. Admittedly a certain amount of authoritarianism is inseparable from a military government. It is by its very nature a régime of force. The whole orientation of the military is based upon command – unified and hierarchical command – discipline and regimentation, and they would naturally be prone to carry this into government. Perhaps one can best arrive at a picture of the character of these military governments by considering to what extent the elements of constitutionalism are accommodated within them.

First, no question arises of the government being subject to a supreme constitution. There is often no *formal* constitutional code as such, from which any limitations upon the powers of the military government can be enforced, and even when there is, the government enjoys a sovereignty that is both absolute and supreme over the constitution. The attempt of the Nigerian supreme court to imply a limitation on the powers of the Nigerian military government from the doctrine of necessity is, as has been explained, unwarranted, and has, not surprisingly, provoked the government to an assertion of its absolutism and supremacy. The constitution of a revolutionary military government may, and usually does, pre-scribe a procedure for legislation. Such a prescription, as has been explained, operates to control, though not to limit or exclude, the sovereignty of the government, and therefore to maintain the supremacy of the constitution. It will enable the courts to pronounce invalid any law enacted in violation of the prescribed procedure. Even this limited control by the constitution of the sovereignty of the government is not possible under a revolutionary military government, since invariably there is an express ouster of the juris-diction of the courts to inquire into the validity of the enactments of the military government. That cornerstone of constitutionalism, the judicial review of the constitutionality of legislation, is thus absent in a revolutionary military government. The Supreme Court of Nigeria has tried to get round this by drawing a distinction between a judicial inquiry which draws into question the *validity* of an enactment and one which questions the *source of the authority* of the military government to make laws. It held that when Section 6 of the Constitution (Suspension and Modification) Decree No. 1 of 1966 provides that the validity of a decree of the federal military government or an edict of a state military government shall not be inquired into in any court of law, this 'does not preclude the Court from inquiring into any inconsistency that may arise (i.e. between a decree or edict and the Constitution), but merely bars the courts from questioning the validity of making the decree or an edict on the ground that there is no valid legislative authority to make one.'[41] In other words, the courts are only precluded from questioning the legal basis of the military government, whether it has legal authority to make, not the particular law in question, but any law at all. This distinction reflects the court's unsupportable assumption that, while the grant of power to the military is legally justified by the law of necessity, that power is nevertheless governed and limited by the Constitution. The Constitution Decree presupposes the validity of the military government's legislative authority, the criterion for which may be predicated either upon the law of necessity or upon the success and effectiveness of the revolution. Section 6 precludes not only any question as to the legal validity of this authority, but, perhaps primarily, any question whether this authority, assuming it to have been legally acquired, has been validly exercised in any particular case in accordance with the Constitution.

Secondly, the absence of a formal constitution means also no bill of rights. As the Pakistani case of the *State v. Dosso* illustrates, the destruction of the constitution by a revolution means that no individual can enforce against the revolutionary government in its legislative capacity any of the fundamental rights guaranteed to him by the annulled constitution. The Nigerian military government is perhaps uniquely liberal in preserving parts of the old Constitution, including particularly the fundamental human rights chapter, but the value and efficacy of this to the individual is not much, as the case of *Lakanmi v. Attorney-General (West)*[42] shows. For, since the federal military government is supreme over the Constitution, any law which it makes in violation of a guaranteed right operates as an amendment of the Constitution. The practice has been to suspend the bill of rights expressly for the purposes of specific enactments. Nonetheless the preservation of the bill of rights has some value. It operates as a limitation upon executive action; this is of course also the case in all common law jurisdictions, whether the bill of rights is preserved by the revolutionary government or not. Thus, although in the case of Nigeria, a particular enactment may have expressly excluded the application of the human rights chapter, any executive action taken under the enactment is only legally justifiable if it complies strictly with its provisions,[43] otherwise it will be open to challenge, though again, regrettably, the enactment itself may confer immunity upon executive actions otherwise unlawfully done under it. Secondly, the preservation of the Bill of Rights by the Military Government of Nigeria limits the legislative powers of the state military governments, whose powers are still subject to the Constitution and to decrees of the federal military government. The preclusion of the courts' jurisdiction to inquire into the validity of an edict may conceivably diminish the efficacy of this restriction, but, as previously stated, the efficacy of law as an instrument of restraint lies perhaps equally in its sanctity as in enforcement. However, the Federal Military Government (Supremacy and Enforcement of Powers) Decree, 1970, seems now by implication to recognise that the courts may pronounce upon the validity of an edict alleged to be inconsistent with the Constitution or with a decree. It is doubtful, however, whether a mere implication arising from an omission to include edicts within the provisions of the Supremacy Decree is enough to amend the express preclusion of the court's jurisdiction under Section 6 of the Constitution Decree No. 1 of 1966.

More important in providing an insight into the character of the military governments is the extent to which they have in fact encroached upon individual liberty and freedom. In some cases, notably Ghana, the seizure of power by the military was avowedly for the purpose of restoring freedom eroded by the civilian government. In accordance with this purpose the military governments in Nigeria, Ghana, and Uganda, promptly released political detainees. This may, however, be viewed as part of the general moratorium on politics, and is matched by the detention of former ruling politicians to put them out of the way of political agitation. The dissolution of political parties is universal, and in Nigeria where various types of tribal unions have infested politics, dissolution is extended to all organisations except *bona fide* improvement or development unions at the town level, or sports, religious, cultural, charitable or co-operative societies. All political activities, meetings and processions are also banned. Freedom of the press is maintained; indeed one of the very first acts of the Federal Military Government of Nigeria was to lift the ban imposed by the politicians on the circulation of certain newspapers within their area. Yet the authoritarian nature of a military government has inclined it to be intolerant of newspaper criticism, and on that ground some newspaper editors had been detained in Nigeria while in Ghana four editors of government-owned newspapers had been dismissed.

As a régime of force, a military government does not admit of opposition. With the moratorium on political activities, organised opposition is of course out of the question, nor is individual opposition very much tolerated. The ordinary man thinks of opposition to the military as a foolhardy undertaking. He tends to associate the military in his mind with the gun and shooting, and he is likely to take the view that discretion is the better part of valour; better to hold one's peace than risk being shot.

Apart from the restrictions upon political liberty, it must be conceded that, by and large, individual civil liberties have been respected by many of the military governments in Africa, especially those of Nigeria and Ghana. These governments have tried to maintain the conditions of a free society and the rule of law; there are no police state methods, and no regimentation of the individual's life, such as characterises the society of totalitarian states.

Then there is the question of structure which, as previously explained,[44] has an important bearing upon constitutionalism. The unified and hierarchical structure of military organisation inevitably imposes its impress upon the structure of a military government. Its structure tends to be monolithic, characterised by a concentration of powers. The military government of Ghana, for example, comprised only one structure, the national liberation council, in which all powers, legislative and executive, were concentrated. The absoluteness of its sovereignty meant that the judicial power was also subsumed in it, though in actual fact there was little usurpation of the judicial function, which continued to be exercised by a separate Judiciary. The composition of the NLC was originally restricted, but was later expanded; even as so expanded it comprised only military and police officers, though it is said to have been nationwide in ethnic, regional and religious terms, comprising Ewes, Ashantis, and people from the Volta, Central and Northern regions as well as Roman Catholics, Presbyterians, Methodists, Anglicans and Muslims.[45]

The Nigerian Federal Military Government has preserved, in form at least, the tripartite structure of the Legislature, Executive and the Judiciary, except for a brief period when legislative and executive powers were united in one body. A supreme military council, made up of only military officers, the commander-in-chief, the navy commander, the chiefs of staff of the armed forces and of the army, and the state military governors,[46] acts as the legislature. The executive authority is the federal executive council, which has the same composition as the supreme military council but with the addition of the inspector-general and deputy inspector-general of police. A government comprising only army and police personnel faces the danger of losing touch with the public and acquiring an isolationist outlook. The Nigerian military governments have been alive to this danger, and have sought to maintain a link with the public through the appointment of civilian commissioners in charge of ministries and their inclusion in the executive councils. They are not, however, made members of the supreme military council. The separateness of the judiciary is maintained, though as the case of *Lakanmi v. Attorney-General (West)* and the Federal Military Government (Supremacy and Enforcement of Powers) Decree 1970 show, the judicial power has ceased to be independent and been submerged in the absolute legislative sovereignty of the federal military government.

Furthermore, in actual fact legislative and executive powers are more concentrated than divided, owing to the fact that the head of the federal military government is president of both the supreme military council and the federal executive council. His position reflects the projection into the governmental sphere of the unified command system of the armed forces, a fact that is particularly evident with regard to legislative functions. Although we have earlier stated that the supreme military council acts as the legislature of the military government, this is nowhere expressly so provided. The Constitution (Suspension and Modification) Decree No. 1 of 1966 merely says that the federal military government shall have power to make laws, and laws are made with the enacting words, 'the Federal Military Government hereby decrees.' It is not defined who is or what constitutes the federal military government for this purpose, but, whatever it means, it clearly does not mean or include the federal executive council. This is evident from Section 130 of the Constitution which charges the federal executive council with the responsibility of preparing the annual estimates and laying them before the federal military government. It follows from this that the federal military government is a body apart from the federal executive council and must mean either the head or the supreme military council or both jointly. More probably it is the supreme military council, since it is before it that the annual esimates are laid, and since in the legislative lists the supreme military council replaces parliament with respect to the latter's power to declare, for example, which roads are to be federal trunk roads. Yet the supreme military council's role in legislature appears to be limited to matters of policy. Once policy has been discussed and decided in the council, the form of the legislation implementing it is generally left to the head of the federal military government, and this means in effect the federal executive council or perahps more accurately the permanent secretaries. A decree is validly made once it is signed by the head.[47] It was the Constitution Decree No. 8 of 1967, implementing the Aburi Agreement, which expressly vested legislative and executive powers in the supreme military council, and thereafter laws were expressed to have been decreed by the council. However, Constitution Decree No. 8 was in operation for barely two months, from March 17 to May 27, 1967, when it was repealed, and Constitution Decree No. 1 of 1966 was revived.

With regard to executive government, the responsibility therefore belongs to the federal executive council, although it is in the head that the executive authority is formally vested.[48] The federal executive council has the general direction and control of the departments of government.[49] Furthermore, functions conferred by existing laws on the president, prime minister, minister, council of ministers, house of representatives or senate now vest in the federal executive council.[50] In reality the federal executive council is subject to the control of the head, by virtue both of his presidency of it and of his authority as the commander-in-chief. It is by him that all its members are appointed, Moreover, it is not as if the council is a representative body; it is an organ of the military government whose ultimate authority rests upon force represented by the armed forces of which the head is the commander-in-chief.

Nor has the federal set-up of the country escaped the impact of the unified and hierarchical structure of the armed forces. The size and diversity of the country made some devolution of powers expedient, if not also necessary, but a strict federal division of powers was incompatible with the military power structure. Accordingly the federal military government assumed to itself power to make laws on all matters whatsoever. Subject to the federal military government's unlimited power of law-making, the military governor in charge of a state can still legislate on matters previously within the exclusive competence of a region, and, with the consent of the federal military government, on concurrent matters. But he has no independent executive power, such as a regional government previously had. The entire executive authority of the country is now lodged at the Centre, and a military governor exercises only delegated executive power, though the executive powers of the former regional government were deemed to have been automatically delegated. The regional military governments are further subordinated to the centre by the fact that the military governors are appointed by the head of the federal military government, and in true military tradition of a hierarchy of command, responsible to him.

By the ill-fated Constitution Decree No. 34 of May 24, 1966, the unified structure of the armed forces made a more drastic intrusion into the structure of the government. Federalism was formally abolished. The regions, now renamed groups of provinces, lost what independent power of legislation was left to them by the Constitution Decree No. 1. They now legislated only as delegates of the national military government on matters specified in the delegation, and edicts made by a military governor of a region before May 24, 1966, took effect thereafter as a decree applying only to the group of provinces which corresponded to the region. They were now meant to operate more in the executive field wherein they still retained all the powers of the former regional government deemed to have been delegated under the Constitution Decree No. 1. There was no provision, such as was contained in Constitution Decree No. 1 in respect of executive powers, to the effect that the powers of legislation of a former region should be deemed to have been automatically delegated. However, a military governor could exercise his executive powers by means of edict, regulation, order or instrument. This unification decree, as it became known, aroused deep resentment and fear in the North, and was the occasion for the massacre in May 1966 of Ibos resident there, and for the counter-coup of July 1966 in which Ironsi, the head of the national military government, was killed while on a visit to Ibadan to address a meeting of the traditional rulers and chiefs. It was repealed on September 1, 1966, by the new military government of Gowon by Constitution Decree No. 59, which revived the quasi-federal structure of Constitution Decree No. 1.

The mainstay of the military governments in all the countries is of course the bureaucracy. Theirs was the unseen hand directing affairs on behalf of the military men unaccustomed, as they are, to the intricacies of government. The permanent secretaries replaced the former ministers in all but name. The introduction into the military government of Nigeria of civilian commissioners has created a problem as to what is the exact relationship between them and the permanent secretaries. Is the status of a commissioner the same as that of a minister under the civilian government, implying therefore a power of general direction and control over the ministry and its permanent secretary? A commissioner has no such power of general direction and control, this being by the Constitution, as modified, vested in the federal executive council,[51] or, as regards a state, in the military governor.[52] Subject to this, the Constitution recognises the permanent secretary as the boss of his ministry, with a power of supervision. Yet the commissioner has succeeded to much of the powers of the former minister, except for that of general direction and control over a ministry. A commissioner appointed to a ministry has vested in him all functions previously vested in, or delegated to, a minister under existing laws (other than the Constitution).[53] No doubt for the execution of such functions and powers within the ministry, the permanent secretary is under the authority of the commissioner. The position appears therefore to be that a permanent secretary exercises supervision over his ministry subject to the general direction and control of the federal executive council (or a military governor), as well as subject to the authority of the commissioner as regards the statutory functions and powers vested in the commissioner. The Commissioner for Justice, who is also the Attorney-General, has wider powers. He has power of general direction and control over the ministry of justice, subject to the overall authority of the federal executive council[54] (or the military governor in a state).

The bureaucracy represent the element of continuity between the old and the new order, and their ability in maintaining this continuity is perhaps the most striking feature of the military régimes. The facility with which they fitted themselves and the whole administrative machinery into the structure of the military government was almost as if nothing had happened. As Gutteridge observed concerning the military government in Ghana, 'almost without a break the administration of the country was picked up by the national liberation council (NLC) acting through these men.'[55] The same forms and the same administrative procedures continued in use as in the past.

However, although government still proceeds upon set procedures and rules, which thereby limit arbitrariness, yet a military government is inherently authoritarian, and a certain degree of arbitrariness is unavoidable in an autocracy. Regarded as a temporary régime, concerned to administer, and not to govern, to correct the mess of politics, to 'wipe the political and constitutional slate clean' in order to enable a fresh start in constitutional government to be made, military government may be tolerated as a necessary tonic to decadent constitutionalism in the emergent states.

REFERENCES

1. Ruth First, *The Barrel of a Gun: Political Power in Africa and the Coup d'Etat*, 1970, pp. xii-xiii; M. Drake, *Sunday Times of Zambia*, March 28, 1971.
2. Ruth First, *op. cit.*; W. F. Gutteridge, *The Military in African Politics*, 1969.
3. E. S. Corwin, *The President: Office and Powers*, 4th ed., p. 37.
4. Quoted from E. S. Corwin, *op. cit.*, p. 332.
5. Quoted from E. S. Corwin, *op. cit.*, p. 336.
6. *Ibid.*, p. 37.
7. XXII Amendment.

8. *The Ghana Coup*, p. 31.
9. Gutteridge, *op. cit.*, p. 100.
10. Gutteridge, *op. cit.*, p. 93.
11. See Abbey Maine, *The Sunday Times of Zambia*, March 28, 1971.
12. *General Theory of Law ana State*, 1945, pp. 111-18.
13. Const. S.C.S./70 of April 20, 1970, by the Ghana Court of Appeal sitting as the Supreme Court (unreported).
14. *The State v. Dosso*, P.L.D. 1958, S.C. 533.
15. Feldman, *Revolution in Pakistan*, Ch. II.
16. *Ibid.* at pp. 538-9.
17. At p. 540. My italics; contrast Justice Archer above.
18. In *Awoonor–Williams v. Gbedemah* Const. S.C. 1/69 of Dec. 8, 1969, the Supreme Court of Ghana disclaimed any jurisdiction to strike down a decree of the N.L.C. as unconstitutional.
19. Kelsen, *op. cit.*, p. 118.
20. *Madzimbamuto v. Lardner-Burke* [1969], 1, A.C. 645 (P.C.); (1968) (2), S.A. 284. For other aspects of the case, see supra pp. 210-16.
21. *Ibid.* at p. 725.
22. *Ibid.* at p. 725.
23. *R. v. Ndhlovu* (1968) (4), S.A. 207.
24. *Uganda v. Commissioner of Prisons, Ex parte Matovu* (1966), E.A. 514; quoted with approval by the Privy Council in *Madsimbamuto v. Lardner-Burke, ibid.*
25. *Lakanmi v. The Att.-Gen. (West)*, S.C. 58/69 of April 24, 1970 (unreported).
26. *Vajesingji Joravarsingji v. Secretary of State for India* (1924), L.R. 51. Ind. App. 357; quoted with approval by the Privy Council in *Hoani te Heuheu Tukino v. Aotea District Maori Land Board* [1941], A.C. 308. For a discussion of the cases applying this principle, see Nwabueze, *Constitutional Law of the Nigerian Republic*, 1964, p. 26; *Machinery of Justice in Nigeria*, 1963, pp. 3-4.
27. Per Chief Justice Chase delivering the opinion of the Court in *Texas v. White*, 7, Wall 700, p. 720.
28. Carl J. Friedrich, *Constitutional Government and Democracy*, revised ed., p. 16.
29. *The State v. Dosso, op. cit.*, p. 539.
30. *Sammut v. Strickland* [1938], A.C. 678.
31. Art. 40.
32. *Doss v. Secretary of State for India in Council* (1875), L.R. 19 Eq. 534.
33. *Cook v. Sprigg* [1899], A.C. 572 at p. 578 (P.C.); *Sobhuza II v. Miller* [1926], A.C. 518; *Hoani te Heuheu Tukino v. Aotea District Land Board* [1941], A.C. 308.
34. *Doss v. Secretary of State for India in Council, ibid.*
35. *Op. cit.*, p. 117.
36. *Ibid.*, pp. 117-18; my italics.
37. *The State v. Dosso, ibid.* at p. 541.

38. Normally, the term military government is used to refer to the government set up in a conquered country by the victorious army, such as that set up by the Allied Powers in Western Germany after the Second World War: see Carl Friedrich, *Constitutional Government and Democracy*.
39. Emerson, *From Empire to Nation*, 1962, pp. 283-4.
40. N. B. Graham-Douglas, in 'Legal Aspects of Military Rule in Nigeria, a lecture delivered under the auspices of the Faculty of Law, University of Ife, May 7, 1971, claims for the Nigerian Military Government that it is 'a respectable contribution to the development of the concept of military democracy.'
41. *Adamolekun v. The Council of the University of Ibadan*, S.C. 378/1966 of August 1967.
42. Supra pp. 203 and below p. 250.
43. *Chief Alhaji Agbaje v. Commissioner of Police, Western State*, Suit No. M/22/69; *Adeoye v. Commissioner of Police, Western State*, Suit No. M/42/70.
44. Supra, Ch. I.
45. Gutteridge, *The Military in African Politics*, 1969, p. 110.
46. Since the increase of states from four to twelve, there are now police officer Military Governors and one state civilian administrator in the Council.
47. S. 4 (1) Constitution Decree No. 1, 1966.
48. S. 7 (1) Constitution Decree No. 1, 1966.
49. S. 97 Constitution of the Federation, 1963.
50. S. 12 (3) Constitution Decree No. 1, 1966. Since May 26, 1967, by the Constitution (Miscellaneous Provisions) (No. 2) Decree, 1967, statutory functions vested in the President or Prime Minister have been transferred from the Federal Executive Council to the Head.
51. S. 97 Constitution, 1963.
52. Constitution (Miscellaneous Provisions) Decree, 1967.
53. Constitution (Miscellaneous Provisions) (No. 2) Decree, 1967.
54. S. 88 (1), Constitution, 1963.
55. Gutteridge, *op. cit.*, p. 109.

CHAPTER IX

SECESSION AND ITS IMPLICATION
FOR CONSTITUTIONALISM
AND LEGALITY

Secession is another of the violent maladies that afflict constitutional government in the emergent states. Like the coup, it is directed against the constitution, the aim being to overthrow its authority in parts of the country. If it succeeds, it becomes a revolution, and creates a new legal order for those parts of the country affected, whereas its failure makes it the crime of treason. To this extent, it is essentially of the same nature as a coup, except that it does not seek to destroy the existing legal order completely but only in respect of a section of the country. There is yet another difference which has an important bearing upon constitutionalism. Usually a coup either succeeds or fails immediately. There is no prolonged period of uncertainty, during which two governments contend for ascendancy. If the coup succeeds, its organisers become immediately the new rulers for the whole country, and their régime is legitimised by the success of the coup and the effectiveness of their control. If it fails, its leaders are rounded up at once, and there is *usually* no question of a rival government operating in competition with, or in opposition to, the legitimate government for a period of time. This means that there is *usually* no civil war. None of the coups in Africa has resulted in a civil war. Secession, on the other hand, invariably leads to the establishment of a secessionist government, and to a military confrontation to crush the rebellion. Almost invariably, too, the secession is crushed, but only after a period (which may extend over some years) of illegal government in the secessionist area, and of war. Now constitutionalism presupposes legality; it is government according to law, but a rebel government is essentially government in opposition to law, and is therefore anti-constitutionalist. And war, too, as has been pointed out, is antithetical to constitutionalism.

Causes of Secession

The grant of political power and the eventual withdrawal of the colonial power brought about a recrudescence of hostility between

257

the various tribes or races comprised in the new states. This has sometimes taken the form of a demand for separation or for a regrouping of peoples arbitrarily separated or stuck together by the European colonisers. For example, the Sanwi, an Akan tribe, living on the eastern border of the Ivory Coast had demanded to be allowed to secede to Ghana to join the main Akan community there; the Ewe, living on the eastern border of Ghana, wish to be integrated with their fellow tribesmen in Togo; and Somalia wishes to unite with Somalis in Kenya, Ethiopia and French Somaliland in an all-embracing Somali Republic. Southern Cameroon, formerly administered by the British as part of Nigeria, has already been joined with French Cameroon in 1960, and agitation continues for the reunification of part of Cameroon still remaining in Nigeria, now known as Sardauna Province. There have been other similar demands for boundary readjustment to bring together members of the same tribe torn apart as a result of the European partition of Africa in the late nineteenth century. While admittedly the separation of people involved in the existing arbitrary boundaries is unsatisfactory, yet to attempt to redraw them now would be likely to light a flame which might consume the continent. The Organisation for African Unity has therefore wisely ruled that the present boundaries, with all their artificiality, should be maintained in the interest of the peace of the continent.

But the demand for the separation of groups within a single state, though a local issue since it does not directly involve other states, can also create a danger equally destructive of peace and orderly development in the continent. For a large-scale state organisation is essential to economic development. Nonetheless, in the larger African states, the mutual antagonism between the major tribes has been so acute and embittering that the obvious advantages of belonging to a large-scale organisation have not prevented demands for secession. Thus, within the last decade, in Chad, Nigeria, Ethiopia, Uganda, Kenya, Sudan, and the Mali federation, threats of secession have been made openly. In three of these, Congo, Mali and Nigeria, the threats have actually materialised, and it may be as well to examine briefly the circumstances that gave rise to it.

Secession in the three countries differed markedly in its origins. The secessionist province in the Congo, Katanga, had had a separatist aspiration for some time before the event. Its separatist aspiration was the result of a resentment felt by the indigenous Katanga tribes against the dominance in Katanga of people from other parts of the country. The indigenous Katanga tribal communities had rather sparse populations who were not as receptive

to modernising influences as their neighbours. The result was that
when the mining company, the Union Minière, began mining
operations in 1920, it had to recruit much of the labour force needed
from outside Katanga, mostly from the Kasai Balubas who had
shown an unusual capacity for upward mobility and receptivity to
European influences and social change. In course of time these
'strangers' came to predominate in the urban mining towns, to the
extent of winning the first municipal elections in the two Katanga
cities of Elizabethville and Jadotville and so producing the burgomasters for the two cities. This, and the suspicion that the new
'stranger' burgomasters were favouring Kasiens in the allocation
of public housing and of residence permits, soon gave rise to a fear
among 'authentic' Katangans that 'unless vigorous action were taken
immediately, the social hegemony of Kasai Baluba, reinforced by
political leadership, would result in a permanent caste system with
themselves frozen at the bottom.'[1] The immediate action so advocated was the formation of a specifically Katangan organisation,
the Confédération des Associations Tribales du Katanga, otherwise
known for short as Conakat, whose objects were, *inter alia*, to secure
priority for Katangans in appointments in the companies, and 'to
avoid any repetition of the result of the municipal elections.'

Power politics did not yet exist in the country. In January 1960,
the Belgian Government summoned Congolese leaders to Brussels
for a conference on constitutional development. The Conakat
delegation went to the conference with a brief for provincial
autonomy within a loose federation. While the round table conference was going on in Brussels, the Conakat, meeting at home,
resolved that, if the conference rejected the Katangan demand for
autonomy in favour of a unitary régime advocated by Patrice
Lumumba and his group, they would take Katanga out of the
Congo unilaterally. However, the conference did agree upon a
type of decentralisation which, while it fell short of the degree of
autonomy envisaged by the Conakat, was nevertheless accepted as
satisfactory by its leader, Moise Tshombe. Yet the desire for separation remained always present in the background, ready to reassert
itself at any time. Thus, when Tshombe, later president of the
Katanga provincial government under the provisional constitution,
failed to get the ministries he had asked for in the central government formed by Lumumba, and what was worse, when his arch-
rival in Katanga, Sendwe, the Baluba leader from northern
Katanga, was designated central government high commissioner for
Katanga, he began to work actively for secession. Congo had acceded
to independence on June 30, 1960, and on July 5 the army mutinied
in protest against harsh conditions and absence of promotion

opportunities. At the request of Tshombe, Belgian troops were sent to Katanga to restore order in its cities. Meeting at an emergency session on July 10, the Katangan cabinet decided that the moment had come for a declaration of independence, and the following day, Moise Tshombe solemnly declared Katanga a sovereign and independent state. Katangan independence lasted until January 14, 1963, when Tshombe proclaimed secession to be at an end. Tshombe's declaration of independence was, however, not accepted by the Balubas of northern Katanga, who, under the leadership of their party, the Balubakat, proclaimed their secession from Katanga and reaffirmed their loyalty to the Congolese state.

A major factor in Katangan secession was its enormous wealth in minerals, copper, cobalt, uranium, zinc, germanium, cadmium, tin and other precious metals. Thus revenue from Katangan mines subsidised Congo state revenue to the tune of about 45 per cent. The mining operations were by a Belgian company, the Union Minière, which also had substantial British and South African interests. The company had in its employ in Katanga a large European community. Actuated by a desire to preserve their privileged position in Katanga, these white settlers had as far back as 1920 started to demand the separation of Katanga from the rest of the Congo as an independent entity under white settler control. An independent Katanga dominated by the white settlers on something like the Rhodesian pattern would assure a continuation of these privileges, whereas a unified Congo ruled by radical nationalist leaders in Leopoldville would spell a loss of them. When therefore the Katangans began to nurse ideas of Katangan separatism and formed the Conakat, they found ready support in the white settlers who, their dreams of a white-dominated Katanga having been shattered by the sudden and unexpected turn in the constitutional development of the country, promptly allied themselves with the Conakat. It was a union of separatists. No doubt the Katanga leaders were lured by the vision of controlling Katangan wealth to the exclusion of the rest of the country, but it was the white settlers and the Union Minière itself who urged them along the path of secession. The whole grand plot was indeed masterminded by this group. When secession was finally declared it was the company which provided much of the financial support, while the settlers served as expert advisers. The Belgian Government was also implicated. The readiness with which it responded to Katanga's appeal for military and technical assistance showed it as an accomplice, if not an instigator of the secessionist plot. And behind Belgium, of course, were some of its NATO allies, notably Britain and France.

The first point of difference between the Katangan secession and the secession of the former Eastern region from Nigeria is that the principal actors in the latter, the Ibos, far from being separatists, were the most ardent advocates of Nigerian unity. With them Nigerian unity was almost an article of faith. 'Having considered themselves citizens of the world,' writes Stanley Diamond, 'the Ibos had nurtured the idea of common citizenship with all people among whom they lived. To inquire into the precise identity of an Ibo was to insult his sense of fraternity with other Africans in Nigeria. Being an Ibo was a private affair, perhaps a source of pride; but the public image was Nigerian.'[2] It is possible that the pan-Nigerian outlook of the Ibo was a product of his social and political organisation which seldom recognises any political authority higher than the village-group, and which, within the village-group itself, diffuses power among the component villages and families, and among elders, age-group organisations, title and secret societies and various other associations. Such a fragmented political structure might be too feeble to hold the loyalty of its members in the context of the modern world, hence the search by the Ibos for larger loyalties extending beyond the boundaries of the village-group. They tried therefore to foster a sense of identity, first, within a cultural framework through the establishment of various town or clan unions which federated at a divisional or provincial level and finally at a pan-Ibo level. These cultural unions represented, however, only an intermediate focus for a higher loyalty which they identified with the ideal of a Nigerian nation. There might also have been an economic aspect to the pan-Nigerian outlook of the Ibo. Faced with over-population, lack of opportunities and an agriculturally poor soil, the Ibos might have desired a Nigerian nation in order not only to ensure free mobility of people but also to safeguard the careers of their members already resident in other parts of Nigeria. This is not to say the Ibo ideal of a Nigerian nation was actuated mainly by economic self interest, for, as Stanley Diamond remarked, 'to explain the basis for this Ibo concern does not invalidate it, for the Ibos were genuine Nigerian nationalists.'

It is an irony of history that the same people who had been the most active advocates of Nigerian unity should also have sponsored secession. The explanation seems to be that secession was forced upon them by a combination of tragic events. The planned massacre in 1966 of thousands of Ibos resident in the North, the unwillingness or inability of the federal government to protect them and their properties against such acts of wanton destruction, the constant state of fear and insecurity in which they had to live, the possibility

that the pogrom might be re-enacted following the cyclic pattern
it had taken in May, July, August and September 1966, the consequent mass exodus of Ibos (numbering between one and two
millions) from the rest of Nigeria back to the safety of their homes
in Eastern Nigeria, the failure to keep faith over the agreement
reached among the military leaders at Aburi, Ghana, on the form
of association for Nigeria – these and other acts of oppression
combined to produce in the Ibos a feeling that they were no longer
wanted in the federation.[3] Federalism in government is the aggrega-
tion of different communities for the purpose of pooling together
their resources, human, economic, etc. for the common good. Of
these recources, the human is the most important. Once, therefore,
the human element has been torn apart, the federation is like a
disembodied object. It is true that Eastern Nigeria, like Katanga,
has vast mineral resources, in this case oil. A desire for the exclusive
control of this oil wealth might well have been an operative factor,
but the mass of the people who demonstrated demanding secession
were moved by the bitter emotion of their relatives killed or maimed
in the North, and by the agonising spectacle of the wretched condition of those who managed to escape the slaughter to return home.

Whereas Katangan secession was an act of the Katangan cabinet,
the secession of Eastern Nigeria proceeded from widespread popular
demand manifested in mass demonstrations, and finally canalised in
a resolution of a joint meeting of the Eastern Nigerian consultative
assembly and the advisory council of chiefs and elders, which
mandated the military governor for Eastern Nigeria, Lieutenant-
Colonel Odumegwu Ojukwu, 'to declare at the earliest practicable
date Eastern Nigeria a free, sovereign and independent state by the
name and title of the Republic of Biafra.'[4] It was on the authority
of this mandate that the military governor made the proclamation
of indepencence on May 30, 1967. The consultative assembly could
claim to be broadly representative of the people. As originally
constituted, it consisted of four members appointed by the military
governor to represent each of the provinces in Eastern Nigeria, but
it was later enlarged by the addition of six more members selected
from each province by certain representative bodies within its
divisions and counties. The council of chiefs and elders had a
uniquely representative character. The office and authority of a
chief rest upon tradition sanctioned by the general acceptance and
consent of the community. As the pivot of his community and the
symbol of its unity, representation by the chief might be considered
more meaningful to the vast majority of people in the remote
villages.

Perhaps the most dramatic of unilateral secessions, and certainly the only successful and bloodless one in Africa, was Senegal's withdrawal from the Mali federation on August 20, 1960. Until the creation of the French community by the Constitution of the Fifth French Republic in 1958, the eight French West African territories had been administered as a federation, with headquarters in Dakar, Senegal. After the dissolution of this federation enthusiasm for federation still persisted among some of the nationalist leaders of whom the foremost advocate was Leopold Senghor of Senegal. Meeting on December 29, 1958, in Bamako, Soudan (now Mali), leaders from Senegal, Soudan, Upper Volta and Dahomey decided to form a federation, and on January 20, 1959, the federation was created with the name of the Mali federation under a Constitution which had been adopted by an assembly set up by the Bamako meeting of 1958. The Constitution was, however, never ratified by Upper Volta and Dahomey, both of which backed out of the arrangement immediately thereafter, thus leaving Senegal and Soudan as the only constituent units of the federation. On June 20, 1960, the Mali federation acceded to independence. Unhappily, independence soon unleashed a storm that eventually battered the federation to death.

The demise of the federation arose largely from the conflicting ambitions and ideologies of its Senegalese and Soudanese leaders. Anxious to preserve their power base in Senegal, the Senegalese leaders wanted a federal structure that would, in Senghor's words, guarantee 'the autonomy of the Senegalese soul',[5] while the Soudanese advocated centralisation. The federation had been built upon the principle of parity between its two units in the distribution of offices and amenities. Not surprisingly the application of this principle provoked disagreement among the two sides as to whether executive power should be concentrated in the head of state or divided between him and a prime minister. The centralisers (Soudanese) favoured the former, though the latter was the scheme eventually adopted. These disagreements on matters of principle were exacerbated by politics. At the time of federation each country had its own dominant ruling party. These remained after federation, but a federal party was inaugurated upon the birth of the federation. Disagreement arose as to what role the federal party should play in the politics and government of the federation and its component units. While the Soudanese advocated political integration by giving the federal party control over both the federal and territorial governments and by making membership of the territorial party of each unit open to the natives of the other unit resident in the former, the Senegalese sought to maintain control over internal

Senegalese politics within the framework of their territorial party. Then there were the manoeuvrings over the candidature for the presidency. For the Senegalese, Senghor was their man. On the other hand the Soudanese were determined to forestall him, and to that end began a secret campaign among certain influential groups in Senegal. The struggle between the two sides for the control of the federation was now coming increasingly into the open, and seemed to have reached a head over the appointment of a chief of staff of the federal army. The two candidates for the post were a Senegalese colonel and a Soudanese colonel. The former was favoured by the Federal Minister of Defence, himself a Senegalese, but Modibo Keita, the Federal Prime Minister, a Soudanese, appointed the Soudanese colonel and had him gazetted despite the Defence Minister's refusal to coutersign his nomination.

A crisis situation was now building up, and the Senegalese began making warlike preparations. When he noticed the movement of armed people, Modibo Keita ordered out the federal army who then surrounded all public buildings and installations in Dakar, but the Senegalese contrived to get the soldiers back in their barracks, and posted the territorial gendarmerie instead to guard the public buildings and to surround the houses of some of the Soudanese officials. On August 20, 1960, the Senegalese territorial assembly was called into a special midnight session, which proceeded to declare the independence of the Republic of Senegal from the Mali federation. Modibo Keita then appealed, but without favourable response, to France for troops to preserve the integrity of the federation. Finally, on August 22, he and the other Soudanese functionaries in Dakar were put in a special sealed train and sent back to Bamako, capital of Soudan. And so perished the Mali federation, though to perpetuate its name the Soudanese leaders decided to change the name of their country from Soudan to the Republic of Mali.

The breakup of the Mali federation illustrates the danger, of which we have spoken earlier,[6] of forming a federation with only two units. As Ernest Milcent remarked, 'a federal state cannot be firmly established unless the federal authorities are capable of arbitrating between the federated states. The government of Mali could not play this role, however, because the federation included only two states . . . Thus any conflict between the states had its repercussions at the summit of the federation. In other words, there was no possibility of arbitration in case of conflict between Senegal and the Soudan.'[7] The other federation of two units, Pakistan, fought a civil war over the secession of its eastern wing, which is separated from the West by a thousand miles of Indian territory.

We have already noted, albeit in very brief outline, the cata-strophic sequence of events in trouble-torn Pakistan since its creation in 1947 – the declaration of a state of emergency by the Governor-General, Ghulam Mohammad, in October 1954; his sacking of the constituent assembly in the same month; the invalidation by the court of all the forty-four constitutional laws enacted by the assembly without the governor-general's assent; the near collapse of the machinery of administration in consequence of this; the breakdown of law and order in East Pakistan following the defeat of the Muslim League in the elections there; the suppression of the East Pakistan provincial government and the personal rule of General Mirza as federal-government-appointed governor; the sad experience with the new Constitution enacted by the new constituent assembly in 1956, especially the fighting in the East Pakistan provincial assembly in 1958 which resulted in the death of the deputy speaker; and finally the annulment of the Constitution and the proclamation of martial law on October 7, 1958, by Mirza who had since become president of the country. By the Laws Continuance in Force Order promulgated by Mirza on October 10, 1958, Pakistan was to be governed as nearly as might be in accordance with the annulled Constitution. Under this, General Ayub Khan, commander-in-chief of the Pakistani armed forces, who had earlier been made the chief martial law administrator, was appointed prime minister on October 24. On October 28 he ousted Mirza as president, and instituted a military rule that lasted from 1958 to 1962. In the latter year he returned Pakistan to civilian rule under a new constitution with himself as executive president.

The great achievement of Ayub Khan was in giving Pakistan a measure of stable administration for the first time since 1947. Yet, by 1965 Ayub's administration and his grip upon the country had begun to weaken. His settlement with India at Tashkent in the U.S.S.R. which brought to an end the ruinous Indo-Pakistan war over Kashmir was viewed by his critics as a sell-out, and was exploited by his foreign minister, Bhutto, to arouse the public to indignation and disaffection against Ayub. Bhutto was relieved of his post and clapped into detention, whence he eventually emerged as a national hero. At the same time opposition was mounting from the Bengalis of East Pakistan. And by the closing months of 1968, public opposition to Ayub had reached such a pitch that he was obliged, apparently under mild pressure from his army, to step down in favour of his army chief, General Yahya Khan, who, as had been done in 1958, annulled the Constitution and proclaimed martial law throughout the country.

The disaffection among the Bengalis stemmed from a variety of causes. First, as has been noted, their own half of the country is separated from the other half, the West, wherein is located the seat of government and of public activities, by a thousand miles of Indian territory. The two are really different peoples, different in culture and language; Islam is the main unifying factor. Communication is difficult and consequently minimal. Military rule had produced the rather abnormal situation of a minority ruling the majority, always an embittering state of affairs. For, although the Bengalis number seventy million as against West Pakistan's fifty million, the number of Bengalis in the army had been estimated at below one per cent. Ayub himself is a West Pakistani and so are most of the other officers from whom the leaders of his régime were inevitably drawn. His handing over to Yahya Khan, another West Pakistani, was believed to have been a mutually agreed plan to perpetuate West Pakistani hegemony. Under the martial law administration, East Pakistan was being ruled almost as a colony of the West, the martial law administrators in the East being invariably West Pakistani army officers. The predominance of West Pakistanis in the army was of course a legacy from the colonial past. Strong and big in build, with a predominantly peasant and feudalistic social structure, the West Pakistanis have had a martial tradition, and so provided for the British ready recruits into the then Indian imperial army. The Bengalis, on the other hand, were a different type, being more inclined towards politics, poetry, music, painting and drama, and, as Pauline Walton observed, 'inquiring critical minds do not provide enthusiastic army recruits.'[8]

Owing to the Indo-Pakistani war a disproportionate part of the country's revenue, about 60 to 65 per cent, was spent on the armed forces. Naturally the Bengalis were resentful at having to support an army which was garrisoned almost entirely in the West, an army in which they were not represented, and which frequently served as an instrument for their own subjugation. Furthermore, the Bengalis felt no concern in the Indo-Pakistani war. It was not really their war; besides, the stoppage of trade with India which the war entailed had had a particularly disruptive effect on their economy.

Bengalis were also smarting under a sense of exploitation from other sources. They felt neglected in the distribution of amenities and the siting of industrial projects, and this rankled particularly since the foreign exchange used to finance these projects was earned mostly through Bengal's export trade in jute and tea. This concentration of social amenities, industrial projects and other kinds of investment in the West has changed its infrastructure from a feudal to an industrial one, while leaving the East still relatively undeveloped, to serve only as a market for the West's manufactured products.[9] Then there is the grievance over the soaring rate of unemployment in the East, a situation which, the Bengalis argue, could have been considerably relieved if they had been given a representation in the army and in the bureaucracy commensurate to their population.

The current troubles in the country result from a struggle for political dominance between the two halves of the country, with the minority Punjabis of the West trying to maintain their hegemony and the Bengalis trying to assert the political leadership to which their numbers entitle them. In the election of December 1970, the Bengali party, led by Sheikh Moujib Rahman, emerged with a majority in the national assembly. Moujib claimed that he should be appointed prime minister on the basis of the results, and also issued a six-point programme in which, among other things, he demanded autonomy for each province over all aspects of government except foreign policy and defence, which were to be the only subjects to be reserved to the centre. Both his claim to the premiership and his demand for provincial autonomy were resisted by Bhutto, leader of the West Pakistani Peoples' Party, whose boycott of the national assembly on this ground precipitated the present crisis. Moujib's demands were also unacceptable to President Yahya Khan. To the President, what was called the Bengali problem required to be solved by military action, and so was launched the invasion of Bengal by troops from West Pakistan. Moujib's reaction was to proclaim East Pakistan a sovereign, independent state with the name of Bangladesh on March 23, 1971. The independent state of Bangladesh has since become a reality, after months of bitter fighting in which Indian troops played a decisive role.

As has been observed, secession has three main implications for constitutionalism and legality, viz. the constitutionality or otherwise of secession, the emergency measures of a civil war, and the constitutional status of the secessionist régime and of acts done by it or under its orders. These will now be considered in turn.

Constitutionality of Secession

That a proclamation of secession is based upon popular mandate, even if the mandate has been given directly by the people at a referendum as in some of the Southern States of America during the rebellion there in 1861, does not make it any the more or less constitutional. Such a mandate is no more than an assertion of what is generally referred to as the people's right of revolution, the right of the people to throw off their allegiance to an oppressive government. This right is nowhere more eloquently stated or more forcibly asserted than in the American Declaration of Independence of July 4, 1776. 'When,' declared the American revolutionaries, 'a long train of abuses and usurpations, pursuing invariably the same object, evinces a design to reduce them (i.e. the people) under absolute Despotism, it is their right, it is their duty, to throw off such Government, and to provide new Guards for their future society.' The purpose of government, asserts the theory, is the protection and well-being of the people, and a government which has become destructive of that purpose forfeits its claim to the allegiance of the people. The correlation of protection and allegiance, it may be said, is both a matter of political theory and of law. As Earl Jowitt, Lord Chancellor of England, said:

'The principle which runs through feudal law and what I may perhaps call constitutional law requires on the one hand protection, on the other fidelity; a duty of the sovereign Lord to protect, a duty of the liege or subject to be faithful. Treason . . . is the betrayal of a trust: to be faithful is the counterpart of the duty to protect.'[10]

It does not follow, however, from the correlation of protection and allegiance that they are both equally buttressed by law. While the subject's duty of fidelity is enforceable by the sanction of the law of treason, there is no means whereby the subject can *legally* enforce upon the sovereign his duty to protect. Its sanction can only be political. It is generally conceded both by political theorists and constitutional lawyers that the people may be morally justified in resisting by force a government which has persistently abandoned its responsibility to protect them and to cater for their well-being.[11] Thus, to the question whether a constitution, by virtue of being the supreme law, is binding *morally* upon all citizens in all circumstances, Sir Kenneth Wheare, the celebrated English constitutional lawyer, has given an emphatic no. Discussing this question in relation to the rebellion of the Southern States of America in 1861-5, he writes:

'There are circumstances in which it is morally right to rebel, to refuse to obey the Constitution, to upset it. A Constitution may be the foundation of law and order in a community, but mere law and order is not enough. It must be good law and good order. It is conceivable surely that a minority may be right in saying that it lives under a Constitution which established bad government and that, if all else is tried and fails, rebellion is right. No doubt it is difficult to say just when rebellion is right and how much rebellion is right, but that it may be legitimate is surely true.'[12]

But the legitimacy of rebellion in *appropriate circumstances* (it is necessary to distinguish this from an absolute right of self-determination)[13] is only a moral one. It cannot support secession as a matter of law. To concede that it can would involve the absurd proposition that the constitution can legalise its own destruction by force, that there can be resistance to government under the authority of government itself, and that the law sanctions violent opposition to itself. If a legal right of secession exists in any case, it can only do so under the terms of the constitution[14] or of some other legal principle upon which the constitution rests, and not by virtue of the right of revolution.

Could, then, the secession of Eastern Nigeria be predicated upon the constitution and laws of Nigeria? That the question could be asked at all is because the Nigerian Constitution was a federal one. It can be stated right away that the Constitution itself contains no provision expressly creating a right in a constituent state unilaterally to secede from the federation. In the absence of any such provision, it may be said that the very nature of a federal constitution gives rise to certain implications which are inherently incompatible with the right of a state to secede either through the action of its government or of its inhabitants.

First, the Constitution of the federation of Nigeria declared itself to be the supreme law throughout the country, overriding any other law, including the constitution of a region, which might be inconsistent therewith. It needs hardly be said that a proclamation of secession, apart from being inconsistent with certain specific provisions of the constitution, was calculated to destroy or impair its supremacy generally. Section 3 specified by name the constituent units of the federation and defined their respective territories. It is from this section that the regions derived their existence, and, since no region was competent to amend any provision of the constitution, secession was unlawful and void as an unconstitutional attempt to alter Section 3. The Constitution of the U.S.A. contains no provision similar to Section 3 of the Nigerian Constitution, though the original states are indirectly named in the section which apportions seats in the house of representatives. However, the Constitution is ordained and established for 'the United States of America,' and it is provided that 'the ratification of the convention of nine states shall be sufficient for the establishment of this constitution between the states so ratifying the same.'[15] Thus, it may be said, ratification had the effect, by implication, of incorporating the ratifying states by name into the constitution, and the same is true of the Acts of Congress admitting new states into the Union. These invariably enact that the named state 'shall be, and is hereby admitted into the Union, upon an equal footing with the original states, in all respects whatever.'[16] Upon these considerations, coupled with the circumstances giving rise to the Union, the U.S. Supreme Court has held that the Constitution not only created a Union among the states but also that the Union is indissoluble except by the consent of all the states. It affirmed that the long-standing association of the American states had 'received definite form, and character, and sanction from the articles of confederation. By these the Union was solemnly declared to be "perpetual." And when these articles were found to be inadequate to the exigencies of the country, the constitution was ordained "to form a more perfect union." It is difficult to convey the idea of indissoluble unity more clearly than by these words. What can be indissoluble if a perpetual Union, made more perfect, is not?'[17] Like its American counterpart, the preamble to the Nigerian Constitution also recited the 'firm resolve' of the people of Nigeria 'to establish the Federal Republic of Nigeria, with a view to ensuring the unity of our people and faith in our fatherland.'

The significance of the supremacy of a federal constitution is underlined by the difference between a federal state and a confederacy of states. A federal government does not, like a confederate organisation, derive its authority by delegation from the component states, but exists independently of them. Within the area of competence assigned to it by the constitution, it has independent and direct authority over the territory and people of each state; it is as much a part of the government of the people, and as such is entitled to their allegiance. The language 'the territory and people of a state' is often apt to create an erroneous impression that the right of the state government over the territory and people within its boundaries is superior to or exclusive of that of the federal government. So far from that being the case, the title or authority of the state government in relation to the territory and people within the state is of the same quality and nature as that of the federal government. Given thus the equal right of both, within their respective spheres of competence, to exercise governmental authority over the territory of the state and to claim the allegiance of the people, there can be no question of the state government having the right unilaterally to oust the federal government from the state. An act of secession by a state is therefore clearly inconsistent with the provision of the federal constitution dividing governmental powers between the federal and state governments, and making each independent of the other with respect to their respective areas of competence. In the case of Nigeria, indeed, encroachment by a regional government upon the federal sphere of power was positively prohibited by a provision in the federal constitution that the executive authority of a region 'shall be so exercised as not to impede or prejudice the exercise of the executive authority of the federation or to endanger the continuance of federal government in Nigeria.'[18]

Should a regional government contravene this provision, the federal government was empowered to assume additional powers in the state to an extent necessary to check the contravention.[19]

Thus, it can be seen that secession is incompatible with federal government. For, if pushed to its logical conclusion, it would ultimately result in the complete destruction of the federal government if all the component states were unilaterally to withdraw from the Union. As the U.S. Supreme Court has rightly said, 'without the states in union, there could be no such political body as the United States.'[20]

It has been sought to justify secession legally by reference to contract, an institution whose legal authority and sanction is unquestioned. There is judicial authority for the view that a federal constitution may be regarded as a compact,[21] the compact being either between the component units[22] or between the people as a whole.[23] The notion of a federal constitution as a compact was perhaps the strongest weapon in the armour of the protagonists of secession in America both at the time of the adoption of the constitution and during the period of the rebellion. From the provision of Article vii that the 'ratification of the conventions of nine states shall be sufficient for the establishment of this constitution between the states so ratifying the same,' it was contended that the constitution derived its existence and authority from a compact between the state governments *inter se*, and that the authority so given could be revoked by the donors at any time. The provision relied upon clearly does not establish the right claimed for the state government, for it refers to ratification, not by the legislature or any other regular organ of the state government, but by a convention elected by the people, a body with no basis whatever in the state constitution. It seems clear, moreover, that 'state' in the context of this provision cannot possibly refer to government – 'conventions of nine governments' conveys no meaning at all. It must therefore be taken to refer to the people inhabiting the territory of the state. In *Texas v. White*,[24] the U.S. Supreme Court had occasion to distinguish three senses in which the word 'state' is used in the constitution, viz. as a political community of free citizens occupying a territory of defined boundaries, and organised under a government sanctioned and limited by a written constitution; as a territory; and lastly as a people. It observed that, when used in the last sense, 'a plain distinction is made between a state and the government of a state.'

Granted that the reference in the clause about ratification is not to the state government, the state righters, as the protagonists of secession in America were called, further argued that the constitution must be regarded as having been established by the people of the several states, acting not as individuals, but 'as so many sovereign political communities, since in the first place, it is only a sovereign political community that can enact law and since, in the second place, the states were in 1787 the only sovereign political communities on the continent.'[25] As has been shown,[26] the argument that law making is a function exclusively of governments, and that the people in their mass, by means of a referendum or a special convention or constituent assembly, cannot enact laws, has no validity any longer, if it ever had any. In the face of this, the contention in favour of a state's right of secession has to be shifted to a new premise, which asserted that it was the people of the several states, *as individuals*, who gave the constitution its legal authority, and not the people of the U.S. as one single, indivisible people. An antithesis was thus erected between the people of the U.S. and the peoples of the states. In the words of Madison:

'This assent and ratification is to be given by the people, not as individuals composing one entire nation, but as composing the distinct and independent states to which they respectively belong . . . The act, therefore, establishing the constitution, will not be a *national* but a *federal* act . . . Were the people regarded in this transaction as forming one nation, the will of the majority of the whole people of the U.S. would bind the minority . . . Each state, in ratifying the constitution, is considered as a sovereign body, independent of all others, and only to be bound by its own voluntary act.'[27]

From this again the conclusion was drawn that the people of the several states, in their individual capacity, and not through their state governments, could take away what they had given. Articulating this inference, Madison again, after stating the different senses in which the word state has been used in the constitution, concludes that it was in the sense of 'a people' that 'the constitution was submitted to the "states"; in that sense the "states" ratified it; and in that sense . . . they are consequently parties to the compact from which the powers of the federal government result . . . The states then, being the parties to the constitutional compact, . . . it follows of necessity that there can be no tribunal above their authority to decide.'[28] It was in reliance upon this theory that some of the Ordinances of Secession of the Southern States in America were submitted to the ratification of the people at a referendum.

Yet, even assuming that the notion of a compact is appropriate to describe a constitution, and that the compact is either between the state governments *inter se* or between the peoples of the several states as individuals, the conclusion based upon it cannot be supported in law. In the absence of express provision in a contract, it is not open to a party to it unilaterally to terminate it. Should he attempt to do that, the other party can rightly ignore the pretended unilateral withdrawal, treat the contract as still subsisting and proceed to perform his part of it. Alternatively he may accept the other's withdrawal and sue for damages for breach. The state righters then say that where the federal government or the section of the people represented by it (i.e. the Northern States) have by their conduct shown such a disregard of the terms of the compact, a breach or repudiation was thereby committed, entitling them to rescind it. This ignores the fact that the contract upon which the constitution is founded is a special one. For once established, the constitution binds not only the organs of government created by it, but equally also the people themselves, so that neither the former nor the latter can change it *legally* except in the manner prescribed therein. In any case, it is now generally accepted that the American Constitution was ordained and established, not by the people of the several states, but by the people of the U.S., acting as one people, though within the several states.[29] 'The people of the United States are an integral, and not a composite mass, and their unity and identity, in this view of the subject, are not affected by their segregation by state lines for the purposes of state government and local administration.'[30] Regarded therefore as one indivisible entity, no section of it has the right unilaterally to withdraw its allegiance to the constitution.

The argument based upon contract can hardly have any application to the Nigerian Constitution. Unlike in America, Australia and Canada, the federation of Nigeria originated by the disaggregation of an existing unitary state. The decision for this was that of the British Government, and was first announced in the House of Commons, after the Kano Riots in 1952, by the secretary of state for the colonies without prior consultation with the people of Nigeria.

In view of all that has been said, it is indisputable that, considered as a transaction under the Constitution, the proclamation of Biafran independence was, like that of the Southern States in America, without any sanction of law and therefore an absolute nullity.[31] The same is true of the Katangan secession.

(i) *Implications of the nullity of secession*

Does a proclamation of secession, notwithstanding its nullity, have the effect of temporarily taking the rebel state or states out of the federation for the duration of the rebellion? Do the rebel states, in other words, cease for the duration of secession to be component units or members of the federal union? This question has been agitated in the U.S., but it should not really arise, for, if secession is void *ab initio*, it is as if it never took place at all, so that the seceding states' continued membership of the federation could not have been affected. 'If this were otherwise,' said the U.S. Supreme Court, 'the state must have become foreign, and her citizens foreigners. The war must have ceased to be a war for the suppression of rebellion, must have become a war of conquest and subjugation.'[32] But for the federal character of the state, the question would not have been raised at all. It could not have been supposed that an individual citizen would cease to be such because he attempted to overthrow the government of his country by unlawful means, nor that a section of a unitary state in revolt against the government would cease to be part of the state for the period of the rebellion.[33]

If the rebel state remains part of the state notwithstanding the attempted secession, it follows that the legal system must also remain in operation, at least that part of it that regulates ordinary social life of the people in the secessionist state. Rebellion is not to be regarded as destroying society and the rules of law that regulate social intercourse. Accordingly the U.S. Supreme Court has held that:

'These laws (i.e. the ordinary laws of the land), necessary in their recognition and administration to the existence of organised society, were the same, with slight exceptions, whether the authorities of the state acknowledge allegiance to the true or the false federal power. They were the fundamental principles for which civil society is organised into government in all countries, and must be respected in their administration under whatever temporary dominant authority they may be exercised.'[34]

It follows too that the obligations of the seceding state and its inhabitants to respect the constitution and laws of the federal state remain unimpaired. Secession does not make acts done *after its proclamation* any the less treasonable; such acts are as treasonable as the initial proclamation of secession itself. Only if secession is regarded as effective to take the revolted state temporarily out of the union will the citizens of the state escape from the sanction of the law of treason for acts done after secession in aid thereof, since in that case those citizens would have become foreigners bound by no duty of allegiance to the federal union. Treason, being a breach of the duty of allegiance, no act, however hostile to a government, can be such unless done by one who owes allegiance, whether permanent or temporary. Thus, a British citizen, resident in Britain, who organised the running of guns and other military stores to the secessionist states in America was held not to have committed treason against the U.S.[35]

However, although obligations remain unimpaired, rebellion does affect the *rights* of the insurgent state and its inhabitants. It operates to suspend their civic rights, though it does not destroy them completely. 'During this condition of civil war,' the U.S. Supreme Court has held, 'the rights of the state as a member, and of her people as citizens of the Union, were suspended. The government and the citizens of the state, refusing to recognise their constitutional obligations, assumed the character of enemies, and incurred the consequences of rebellion.'[36] For example, the right of the state to appoint senators and of its citizens to elect Representatives to Congress was held to be lost temporarily. Furthermore, as enemies, the property of the insurgent citizens was subject to capture in certain circumstances.

(ii) *The effect of general pardon or amnesty*
It is usual to grant a general pardon or amnesty to the insurgents at the end of the rebellion. What is the effect of this upon the insurgents' liability and disabilities in connection with the rebellion? The position has been explained by the U.S. Supreme Court to be that:

'A pardon reaches both the punishment prescribed for the offence and the guilt of the offender; and when the pardon is full it releases the punishment and blots out of existence the guilt, so that in the eye of the law the offender is as innocent as if he had never committed the offence. If granted before conviction, it prevents any of the penalties and disabilities, consequent upon conviction, from attaching; if granted after conviction, it removes the penalties and disabilities, and restores him to all his civil rights; it makes him, as it were, a new man, and gives him a new credit and capacity.'[37]

Every individual, unless excluded by its terms, is covered by the general pardon or amnesty as fully as if he had been specifically named therein.[38]

The question concerning the effect of a pardon had arisen in America in relation to certain acts of Congress imposing disabilities upon persons who had given aid or comfort to the rebellion or who had consented to their property being used in aid of it. The statutes authorised the confiscation of property so used. With regard to persons who gave aid or comfort, any property of theirs which had been captured or been abandoned was to be sold and the proceeds appropriated absolutely to the federal government. The U.S. Supreme Court has, however, held that a pardon relieved from much of this penalty provided the proceeds had in fact been appropriated to the United States;[39] a pardon also relieved the individual concerned from proving that he did not give aid and comfort, since the pardon is equivalent to actual proof of his unbroken loyalty.[40] Of these disabling statutes perhaps the most drastic was that which required every person elected or appointed to any office of honour or profit under the government of the U.S., either in the civil, military or naval departments of the public service, and also attorneys and counsellors of the courts of the U.S. to take the following oath:

(i) That the deponent has never voluntarily borne arms against the U.S. since he has been a citizen thereof;

(ii) That he has not voluntarily given aid, countenance, counsel or encouragement to persons engaged in armed hostility thereto;

(iii) That he has never sought, accepted or attempted to exercise the functions of any office whatsoever, under any authority or pretended authority in hostility to the U.S.;

(iv) That he has not yielded a voluntary support to any pretended government, authority, power or constitution, within the U.S., hostile or inimical thereto; and

(v) That he will support and defend the constitution of the U.S. against all enemies, foreign and domestic, and will bear truth, faith and allegiance to the same.

In *ex parte Garland*[41] the petitioner who, during the civil war, had been successively a member of the lower house and of the Senate of the Confederate States, asked permission after the war to continue to practice as an attorney and counsellor of the court without taking the prescribed oath. He had received an unconditional pardon from the President. The U.S. Supreme Court held by a majority that, as the petitioner could not take the oath without perjuring himself the effect of the statute was to exclude him permanently from practising his profession, that such exclusion was clearly a punishment for his past participation in the rebellion, and as such it was a negation of the pardon. As the power of pardon belonged to the President under the constitution, it was incompetent to the Congress to limit or negate its effect. Accordingly it was not within the constitutional power of Congress thus to inflict punishment beyond the reach of executive clemency. The statute was accordingly declared unconstitutional on this ground as well as on the ground that it partook of the nature of a bill of attainder and of an *ex post facto* law, both of which were prohibited by the constitution.

Constitutionalism and Civil War

Rebellion almost invariably calls forth on the part of the lawful government military action to suppress it, which, if resisted by the secessionists, leads to a civil war. Thus, in the U.S. and in Nigeria there was, consequent upon the rebellion, a civil war which lasted for over four and two and a half years respectively. In the Congo, where the rebellion also lasted for two and a half years, the intervention of the United Nations' troops prevented a civil war as such though there had in fact been an abortive invasion of Katanga by the federal government of Lumumba. The secession of Baluba from Katanga also provoked military action by the Katangan government, with sporadic fighting going on there for the whole period of the crisis. And in Pakistan civil war had raged between the federal government and the secessionist state of East Pakistan until the final defeat of the federal forces.

Now as has been stated,[42] war calls for emergency powers going beyond the normal constitutional limitations upon government. In Nigeria the federal government was already a military and consequently an autocratic one when the rebellion broke out, but it nevertheless thought it expedient to assume further power by declaring a state of emergency which freed it from the remaining vestiges of restraint upon its power. On the rebel side, the régime, also military, was anything but constitutional; there was no limitation of any kind upon its power and the exercise of power was entirely arbitrary. So also during the American civil war, although representative institutions continued to function, the President made rather ample use of his war powers, sometimes exceeding the proper constitutional limits of those powers. Martial law, military commissions, arbitrary arrests, the suspension of the habeas corpus acts and other arbitrary exercise of power were all used.[43] An Indemnity Act had to be passed in 1863 to protect the executive against the excesses of power. And, as already noted, there were various Acts of Congress authorising the confiscation of property of those involved in the rebellion.

The Constitutional Status of the Secessionist Régime and of Acts Done by it or under its Orders

If secession is unlawful and a nullity, it necessarily follows that the rebel régime, being a direct product of the proclamation of secession, can have no legal existence. It is an entity unrecognised by the constitution. Thus the Republic of Biafra declared on May 30, 1967, lacked any kind of legal identity, just like the Confederate States of America. The same is true of the Republic of Katanga. But does it follow from this that all legislative or executive acts done by it or on its order were equally devoid of legal validity? Here the consequences must differ according as the state is a unitary or federal one. In a federation, secession by a constituent

T

unit is unconstitutional because it implies the usurpation of powers belonging under the constitution to the federal authorities. Whereas in a unitary state every act of a rebel régime is necessarily a usurpation, in a federation, on the other hand, such powers as under the constitution are within the competence of a region cannot be affected by the act of secession, and the exercise of them by the seceding state after secession cannot be a usurpation and must therefore, in general, be accepted as valid, provided that such exercise of them is otherwise in accordance with the constitution of both the federation and the region concerned. The point is well stated in the following dictum of the U.S. Supreme Court:

'Whilst thus holding that there was no validity in any legislation of the Confederate States which this court can recognise, it is proper to observe that the legislation of the States stands on very different grounds . . . As far as the Acts of the States do not impair or tend to impair the supremacy of the national authority, or the just rights of the citizens under the constitution, they are, in general, to be treated as valid and binding. As we said in *Horn v. Lockhart* . . . "The existence of a sate of insurrection and war did not loosen the bonds of society or do away with civil government or the regular administration of the laws. Order was to be preserved, police regulations maintained, crime prosecuted, property protected, contracts enforced, marriages celebrated, estates settled, and the transfer and descent of property regulated, precisely as in the time of peace. No one that we are aware of seriously questions the validity of judicial or legislative Acts in the insurrectionary states touching these and kindred subjects, where they were not hostile in their purpose or mode of enforcement to the authority of the National Government, and did not impair the rights of citizens under the constitution".[44]

The application of this principle may, however, raise a difficulty. When a state in a federation secedes from the federal union and proclaims itself an independent, sovereign state, all its acts thereafter are done in its new capacity. And if in that capacity it has no legal existence, should it not follow logically that all such acts can also have no legal validity? It is not as if a state, while remaining such, usurps the powers of the federation. This problem did not arise in the United States. There, as in Nigeria and the Congo, each of the southern states had, by its ordinances of secession, declared itself 'a separate and sovereign state.' But they hardly functioned in that capacity. While retaining their constitutions as they were before, they immediately organised a new federal government by the name of the Confederate States of America, investing it with all the powers formerly belonging to the United States in the insurgent states. Thereafter the states resumed their original capacity of states, thus enabling a clear separation to be made between them and the usurping body, the Confederate government. Concerning the latter the U.S. Supreme Court has rightly maintained that it had no legal existence, and accordingly that its pretended power being a usurpation of power lawfully belonging to the United States, its legislation could have no legal validity. If, in the Nigerian case, the Republic of Biafra, like the Confederate States of America, must be deemed never to have existed *in law*, then it follows that the only entity of which the law can take account during the period of rebellion was the Eastern Region, which on the eve of the rebellion had been split into three states. All acts purported to have been done by the non-existent Republic of Biafra are therefore to be deemed to be acts of the state governments. And, on the principle as laid down by the U.S. Supreme Court, such of them as were within the competence of a state should in general be recognised as valid. But those that amounted to a usurpation of the powers of the federation would be void. This is in line with the decision of the U.S. Supreme Court that a statute purported to have been enacted by the legally non-existent Confederate government could be regarded, if at all, only if it had been adopted by a state government, though it would then operate, not as an enactment of the Confederate government, but of the state which had adopted it. 'Any enactment,' said the court, 'from whatever source originating, to which a state gives the force of law is a statute of the state . . . By the only authority which can be recognised as having any legal existence, that is, the state of Virginia, this Act of the unauthorised Confederation was enforced as a law of the Commonwealth.'[45]

As the statement of the U.S. Supreme Court makes clear, the validity of an act of a rebel state government within the limits of its jurisdiction is subject to the qualification that it should not be in aid of the rebellion or violative of the constitutional rights of citizens. This qualification is well illustrated by the case of *Williams v. Bruffy*.[46] There, the plaintiffs, who were resident in the non-insurgent state of Pennsylvania, had before the rebellion sold and delivered certain goods to the defendant in Virginia, one of the revolted states, wherein the defendant resided. During the rebellion, the Confederate government enacted a statute sequestrating the lands, goods, chattels, rights and credits within the confederate states belonging to any alien enemy; any person holding any such land, etc., on behalf of such alien enemy was required to transfer them to the receiver of the Confederate government, such transfer to operate as a discharge for the person so transferring them. In pursuance of this the defendant paid to the receiver the amount representing the price of the goods sold to him by the plaintiffs. When after the end of the rebellion the plaintiffs sued him to recover the price of the goods he pleaded the confederate statute as having discharged him from liability to make further payment to the plaintiffs. Considered as a statute of the Confederate government, an unlawful organisation, the Sequestration Act had no legal validity whatever, but since it had been enforced by the government of the state of Virginia, it was conceded that it might have validity as a law of that state. Even as so treated the Supreme Court nevertheless held it to be invalid for repugnancy to the constitution of the United States, because:

(i) it impaired the obligation of the contract between the plaintiffs and defendant, contrary to the constitutional guarantee of liberty;

(ii) it discriminated against the plaintiffs as citizens of a loyal state by denying them the same privileges accorded to the citizens of Virginia, contrary to the constitutional guarantee of equality of treatment;

(iii) it was an Act in aid of rebellion, having been enacted as a means of raising funds for the prosecution of the war against the U.S.

This last ground has been the all-pervading criterion for the validity of the acts of the rebel governments. 'Nothing,' said Justice Swayne, 'is better settled in the jurisprudence of this court than that all acts done in aid of the rebellion were illegal and of no validity. The principle has become axiomatic.'[47] The principle has been applied to invalidate a statute sequestrating shares in a gas company held by loyal citizens,[48] or under which a loyal citizen was prosecuted for assisting the federal forces[49] or authorising the issue of treasury notes to raise money for prosecuting the war.[50] The leading case of *Texas v. White*[51] was one of contract by which the Military Board of Texas, a body created for the purpose of prosecuting the war against the U.S., obtained the supply of a large quantity of cotton cards, and medicine from certain individuals to whom it transferred certain bonds of the State of Texas by way of payment. On behalf of the suppliers it was contended that the contract, being for the purchase of cotton cards and medicines, was not a contract in aid of rebellion, but one for obtaining goods capable of a use entirely legitimate and innocent. It was held that, even ignoring the unlawful character of the Board, the contract was, from the available evidence, clearly in aid of rebellion and void. The principle applies also to contracts between private individuals, so that a seller of goods under such a contract cannot recover the purchase price.[52]

As already noted, an act of a rebel legislature passed in aid of the rebellion cannot be pleaded by an individual as absolving him from his contractual liability to another. Where, too, a person prosecuted and acquitted of the charge of treason by a confederate court brought an action for malicious prosecution against the judge of the pretended court, its clerk, the prosecuting district attorney and a newspaper editor alleged to have incited the prosecution through the medium of his newspaper, the court held that the confederate court being illegal, 'the form of law with which it clothed its proceedings gave no protection to those who, assuming to be its officers, were the instruments by which it acted.'[53] The trial court had directed the jury that if the plaintiff had himself been a traitor he could not recover, unless his support of the rebellion was under an honest and rational apprehension of persecution, loss of life, liberty or property. Disapproving of this direction, the U.S. Supreme Court said:

'As a matter of law, we do not see any connection between the two elements of this proposition. Giving aid to the troops of the United States, by whomsoever given, and whatever the circumstances, was a lawful and meritorious act. If the platintiff had before co-operated with the rebels there was a *locus penitentiae*, which, whenever he chose to do so, he had a right to occupy. His past or subsequent complicity with those engaged in the rebellion might affect his character, but could not, as a matter of law, give impunity to those by whose instrumentality he was seized, imprisoned and tried upon a capital charge for serving his country. Such a justification would be a strange anomaly. Evidence of treasonable acts on his part against the United States was alien to the issue before the jury. To admit it, was to put the plaintiff on trial as well as the defendants . . . The guilt of the plaintiff, if established, could in nowise affect the legal liability of the defendants; nor could the fact be received in mitigation of damages.'[54]

These, then, are the conditions governing the validity of acts of a rebel state government. The presupposition is of course that the state government is lawfully constituted. In the context of the Eastern Nigerian rebellion, legal validity of acts of the secessionist régime so far as they related to matters within state competence presupposes that Ojukwu was or remained during the period of the rebellion the lawful military governor of any of the states in the insurrectionary territory. Before secession, he had been the lawfully appointed military governor for Eastern Nigeria. As previously noted, however, Eastern Nigeria was just before the proclamation of secession split into three states by the federal military government, namely the East Central State, the South Eastern State and the Rivers State. To the last two, it appointed other persons as military governors, and subsequently dismissed Ojukwu both from the Nigerian army and from his office of military governor of the East Central State, replacing him in this latter position with a civilian administrator. By these actions of the federal military government, Ojukwu ceased to be the lawful governor of any part of the secessionist territory, though he remained still in *actual* control of the seats of power and of public offices in the three Eastern States, providing, indeed, the only government in those territories until their liberation by the federal forces, culminating eventually in the total collapse of the rebellion.

Could it then be said that all the acts of Ojukwu as *de facto* military governor ceased to have effect from the time of his dismissal, or, as regards the South Eastern State and Rivers State, from the time of their creation? For precedent we have again to consult American experience. Not all the insurgent state governments in America had been lawfully elected. Texas was a notable example of this. There, the lawful governor elected before the secession had been summarily ejected from office together with his Secretary of State for refusing to take an oath of fidelity to the constitution and laws of the Confederacy. A convention, called without authority, but subsequently sanctioned by the regularly elected Legislature, had adopted an ordinance of secession, appointed a committee of public safety, and adopted an ordinance authorising the committee to take measures for obtaining possession of the property of the U.S. in Texas, and for removing the U.S. troops from the state. Commissioners were also appointed, and a military force organised. After the ordinance of secession had been ratified by the majority of the people at a referendum, the convention applied for membership of the Confederation of American States, pledging the adhesion of Texas to its provisional Constitution, and thereafter proceeded to make the changes in the state Constitution which this adhesion made necessary. When the war ended, the insurgent government of Texas disappeared. The chief functionaries left the state, and so did many of the subordinate officials. A provisional government was appointed for the state by a Proclamation of the President of the U.S. In accordance with the provision of the Proclamation, a convention was assembled, the Constitution of the state amended, elections held, and a new state government, acknowledging its obligation to the U.S., established.

The U.S. Supreme Court took the view that the government organised in Texas for prosecuting war against the U.S. was unlawful.[55] It also held that any rebel legislature whose members had not taken the oath prescribed for such members by the Constitution of the U.S. was unlawful.[56] Further, that after the adoption of the ordinance of secession and of the ordinance by which a state acceded to and became a member of the insurrectionary confederacy, the state legislature, though regularly elected before the rebellion, ceased to represent the state as a constitutional member of the Federal Union.[57] The court nevertheless went on to acknowledge the historical fact that the unlawful government was the state's only actual government. In regard to Texas, it held that the new government, having displaced the regular authority, and having established itself in the customary seats of power and in the exercise of the ordinary functions of administration, constituted, in the strictest sense of the words, a *de facto* government, so that its acts, during the period of its existence as such, were, in general and subject in particular to the conditions noted above, effectual and valid.[58] 'It is not necessary,' said Chief Justice Chase, delivering the opinion of the court, 'to attempt any exact definitions, within which the Acts of such a state government must be treated as valid or invalid. It may be said, perhaps with sufficient accuracy, that Acts necessary to peace and good order among citizens, such, for example, as Acts sanctioning and protecting marriage and domestic relations, governing the course of descents, regulating the conveyance and transfer of property, real and personal, and providing remedies for injuries to person and estate, and other similar Acts, which would be valid if emanating from a valid government, must be regarded, in general, as valid when proceeding from an actual, though unlawful government; and that Acts in furtherance or support of rebellion against the United States, or intended to defeat the just rights of citizens, and other Acts of like nature, must, in general, be regarded as invalid and void.'[59] Reaffirming this view in a subsequent case the court observed that it is only 'when the functions necessarily reposed in the state for the maintenance of civil society were perverted to the manifest and intentional aid of treason against the Government of the Union, that their Acts are void.'[60] Thus, a statute of a state legislature creating corporations for purposes of ordinary civil functions not connected with the rebellion was upheld.[61]

However, the position of Ojukwu's rebel government differed from that of the rebel state governments in America in two respects. Whereas the latter had no lawful rivals in matters within state competence, Ojukwu's had. There was, as has been pointed out, a lawful civilian administrator for the East Central State, and a lawful military governor for each of the two other states in the East, the South Eastern State and the Rivers State. These lawful state governments remained in existence throughout the period of the rebellion, and continued to assert their authority over their respective territories, and were making effort through the federal military government to regain control. In relation to them Ojukwu was a usurper, and as such could claim no *de facto* status for his rebel government. This conclusion follows from the decisions of the U.S. Supreme Court regarding the Confederate government (discussed below), and from that of the Privy Council concerning the rebel government of Ian Smith in Southern Rhodesia. 'The *de facto* status of sovereignty,' said Lord Pearce, 'cannot be conceded to a rebel government as against the true Sovereign in the latter's courts of law.'[62]

In the second place, the Nigerian Regions under the military régime had no area of *exclusive* competence except for a brief period, March 17 to May 26, 1967.[63] Right from the inception of military rule, the federal military government assumed to itself power to legislate for the peace, order and good government of Nigeria or any part thereof with respect to any matter whatsoever. This unlimited power it resumed again on May 27, 1967,[64] after its brief relinquishment from March 17 to May 26, 1967. So that on May 30, 1967, when the former Eastern Nigeria was declared an independent, sovereign state, the federal authority extended over the whole of what were formerly areas of regional competence. It follows therefore that the secession was, in respect of every exercise of power by the secessionist government, a usurpation of the federal power. The position of Ojukwu's rebel government is thus analagous in every respect to that of the Confederate government in America.

The de facto *Character of a Rebel Government with respect to the Exercise of Power outside State Competence*
What has been said so far about the *de facto* character of a rebel government relates only to the exercise of power with respect to matters within state competence. Yet it is equally a fact that, for the duration of the rebellion, the rebel government exercises actual authority over the rebel territory with respect to matters within federal competence. The Confederate government did so in America, and likewise Ojukwu's and Tshombe's governments in Eastern Nigeria and Katanga respectively. Could not such a government constitute the *de facto* government of the area for purposes of federal powers just as in the case of state powers? This point has greatly agitated the U.S. Supreme Court concerning the Confederate government. It was urged upon it that, although the Confederate government lacked legal existence, it should nevertheless be recognised as a *de facto* government. In attempting to answer this question,

the court had had to go into a detailed examination of the nature
of a *de facto* government, and the definition which it arrived at is
that, in the strictest sense of the term, a *de facto* government is one
which has expelled the regularly constituted authorities from their
seats of power and public offices and established its own functionaries in their places, so as to represent in fact the sovereignty of the
nation.[65] The Government of England under the Commonwealth
established upon the execution of King Charles I and the overthrow of the Loyalists was cited as an example of this. Judged by
this definition, the Confederate government did not, in the court's
opinion, qualify as a *de facto* government, because:

'It never represented the nation; it never expelled the public
authorities from the country; it never entered into any treaties,
nor was it ever recognised as that of an independent power. It
collected an immense military force, and temporarily expelled
the authorities of the United States from the territory over which
it exercised an unusurped dominion; but in that expulsion the
United States never acquiesced; on the contrary, they immediately resorted to similar force to regain possession of that
territory and re-establish their authority, and they continued to
use such force until they succeeded. It would be useless to comment
upon the striking contrast between a government of this nature,
which with all its military strength, never had undisputed possession of power for a single day, and government like that of the
Commonwealth of England under Parliament or Cromwell.'[66]

This opinion was rendered in 1878. Ten years earlier when
confronted with a similar question in *Thorington v. Smith*,[67] the
court, whilst accepting that the Confederate government was not a
de facto government in the strict sense described above, stated that
there is another description of government, also classified as *de facto*
by publicists, but which might perhaps be more aptly denominated
as a government of paramount force. Such a government is characterised by the fact that its existence is maintained against the
rightful authority of an established and lawful government, by
active military power which compels the obedience of the citizens
as a matter of necessity, if not of duty. The usual example of this is
where one country occupies part of the territory of another with
which it is engaged in lawful warfare. Although the Confederate
government differed from a *de facto* government of this type in the
circumstance that its authority did not originate in lawful acts of
regular war, the court nevertheless thought that it could be equated
with it, since its control was no less actual or supreme, and its
supremacy, while not justifying acts of hostility to the U.S., made
obedience to its authority in civil and local matters not only a

necessity, but a duty. 'To the extent,' said Chief Justice Chase, 'then, of actual supremacy, however unlawfully gained, in all matter of government within its military lines, the power of the insurgent government cannot be questioned.'[68] As Justice Nelson put it while delivering the opinion of the court in another case:

'It cannot be denied but that by the use of these unlawful and unconstitutional means, a government, in fact, was created greater in territory than many of the old governments in Europe; complete in their organisation of all its parts; containing within its limits more than eleven millions of people, and of sufficient resources, in men and money, to carry on a civil war of unexampled dimensions . . . the so-called Confederate States were in the possession of many of the highest attributes of government, sufficiently so to be regarded as the ruling or supreme power of the country.'[69]

However, in *Ford v. Surget*,[70] decided in 1878, the majority of the court, without expressly referring to *Thorington v. Smith*, renounced the position there taken up, maintaining that the Confederate government had, *as a government*, no *de facto* existence of any kind, and can be regarded by the courts in no other light than as simply the military representative of the insurrection against the authority of the U.S. In a powerful dissenting judgment Justice Clifford reaffirmed the unanimous opinion of the court in *Thorington v. Smith* that the Confederate government should be accorded the character of a government of paramount force, pleading passionately that:

'Unless the Confederate States may be regarded as having constituted a *de facto* government for the time or as the supreme controlling power within the limits of their exclusive military sway, then the officers and seamen of their privateers, and the officers and soldiers of their army were mere pirates and insurgents, and every officer, seaman, or soldier who killed a federal officer or soldier in battle, whether on land or the high seas, is liable to indictment, conviction and sentence for the crime of murder, subject of course to the right to plead amnesty or pardon, if they can make good that defence.[71] Once enter the domain of strife, and countless litigations of endless duration may arise to revive old animosities and to renew and inflame domestic discord, without any public necessity or individual advantage. Wisdom suggests caution, and the counsels of caution forbid any such rash experiment.'[72]

The decision in *Ford v. Surget* was handed down in November 1878, seven months after *Williams v. Bruffy* referred to above. In the latter case the court, though not renouncing *Thorington v. Smith*, gave it a limited interpretation as meaning that, 'as the actual supremacy of the Confederate government existed over certain territory, individual resistance to its authority then would have been futile, and, therefore, unjustifiable. In the face of an over-whelming force, obedience in such matters may often be a necessity and, in the interests of order, a duty. No concession is thus made to the rightfulness of the authority exercised.'[73] This seems to represent a compromise between the two views, the effect of which may be stated as follows: every legislative act of the Confederate govern-ment was void, and the existence of hostilities could not bestow validity upon it. An individual could not set up such act as justifica-tion for his action or as relieving him from an obligation owed to another. But an action imposed upon him by the application or threat of force, resulting from the irresistible power of the Con-federate government may excuse from liability. Purely executive acts of such a government enforced upon the community with a view to the preservation of order and ordinary social intercourse may also be taken cognisance of. To illustrate: a U.S. postmaster in an insurgent state, who in obedience to an Act of the Confederate congress and an order of its postmaster-general, transferred certain U.S. bonds in his possession to a mail carrier in payment for an amount due to him from the U.S. as remuneration for his services was held liable to make good the value of the bond, the court observing that 'whatever weight may be given under the circumstances to its acts of force, on the ground of irresistible power . . . the Acts of the Confederate congress can have no force, *as law*, in divesting or transferring rights, or as authority for any Act opposed to the just authority of the Federal Government.'[74] As to whether in fact the payment was compelled by an act of force emanating from the irresistible power of the Confederate government, the court held that it was not enough that the defendant was resident within the insurgent states and that the Confederate government had force sufficient to enforce its orders, and did enforce them in the area where the defendant resided. It must be shown that the payment was made as a result of the application of physical force to compel him to pay. For it is consistent with the evidence that the defendant might have been desirous and willing to make the payment. There was no evidence of any effort or endeavour on his part to secure the funds in his hands to the government, to which he owed both the money and his allegiance. Nor was there evidence that he would have suffered any inconvenience or been punished by the Confederate authorities if he had refused to pay the draft of the insurrectionary post office department. 'We cannot concede,' said the court, 'that a man, who, as a citizen, owes allegiance to the U.S., and as an officer of the government holds its money or property is at liberty to turn over the latter to an insurrectionary government, which only demands it by ordinances and drafts drawn on the bailee, but which exercises no force or threat of personal violence to himself or property in the enforcement of its illegal orders.'[75]

In *Williams v. Bruffy*[76] where the court refused to recognise a sequestration Act of the Confederate government as relieving the purchaser of goods from his contractual obligation to pay for them, notwithstanding that he had already, pursuant to the Act, paid the money to the receiver of the Confederate government, the court nevertheless conceded that parties residing in the insurrectionary territory, who may have had taken from them by force property held by them as trustees or bailees of loyal citizens, may perhaps be released from liability. But, debts not being tangible things subject to physical seizure and removal, the debtors cannot claim release from liability to their creditors, by reason of the coerced payment of equivalent sums to an unlawful combination.

The question in *Thorington v. Smith* was as to what recognition, if any, should be given to rebel currency notes. (The Republic of Biafra issued its currency notes in 1968.) The court affirmed that the notes, considered as contracts in themselves, were nullities, having been issued in furtherance of an unlawful attempt to overthrow the government of the U.S.; as such they imposed no legal obligation upon the lawful government after the suppression of the rebellion to pay money to persons holding them. This is the view which the federal military government of Nigeria has adopted in a decree upon the matter. But the court held nonetheless, that, as the currency notes provided the only medium of exchange in nearly all business transactions of many millions of people, which made their use a matter of almost absolute necessity, they must be regarded as a currency imposed on the community by irresistible force. 'It seems to follow,' the court concludes, 'as a necessary consequence from this actual supremacy of the insurgent government, as a belligerent, within the territory where it circulated, and from the necessity of civil obedience on the part of all who remained in it, that this currency must be considered in courts of law in the same light as if it had been issued by a foreign government, temporarily occupying a territory of the U.S.'[77] Contracts made on the basis of the currency were not therefore, on that account alone, illegal or void. For as the court observed in another case, 'it would have been a cruel and oppressive judgment, if all the transactions of the many millions of people composing the inhabitants of the insurgent states, for the several years of the war, had been held tainted with illegality because of the use of this forced currency, when those transactions were not made with reference to the insurrectionary government.'[78] Accordingly, a party entitled to be paid in the rebel currency can, after the suppression of the rebellion, recover their actual value at the time and place of the contract, in lawful money of the U.S. In the view of the court there was no great difficulty in ascertaining the value of the rebel notes in terms of lawful U.S. dollars, since their widespread use 'gave them a sort of value, insignificant and precarious enough it is true, but always having a sufficiently definite relation to gold and silver, the universal measure of value.'[79]

It seems also to be clearly implied in the cases in which the U.S. Government had claimed and been awarded property belonging to the Confederate government in the hands of agents holding the same for that government, that the Confederate government had sufficient *de facto* capacity to acquire, hold and dispose of property, at any rate personal property.[80]

The Case of Southern Rhodesia

As previously stated,[81] Southern Rhodesia was annexed as a British colony in 1923, becoming thereby part of Her Majesty's dominions. In British constitutional law, the British Parliament has absolute sovereignty over not only the United Kingdom but over every part of Her Majesty's dominions outside the United Kingdom, except those that have attained independence. In 1961 Southern Rhodesia was granted a Constitution which gave her full internal self-government, including indeed power, in accordance with a prescribed procedure, to amend the Constitution itself, but the amendment of certain provisions was reserved *exclusively* to Her Majesty in Council in the United Kingdom. These provisions were those relating to the office of Governor, his powers and duties (Sections 1, 2, 3, and 5), the definition of the legislature as consisting of Her Majesty and the Legislative Assembly (Section 6), the assent to bills by Her Majesty or the Governor on Her behalf (Section 29), the power to disallow bills (Section 32), the vesting of executive authority in Her Majesty (Section 42), the prerogative of mercy (Section 49), and the amending procedure itself (Section 111). It is important to emphasise again that the amendment of these provisions is not concurrent to the Rhodesian legislature and Her Majesty in Council, but is vested exclusively in the latter. Furthermore, certain other provisions of the Constitution, notably the declaration of rights and the right of appeal to the Privy Council, though amendable by the Rhodesian legislature with a two-thirds majority, could only be so amended with the approval of Her Majesty in Council or in the alternative with the concurrence of a majority of all the four principal racial groups in the country, in a referendum in which every adult citizen of over twenty-one years of age, white or black, is entitled to vote, notwithstanding that in the case of an African he cannot ordinarily vote (Sections 107(2) and 108). Wide as is therefore the power of the Rhodesian government under the 1961 Constitution, it falls short of full independence. The British Government retains ultimate responsibility for it, so that the status of the territory remains that of a British dependency or colony.

It has been contended that the frame of the 1961 Constitution involved a division of sovereignty analogous to that in a federal system between the federation and its component units, and that accordingly the usurpation involved in the unilateral declaration of independence by Prime Minister Ian Smith and his ministers on November 11, 1965, was limited to powers which under the Constitution belong to the British Government either exclusively or concurrently with the Rhodesian Government.[82] In respect of such powers, the rebel government set up by Ian Smith following upon UDI could not, it was generally conceded on all hands, be recognised as a *de facto* government. As regards matters within the exclusive competence of the Rhodesian legislature and government, however, the appellate division of the Rhodesian high court held, by a majority, that the rebel government should be accorded a *de facto* status. The reasoning of the court was succinctly stated by Sir Hugh Beadle, the Chief Justice, as follows:

'(1). Southern Rhodesia before the declaration of independence was a semi-independent state which enjoyed internal sovereignty and also a large measure of external sovereignty, and her subjects, by virtue of the internal sovereignty she enjoyed, owed allegiance to her, but they also owed a residual allegiance to the United Kingdom by virtue of the external sovereignty which that country enjoyed. (2). The status of the present Government today is that of a fully *de facto* government in the sense that it is in fact in effective control of the territory and this control seems likely to continue. At this stage however it cannot be said that it is yet so firmly established as to justify a finding that its status is that of a *de jure* government. (3). The present Government having effectively usurped the governmental power granted Rhodesia under the 1961 Constitution, can now lawfully do anything which its predecessor could lawfully have done, but until its new constitution is firmly established and thus becomes the *de jure* constitution of the territory, its administrative and legislative acts must conform to the 1961 Constitution.'[83]

Yet, once admit that Southern Rhodesia is not fully independent, and is therefore still a colony, it remains subject to the sovereignty which the British parliament possesses over the whole of Her Majesty's dominions outside the independent ones. That sovereignty is absolute and unlimited in law. But it was contended that in relation to Southern Rhodesia that sovereignty is now limited by the convention whereby the British parliament does not legislate for Southern Rhodesia in matters within the competence of its legislature, except with the agreement of its government, a convention which was reaffirmed by the British Government in a statement in 1961.[84]

The Privy Council rejected the view that the grant of internal self-government to Southern Rhodesia under the 1961 Constitution involved any kind of division of sovereignty betwen it and the United Kingdom (assuming that to be possible under the British system), or that the grant in any way diminished the absolute sovereignty of the British parliament over the colony as part of Her Majesty's dominions. Further, that, important as the convention referred to is politically, it can have no legal effect in limiting the legal power of parliament, so that if parliament should choose to disregard it in any particular situation, as it did in passing the Southern Rhodesia Act, 1965, which declared Southern Rhodesia to be still the responsibility of the British Government and which authorised Her Majesty in Council to make provision for its government during the period of the rebellion, the courts must accept without question the legality of the action taken by parliament, conventions not being the concern of the courts.

In any case, however, although a disregard by the British parliament of the convention before 1965 may have been considered unconstitutional (i.e. politically improper), yet it may be said that 'the unilateral declaration of independence released the United Kingdom from any obligation to observe the convention.'[85]

Accordingly, the Board held that the exercise of power by the rebel régime of Ian Smith was in every respect a usurpation of the sovereignty of the British parliament, and that that precluded the concession of a *de facto* status to it by the courts of the lawful sovereign.

As may be recalled,[86] it was also contended that, even if the rebel government could not be accorded any *de facto* status, yet certain of its acts, both legislative and administrative, ought to be recognised as valid on the basis of necessity or implied mandate from the lawful sovereign, in so far, at any rate, as they might be necessary to preserve law and order. The Privy Council held that, while 'it may be that there is a general principle, depending on implied mandate from the lawful sovereign, which recognises the need to preserve law and order in territory controlled by a usurper,'[87] in the circumstance of the Rhodesian situation it was unnecessary to decide the question, since the lawful sovereign has by express enactment categorically prohibited any exercise of power by the rebel government, no matter how necessary such exercise of power might be to the preservation of law and order. But Lord Pearce, in a dissenting judgment, took the view that necessity demanded that recognition be given to such of the measures, both legislative and executive, of the rebel régime, as were reasonably required for the preservation of law and order. In this view the learned Lord of Appeal purported to base himself upon certain of the U.S. Supreme Court decisions in the Civil War cases. But, as has been pointed out earlier,[88] the decisions relied upon were concerned with the position of the rebel state governments whose powers were not a usurpation of those of the United States or of any other lawful government, and who for that reason were accorded recognition by the court as *de facto* governments. The position of the rebel government in Southern Rhodesia may be equated to that of the Confederate government in America, both being usurpers of the authority of the lawful government. Although the U.S. Supreme Court had vacillated as to the extent to which executive acts of the Confederate government might be given recognition by the courts, it had consistently refused to countenance the validity of its legislation on any ground. But this was the very thing that Lord Pearce tried to do in the Rhodesian case.

The Rebel Government as the Military Representative of the Insurrection: Belligerent Rights

All are agreed in conceding recognition to the Confederate government in its military capacity. What is the basis of this concession, and what acts are covered by it? The concession arises from the existence of a state of belligerence. Rebellion, though unlawful, may give rise to a state of belligerence, when the rebellious party is in control of a sizeable portion of the territory of the rightful sovereign and has organised armies and raised supplies sufficient enough to oppose and, if possible destroy, the lawful government. A rebellion which has attained such proportions becomes a civil war, and as such is recognised in international law as entitling both parties to the rights of war – belligerent rights as they are called – just as if it was a public war between two independent nations. The reason for treating the two parties to a civil war as public belligerents is explained to be that 'civil war breaks the bands of society and government, or at least suspends their operation and effect; it produces in the nation two independent parties, who consider each other as enemies, and acknowledge no common judge. These two parties, therefore, must necessarily be considered as hence-forward constituting, at least for a time, two separate bodies, two distinct societies. Though one of the parties may have been to blame in breaking the unity of the state and resisting the lawful authority, they, the two parties, are not the less divided in fact . . . They stand, therefore, in precisely the same predicament as two nations who engage in a contest, and being unable to come to an agreement have recourse to arms.'[89] Placed in such a position of mutual enmity and hostility, it is usual that both parties should concede to each other belligerent rights, upon grounds of humanity and expediency, in order to prevent the cruelties of reprisals and retalia-tions, since otherwise the war will become more destructive to the nation. It is not necessary that the independence of the rebellious party should be acknowledged in order to constitute it a party belligerent in war, according to the law of nations. Nor is it neces-sary, either, that the pretended government of the rebellious state should be recognised as the *de facto* government thereof. But the concession of belligerent rights implies at least its recognition as the military representative of the insurrection against the authority of the *de jure* government.

The acts that may lawfully be done in pursuance of belligerent rights must, however, be directly connected with the mode of prosecuting the war; that is to say, acts of legitimate warfare. No liability attaches to soldiers and officers of the rebel army who commit such acts. But belligerent rights do not extend to matters of civil government not connected with the mode of prosecuting the war. Outside acts of legitimate warfare, 'it conferred no further immunity or any other rights . . . it sanctioned no hostile legislation; it gave validity to no contracts for military stores; and it impaired in no respects the rights of loyal citizens as they had existed at the commencement of hostilities.'[90]

Two questions arise concerning the limits of belligerent rights. Are the acts of legitimate warfare protected by them limited to acts of a purely military character, like death or other kinds of destruc-tion? Secondly, must the protected acts have been done by a member of the armed forces in the military service of the rebel government? In *Ford v. Surget*[91] 200 bales of cotton belonging to the plaintiff had been burned during the civil war in America by the defendant, a civilian, in obedience to an order of a rebel com-manding general, acting under the authority of an Act of the Confederate Congress, which enjoined upon all military com-manders a duty to destroy all cotton, tobacco or other property that might be useful to the federal forces, whenever in their judg-ment the same should be about to fall into the hands of those forces.

Large quantities of these articles were destroyed in this way. The plaintiff sued after the suppression of the rebellion to recover the value of the cotton from the defendant. The U.S. Supreme Court held, first, that whether the destruction of the cotton might be justified as an act of legitimate warfare must be decided without reference to the Act of the Confederate Congress. For, having neither a legal existence nor even a *de facto* status in the strict sense of the term, the Confederate government could pass no valid legislation. Accordingly, the Act was to be regarded as nothing more than a declaration upon the part of the military representative of the rebellion, addressed to the rebel commanders, as to the circumstances under which cotton within the limits of the insurrection might be destroyed by the military commanders. 'It assumed to confer, however, upon such commanders, no greater authority than, consistently with the laws and usages of war, they might have exercised without the previous sanction of the rebel legislative authorities.'

As to whether the destruction was directly connected with the mode of prosecuting the war and therefore an act of legitimate warfare, the court thought that the rebel commander had 'the right, as an act of war, to destroy private property within the lines of the insurrection belonging to those who were co-operating, directly or indirectly, in the insurrection against the Government of the United States, if such destruction seemed to be required by impending necessity for the purpose of retarding the advance or crippling the military operations of the federal forces. Of that mode of conducting the war, on behalf of the rebellion, no one could justly complain who occupied the position of an enemy of the U.S., by reason of voluntary residence within enemy territory.' Cotton occupied a position of peculiar importance to the two sides in the war. It was the rebel government's chief reliance for means to purchase the munitions of war in Europe. Secondly, the insurgent states were the main suppliers of cotton to the rest of the U.S. and to the world. So the insurgent government might either use it to purchase munitions in Europe or withdraw it from the world market, thereby causing such a scarcity of it as might force the U.S. to call off the war. To allow it to fall into the hands of the federal troops would therefore be calculated to strengthen the position of those troops against those of the rebel government. Its destruction was therefore peculiarly an act of legitimate warfare, for which the destroyer was relieved from civil liability at the suit of an owner voluntarily residing at the time within the lines of the insurrection.

On the question whether the protection was limited to regular members of the rebel armed forces, it was held that it extended not only to soldiers but also to all persons acting under the power and compulsion of the rebel military authorities. But a mere volunteer, i.e. a person under no military order to do acts necessary for the conduct of the war, is apparently not covered. Since, therefore, the defendant, though a civilian, acted under military order and compulsion, he was entitled to make the same defence as any soldier, regularly enlisted in the rebel army, and acting under like order, could have made.

The decision in this case seems to limit the protection to acts done in relation to persons voluntarily resident within the rebel area and who co-operated with the rebellion. But what about acts against persons resident in the loyal states or persons whose residence within the rebel territory was temporary or constrained; or persons who, though permanetly resident therein, are loyal to the lawful government? The court thought the belligerent rights do not avail against the first class of persons, but as to persons in the last two categories, it left the point open. There is clearly no justification for so limiting the concession. Once concede that a rebellious party is a belligerent, and as such entitled to do acts of lawful warfare to save themselves from being crushed, on what ground could it be maintained that such acts could not be done against loyal citizens? This view of the matter finds some support in the opinion expressed by the court in *Williams v. Bruffy* that, although the plaintiffs whose rights were sequestrated were resident in a loyal state, the defence of belligerent rights might have availed against them in certain circumstances.

The concession of belligerent rights would appear, therefore, to be an exception to the rule invalidating all acts in aid of rebellion. For acts of warfare are manifestly of that nature.

REFERENCES

1. Crawford Young, 'The Politics of Separatism: Katanga, 1960-63,' in Carter, ed., *Politics in Africa: Seven Cases*, 1966, p. 173, on which this account is largely based.
2. 'The Biafran Possibility,' *Africa Report*, February 1969.
3. For details, see Nwankwo and Ifejika, *The Making of a Nation: Biafra*, 1969.
4. Meeting of May 27, 1967.
5. Quoted in William J. Foltz, 'An Early Failure of Pan-Africanism: The Mali Federation 1959-60,' in Carter, ed., *Politics in Africa: Seven Cases* (1966), p. 55 – an excellent account of the break-up of the Mali Federation.
6. Supra, p. 112.
7. Carter, ed., *African One-Party States*, 1962, p. 107.

8. Pauline Walton, 'Yahya's Bitter Half,' *Sunday Times of Zambia*, April 11, 1971.

9. See an article by Hasan Rabbi in the *Sunday Times of Zambia*, April 11, 1971.

10. *Joyce v. D.P.P.* [1946], A.C. 347. This dictum was uttered in the course of a judgment affirming the conviction for treason of an American citizen who, while in Germany under a British passport, broadcast for the Germans during the Second World War.

11 See Carl Friedrich, *Constitutional Government and Democracy*, revised ed., Chs. VII and VIII.

12. *Modern Constitutions* (1966), p. 64.

13. As to which, see Emerson, *From Empire to Nation.* 1962, Chs. XVI and XVII; as applied to Katanga, see Crawford Young, *op. cit.*

14. There are only three cases where the constitution expressly sanctions secession, the U.S.S.R., Burma and Malaysia, but as Emerson remarked, the right of secession in the U.S.S.R. is a mere 'window dressing which lacks all political reality save its propaganda value,' *op. cit.*, p. 300.

15. Art. VII.

16. See *Hanauer v. Woodruff*, 15, Wall 439.

17. *Texas v. White*, 7, Wall 700 (1869) at pp. 724-5 per Chief Justice Chase delivering the opinion of the court.

18. S. 86.

19. S. 71.

20. *Lane Co. v. Oregon*, 7, Wall 71, at p. 76 (1869).

21. Per Lord Wright in *James v. Commonwealth of Australia* [1936], A.C. 578, at p. 613 (P.C.).

22. Per Griffith, C. J. In the *Railway Servants' Case* (1906), 4, C.L.R. 488, at p. 534 (Australia).

23. Per Curiam in *The Engineers' Case* (1920), 28, C.L.R. 129, at p. 142 (Australia).

24. *Ibid.* See also Corwin, *The Doctrine of Judicial Review*, 1963, p. 99, n. 33.

25. Corwin, *op. cit.*, p. 82.

26. Supra, p. 4.

27. *Federalist*, No. 39; my italics.

28. Quoted in Corwin, *op. cit.*, p. 103.

29. Corwin, *op. cit.*, p. 82, p. 98.

30. *White v. Hart*, 13, Wall 646, at p. 650 (1872).

31. *Cf. Texas v. White, ibid.*; *White v. Hart, ibid.*

32. *Texas v. White, ibid.*, p. 727.

33. *Cf. White v. Hart, ibid.*

34. *Sprott v. U.S.*, 20, Wall 459, at p. 464 per Justice Miller delivering the opinion of the court (1874).

35. *Young v. U.S.*, 97, U.S. 39 (1878).

36. *Texas v. White, ibid.*, at p. 727.

37. *Ex parte Garland*, 4, Wall 333, at pp. 380-1.

38. *Sprott v. U.S.*, 20, Wall 459 (1874); *Lamar v. Browne*, 92, U.S. 195; *Miller v. U.S.*, 11, Wall 305.

39. *Armstrong's Foundry v. U.S.*, 6, Wall 766 (1868).
40. *Armstrong v. U.S.*, 13, Wall 154; *U.S. v. Klein*, 13, Wall 136; *U.S. v. Padelford*, 9, Wall 531.
41. 4, Wall 333.
42. Ante, p. 182.
43. See Randall, *Constitutional Problems under Lincoln*, revised ed., 1964, particularly Chs. VI-IX.
44. *Williams v. Bruffy*, 96, U.S. 176 (1878); quoted with approval in *Taylor v. Thomas*, 22, Wall 479 (1875).
45. *Williams v. Bruffy*, 96, U.S. 176 at p. 183.
46. *Ibid.*
47. *Dewing v. Perdicaries*, 96, U.S. 193, at p. 195 (1878).
48. *Dewing v. Perdicaries, ibid.*
49. *Hickman v. Jones*, 9, Wall 197.
50. *Taylor v. Thomas*, 22, Wall 479 (1875).
51. 7, Wall 700 (1869); also *Thomas v. Richmond*, 12, Wall 349 – a statute of the state of Virginia validating notes issued as currency by the city of Richmond was held void as being in aid of rebellion.
52. *Hanauer v. Doane*, 12, Wall 342 (1871).
53. *Hickman v. Jones, ibid.*, p. 201.
54. At pp. 202-3.
55. *Texas v. White, ibid.*
56. *U.S. v. Home Insurance Co.*, 22, Wall 99 (1875).
57. *Taylor v. Thomas*, 22, Wall 479 at p. 489 (1875).
58. *Texas v. White*; also *U.S. v. Home Insurance, ibid.*
59. *Texas v. White, ibid.*, pp. 732-3; also *Thomas v. Richmond*, 12, Wall 349 at p. 357 (1871); *Taylor v. Thomas*, 22, Wall 479.
60. *Sprott v. U.S.*, 20, Wall 459 (1874).
61. *U.S. v. Home Insurance*, 22, Wall 99 (1875).
62. *Madzimbamuto v. Lardner-Burke* [1969], 1, A.C. 645, 732; discussed supra, pp. 210-11.
63. Constitution (Suspension and Modification) Decree, 1967 No. 8.
64. The Constitution (Repeal and Restoration) Decree, 1967 No. 13.
65. *Williams v. Bruffy*, 96, U.S. 176 (1878); *Thorington v. Smith*, 8, Wall 1 (1869); *Ford v. Surget*, 97, U.S. 594.
66. *Williams v. Bruffy, ibid.* at p. 185.
67. *Ibid.*
68. *Ibid.* at p. 11.
69. *Mauran v. Insurance Companies*, 6, Wall 1 at p. 14.
70. 97 U.S. 594.
71 This particular danger is obviated by the concession of belligerent rights discussed below.
72. *Ibid.* at p. 623.
73. *Ibid.* at p. 189 per Justice Field delivering the opinion of the majority. Justice Clifford again dissented.
74. *U.S. v. Keehler*, 9, Wall 83 at p. 87 (1870) per Justice Miller, delivering the opinion of the court.
75. *U.S. v. Keehler, ibid.* at pp. 87-8.

76. *Ibid.*
77. *Ibid.* at p. 11.
78. *Hanauer v. Woodruff*, 15, Wall 448; quoted with approval in the *Confederate Note Case*, 19, Wall 548.
79. See to the same effect *Thomas v. Richmond*, 12, Wall 349. The exchange value of the rebel notes in certain rebel areas was $20 to one U.S. lawful dollar two years after the war started, and $40 to one U.S. lawful dollar a year later. After the war many of the rebel States passed what were known as Sealing Acts fixing the exchange value of the rebel notes at different times. In the Republic of Biafra the exchange rate was £20 rebel notes to one shilling lawful Nigerian money towards the close of the war.
80. See *U.S. v. McRae*, 8, L.R. Eq. Cas. 69; *U.S. v. Prioleau*, 2, Hem and Mill Ch. Cas. 559. Both of these cases were cited with approval in *Sprott v. U.S.*, 20, Wall 459.
81. Supra, p. 208.
82. *Madzimbamuto v. Lardner-Burke* [1969], 1, A.C. 645 (P.C.); (1968) (2), S.A. 284.
83. (1968) (2), S.A. 284, 359-60.
84. (1961) Cmnd. 1399.
85. [1969], 1, A.C. 645, 723.
86. Supra, pp. 209-11.
87. *Ibid.* at p. 729.
88. Supra, p. 213.
89. Vattel, *Law of Nations*, p. 245; quoted by Justice Field in *Williams v. Bruffy*, *ibid.* at p. 191 and by Justice Clifford in *Ford v. Surget*, *ibid.* at p. 613.
90. Per Justice Field in *Williams v. Bruffy*, *ibid.* at p. 187.
91. 97 U.S. 594 (1878).

CHAPTER X

CONCLUSION

The subject-matter of Chapter IX – secession – is apt to give the impression that the state itself in the emergent nations is in the process of disintegration. Far from this being the case, the state exhibits every mark of permanence and continuity, its acknlowedged artificiality notwithstanding. Indeed secession has had a rather limited incidence, and this gathering storm seems to be abating as the new states begin to settle down after the excitement over who should inherit power from the departing European colonisers. It was independence that gave impetus to secessionist demands among groups within the new state, who feared that the removal of the imperial protective power, with its professed solicitude for the interest of minorities, might leave them a prey to the tyranny of their more populous brethren. As the first decade of African independence passes by, these fears tend to diminish. The futility of secessionist demands has compelled a willingness to seek and accept accommodation with one's neighbours, and a realisation that one's interest is best served by trying to work out one's destiny within the inherited state rather than by devising a new one. The Masais and Somalis in Kenya are beginning to reconcile themselves to life in an independent Kenya Republic, as are the Ewes in Ghana, the Sanwis in the Ivory Coast and the Baganda in Uganda.

In the two African states, Congo and Nigeria, in which secession was actually attempted, its failure has been an object lesson, demonstrating the futility, the wanton waste of lives and resources, the misery and horror that result. In both countries, the secessionist region has been reintegrated into the state, and the fears and cleavages which gave rise to secession, together with the bitterness generated by the conflict, are giving way to a new sense of fellow-feeling, of belonging together, and to a greater mutual respect for the worth and importance of other groups in the state. Out of the bitterness and suffering of the experience has been born a new society in which, it is hoped, the bigotry and prejudices of the past will gradually die away, and be replaced by a broadened outlook and a new spirit of mutual tolerance and fraternity. The reintegration of the Ibos into the new Nigerian nation has been greatly facilitated by the enlightened and benevolent policies of General

299

Gowon's federal military government. The spirit of forgiveness and of reconciliation is transcendent. Never before in history has an armed conflict, fought with so much brutality and unbridled vituperation, ended with no reprisals, no trials and no shootings. But almost overnight in Nigeria former enemies mingle together again with apparent cordiality, as if nothing had happened. The Ibos are back in Lagos, at their homes, their businesses and their jobs. Reconstruction of the war-ravaged areas of the East is going ahead. Progress may be slow, but that must be judged by the magnitude of the job and the difficulties facing a country just emerging from two and a half years' continuous warfare, which engaged the better part of its resources. When one reflects upon the history of reconstruction in the United States after the Civil War in 1865, one cannot but be impressed by the magnanimity displayed by General Gowon and his government. In the Congo, the leader of secessionist Katanga, Moise Tshombe, was later to become the prime minister of the country, and the recent announcement that the Nigerian federal military government would welcome Odumegwu Ojukwu back to the country whenever he should choose to return demonstrates more forcefully than anything else the spirit of forgiveness and reconciliation on the part of the Government. The new twelve-state structure of the Nigerian Federation, although in origin it might have been intended as a solution to what was then regarded as the 'Ibo problem,' is unquestionably one of the great milestones in the country's constitutional and political evolution. For it was the old three- (later four-) state structure and the enormous, if unequal, size of the states that accounted for much of the country's ills. When the country has recovered sufficiently from the ill-effects of the war, one hopes that an opportunity would be provided for an adjustment here and there in the boundaries of the states so as to try to remove the remaining sources of friction.

The new states in Africa have definitely come to stay. They are colonialism's great legacy to the continent. They must be nurtured to maturity, for they provide the best hope of salvation through economic development. Instead of secession, we should be working towards greater regional co-operation on lines similar to those of the East African Community.

Leaving aside the impression of disintegration which secession is apt to engender, it might be thought that the picture of constitutionalism – one of failure – painted here is somewhat unduly pessimistic if not altogether too sombre. It might indeed be questioned whether constitutionalism can really be said to have failed in the emergent states. Does not failure connote a more or less permanent state of affairs, and is the present state of constitutionalism in these countries not a manifestation of the normal teething trouble associated with infancy? Perhaps failure is somewhat too harsh.

Erosion of the foundations and principles of constitutionalism there certainly has been. This erosion has had many causes and has taken various forms, as we have tried to show in the preceding chapters. Underlying these causes is the constitution's lack of legitimacy for the masses, and perhaps more disastrous, for the ruling politicians. Politicians in developing countries are yet to develop the right attitude towards the constitution; they are yet to learn to regard and respect it as an 'umpire above the political struggle,' and not as 'a weapon in that struggle which can be used and altered in order to gain temporary and passing advantages over one's political opponents.'[1] The constitution lacks sanctity because the values and ideas which it enshrines are different and opposed to those of the rulers and society alike. While a constitution is meant to be a check upon power, a limitation upon the arbitrariness of discretion, the politicians' orientation is authoritarian. They tend to be impatient with, and want to break away from all, constitutional restraints; and if the constitution proves an obstacle, then it must be bypassed or be made to bend to their desires. The result, as we have seen, is a systematic perversion of the institutions and processes of government coupled with a spate of amendments to the constitution where it is thought necessary to maintain some facade of legality.

This is the basic problem facing constitutionalism in the emergent states. The problem is largely human rather than institutional. And the motivation for the politicians' authoritarian tendencies is power together with its wealth and prestige. Disproportionate premium is attached to wealth in a community where poverty is the general condition for the overwhelming majority of the population. The ability to help one's friends and relatives with jobs and contracts is highly prized in a country in which unemployment is widespread, and in which the government is the main employer of labour. From this a flicker of hope appears, however dimly, on the distant horizon. Poverty and unemployment cannot remain a permanent condition of the emergent states. Development has been launched upon its difficult and desultory course, yet no matter how long-drawn it is going to be, the experience of the developed societies gives ground for an optimistic future. When the new states have attained a sufficient degree of development in education, technology and industrialisation, the craze for power and wealth should diminish, and political power would then be cut to its proper dimensions. It

x

would then lose some of its present appeal and cease to be regarded as the supreme object of human existence.

There is another ground for hope. It is perhaps not altogether surprising to encounter authoritarian tendencies in the first generation of rulers. Any new thing has a flattering and infatuating appeal, and the inheritance of the power of the white colonisers, with all its glory and myth, must be more than infatuating; it has indeed been intoxicating. The present generation of rulers were the leaders of the nationalist movement, and rightly consider themselves the founders of the new states. Herein lies their belief that they have a peculiar title to rule in order to safeguard the fruit of their revolution. Opposition is considered an attempt to destroy the revolution, a struggle in which they have sacrificed so much, borne so much humiliation and deprivation. The argument of the rulers is that 'we shall not sit by and allow others to snatch the fruit of our labour from us. Whatever amenities the people enjoy today, in the way of jobs, education, medical services, etc., they owe to us as the authors of the revolution.' The argument sounds somewhat naïve, yet it impresses the unsophisticated masses. This is the attitude to power which has brought the ruling élite into conflict with other classes of the élite, who refuse to accept that the fact of having led the nationalist movement gives the rulers a right to govern indefinitely. The younger élite have their own pretensions to power which they are not prepared to subordinate to the perpetual dominance of the present rulers. It is a characteristic of all élites in the emergent states that they believe rulership to be their right by the very fact of being an élite. The challenge of the younger élite to their elders' claim of a pre-eminent title to rule is well calculated to provoke class conflict, and accounts in great measure for the incidence of coups in the emergent nations.

The point that it is necessary to make here is that this particular threat to constitutionalism is likely to prove ephemeral. It should not last longer than the situation that excites it. The generation of the élite that led the nationalist movement and succeeded to the power of the colonial government cannot be immune to the effect of the natural laws of wear and tear and age. It is true that at eighty some of them are still hanging on to power, but the alert and active octogenarian is a rare creature. When their era is over, as it will be sooner or later, then their claim to the state as a personal fief will have perished, and with it the myth of messianic or charismatic authority. Struggle for power among the younger and on-coming élites will not thereby be abolished, for that is the very essence of politics, but the repressive and perverse methods of the present day, which are primarily designed to maintain the 'founder' rights of the authors of the nationalist revolution, would, one hopes, disappear. The danger of course is that practice often stamps its imprint upon the course of historical development; once originated, it serves as an example which might be resorted to in future by those who find in it an easy way out of a given situation. It would be a tragedy if the coming generation of rulers in the emergent nations should succumb to the temptation to resort to the methods of their predecessors. They have no 'founder' rights, the preservation of which would provide justification for such a course. Our hope is that the intoxication of power would have worn off sufficiently to permit a regular succession in the rulership, and to imbue the contenders for power with a willingness to accept the verdict of the ballot box and the restraints of the constitution. One hopes that the time will come in Africa when a leader, after two terms of office, will voluntarily retire to make way for a new man with a fresh idea and a new approach. The argument about the indispensability of a particular leader is a myth, and underrates the leadership potentials of the new states.

The role of inexperience in the behaviour of African politicians has generally not received due attention. In many of these countries independence had come about unplanned; overnight, as it were, men who only the other day had been told they were unfit to be entrusted with responsibility found themselves in the position of having to shoulder the high responsibility of administering the state, with scarcely any previous experience of its working. The colonial approach to government had deprecated co-operation between the rulers and the ruled. The mechanisms of government had to be kept away from the people, as if they were a secret; what was primarily expected of them was to obey the constituted authority and its laws and to provide the labour and pay the taxes needed to run the administration. And so it happened that when power was transferred, the nationalist leaders came to it quite innocent of its intricate mechanisms, and were left to grope about like an illiterate peasant left in charge of highly complicated machinery. The zeal of inexperience mingled with the determination not to fail, and produced in the new rulers an inclination towards intolerance and authoritarianism. Government is an art, and like all arts it grows by experience gained from practice over a long period of years. Each generation of rulers learns from the experience of its predecessors, and the accumulation of this experience will after many generations infuse into the population the habits and ideals of democratic behaviour.

Loyalty to the nation requires even longer experience. With one or two exceptions, the modern state in Africa is nowhere older than one century, nearly nine-tenths of which was covered by the colonial era with its deliberate discouragement of the development of national identity among the various component groups. This means that the new states have had barely a decade to undo the work of colonialism and foster the integration of their societies. Loyalty to the state is not like economic development. Capital may be generated in a variety of ways, through foreign aid and the exploitation of the country's natural resources; with this capital one might hope to achieve in one decade what in the older states had taken several. The development of a feeling of loyalty and love for the state is necessarily a much slower and protracted process because, being a matter of the mind, it cannot be forced nor can it be bought. It takes other things to nurture besides economic progress. It has to be nursed by teaching and by precepts among children at school, among the members of various organisations and associations, and among the society generally.

Another point that requires to be made in favour of the new African states is that, in spite of the erosions of constitutional democracy, in spite of the tendency towards authoritarianism, none of them can really be said to be totalitarian. The rule of one party is presently in vogue, and this is manifestly inimical to constitutionalism. Yet the single party in all these countries is a mass party, thriving upon mass participation and popular consultation, manipulated and controlled though it may be. Authoritarianism, however, is not the same thing as autocracy, much less is it the same as totalitarianism. It may be difficult to say at what point one shades off into the other, but still there is a difference in the amount of freedom they permit. 'Autocracies are governments that permit little personal freedom, little organisational autonomy (either in government or society), and little legitimate political competition.'[2] Totalitarianism 'magnifies the elements of autocracy to their farthest limits – it is a form of rule in which all governmental structures are hierarchically integrated, all human relations subsumed to government, and all legitimate political activity mobilised to support the governmental structure.'[3] Governmental control attempts to be *total*, reaching out into every facet of human life and activity. To quote Eckstein and Apter again, 'the essence of totalitarianism, then, is that it annihilates all boundaries between the state and the groupings of society, even the state and individual personality. At any rate, that is the intention of totalitarianism . . . Certainly no other social order . . . has tried to integrate so many aspects of human existence: family life, friendship, work, leisure, production, exchange, worship, status, art, manners, travel, dress – even that final assertion of human privacy, death.'[4]

From this description of autocracy and totalitarianism the contrast between them and the African régimes becomes clear. Even Dr. Nkrumah's government in Ghana, perhaps the most authoritarian of all, was less than an autocracy, and much less than a totalitarian régime. It can be said that in all African countries individual liberty in non-political matters is allowed quite ample scope. The individual is not regimented in his life, he is free to move about, to choose his occupation, to acquire wealth and property, to indulge in as much leisure and luxury as he can afford, to form friendships and business associations, to train his children in the way he likes. If he can stay away from politics, as most do, he can live a full life without ever experiencing the repressive power of government. There is thus ample scope for the enjoyment of personal and organisational autonomy in non-political matters. Nowhere are there any of the secret police methods and the special tribunals of the totalitarian state. It is in political matters that the government's authoritarianism becomes evident. In the one-party states, all organisations with an active political role, trade unions, farmers' association, women's and youth associations are integrated into the party; political opponents are repressed by preventive detention and other methods of coercion. This is not to say that political debate is completely disallowed. The single party still tolerates debate but insists that it must be within the party. More important, perhaps, the ordinary courts still function as the guardian of the individual's rights against the executive, though their effectiveness is greatly undermined by the absence of a justiciable constitutional guarantee of rights in some of the one-party states and by political interference – the most outrageous example of such interference being the dismissal by Nkrumah of his Chief Justice and other judges for acquitting certain politicians accused of involvement in the alleged plot to assassinate him, and the reversal of that acquittal by statute.

Immanuel Wallerstein has noted an inherent limitation upon the African one-party states. For they are

'not integrated organisms but integrating organisms. That is, they are carefully built conditions, in need of constant nurture, whose primary aim is to keep the country together. The principal method of maintaining party unity, indispensable to national unity, is the constant balancing of interests. The allocation of seats in the legislature, or expenditures of the public works department, are the result of hard bargaining and careful calculation, which bear comparison with the interplay of special interests in Western parliaments. The image of a small élite imposing their will, through the party structure, on an inert mass fails to take account of the real dispersion of powers that still exists in every African country.'[5]

Allowing for the author's indulgent advocacy of the African one-party system, there is some truth in this. The diversity of the interests represented within the single party inhibits excessive authoritarianism.

In those states which have not adopted the one-party system, the integration of organisations and associations into the ruling party is desired but not enforced, and the degree of repression is less. Nor are the military régimes which have sprung up in many parts of Africa as autocratic as might be thought. Personal freedom in non-political matters is largely maintained, in spite of the military's leaning towards command and hierarchy. None rules with the degree of repression associated with the military government of a conquered territory. And, except in Pakistan from 1958 to 1962, martial law has never been resorted to.

There can be no more eloquent testimony to the African's distaste for totalitarianism than that after a decade of vigorous effort communism appears to be making hardly any headway on the continent. Nigeria's flirtation with the U.S.S.R. was forced upon her by the exigency of the civil war, and the fear of possible communist influence in the country's economic and political system has so far proved unfounded. There is no indication that communism has made any impact upon the practice and thinking of the Nigerian government. The outlook of the leaders is strongly individualistic as regards both private enterprise and private property. The masses, at any rate in the South, are equally individualistic, with a distinct distaste for governmental regimentation. Even the North, which was thought to be a fertile ground for communist penetration, has proved unreceptive. The feudalistic hold of the Northern Emirs upon the society is perhaps more difficult to break down than the individualism of the Southerners. Moreover, the Northern society has changed and is changing fast in the direction of individual self-determination, thanks to the educational revolution in the two decades just before and since independence.

Admittedly, the existence of so many military régimes on the African continent is like a malignant excrescence which needs to be excised. Ghana, the first of the black African colonies to become independent, set yet another example by the action of its military government in handing over power to a civilian government popularly elected under a democratic constitution drafted by an independent commission and enacted by a constituent assembly after much consultation and discussion. By this action, it was generally thought, a bright trail was lighted in the somewhat darkened image of constitutionalism on the continent. We rejoiced at the prospect, which the Ghana example was thought to herald, of a general return from military to civilian government, and of a fresh start in democratic government under a new crop of leaders sobered by a period of enforced rustication by the military and an opportunity for quiet reflection on the crudities and excesses of the past. The restoration in Ghana offered a unique opportunity to the new civilian government of Dr. Busia to demonstrate to the world that the African was not an unrestrainable tyrant, incapable of democratic government and of cultivating the spirit of tolerance which it demands. Busia himself had had a full measure of life in opposition, during which he had experienced its trials and hazards and denounced Nkrumah's authoritarian methods. The restoration in Ghana thus placed upon him a particularly heavy responsibility to show that he could practise what he had preached while in opposition. It was a challenge to his integrity and to his moral conscience. One would hate to think that he betrayed this responsibility, though his record seems to indicate that he was not free of vindictiveness, the very thing which he had consistently condemned in Nkrumah. One feels, however, that, though he might have displayed a reprehensible trait of vindictiveness, and even of vanity and waste, he should have been given the chance of one term in office. It may be too, as is alleged, that as leader he was colourless and failed to inspire enthusiasm and confidence, yet, having been constitutionally elected, he still deserved to be left to serve his term. Thereafter it would be for the electorate, as the constitutional arbiter, to refuse to return him if they thought his stewardship discreditable or uninspiring. For this reason, the second military coup in Ghana in January 1972 was a retrograde step. It dashed the hope that at last the era of direct military intervention in politics in Africa is drawing to an end.

REFERENCES

1. Ghai and McAuslan, *Public Law and Political Change in Kenya*, 1970, p. 511.
2. Eckstein and Apter, ed., *Democracy and Totalitarianism in Comparative Politics*, 1965.
3. *Ibid.*
4. *Ibid.*
5. Immanuel Wallerstein, *Africa: The Politics of Independence*, 1961. p. 161.

INDEX

ABURI AGREEMENT, 250, 262
Action Group (Western Nigeria),
102-5, 115, 125, 128, 131, 133-4,
143, 145, 147, 151-5, 162-3, 175,
177; *see also* Nigeria
Adebo, *see* Phillipson and Adebo
Adegbenro, Chief, 133, 147
Ademola, Chief Justice, 74, 203-4
Africa: The Politics of Independence, see
Wallerstein, Immanuel
African Unity, Organisation for
(O.A.U.), 258
Afrifa, Colonel, 225
Agbonmagbe Bank Ltd. (Nigeria),
103
Aguiyi-Ironsi, Major-General, 196-7,
201, 252
Ahomadegbe, Justin, 227
Akan tribe, *see* Sanwi
Akintola, Chief, 128, 133-5, 143, 145,
150, 152, 154, 175-6, 196, 226
Alafin of Oyo, 141
Alexander, Justice, 117, 163
Algeria, 38, 158, 226, 245; *abortive
coup*, 1967, 220; *constitutional council*,
38; *coup d'état*, 219
Allison, 104
Aluko, Dr., 151
America, United States of, 5-6, 16-17,
25, 36, 41, 47-8, 78, 82, 86, 90, 112,
122, 213, 222-3, 270-89, 292-5;
Bill of Rights, 16, 41, 44, 48; *Civil
War*, 274-89, 292-5, 300; *Congress*,
68, 78, 183; *Constitution*, xii, 6, 9-10,
14, 16-17, 26, 29-30, 48, 63, 69,
182-3, 223-5, 269, 273, 280, 283;
Declaration of Independence, 267-8;
federal courts, 70; *New Deal Legislation*,
48; *Pearl Harbour*, 182-3;
Presidential system, 63, 65, 68;
Second World War, 182, 224; *Supreme
Court*, 16, 20, 46-7, 182, 213, 236,
269, 271, 274-6, 278-89, 292, 294-5;
Southern States (Confederate government)
267-8, 272-89, 292-5
Amin, General, 245
Anglicans, 249
Anglo-Israeli Bank (London), 104
Anin, Justice, 239
Ankara, 189
Anne, Queen of England, 201
Anne, Queen of Scotland, 201
Anson, Sir William, 199
Apaloo, Justice, 230, 243
Apithy, President, 227
Apter, *see* Eckstein and Apter
Arab Bros. (Motors), Ltd. (Nigeria),
104-5, 107
Archer, Justice, 231, 234
Ashanti, 249
Asia, 173-4
Ataturk, Kemal, 91
Atkin, Lord, 34-5, 39
Australia, 33, 69-70, 122, 273
Awolowo, Chief, 133-4, 162
Awo National Brigade, 143
Azikiwe, Dr. Nnamdi, 58, 60, 89, 124,
197

BACON, SIR FRANCIS, 198
Baganda, 299
Balewa, Sir Abubakar Tafawa, 63-4,
131, 145, 196
Baluba, 277
Balubakat, 260
Balubas, 259-60

309